Reading Joyce

James Joyce; photograph by Berenice Abbott, Paris, 1928

Source: Berenice Abbott/Commerce Graphics NYC

Reading Joyce

David Pierce

PEARSON
Longman

Harlow, England • London • New York • Boston • San Francisco • Toronto
Kong • Seoul • Taipei • New Delhi
sterdam • Munich • Paris • Milan

Pearson Education Limited

Edinburgh Gate
Harlow CM20 2JE
United Kingdom
Tel: +44 (0)1279 623623
Fax: +44 (0)1279 431059
Website: www.pearsoned.co.uk

First edition published in Great Britain in 2008

© Pearson Education Limited 2008

The right of David Pierce to be identified as author of this work has been asserted by him in accordance with the Copyright, Designs and Patents Act 1988.

ISBN: 978-1-4058-4061-3

British Library Cataloguing in Publication Data
A CIP catalogue record for this book can be obtained from the British Library.

Library of Congress Cataloging in Publication Data
Pierce, David, 1947–
   Reading Joyce/David Pierce.
      p. cm.
   Includes bibliographical references and index.
   ISBN 978-1-4058-4061-3
   1. Joyce, James, 1882–1941—Criticism and interpretation. 2. Joyce, James, 1882–1941—Appreciation.
3. Joyce, James, 1882–1941—Study and teaching.   I. Title.
   PR6019. 09Z7819 2007
   823'. 912—dc22

2007038448

10 9 8 7 6 5 4 3 2 1
12 11 10 09 08

Set by 73 in 10/13.5 pt Sabon
Printed by Ashford Colour Press Ltd., Gosport

The Publisher's policy is to use paper manufactured from sustainable forests.

For Mary and Matt, home again

Also by David Pierce

Attitudes to Class in the English Novel (with Mary Eagleton), London: 1979;
W. B. Yeats: A Guide Through the Critical Maze, Bristol: 1989; *James Joyce's Ireland*, London and New Haven: 1992; *Yeats's Worlds: Ireland, England and the Poetic Imagination*, London and New Haven: 1995; *Sterne in Modernism/Postmodernism* (co-editor with Peter de Voogd), Amsterdam: 1996; *W. B. Yeats: Critical Assessments*, 4 vols, Robertsbridge: 2000; *Irish Writing in the Twentieth Century: A Reader*, Cork: 2001; *Light, Freedom and Song: A Cultural History of Modern Irish Writing*, London and New Haven: 2005; *Joyce and Company*, London: 2006.

Contents

List of illustrations

Acknowledgements

A short extract from Chapter 7 appeared in *Joyce and/in Translation*, edited by Rosa Maria Bollettieri Bosinelli and Ira Torresi (Rome: Bulzoni, 2007). This is also the place to record a debt of gratitude to the following individuals who have helped me with various parts of this book: Austin Briggs, Iris Bruderer, Teresa Caneda, Vincent Caprani, Diane Evans, Rosa Gonzalez, Anthony Green, Irena Gubrica, Ian Gunn, Dan Harper, Mary Haugh, Josephine Hilton, Maureen Luxton, Jürgen Partenheimer, Laura Pelaschiar, Jörg Rademacher, Fritz Senn and John Smurthwaite. As ever, my chief debt is to Mary Eagleton. I would also like to take this opportunity to thank Philip Langeskov and his team at Pearson for their enthusiasm and support through all the stages in the production of this book.

Publisher's Acknowledgements

We are grateful to the following for permission to reproduce copyright material:

Pages ii and 19 Berenice Abbott/Commerce Graphics NYC; Page 14 ADAGP, Paris & DACS, London 2007; Pages 16 and 26 Estate of Gisèle Freund/John Hillelson; Pages 30, 83 and 99 Dan Harper; Pages 79 and 325 The Department of Irish Folklore, University College, Dublin; Page 132 Courtesy of InBev; Pages 171 and 214 Editions Gallimard; Page 181 Fr Bruce Bradley S.J.; Pages 209, 224 and 330 James Joyce Collections at Morris Library/Southern Illinois University; Page 223 Phil Phillps Collection/ Rosenbach Museum & Library; Page 227 Reproduced from *Dublin 1660– 1860* by permission of Maurice Craig and Liberties Press; Pages 232 and 257 Courtesy of the National Library of Ireland; Page 233 Ian Gunn & Clive Hart/James Joyce's Dublin/Thames & Hudson & Stephen Paterson/ Napier University; Page 264 Richard Hamilton, All Rights Reserved, DACS 2007; Page 269 Dedalus Foundation, INC/DACS, London/VAGA, NY 2007; Page 306 University of Washington Press; Page 336 © ARS, NY and DACS, London/Tony Smith Estate, courtesy Matthew Marks Gallery, New York.

Every effort has been made to trace copyright holders, but if any have been inadvertently overlooked the publisher will be pleased to make the necessary arrangements at the first opportunity.

Abbreviations

D	James Joyce, *'Dubliners': Text, Criticism, and Notes* (eds Robert Scholes and A. Walton Litz), New York: Viking, 1969.
E	James Joyce, *Exiles* (intro. Padraic Colum), London: Granada, 1979.
FW	James Joyce, *Finnegans Wake*, 1939; London: Faber & Faber, 1964. Page number is given first, followed by line number.
P	James Joyce, *'A Portrait of the Artist as a Young Man': Text, Criticism, and Notes* (ed. Chester Anderson), New York: Viking, 1969.
U	James Joyce, *Ulysses: The Corrected Text* (ed. Hans Walter Gabler with Wolfhard Steppe and Claus Melchior), London: The Bodley Head, 1986. Chapter number is followed by line number.
Letters	*Letters of James Joyce* (ed. Stuart Gilbert), London: Faber & Faber, 1957.
Letters II	*Letters of James Joyce*, vol. II (ed. Richard Ellmann), New York: Viking, 1966.

Guy Davenport's humorous caricature of Joyce dangling a pair of bloomers, complete with an equally intriguing view of two other popular performers, this time from the fields of early cinema and the Greek classics. Bloom, Chaplin, Odysseus. Odysseus, Chaplin, Bloom. From Hugh Kenner, *The Stoic Comedians* (1964).

CHAPTER 1

Introduction

Opening remarks

In the closing moments of his final almost impenetrable work, Joyce asks a question that many of his readers over the years must have thought about him, 'Is there one who understands me?' (*FW* 627:15). There will always be a doubt about *Finnegans Wake*, but to some extent the complaint also resonates against his work as a whole. For Joyce, both as a man and as a writer, is a puzzle, and he has been so for what is now several generations of readers round the world. Joyce half-knew he would be a puzzle and to some extent he was responsible for his fate, for, as he once remarked about *Ulysses*, 'I've put in so many enigmas and puzzles that it will keep the professors busy for centuries arguing over what I meant, and that's the only way of insuring one's immortality' (Ellmann, 1982, 521). The enigma, though, prompted worldwide interest, for as John Banville noted, writing in the *New York Times* on the centenary of Bloomsday in June 2004, '*Ulysses* remains one of the most talked about and least read works of world literature.' Banville's conjunction is instructive. Joyce, who knew how to *in*sure and *en*sure his immortality, is the most talked about *and* least read modern author, as enigmatic today as he was when he first came to the world's notice in the years around the Great War.

This book begins with the enigma that is Joyce and to some extent it ends with the enigma that is Joyce. But, in the light of 40 years reading Joyce and 30 years teaching him, it's also a journey in which I try to make sense of this enigma. He began for me as a dilemma at a Catholic junior seminary when my alter ego Donagh McDonagh, a classmate who was one day my senior, alerted me, with glee in his eyes, to *A Portrait of the Artist as a Young Man*: 'Read that and tell me what you think.' I didn't read it at the time, for I suspected it would be too close to my experience, and, moreover, I had no intention of listening to a renegade while inside the sacred confines of the Church. From that moment on, though, I sensed I had an appointment with destiny, but I put the enigma on one side until I was beyond

7.45 The World of James Joyce

Is There One Who Understands Me? James Joyce was born in Dublin 100 years ago. At the age of 20 he left for Paris to begin a self-imposed exile that was to last most of his life. Dublin, however, remained the inspiration for his writing. This Emmy Award-winning film, complete with many previously unseen interviews, shows the obstacles that lay in the path of *Dubliners, Portrait of the Artist as a Young Man, Ulysses* and *Finnegans Wake*, the books that were to make Joyce one of the most famous and influential writers of this century.
Narrated by **T. P. McKenna**

Script COLBERT KEARNEY
Music SEORISE BODLEY
Programme consultant RICHARD ELLMANN
Produced by SEAN O'MORDHA, RTE
(Joyce in June, *Thursday* 7.40 pm)

Christmas 1982 listing in *Radio Times* of one of the best documentary films on Joyce: *Is There One Who Understands Me?*

adolescence and beyond the immediate circle of his influence. Joyce for me, then, was a writer to return to, but all of us come to him with our own expectations and varying states of readiness. This book is a journey, and part of that journey is about beginnings and imagining what it was like for me beginning to read Joyce and putting myself in the shoes of those embarking on a similar journey today.

Reading Joyce is not for everyone, and nor should it be, but, for those who develop an interest, the habit can be forming and even last a lifetime. For many readers, Joyce is often embarked upon as a matter of obligation or as part of a high-school or undergraduate programme. This book is written to convey something of the pleasure in reading Joyce, and it is informed therefore by a spirit of humour and appreciation. It issues from a belief that the reader new to Joyce needs a certain amount of guidance, but not an excessive amount. I look to the reader, therefore, who appreciates a challenge and who, long after the prompt books have been put down, will continue reading 'the porcupine of authors', as his biographer Richard Ellmann once called him (Ellmann, 1982, 6). Indeed, the reader I have in mind is sceptical of reading books with 'notes' in the title and is looking for a critical engagement with a writer who is so highly regarded. Not 'this means that' but 'Why should I read this at all?' and 'How does any of this connect with my life?' and 'Please tell me things but make it interesting.'

Fabulous Voyager: James Joyce's 'Ulysses' is the title of a much-admired study by Richard Kain (1947), and what the author stresses throughout is that it is the reader who is the 'fabulous voyager'. I think that's right. The central person in my book is not me or James Joyce, or the voyages of Joyce's characters or the flight of his imagination, but the reader. It is the reader who is on a journey, and the journey being offered is to my mind a fabulous one; fabulous meaning great, beautiful, exquisite; fabulous also meaning made-up, a fable, an extraordinary narrative. Both meanings are in evidence here but it is the second one that is most suggestive, for what Joyce offers his reader is something unimaginably realistic and for that very reason fabulous. Begin here and recall this moment when you come to the end of the voyage, for, more than most writers, reading Joyce is an unbelievably fabulous experience and you can't be sure where that experience will end.

Most books, be they a collection of stories about a neglected colonial city at the turn of the twentieth century or a work of literary criticism, have a story behind them. This one is no different. In 2005 the Acquisitions Editor for Literature at Longman, Philip Langeskov, contacted me asking if I would consider writing a book on Joyce that would be both educational and informative and at the same time come with a personal stamp on it. I thought, with my previous books on Joyce for Yale University Press and Continuum, I had done enough on the great man, and I wasn't sure I had anything new to say. Philip persisted. Had I read W.G. Sebald's *The Rings of Saturn* (1998) or Janet Malcolm's *Reading Chekhov: A Critical Journey* (2001)? Flattery works with most of us, but this was distinctly heady company. Sebald's work is very special and he is a great storyteller. One minute we are in a parish church in Suffolk, the next in the early modern period with new immigrants from the Low Countries, and, then, in one fell swoop, we are looking up at the sky watching German bombers menacingly overhead. The arts of war and peace brought into alignment, and all from a central European perspective. I couldn't get anywhere close to that, I told Philip. My experience is simply too limited to carry so much weight. He persisted.

What about Janet Malcolm, then? She had undertaken a journey to the places associated with Anton Chekhov's short stories, and she makes much of her conversations with her tour guide and the possibility of touching and recuperating the Russian writer through association. This, too, is a very special book, partly because it is so beautifully written and partly because Janet Malcolm is so intelligent when it comes to human psychology. The insights I have, I told Philip, are more pedestrian, so anything I would tackle would, again, of necessity be limited. What I did do, however, on a more practical level, just in case, was return to Dublin and Paris and take some more photographs of places connected with Joyce, and some of these appear here for the first time, adding to the texture and by implication the argument of my book as a whole.

I was tired. For 15 years and more I had been producing books without a break in an unsupportive university environment. Philip didn't give up. For some years he had been keen to publish a book that would rescue Joyce from his reputation as a difficult writer. As he rightly insisted to me, 'Isn't it odd that Joyce often turns up at the head of lists of both the most influential books and the books least likely to be read. There's something a bit funny about that, isn't there?' On two occasions in 2006 he came up to York and bought me lunch. How could I refuse? I started writing but had to wait for some months before I could settle on the right tone or discern a sufficiently clear line. Stepping outside the conventional boundaries of writing is never easy, but I've always been keen on trying something different. Philip wanted a book where the images were integrated, rather than juxtaposed, with the text. Again, another challenge, which could only be seen as successful, if at all, in retrospect. So, I would need to allow time at the end for polishing and ensuring a happy mix of caption and narrative flow.

That's how the book you have in your hands began. I am quite certain there wouldn't be a book if it weren't for the persistence of an editor at a large educational publishers. The story's worth recounting because it helps to set the scene for what's to come. I took the view that if discursiveness wasn't to become a burden for the reader, then I had to ensure a familiar structure based on Joyce's fictional texts. Not everything in a book of discovery should be subject to discovery. Hence there are four chapters on *Dubliners*, one on *A Portrait of the Artist as a Young Man*, three on *Ulysses*, and a final chapter on *Finnegans Wake*. Throughout, I also include references to Joyce's other writings, such as his play *Exiles* and his poetry, but my attention is focused on those texts which constitute the Joyce canon and which, with the exception of *Finnegans Wake*, regularly appear on course lists.

I begin with a biographical chapter on Joyce at 22 and the year of 1904 when, with the entry of his future partner into his life and the printing of the first stories of *Dubliners*, the world began to change significantly for him. Joyce the man and Joyce the writer – what was he like and what distinguishes his writing? I devote quite a lot of energy in the first part of this book to this question in the belief that orientation and first impressions tell us not all we need to know but a surprising amount of potentially useful information. The complex relationship between Joyce the man and Joyce the writer is touched on throughout this book, but I thought it would be helpful to spend time at the beginning reflecting on that moment when a line was being drawn between his past and his future.

With that complex relationship in mind I also include a brief section below on 'Snapshots of Joyce' as a way of introducing how Joyce has sometimes been portrayed by visual artists and how such images also inform our impressions of him and therefore our reading of him. In a final section on 'Home, sweet home' I explore places associated with Joyce, places where he can still be felt, and the meaning that exile had for him. As the references to 'Dublin 1904, Trieste 1914' at the end of *A Portrait of the Artist as a Young Man*, and to 'Trieste, Zurich, Paris, 1914–1921' at the end of *Ulysses* remind us, Joyce was an exile whose thoughts from abroad were dominated by the meaning of home, places in-between, and times past.

There is a variety of material on display in this book, but all of it is designed to intrigue or entice or encourage. The illustrations are built into the text and can be enjoyed for themselves or mulled over at leisure. It's a big book, but I have tried to break up the text in ways that enhance the argument and reading experience. It's also a critical journey in that it deals with my journey as a critic reading Joyce over four decades. How has my reading of Joyce changed? What do I get out of reading him? How have the students I have taught over the years responded to his writings? It's a personal book, therefore, with personal narratives interspersed throughout with critical and contextual comments. I wrap my personal narratives inside the covers of this book to insist on my involvement with Joyce and how this arises from more than simply a concern with writing. After ten books, I feel I can now come clean and say what I wanted to say all along. It's never quite like that of course, but, given the demise of critical monographs, there's something to be said for trying to take criticism into areas that might prove more attractive for today's reader.

The Introduction to my Cork *Reader* (2001) includes some remarks on my Irish background, and there are further personal reflections in *Joyce and Company* (2006) on my Catholic education as well as on visits to universities in the German Democratic Republic in the 1980s. Here in this book I recall attending an American Wake in the mid-1950s in the west of Ireland as well as other moments that suggest something of a common culture I (and others) share with Joyce. His Catholic upbringing will be readily appreciated by most Catholic readers, whether or not they are Irish. My upbringing was slightly more intense in that I spent my teenage years in seminaries, first in Sussex and then in Surrey. I reflect more on that experience and how it impacts on my interpretation of *A Portrait*. But I launch my personal story with experiences at university in the hope that this might establish a rapport with my reader. Chapter 2, in a section I have called 'At 22', begins with what it was like for me going to university in the north of England in the 1960s. Other experiences include teaching in adult education, in a community college in Northern California, and with the British Council in Madrid when I was a newly qualified graduate – all this material, tied to the Joycean yoke, surfaces in this book of many words.

Difficulty and delay

The things I like about Joyce will become apparent as we go along, but let me at the outset offer a couple of pointers or signposts. The issue of difficulty means that we have to spend time attending to detailed textual matters. The word I see I'm fond of in this book is 'delay'. Joyce encourages us to delay on words and phrases, on grammar and punctuation, and on meaning. As it happens, many first-time readers encounter difficulty not head-on but indirectly, when they arrive at the end of a story in *Dubliners* and are puzzled: 'Is that it? Have I missed something? Why is such writing considered special?' If you read for meaning you can miss a lot, but if you don't catch the meaning you can also miss a lot. It would be nice if this wasn't the case and the Joycean mood music was different, but, as I say, we are obliged to delay and spend time reflecting. I have deliberately delayed in the early part of this book on individual stories of *Dubliners* to ensure the reader new to Joyce gets on the right track and doesn't miss things.

Some of the best readers of Joyce are those whose first language is not English, for, repeatedly, they have to delay over a word or a phrase that for native speakers presents no immediate problem and is often glossed over. I enjoy perusing translations of Joyce's work, for you can sometimes discern at a glance what may have delayed someone else. The word 'gesabo' (*U* 18:1493), for example, is how Molly Bloom describes her house. It's not an English word and neither is it easy to identify its meaning from the context. I find myself pausing and deliberating on this one word in Chapter 9, drawing on how the word is translated into other European languages. Is her house a mess, a pigsty, a glory-hole, a holy show, a transit camp, too big, or what? Delay in this case reminds us of curiosity rather than difficulty, and it involves us as readers in the continuing construction of meaning. Many authors yield their treasures too quickly or within a generation or so, but this is not the case with Joyce, and in part this is because of his difficulty. Difficulty and complexity here begin to overlap, for not everything has been settled by the critics and scholars, and we can still encounter words or phrases that have the potential to shake the known or conventional interpretation.

Delay seems built into his writing, and the more we delay the more we can discern what's there. This is why I prefer the word 'delay' to 'difficulty' when speaking of Joyce, for difficulty suggests a cul-de-sac, but delay an opening. To take another example, which will be more familiar to readers of Joyce but which can be given a different gloss. Consider the opening word and phrase in *A Portrait*, 'Once upon a time'. When a native speaker reads such an opening to *A Portrait*, s/he reads on, perhaps fascinated by the technique of starting a novel in this way inside the consciousness of a child. But if we considered how a non-native speaker would translate such a phrase into their own languages, it might make us pause, for there is often no easy equivalent. In English the phrase marks the opening to a children's fairy story, but detach 'once' from 'once upon a time' and we are involved in something other than a children's story. Now something else happens, and we perhaps begin to discern an encounter between history and myth, how the young boy will drop into language and history and learn eventually to read his life in terms of history and language. 'Once' also reminds us that we only come into the world but once and are therefore part of history. 'Once upon a time', by contrast, suggests a more permanent state, that of childhood, outside of history.

It's worth teasing out, therefore, what we mean by difficulty. Difficulty comes in various shapes and sizes, and, more than most writers, Joyce makes certain assumptions, some of which can appear unwarranted. We are obliged almost to become familiar with his personal history, his attitude towards his mother and father and towards his teachers and friends at school and university, and it behoves us to learn something about his relationship with his partner Nora Barnacle, especially when considering his portrayal of female characters such as Gretta Conroy in 'The Dead' or Molly Bloom in *Ulysses* or Bertha in *Exiles*. We also need to develop a certain familiarity with his Irish background, which will include his rejection of Roman Catholicism and his sense that the Irish people repeatedly betrayed their leaders. His work is overshadowed by the loss of faith and by the fall of Charles Stewart Parnell, the leader of the Irish Parliamentary Party. In Committee Room 15 of the House of Commons in December 1890, Parnell, who nearly won Home Rule for Ireland in the 1880s, was brought down by his own party after the affair he was conducting with Kitty O'Shea, the wife of one of his Parliamentary colleagues, was drawing too much fire from the Catholic Church in Ireland and from Protestant opinion inside Gladstone's Liberal Party. The paralyis that ensued in Ireland informs an important element in Joyce's view of contemporary politics, and it also informs the stories of *Dubliners*, where it receives a special focus in 'Ivy Day in the Committee Room'.

Joyce also delighted in realistic texture and he was quite obsessive about transcribing accurately the details connected with his native Dublin. He effectively left Ireland in 1904 and became an exile, but, with the exception of *Giacomo Joyce* (1968), all his fiction is rooted in the Dublin of his childhood and youth. His memory was prodigious, but he also relied on reference books such as *Thom's Official Dublin Directory* of 1904 – which listed all the streets, all the houses, and the names of their occupants – and on the knowledge of his family to help him out. He wanted to determine, for example, whether it was possible to climb over the area railings and enter 7 Eccles Street via the basement (as happens to Bloom at the end of *Ulysses*). *Ulysses* furnishes us with so much information that Joyce believed, somewhat fancifully, if Dublin were ever destroyed, it could be rebuilt using the information contained in his novel. Shops, offices, churches, pubs, streets, statues, signs, bridges, hospitals, libraries, hotels, lamp-posts, railings, tram routes, clocks, all are accurately described *in situ*. Even the flow of the river running through the city is measured so that the same piece of paper dropped into the water can be observed by different people at different places at different times of the day. Understanding place, then – and Dublin in particular – constitutes one of the many challenges in reading Joyce.

If this wasn't enough, there is an added piquancy to Joyce's obsessive imagination. As his name suggests, Bloom is given to bloomers, but Joyce himself is rarely wrong, so that those who time any of the walks across the city undertaken by his characters in *Ulysses* simply confirm that he got it right. Such knowledge can be quite daunting for readers new to Joyce, especially as there isn't a book on 'Backgrounds to Joyce' that foots the bill. I'm tempted to say, 'Enjoy Joyce's reconstruction of a city', for in many respects it's enough to be getting on with. For those who want to follow the routes round the city by various characters in *Dubliners* and *Ulysses*, I have provided some examples of these in the chapters that follow. But none of us can match Joyce's obsession, nor his comprehensiveness, nor the often exhausting way he proceeds to portray his city. We might legitimately feel that whatever insights we possess deserve to be more than merely those that supplement or confirm the author's original intention or achievement.

Difficulty in *Ulysses* is of a higher order than the difficulty we encounter in *Dubliners* or *A Portrait*. Partly this is to do with the reasons outlined above, but part of it concerns the sheer number of allusions to the mountain that forms the heritage of Western culture and history. In the past, the educated person might have been expected to be familiar with such knowledge, but most of us today will have to spend time searching the internet for such things or referring to Don Gifford and Robert Seidman's *Ulysses Annotated* (1989). By the age of 12, John Stuart Mill (1806–73) had read most of the classics and in the original languages of Latin and Greek. Joyce, who was also brought up in a nineteenth-century ethos, isn't this gifted but he did range widely and profitably in his reading and he was in possession of a remarkable memory. Most of us notice things and pass on, but Joyce is one of those people who seem incapable of letting things pass. Who knows, but perhaps 90 per cent of his sense impressions he put to use in his fiction. Whereas his eyes gave him trouble throughout his life, his mind seemed to compensate for such weakness, giving his impressions an added relish and storage space. Moreover, he enjoyed an education in Ireland at the hands of the Jesuits, who were experts at moulding their charges and who, quite simply, gave Joyce a system or habit of ordering the world.

The sheer number of allusions in the first episode of *Ulysses* will stop most readers in their tracks. The episode contains references to the following: the opening of the Latin Mass, the Church Fathers, the Victorian poet Algernon Swinburne, the Greek historian Xenophon, the contemporary Irish poet and mystic George Russell (aka AE), Shakespeare's Hamlet, Matthew Arnold's distinction as outlined in *Culture and Anarchy* (1869) between the Hellenising and Hebraicising impulses in Western culture, lines from William Butler Yeats's early verse, the *Mabinogion* and the *Upanishads*, the Old and New Testaments, Walt Whitman, the eighteenth-century Italian dramatist Carlo Goldoni, Palestrina's Mass for Pope Marcellus, Church heresies, Nietzsche and the superman. Joyce makes as much use of popular culture, so we encounter everything from pantomimes to popular fiction, snatches of contemporary songs to Nelson's words at the Battle of Trafalgar. I could go on, but, as we turn the page, we might be forgiven for thinking 'What on earth's coming next?'

Encountering such information in the first chapter of a modern novel could overwhelm us, especially on a first reading, so, in the first of my three chapters on *Ulysses*, I attempt to show how to cope and read on. All of us need strategies for reading Joyce, which is another way of saying strategies of coping. *Finnegans Wake* takes us to another level of difficulty altogether, and I have included a chapter on this text partly to round out the story and partly to insist on the integrity of the whole of Joyce's work. It's not easy to assign *Finnegans Wake* to a given genre for it's not a novel as we understand that word. It took Joyce some 15 years or so to put together, and he thought that if it had taken this long to write he didn't see why it shouldn't take a similar amount of time to read. The difficulty with *Finnegans Wake* lies in part in the use of portmanteau words and phrases and also in the way these draw on languages others than English. Thus a portmanteau phrase such as 'foenix culprit' (*FW* 23:16) includes at a minimum the following associations: the Church's resurrection motif *felix culpa* or happy fault, that Adam's sin had one important benefit because it brought forth the Saviour; the Phoenix Park to the west of Dublin, where the Chief Secretary to Ireland was murdered by the Invincibles in 1882; the culprit responsible for a possible murder in Sheridan Le Fanu's intriguing novel *The House by the Church-yard* (1863); 'the feelmick's park' (520:1), a crude allusion to some sexual misdemeanour in the park, 'mick' being a slang word in Hiberno-English for penis; the phoenix that rises from the ashes; perhaps the language you might come across in a children's comic 'Foe

The Wellington Monument in the Phoenix Park. An Edwardian postcard.

knicks culprit'; 'Feenichts Playhouse' (219:2) where admission is free. The phrase also betrays a doubt as to whether or not there has been a crime committed, and whether or not there is either a foe or a culprit, a pair who are separated in this instance by nix, nichts, nothing.

'O foenix culprit!' contains all these associations, all these possible associations, and all this history. These portmanteau words and phrases in *Finnegans Wake* are like chords in music and we are invited to listen to the sounds they make, not all of which we can be sure are intended and not all of which are etymologically accurate. 'Culpa' and 'culprit' enter the language at different times; 'culprit' is a seventeenth-century word being primarily legal and linked with the person who commits a 'culpa' or sin. Joyce enforces the link by phonological similarity, a shared syllable, and semantic association. 'Mea culpa', the breast-beating penitent would say in the confessional and at Mass. My fault, my fault, my most grievous fault. But introduce the idea of 'culprit' and the confessional or owning-up context shifts. Perhaps at a deeper level we can discern Joyce drawing attention to the close alignment between original sin, which is a stain on humanity, and the sins, whether venial or mortal, that were subsequently committed by us all; or the alignment between sin and error; or between someone suffering a fault and the person who is responsible for it, or between victim and perpetrator; or, if we go back far enough, the alignment between Adam, the culprit, and Jesus, who died for our sins.

Table 1.1 'Foenix culprit': associations

Foenix	Culprit
felix (Latin for happy)	culpa (Latin for sin, mistake, fault)
felicitous	culpability
Felix	Culapert
felicious	coolpose
finixed	coulpure
Finn MacCool	
phoenix (bird)	
Phoenix Park (linguistic corruption)	
fin (French for end)	
Feenichts Playhouse (nichts, German for nothing)	
foe knicks	
knicks (short for female knickers)	
feelmick's park	
	culprik
fiendish	
Phoenician	

Coping with such a text as *Finnegans Wake* presents an enormous challenge, and in my final chapter I reflect on the notes I made when I first began reading it in earnest. The position we are assigned as readers in *Finnegans Wake* is also relevant and can be observed in something that is more readily accessible. When I embarked on reading the text, perhaps by way of relief, my eye was repeatedly drawn to something adjacent to the difficulty presented by the portmanteau words. If there is one punctuation mark that dominates Joyce's last work, it seemed to be the exclamation mark. In the first chapter alone there are around 194 such marks flying off the page. An exclamation mark is an awkward punctuation mark in English. How are we supposed to respond when we encounter it on a page? Is it a shared moment with the author? The attitude of the author or narrator to what is being described or narrated? A form of exclusion of the reader? A way of forestalling sympathy? A way of responding to our plight as readers, as when we encounter the phrase 'Cry not yet!' in *Finnegans Wake*? Is it a form of encouragement, therefore? Or is the exclamation mark designed to convey a dramatic moment and to remind us we are indeed reading a book and that this is the primary reality? At times, difficulty in Joyce arises from our not being sure what constitutes the disposition of the material. A range of attitudes can be invoked to make sense of what we are reading, but which one? Interestingly, while we might delay in opting for the right one, all the ones just mentioned are in fact knowable, and knowable to most readers.

Even as I'm addressing it all the time, I tend to avoid the word 'difficulty', therefore, in the book that follows. The phrase I stress in the opening chapters is 'unfinished sentences', which itself is another form of delay. As readers, we are not unlike the boy in the first story of *Dubliners* obliged to 'extract meaning' from Mr Cotter's 'unfinished sentences'. Reading Joyce is an interactive affair and involves us in extraction, a word that might well remind us of the dentist's chair or of how minerals are extracted from the earth. But delay allows us to develop something else, namely curiosity. I would ask my students to see if they could discover something to be curious about and share it with the group. Without curiosity, Joyce will remain for all of us nothing but a curiosity. Come up with a question. Why does this story carry this particular title? Why 'Clay'? What was 'Ivy Day'? Could the sisters in 'The Sisters' also be the boy and the priest? Is the snow falling at the end of 'The Dead' to be read as a positive or a negative sign? Formulating questions can help gain confidence in reading Joyce, and, even if there are no neat answers, they provide inside help, as it were, and a first rung on the ladder of interpretation.

Turn round the question of difficulty and come at it from a biographical angle. Let me put this dramatically: Joyce was extraordinarily reluctant to say what he means. As we shall see in a later discussion at the beginning of Chapter 11, the reasons for this belong in part to the general reluctance of Modernists to allow their work to be paraphrased. But here let me draw attention to something Joyce's brother Stanislaus wrote in the early 1950s in a public row with Joyce's one-time friend Oliver St John Gogarty: 'My brother's self-appointed task was to rescue literature from the hands of those who had made it a parody of life, from the "mummers", as he called them' (Stanislaus Joyce, 1954, 53). Joyce was a determined young man who, like Stephen Dedalus at the end of *A Portrait*, sought 'the reality of experience' (*P* 253). The words Stanislaus uses are deliberately confrontational or, we might well agree, Joycean: 'self-appointed', 'rescue', 'parody', 'mummers'. 'Mummers' was a word Joyce had used in his attack on Yeats's Irish National Theatre Society, an early-twentieth-century drama group which was the immediate forerunner of the Abbey Theatre. For Joyce, mummers are those who dressed up in plays or pantomimes, who provided nothing more than what we might consider entertainment at a dumb-show. Joyce, 'self-appointed' or not, was determined to rescue literature from 'keeping mum', as it were, and to give us not a parody of life but life itself.

I would argue, therefore, that Joyce's 'difficulty' is not primarily to do with his special knowledge or, what might be thought, his arrogance or snobbery, but is one of the consequences of his serious purpose, what I term in my Afterword the covenant he sought with the reader. What he was looking for was contact with 'the real' and not the pseudo-real as practised by those in control of the literary and artistic establishment. In this regard Joyce was not so much a rebel without a cause but an ideologically committed writer, who in the early part of his career allied himself with Henrik Ibsen and the cause of truth in the face of bourgeois illusions. Putting it like this doesn't excuse the difficulty, but it may help some readers to identify more with the young man who had ambitions to make a mark on the world and challenge our illusions or beliefs in the field of politics and letters.

This book is about coping with Joyce. I have spent over 30 years watching how students cope with him, and I rely on some of that experience, including student comments and observations, as a way of indicating how other readers might cope. I have also reproduced some of my class handouts and even the notes on the endpapers of my copy of *Finnegans Wake*. My book is in that sense close to the reality of teaching and the classroom experience. If at times it has the look of a workshop, that's intentional. I want the book to be read as an argument about why we continue to read Joyce, but I also want the book to be a practical help for readers who are new to Joyce. What do students today write about Joyce? What gets them excited? Why not include that in your critical journey, I told myself, and show others how Joyce continues to intervene in our culture. As emerges from a reading of Chapter 10, some of the liveliest writing has come out of responses to the Molly Bloom soliloquy, and I have included some of those responses here by way of prompting further thought. At the same time, I'd like the book to be read as a whole, as part of an argument about why we should delay in reading Joyce.

Snapshots of Joyce

Coping with Joyce, then, doesn't have to be like a workout. Reading him normally involves us in stretching and sometimes in mental gymnastics, but it doesn't mean enduring the equivalent of Jane Fonda's burn. Sometimes the visual can say as much if not more than the written, and I have taken this opportunity to use an array of images to complement and augment my argument. Perhaps this is another reason why I am attracted to Joyce, for I like visual material to be varied. Nothing should be automatically excluded, and some things should challenge us by their unexpected nature. Pointing to a painting of Cork in a cork frame in his Paris flat, the punning Joyce

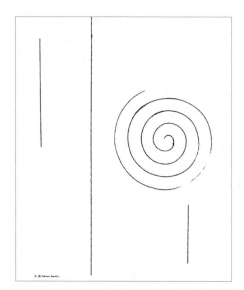

(left) Brancusi's *Symbol of Joyce* was used to accompany Joyce's *Tales Told of Shem and Shaun*, published by the Black Sun Press in Paris in 1929.

(right) *Portrait of James Joyce* by Constantin Brancusi, *c.* 1925. What more was needed to give us a full portrait than a sketch of seven hairs or so on the crown of a head and three on the side, an open mouth, a well-defined chin, and wire glasses in front of a slit (or is it a wound?) for an eye. It's a portrait that ironically suggests there is more tenderness in the artist than in the subject.
Source: ADAGP, Paris and DACS, London 2007

revealed to the Cork writer Frank O'Connor that he was looking at C/cork. Here, then, at the beginning of this visual journey, I thought it might help by way of orientation if we touched on the impression Joyce himself creates in our culture.

Opposite the title page of Richard Ellmann's biography of James Joyce is an iconic image by Constantin Brancusi of a spiral with three straight vertical lines alongside. When Joyce's father was shown the sketch, he humorously quipped that his son had changed somewhat since he last saw him. The image of the spiral is not so much unsettling as intriguing, for the convention with biographies is to select a photograph that provides a sense of immediacy or an insight into the subject's essential character, dressed for the part as it were. A spiral is a geometrical symbol, circular but not a circle, a gesture toward infinity but not itself the sign of infinity. We might record something else from the period and think of Joyce also in this context. According to Adolfo Best-Maugard in a book published in 1929 surveying the history of design and patterns that have come down to us from antiquity, the form of the whirling spiral is 'the fundamental principle of design' (Best-Maugard, 1929, 162).

A spiral is not an obvious choice for the Irish author. If pressed, we might detect an echo of another term from geometry, the 'gnomon' from Euclid's geometry and a word deployed by Joyce in the first story of *Dubliners* and which I discuss in more detail in Chapter 3. It's another form of delay, therefore, but this time from a visual perspective. Or perhaps we might interpret it, as some have claimed, as a 'spiral ear', an image of the aural and the visual combined in the author who wrote as much for the ear as the eye and who called the protagonist in his last work 'Earwicker'. More remotely, perhaps the spiral and the three lines can be read as a conversational, inter-textual reply across the centuries to the whimsical flourish of Corporal Trim's stick in Laurence Sterne's novel *Tristram Shandy* (1759–68). What-ever the case, Brancusi's *Symbol of Joyce* (1929) is, nevertheless, arresting, and confronts us as an enigma or as an epiphany, a moment of revelation whereby Joyce is revealed as worthy of non-representation. In that sense it's not unlike how Yahweh was depicted in non-human form as an all-seeing eye by Jacobean Protestants suspicious of Catholic iconography of God and his saints. Knowing what we now do, we might well agree that into the shell of this ear went all the seas and sounds of the world.

Ellmann could have selected one of Joyce's favourite photos, the one of him with his back to the camera taken by Carola Giedion-Welcker at the Platzspitz in Zurich where the Rivers Sihl and the Limmat meet, but this would hardly do by way of introduction and might be taken up wrongly by

Carola Giedion-Welcker's photograph of Joyce, Zurich 1938.

Portrait of Joyce taken by Gisèle Freund, Paris 1938.
Source: Estate of Gisèle Freund/John Hillelson

his reader. Or he might have picked one from the most evocative series of photos we possess of Joyce, namely those by Gisèle Freund taken in Paris in May 1938, one of which appeared in colour on the cover of *Time* magazine in May 1939 (and the one I used as a basis for the cover of this book). I think it's to his credit that Ellmann chose the image he did, for it sets down a marker by way of introduction to the figure whose life is about to be drawn for us, a figure therefore whose enigmatic status in the culture is insisted on from the outset.

Joyce enters the culture somewhere between word and image, between iconicity and perversity, between being and meaning. He is both a mystery and a person hidden from view, both inviting and off-putting, someone who is a delight for the caricaturist but who resists the easy art of paraphrase. When the visual is to the fore, we notice the gestures – the head to one side as a young man with hands in pocket outside Constantine Curran's greenhouse, or the image of him around 40 years of age with ashplant silhouetted in the doorway of Shakespeare and Company with a young-looking Sylvia Beach, or the magnifying glass close to the failing eye in middle age. But with the word he remains often invisible, not so much turning his back on the reader as insisting on the primacy and the revelatory potential of the reading experience. In this sense, Brancusi's spiral is also an epiphany, an epiphany being Joyce's borrowed term to convey the distinctive character of his collection of stories – the moment, for example, when a character or the reader suddenly understands their destiny or the narrative's destination.

Poster for the International James Joyce Symposium held on the island of San Giorgio in Venice in 1988. This is my favourite Joyce conference poster: the winding canal, Joyce playing, and Stephen Joyce, Michael Yeats, and Mary de Rachewiltz – the offspring of Joyce, Yeats, and Pound – in the one room together perhaps for the only time in their lives. The previous month Ronald Reagan and Margaret Thatcher had been holed up on San Giorgio talking about Star Wars.

A classic photograph of Sylvia Beach and Joyce outside Shakespeare and Company on rue de l'Odéon in Paris in 1920.

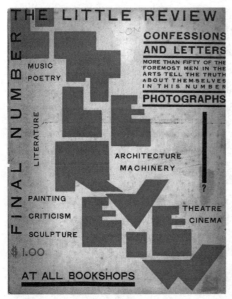

Final issue of *The Little Review*, May 1929, in which the editors hoped to print the truth about the leading 50 figures in the contemporary world of the arts.

Turning Joyce to face the camera has been the historic task of critics ever since. Characteristically, while he drew attention to himself calling his semi-autobiographical novel *A Portrait of the Artist as a Young Man*, when he became famous he took pains to prevent too much direct prying into his own portrait. When he actually sat for his portrait for the painter Patrick Tuohy, what he was most anxious about was not his soul or his character but ensuring the artist got his tie right. Joyce has this uncanny knack of out-flanking or undermining expectations or conventions, and he reminds us that appearances matter, but that, wherever his soul is, it isn't in the painting. The final issue of *The Little Review* in 1929, Margaret Anderson's magazine that first gave *Ulysses* to the world when it published several in-stalments in 1918–20, was devoted to a survey conducted among the lead-ing writers of the time. Included in the ten questions or so sent out were: 'What should you most like to do?' 'What do you look forward to?' 'What do you consider your weakest/strongest characteristic?' 'What is your atti-tude toward art today?' 'What is your world view?' 'Why do you go on liv-ing?' Most authors filled in their replies dutifully. Ezra Pound wrote briefly: 'Print what you've got on hand' (*Little Review*, 41). HD (Hilda Doolittle), who responded at length, ended by saying that for years she went on living 'out of spite or pique' (40). Ernest Hemingway sent a poem which began 'Sing a song of critics/pockets full of lye' (42). Joyce replied that he had been away from home and invited the editor Jane Heap to tea 'when we can talk over the questionnaire' (50). When she left, he telephoned her office with the disappointing news that 'he really could find nothing to say'.

What did Jane Heap expect? Joyce's reaction was hardly surprising given the questions were designed to prise open a door – in Joyce's case to this most private person. We can only guess how he might have answered the various questions. 'What is your world view?' 'Read my books', he might well have replied. 'How can I paraphrase or summarise what constitutes my world view? From "Once upon a time" at the beginning of *A Portrait of the Artist as a Young Man* to "yes", the final word of *Ulysses*, every sentence I've written contains a world view of sorts.' Jane Heap didn't pursue the matter. Instead, she printed the proofs of two pages from 'Work in Progress', which appeared in the first issue of *transition* and which included the phrase of sensible Shaun, Joyce's alter ego: 'I'd like my own company best'. As ever, the two pages were adorned with a string of corrections in Joyce's spidery hand. The photograph used in *The Little Review* piece is one taken by Berenice Abbott in 1926, with an eye-pad over his left eye and Joyce looking away to the right, sporting a spotted bow-tie and striped shirt, his right hand supporting his head in front of his 'spiral' ear.

Berenice Abbott's photograph of Joyce, Paris, 1926.
Source: Berenice Abbott/Commerce Graphics NYC

Home, sweet home

If William Wordsworth's Dove Cottage in the Lake District, or Yeats's Thoor Ballylee on the Clare–Galway border, or Robinson Jeffers's Tor House in Carmel, California, or Emily Dickinson's house in Amherst, Massachusetts still retain something of the presence of their former occupants, where can Joyce can found? We might begin our search with his homes in Dublin and environs in the first 22 years of his life. But which one? Before departing for the continent in October 1904, never effectively to return to live, Joyce had some 12 addresses, and these 12 don't include the years spent at Clongowes Wood College between the ages of six and nine, the nearly three months spent at the Hôtel Corneille in Paris in January–April 1903 while exploring the possibility of becoming a medical student, or the few days he spent at the Martello Tower in Sandycove in September 1904. Listing the addresses confirms the difficulty of finding Joyce at home or of securing any of them for posterity:

41 Brighton Square, Rathgar, 1882–4.
23 Castlewood Avenue, Rathmines, 1884–7.
1 Martello Terrace, Bray, 1887–91.
23 Carysfort Avenue, Blackrock, 1891–2.
14 Fitzgibbon Street, Dublin, 1892–4.

(left) 41 Brighton Square in the new suburb of Rathgar on the south side of Dublin. Joyce was born here on 2 February 1882 and it's nice to imagine that it was here that his father told him a story about a moocow coming down along the road.

(right) 1 Martello Terrace, Bray. Photograph by David Pierce. This is where the Christmas dinner scene in *A Portrait* is staged by Joyce. The house, complete with a boat house, was adjacent to the sea, and it must have been a delight for John Joyce who could indulge his love of rowing.

2 Millbourne Avenue, Drumcondra, 1894–6.
17 North Richmond Street, Dublin, 1896.
29 Windsor Avenue, Fairview, 1896–9.
Convent Avenue, Fairview, 1899.
8 Royal Terrace, Fairview, 1900–1.
32 Glengariff Terrace, Dublin, 1901–2.
7 St Peter's Terrace, Cabra, 1902–4.

As for the addresses he occupied between 1904 and his interment in the Fluntern Cemetery in Zurich in January 1941, these can be quickly indicated, but we would be mistaken if we thought the story would be different. A full list of addresses, which occupy some eight pages, can be consulted in the second volume of *The Letters of James Joyce* (1966). Between 1904 and 1915 Joyce had some ten different addresses in Trieste; eight in Zurich between 1915 and 1920; and some 19 in Paris in the interwar years between 1920 and 1939 – and I have included none of the hotels or guest houses he stayed at in various parts of Britain and continental Europe. Some addresses have a larger claim on him simply because of the time spent there. Nearly three years at the Via Donato Bramante in Trieste between 1912 and 1915; nearly six years at Square Robiac on rue de Grenelle in Paris between 1925

Hôtel du Commerce at St Gérand-du-Puy, where the Joyces stayed in 1940 when fleeing Nazi-occupied Paris. The family were resident here for six months before escaping to neutral Switzerland in December 1940. It was here that Joyce met for the last time his Jewish secretary Paul Léon, who was later murdered by the Nazis. This photograph by Jacques Richard appeared in Patricia Hutchins, *James Joyce's World* (1957), where there is also an account of his walks with his trusty friend Maria Jolas.

and 1931; over four years at rue Edmond Valentin in Paris between 1935 and 1939. But most of his addresses were of fewer than 12 months' duration. If plaques were to be erected outside every door he had a key to, there would be over 50 locations to commemorate. This amounts to not quite one address a year for every year he lived, but close to it.

In 'Coole Park and Ballylee, 1931', a poem composed in his mid-sixties celebrating his friend Lady Gregory and the Big House in Ireland, Yeats lamented:

> Where fashion or mere fantasy decrees
> Man shifts about – all that great glory spent –
> Like some poor Arab tribesman and his tent.
> (Yeats, 1933, 32)

Joyce, too, shifted about, in that delightful, conversational phrase of Yeats, but there was no great glory behind him, simply the pattern his impecunious father had established for the family. In a paragraph in *Finnegans Wake* he groups together the Dublin addresses where he lived with his family and recasts them in the process with images of immiseration. Milbourne Avenue surfaces as 'Milchbroke', Windsor Avenue is hailed as 'Windsewer. Ave', and Royal Terrace is transformed into something decidedly ugly – 'Royal Terrors' (*FW* 420). 'Dining with the Danes' is a phrase used in the same paragraph, and you can just imagine the Joyce children saying to each other, when the removal van arrived, 'Where next? Oxmantown or wherever they buried the Vikings? We'll be dining with the Danes next.' Like his father, Joyce tended to move within cities for financial reasons. In that sense, Joyce kept changing addresses not because of fashion or because he had some whim to satisfy. By the time he left Dublin with his partner Nora Barnacle in 1904, he was destined to keep moving, but there was nothing romantic about any of this. At probably no time in his life was he ever footloose and fancy free. Equally, while he may have been constantly on the move, he was not like 'some poor Arab tribesman and his tent', and – a point worth dwelling on – he betrays almost no sign of a homeless mind. With her broad vowels from the west of Ireland, Nora ensured he was never far from home.

So where might we go to feel Joyce's presence? Put another way, is there a place called home for Joyce? With a typographical slip that could not completely hide its emotional import for the young man setting out on life's course, the telegram he received in Paris from his father on Good Friday 1903 stated simply: 'Nother dying come home father'. Not 'mother' but 'nother'. Home at that time was St Peter's Terrace. His father certainly thought this was home for his eldest son. Four months after receiving the

Joyce family in transit.
Photograph taken by Ottocaro
Weiss in Zurich 1915. Giorgio
was ten, Lucia eight.

telegram, Joyce's mother was dead, her body wasted by cancer. She was 44. Home for Joyce was twelve addresses and nine other children, or, expressed from the vantage-point of his mother, Mary-Jane, 'May' Joyce, on average every other year between 1882 and 1903 witnessed a change of address and a new accession to the family.

Frequent changes of address have their own effect. It's true that to some extent Joyce never cut the umbilical cord linking him with his city and country. But the state of exile was almost programmed into him from the start, bequeathing to him one of the most powerful themes in his imaginative work. *A Portrait of the Artist as a Young Man* (1916), which ends with Stephen Dedalus packing his second-hand clothes for Europe, is a journey into exile; *Ulysses* (1922), which begins with Stephen home again after his sojourn in Paris, is a journey back to his homeland. In *Exiles*, the play that was published in 1918, between 1916 and 1922 that is, Joyce addresses the theme head-on, and probes the view that home is where the heart is. The title sets up the expectation that the play will explore the conventional view that afflicts most exiles, namely the *odi atque amo* theme, the hatred and the love the exile feels at one and the same time for his native country. However, the tension in this play is something more personal.

Richard and Bertha Rowan return to Ireland with their son Archie after being away for nine years, and Richard soon discovers a third person in the marriage, for, in spite of years of exile, his wife and his friend Robert Hand are still fond of each other. Almost from the play's opening scene, the theme of 'exiles from home' gives way to the theme of 'exile from the self' and the playing out of jealousy and betrayal. Its power derives in part from the autobiographical imprint that is undisguised and everywhere apparent. It lets us into discussions that must have taken place in the Joyce household and the reservations Nora and James felt about each other. Like Richard, Joyce was intent on possession of the other, possession of the other's affections, and even possession of a lover's past affections. Joyce's remarkably frank set of notes to the play alludes to Rahoon in Galway (where Nora's boyfriend Michael Bodkin is buried) and to the way 'she' (that is Nora) was known in the convent where she worked as a 'mankiller' on account of the deaths of two boyfriends, Bodkin and Kearns.

Exiles represents Joyce's sharpest view of his own exile. It's a play that is at once honest and painful, a reminder of Joyce's peculiar, under-developed psychology where the soul is compelled to face itself regardless of consequence. When Richard wakes Bertha to inform her he has been unfaithful, he insists to his friend Robert that 'She must know me as I am' (*E* 83). At the same time, he leaves her alone one evening with Robert because 'in the very core of my ignoble heart I longed to be betrayed by you and her' (*E* 87). Richard is caught between wanting Bertha to be independent of him and discovering the pain that ensues from such a release. It's a play, then, that redefines the tension between home and abroad in terms of the heart and sexual betrayal. What Joyce could see, or what perhaps he wanted to see, was that home is where the heart is, and for Joyce this meant not Ireland or his mother or even his male friends, but his emotional attachment to a woman he both loved and wanted to test. There is a homeliness in the language of the old servant Brigid, but, for the writer intent on Europeanising Ireland, she represents the past not the future. Abroad, Bertha recalls the time when she and Richard first met: 'Every day of my life I see that' (*E* 143). The word she inadvertently uses is 'Ourselves', which in Irish is *Sinn Féin* (sometimes translated as 'ourselves alone'). It's a word that causes us to delay, as if certain parallels were being drawn with a wider narrative of liberation. But it doesn't get that far, and we realise that, although their marriage is no longer new, for Bertha and for Richard, a sexual relationship, which acquires intensity by the condition of exile and return, constitutes the primary reality, and not the state or the condition of Ireland.

Of the two houses in the play, both belong to Robert. One represents Edwardian ease and the other – a cottage in Ranelagh used for the liaison with Bertha – intimacy. By contrast, Richard is the returning exile, with no home and, as it transpires, no university appointment. The sun in the first act is 'waning' and by the second act we hear rain falling and gusts of wind causing the lamp to flicker. We are at the end of something. Home for Joyce is circumstance, the place to get away from, associated with being without. If your friends fail you, you go away, and if you go away long enough you learn to adjust. One of the consequences of exile for Joyce was that he was reduced to hearing voices, as Richard does. I say 'reduced', which suggests a certain loss, but in Joyce's case it produced the spiral ear, which in turn gave us all the sounds of his native city and country. So, exile was a condition that had its positive side, and, as Robert somewhat stiltedly reminds us, it gave him 'that food of the spirit by which a nation of human beings is sustained in life' (*E* 127).

Exile prompted or encouraged a curious exchange or reciprocity between presence and absence in Joyce, which meant he never cut the umbilical cord. Look at the more than 150 words for Dublin that Louis Mink has identified in *A Finnegans Wake Gazetteer* (1978) and you can appreciate the strength of Joyce's feelings for his native city and how, as an exile, he enjoyed playing with its name: 'devlinsfirst' (*FW* 3:23), 'Dobbelin ayle' (*FW* 7:12), 'Dyoublong' (*FW* 13:04), 'antidulibnium' (*FW* 310:07), 'Aud Dub' (*FW* 484:21). But in using the word 'exchange' I am drawing attention to something on display throughout the book that follows, namely Joyce's 'economic' way of being or thinking. Like the economy, touch any part of Joyce and there are effects elsewhere, some of them unexpected; and like the economy, as inflation reminds us, there's nothing in one sense that lies outside. Thus, his nomadic existence, for example, allowed Joyce, almost incidentally, insight into the world of the street. Talk about exile and you find yourself talking about home. Talk about home, and you find yourself talking about the street. Talk about Aud Dub and you find yourself asking 'Do you belong?' (Dyoublong). Such moves involve us as readers in keeping up, but, if you focus not on cause-and-effect but on 'economic' patterns, understanding Joyce can become slightly easier.

Streets in Joyce, particularly evident in *Dubliners* and *Ulysses*, are not so much a gulf to be negotiated, as they are in Virginia Woolf, but are, rather, a place that offers a form of security away from the insecurity of home. Through all the changes of address in his first 22 years, the city streets in Dublin remained much the same. It was a comfort of sorts. For most of Joyce's characters, the streets afford different air to breathe, sometimes as in 'An Encounter' an adventure which ends in an encounter with a pae-dophile. As the guide books suggest, *Ulysses* is essentially a novel of the streets, where people are shown walking and bumping into each other, where people notice others walking in the street, and where people pass known landmarks and shops on their way through the city. Dublin comes across as a domestic city, but this stems largely from the portrayal of the street and not the home. Interestingly, one reason Bloom's fate is particularly intense is because his home life keeps 'intruding' on to the street to become public knowledge.

Freund's series of photographs of Joyce in 1938 in Paris are striking not only because of the domestic shots of the Joyce household but also because of the exterior ones, as if she knew instinctively where Joyce is most at home. There is one of Joyce and Adrienne Monnier walking along rue de l'Odéon in Paris, one of his favourite streets. Something in the shop window of Shakespeare and Company has caught both their eyes but they continue walking with a certain amount of purposiveness, she with a long skirt gently billowing in the wind, he with his walking stick tucked under the left arm of his unbuttoned overcoat, his hat pushed back, a parcel under his right arm. Freund has ensured the two occupy only part of the photograph, for most of it is taken up with the street scene – a passer-by behind them,

Gisèle Freund's photograph of Joyce and Adrienne Monnier on rue de l'Odéon, Paris, 1938.

Source: Estate of Gisèle Freund/John Hillelson

street signs, a parked car, an empty handcart – and all overshadowed by the row of shops and apartments above tapering off into the distance, the cross of a pharmacist's separating their two heads. It must be near midday with the sun nearly overhead because Joyce and Monnier, as if they are already part of history or the future, cast almost no shadow.

Streets offered Joyce somewhere else to reflect, a place parallel to but distinct from worry and care, where the mind could meditate and catch itself thinking. And things invariably happen on Joyce's streets – encounters, missed opportunities, relief, talk, gossip, or paying for a taxi, as can be observed in one of Freund's photos where Joyce, hand in purse, looks quizzically at the camera as if to say 'Faith, what do you want a shot of me reaching into my purse and paying for a taxi? What's so special about that? At home I might be special but in the street I'm like everyone else.' From inside favourite restaurants such as La Coupole in Montparnasse, Joyce, glass of white wine in hand, could watch the action on the streets and be reminded of the voices of Dublin. His streets are noisy, human, full of people in transit across the city, closer to a labyrinth than paralysis. Home by contrast was circumstance, one step removed from paralysis, where children are beaten, as in 'Counterparts', or where his mother died an awful death, as we have seen, her eyes glazing, 'staring out of death' (U 1:273), or where the starving Joyce children, perhaps like Maggy Dedalus, 'poured yellow thick soup from the kettle into a bowl' (U 10:285). Bloom, the inside-out character in Ulysses, might have had the Joyce family in mind when he surmises in the Funeral episode: 'The Irishman's house is his coffin' (U 6:821–2).

The question prompts itself. Did Joyce need the constant change of address to remind him of the familiar, the family he came from, to feel reassurance and at the same time to provide a whetstone for his imagination? Some writers, some people, are driven creatures. Like the Beats in the 1950s, they feel the urge to take to the highway and never stop the journey westward or wherever, a compulsion not to put down roots. On the road. No direction home, as Bob Dylan has it. Joyce was a European writer and took to no highway, but, if you spend your life renting rooms, you develop little sense of ownership. There is a positive side to this and Joyce has it in abundance. In his mind, he set about peopling rooms for others and developed an expertise in imagining interior spaces. Think of the tight little spaces in 'The Boarding House', the setting for the female predators lying in wait to trap Mr Doran into marriage, and the dramatic moment, the epiphany, at the end of that story when Polly hears her mother: 'Come down, dear. Mr Doran wants to speak with you' (D 69). Or take the Blooms' large house on Eccles Street with its railings, fanlight over the door and sash windows, or the

Two images of La Coupole in Montparnasse, one of Joyce's favourite places in Paris in the interwar years, taken in the 1930s and 2006. 2006 photograph by David Pierce.

gothic atmosphere of the Misses Morkans' house in 'The Dead' with its high-ceilinged pantry, spacious hallway as a buffer with the outside world, symbolic stairs and banisters, and large drawing room for entertaining. The house in *Finnegans Wake* is full of noises travelling up and down between floors and through the chimney. Only someone who shifted about could give us a sense of so many different houses and interiors.

In life, returning home in the evening was more problematic. What was it like to be part of a family in decline? The heart sinks as the front door opens. No comfort here for the adolescent boy, his whole life overshadowed by something which gnawed at its roots. We might be reminded of a scene from a sentimental Victorian novel or a particularly painful section in the 'Wandering Rocks' episode of *Ulysses* when we glimpse the acute poverty of the Dedalus children. By contrast, in early childhood, on special occasions such as Christmas dinner, the young Joyce would dress for dinner, as Stephen Dedalus does in *A Portrait* with his 'deep low collar and the Eton jacket' (*P* 30). But what happens when, gazing out of the window, Eveline notices the evenings begin to *invade* the avenue, as happens to the female protagonist in *Dubliners* (*D* 36)? Inside and outside the home, the young boy's world closes in. North Richmond Street, the setting for 'Araby', is 'blind' (*D* 29). As Gabriel Conroy comes to realise in a story about Irish hospitality and personal emotions, the freest place in 'The Dead' is not inside his aunts' house or his wife's affections but outside on the snow-capped top of the Wellington Monument in the Phoenix Park.

So where is Joyce to be found? Occasionally he can be discovered in the corrections he made by hand to his manuscripts after they had been typed up, as if his intentions could be deciphered without the interference of type. Joyce understood addition better than subtraction and his insertions frequently allow us to touch him there as it were. The streets of Dublin yield if not intimacy then another kind of connection. The various Joyce houses listed above are more evocative of the family's financial decline than of the person who became the famous writer. A visit to 1 Martello Terrace, Bray, an end-terrace house at the edge of the sea and the setting for the Christmas dinner scene in *A Portrait*, conveys something of the presence of Joyce's father and his interest in rowing. Before it had been 'discovered', coming across a chemist called Vance and Wilson on Main Street, Bray was exciting and somehow seemed close to a trail leading to Joyce. Eileen Vance, who emigrated to Canada and lived to be 100, is the name of the little Protestant girl who plays with Stephen Dedalus at the beginning of *A Portrait* and was related to the former owner of this shop. The Martello Tower at Sandycove, which now houses the James Joyce Museum, is a must for the visitor and contains Joyce's waistcoat and other memorabilia. From the top of the tower, as you gaze across Dublin Bay toward Howth Head, where you are standing marks the opening of *Ulysses,* and the direction in which you are peering marks the closing moments when Molly recalls lovemaking with Bloom and his proposal to her. Behind you are the Dublin Mountains and to the left is Dublin itself, where the bulk of the novel takes place.

The James Joyce Centre on North Great George's Street, on the northside of Dublin off Parnell Square, was established in more recent times by

The actor Eamonn Morrisey, dressed as Bloom, at the top of the Martello Tower at Sandymount. Photograph taken by Dan Harper in October 1985. The same year Morrisey gave a one-man *Ulysses* show for students from York and Leeds taught by myself and Pieter Bekker. It was a memorable afternoon with Morrisey using every inch of the former gun emplacement to give us an impressive take on the different characters in the novel.

Source: Dan Harper

Senator David Norris and Joyce's nephew Ken Monaghan. It contains the door of Bloom's house, 7 Eccles Street, furniture from the Parisian flat of Joyce's secretary Paul Léon, and a room once used by the dancing master Dennis J. Maginni, who has a distinguished walk-on part befitting his status in *Ulysses*. The house on Usher's Island, the setting for 'The Dead', has been saved from the developer. 7 Eccles Street, the one house with perhaps the strongest claim on Joyce's spirit, has long gone. The rebuilt Ormond Hotel, the setting for 'Sirens', advertises itself as the 'Siren Bar' and the 'Sirens Lounge', which is by anyone's standards really over the top. In Joyce's day, confirmed by *Thom's Business Directory of Dublin and Suburbs for the Year 1906*, Mrs De Massey was the proprietor. Unfortunately,

PROFESSORS OF DANCING.

Byrne, Mr. and Mrs. Talbot Leggett, 27 Adelaide road, and 63 Mountjoy sq.

Cottuli, Mrs., 91 Harcourt street, and 53 Charleville avenue.

Cottuli, Theodore, 91 Harcourt street, and 53 Charleville avenue.

D'Vine, Robert, 24 Bridge street, lower.

Graham, R. H., 26 Temple street, north.

Levenston, Mrs. P. M., 35 Frederick st., south.

Maginni, Denis J., 32 George's street, n.

Entry for Maginni in *Thom's Business Directory of Dublin and Suburbs for the Year 1906*, which also lists three pages of 'Professors of Music'.

The Ormond Hotel beside the River Liffey in Dublin. Photograph by David Pierce. This is the setting for 'Sirens', the Music episode in *Ulysses*.

without architectural plans from the period, it has proved almost impossible for Joyce scholars to reconstruct with any degree of certainty the hotel's Edwardian interior. The Gresham Hotel on O'Connell Street, where Gretta and Gabriel spend an unhappy night after his epiphany that her heart is with a former lover, is part of the Joyce story if not terribly integral to it. All over the city there are little reminders of Joyce – the interior of the National Library and its steps, shops from the period, statues of writers and political figures, Guinness barges, quayside walks, churches, priests, the poor.

Hearing voices of home – this is what Joyce constantly experienced abroad. His work is full of Irish voices, and, in hearing him evoke these, we are listening to the master himself. Seeking out the *fons et origo*, the fount and origin, of his inspiration or the immediate contexts for his work will inevitably remind us that he is now dispersed across Europe, across the globe, into the ether. Given that he spent nearly two-thirds of his life outside of Ireland, it would be churlish to imagine we could trace everything back to his formative years. Equally, as Peter Costello's *James Joyce: Years of Growth 1882–1915* (1992) reminds us, the biography of Joyce finishes in one sense in 1915, the year Joyce moved to Zurich. After that date Joyce's life to some extent retreats before us with nearly all his life going into his writing. Remove problems with his eyes, difficulties with securing employment, getting his work published, threats of litigation (and actual court cases), and moving house, what does a record of Joyce's life amount to? The

Switzer and Co., a name that Joyce links in *Finnegans Wake* with Switzerland and refuge from the Great War. The department store on Grafton Street has changed hands but the sign above street level remains. In her soliloquy, Molly recalls Bloom trying to get near 'two stylishdressed ladies outside Switzers window' (*U* 18:1044–5). Photograph by David Pierce.

answer must be – and the contrast with Yeats is instructive – disappointingly thin and unremarkable.

The Joyce country, then, is different from the Yeats country in Sligo or on the Clare–Galway border. Take one look at Ben Bulben and you understand immediately the significance of Yeats's wish to be buried in its shadow. Similarly with the Tower at Ballylee, where you can imagine Yeats in the 1920s climbing the winding stair and pacing the battlements at the top. Some of the best Joycean sites are concerned with his imaginative work, such as the Martello Tower at Sandycove or the various sites connected with Bloom's walks through the city of Dublin. Equally, and this is in part why I agreed to write this book, it's still possible to discover new things about the Joyce country if you put your mind to it. In Chapter 5, I spend time reflecting on North Richmond Street, the setting for 'Araby', in an attempt to bring out the changing face of his city from 1904 to 2006. Eccles Street, where the Blooms lived, invites considerable attention from those interested in the Joyce country, and with the help of a series of photos and drawings I revisit the physical setting and location of their house and home in an attempt to shed new light on a familiar subject.

My great find – and it matches the 1913 postcard with the signatures of Yeats, Ezra Pound and Lady Gregory which I write about in *W.B. Yeats: Critical Assessments* (2000) and which I purchased at a postcard fair in York – are two photos of printing rooms at *The Freeman's Journal* taken around the time when *Ulysses* is set. We now have in our possession the working environment that Joyce is trying to convey for us in 'Aeolus', the Newspaper episode. Among the typesetters is one mentioned by Joyce, and there are possibly others who are so far unidentified. I also include an indenture that I came across some years ago in an antiques shop in Chichester in Sussex. It's a lesser find but it's one for which I have a perverse affection. Complete with red wax seals, the legal document, dated October 1769, concerns the sale of a dwelling house and land by John and Elizabeth Earwicker from the parish of Sidlesham in Sussex to one Joseph Straker. Earwicker was a name Joyce came across in a local guide book while on vacation in Bognor in the summer of 1923, and this is the name he lifted for his protagonist in his final book *Finnegans Wake*. I like my discovery, for normally we work the other way round with Joyce, reading off his fictional creations against people in real life. But here is a new way of reading him, where it is we who do the supplying of information that Joyce knew nothing about. The way we can here outflank Joyce has a perversity that is in its own way Joycean.

Joyce, who has been the subject of considerable attention by scholars and critics round the globe, can still be given a makeover and come up smiling. In the last ten years new information on his Trieste years has come to light, obliging us to revise the account offered in Ellmann's biography. Joyce spent over ten years in Trieste during a very formative period between 1905 and 1915, but, at a time when people who knew Joyce were still alive, Ellmann spent only a few weeks in the 1950s in the Italian city gathering material for his biography. Those years have now been properly addressed by John McCourt in his biography *The Bloom Years: James Joyce in Trieste 1904–1920* (2000), and a more nuanced story emerges. Attending to what Joyce was reading when he wrote *Finnegans Wake* has also yielded new insights not only into the genesis of that text but also into Joyce's characteristic procedures when he was at work on his 'book of Doublends Jined' (*FW* 20:15–6).

Almost inevitably, because we are dealing with a writer of such complexity, whose every word is to be cherished, our view of Joyce will continue to develop and be augmented by new discoveries, particularly arising from his continental sojourn. Sylvia Beach's previously unknown correspondence with Joyce in the 1930s is now available for consultation in the James Joyce Foundation in Zurich, while important drafts and early notes for *Ulysses*, which were acquired by the National Library of Ireland in 2002 from Paul Léon's family, will alter the view we have of the novel. It's not only in what he has to say but also in the legacy he has bequeathed us that Joyce remains our contemporary. In turn, for those involved in his recuperation and his continuing reception therefore, the struggle to spread the word of Joyce has a certain heroic quality which will be best appreciated perhaps by those who come after us.

Joyce continues to resonate inside Irish culture as if he had never left the country and was still alive. Joyce the insider, as opposed to Joyce the outsider – there is a nice tension here which no image can ever quite capture. Even as I stress the Joyce who doesn't face the camera or the Joyce who's never at home or the Joyce who refuses to say what he means, at the

Aerial view of Dublin, Georgia, in a 1950s postcard. Doubling, doubling up, dyoublong, do you belong. Absolutely nothing could tie down Joyce's imagination.

same time I delight in the Joyce who never ceased struggling to say what he meant, who developed our ear for language and for languages, and whose first reference to somewhere called Dublin in *Finnegans Wake* is to Dublin in Georgia in the USA.

Whichever company, then, we put him in, Joyce doesn't quite conform, and it is on this note I want to end this Introduction. All over Ireland, Britain and North America, Yeats lectured about his work and his theatre. If he were alive today, you can imagine him appearing on television chat-shows or being invited to book or literature festivals in Edinburgh or Hay-on-Wye. You can't imagine any of this of Joyce. The public lectures Joyce delivered in Trieste, one of the few occasions he spoke publicly out-side the classroom, promoted Irish history and politics, but they were not about his own work. When he became famous as a writer, as we have ob-served with his responses to *The Little Review*, he was not given to opening up. One conclusion we might draw from this is that while there is something intriguing about Joyce, unlike Oscar Wilde he will always remain in one sense untouchable. But there is another conclusion we might draw and it is one that reverses the terms: because he is in one sense untouchable, for a modern audi-ence with an appetite for enigmas Joyce is as intriguing as it gets.

CHAPTER 2

1904: Joyce's point of departure

Colonial contexts

In this chapter I want to focus on the summer of 1904. What was it like that summer living in Dublin? In some respects the most noteworthy new feature about the city and one that would have given its citizens particular joy and pride was the newly laid electric tramway system, which had been operational for some four or five years. In *Ulysses* Joyce fondly imagines, without irony, the centre of the city being outside the General Post Office on what is now O'Connell Street, where trams departed for all parts of Dublin and beyond. On the other hand, the city was still 'dear, dirty Dublin', the term Lady Morgan had coined for it a century before and the one Joyce enjoyed playing on when he came to write *Finnegans Wake* in the interwar years. Dublin was by turns 'dear dutchy deeplins' (*FW* 76:25), 'dire dreary darkness' (*FW* 136:20), 'Dear Dirty Dumpling' (*FW* 215:13), or simply, when looked on as a person that needed dressing down, 'duddurty devil' (*FW* 196:15).

Child mortality rates, largely due to overcrowding, especially in the tenements, were among the highest in Europe. Water, gas and electricity were slowly being installed throughout the city, and in this regard we might notice that listed in *Thom's Business Directory of Dublin and Suburbs for the Year 1906* are some 30 gas fitters, 3 gas meter makers, around 70 plumbers, 26 sanitary engineers and contractors, and 8 stove and kitchen-range warehouses. The list reminds us that, in spite of ongoing improvements since the 1860s, problems of underdevelopment remained. In cities like Birmingham in the 1870s and 1880s, gas-and-water socialism was the rallying cry, but large parts of Dublin still lagged behind their British counterparts, and, perhaps not surprisingly, its population had seen little growth for several generations.

Politically and culturally, however, things were stirring, and within 12 months the landscape of Ireland was to change for ever. 1905 saw the launch of Arthur Griffith's new party Sinn Féin, the advanced nationalist party which was committed to breaking the historic link with Britain and which was to be associated a decade later with the Easter Rising of 1916. In December 1904 the Abbey Theatre opened its doors for the first time, with performances of Lady Augusta Gregory's play *Spreading the News*, William Butler Yeats's *On Baile's Strand* and *Kathleen Ni Houlihan*, and John Millington Synge's *The Shadow of the Glen*. With its emphasis on de-anglicisation and a return to the people, it was an astute move on Yeats's part and ahead of its time. Moreover, the Abbey Theatre, which was the most visible sign that the Irish Literary Revival was more than a passing fad of poets and dreamers, became almost at once the arena for national debate and argument about the condition of Ireland. Indeed, in January 1907, on cue, there were riots inside the theatre over Synge's *Playboy of the Western World* and police had to be called.

The note that was repeatedly struck among political nationalists and cultural nationalists alike was 'Look. This is the new Ireland in the new century. We are an ancient nation with our own language, culture, and customs. Our long-cherished dreams of independence deserve to be heard either within the Empire or, if not, outside it.' But the Empire thought otherwise, and from its headquarters at Dublin Castle, which contained an armoury designed for 80,000 men, Britain, fresh from recent victories over the Boers in South Africa, administered Ireland with a mixture of good intentions, missionary duty, a 'civilising' mission, benign neglect, occasional ineptitude, a culpability sometimes acknowledged sometimes not, limited horizons and characteristic hypocrisy; and, behind all these mind-control measures, it could call on the ranks of the Dublin Metropolitan Police, a network of Castle informers and forces of the Crown. In addition to the troops stationed at the Castle, Dublin boasted some nine barracks, and, much to the annoyance of nationalists such as Maud Gonne and others, soldiers, as a show of force, continued to parade in the streets, past Union Jacks flying high and postboxes painted red. But the system, as we know, couldn't last for ever.

The summer of 1904 presents a characteristically dual or we might say duel perspective, the official one and the unofficial one. In retrospect, it's a year that forms part of the movement towards independence, and we can now discern more clearly how things were shaping up. Historical novels, from L.A.G. Strong's *The Garden* (1931) to Jamie O'Neill's *At Swim, Two Boys* (2001), have captured that movement with varying degrees of success. At the time, however, it must have looked as if the Union with Britain would never be severed. Among the people, therefore – and Joyce gives us a good insight into this in the character of Miss Ivors in 'The Dead' – there

In the heart of the Hibernian metropolis. Sackville Street (now O'Connell Street) in the late-1890s, when horse-drawn trams gathered below Nelson's Pillar, symbol of British power and influence. Nelson dominated the whole wide street, including the General Post Office where in 1916 Patrick Pearse set up his headquarters and read out the Proclamation of the Irish Republic.

Detail of same scene with statue of Sir John Gray, who helped establish a new water supply to the city in 1868. On the pavement outside the Hotel Metropole figures can be seen in conversation. As Joyce brings out in *Ulysses*, Dublin was a city for close encounters, for watching the world go by, for walking, cycling and catching trams. The sun is high in the sky, the awnings are out, and the man at the top of the tram, an advert for Cadbury's Cocoa just below his left shoulder, is shielding himself with his boater from the sun. One click and you expect the whole scene to start up, precisely what happens when you begin reading *Ulysses*, a city coming to life in movement, talk, and gossip.

was inevitably a mixture of frustration, anger and a sense of failure, together with resolution, determination and hope. It is as if politics was being conceived not in terms of objective circumstances to do with economics and the play of social and historical forces but in terms of character, will and personal commitment. Joyce, as we will see in the chapters that follow, exhibits many attitudes both in himself and in his characters, and, in spite of its dominance, we would do well not to confine his view of Ireland to simply 'paralysis'.

Joyce was in fact responding to many currents in the culture, but through it all what he never stops insisting on is the gulf between the official view of things and the world as seen from below. He was exploring the basis of social life in a colonial setting and little escaped his attention. In his 1930s novel which provides a critique of the Dublin Protestant middle class at this time, Strong noticed the difference between the 'outward shell' of the old order and what gave it 'meaning' (Strong, 1931, 269). It's something that Joyce was also at pains to record about the whole culture. The observances were there, as were the facades, but what gave it all meaning had gone. Empty shells. Joyce understood colonialism from within, that is in his case from below, so that by the time he reached the age of 22 in 1904 he was well on the way to 'decolonising the mind', to adopt the helpful phrase of the contemporary Kenyan writer Ngũgĩ. Moreover, it was true in Ireland, as it has been in other parts of the globe under colonial rule: colonial subservience eventually brings forth its opposite. In this chapter I stress Joyce's defiance particularly in terms of his personality, but we should also remember that defiance belongs to this wider struggle against being defined either by the coloniser or by those seeking to break the connection with the Crown.

At 22

Joyce, then, like his city and country, was on the edge of a new world just coming into view. The summer of 1904 was the period when the first stories of *Dubliners* appeared, when Joyce met his future partner Nora Barnacle, and when the course of his life was changed for ever. Looking back, Joyce also saw this period as decisive, setting his great novel *Ulysses* on 16 June 1904 to commemorate his first date with Nora. 1904 was also the year that witnessed the birth of his semi-autobiographical novel *A Portrait of the Artist as a Young Man*, a novel which in turn carries, as if to signal a triumph over something, two dates – one of which is 1904 – and two cities a thousand miles apart: 'Dublin 1904 Trieste 1914'. That summer, Joyce was 22, a young man, a graduate of two years standing, with no settled job.

His family was slipping from him: the previous August, his mother had died from cancer, and his father's drinking and improvidence showed no sign of abating.

I used to begin my class on *Dubliners* by concentrating on the man as much as on the writer. That way not only do certain aspects of the stories come alive but also contact with someone who is not unlike students themselves can be established. What's it like to be 22 and to imagine you're special? 'Simply by force of personality I can get myself into a career as a fashion journalist.' I would occasionally hear this kind of remark from final year students, and sometimes students do manage to persuade an interviewing panel that they have what it takes. 'Force of personality.' Would that opportunism could break down the doors of privilege. 'But, consider,' I would say to the student in my room, 'consider the people at the top in the media. Do some background research and then tell me how they got where they are. Consider their surnames. Are their family in the media? Who did they know? Where did they study? Here in York you're some way from the golden triangle of London, Oxford and Cambridge. Have you ever managed to see your work in print? Do you have any idea how many media and journalism students graduate every year in Britain? Freedom is the recognition of necessity.' And in case there's any revolutionary spark in need of kindling, I would double-back on myself and add: 'Freedom is also the non-recognition of necessity.' I realise that such advice is a bit of a downer. 'Look, David, I'm not aiming for the very top, but several rungs down, and I only want a job, not the overthrow of the system.' The business over, some students would leave my room with even more determination to become someone.

I wonder what I would have said to Joyce as a young man if he had approached me for advice in the summer of 1904. 'Keep your options open. Do some networking with those who control the cultural and writing outlets. Go to London and curry favour with the literary editors of journals and newspapers. Don't bite the hand that feeds you. You need a job in the meantime that will allow you time to write and get established. Going abroad might help, if the exchange rate is in your favour and the cost of living is cheaper. What about teaching English as a foreign language?' Joyce wasn't obvious material for an academic appointment, and in 1904 such positions were few and far between. I wouldn't, therefore, have raised that possibility with him. The next generation, as Samuel Beckett (1906–89) reminds us, was to enjoy the benefits of university patronage. But I wonder if I would have detected a special quality in Joyce. I would certainly have noticed his force of personality, but then everyone in Dublin did at the time.

As can be observed from his efforts in the previous four years, Joyce had already made a start of sorts on a writing career. In 1900, when he was only 18, a review of Henrik Ibsen's play *When We Dead Awaken* (1899) appeared in the prestigious English journal *Fortnightly Review*. In seeking a name for himself, Joyce couldn't resist the thought that kicking might help, so in 1901 he published a pamphlet entitled *The Day of the Rabblement* attacking Yeats and the Irish Literary Revival. In October 1902 a truculent 20-year-old arranged a meeting with the 37-year-old Yeats, who was himself, like Joyce, a driven creature. Joyce showed Yeats some of his poems and what he described as epiphanies, but the meeting wasn't terribly productive and Joyce is alleged to have told Yeats, 'I have met with you too late. You are too old' (Ellmann, 1982, 103). In 1903, in Paris, he undertook some reviewing for the *Dublin Daily Express* and met Synge, then also beginning to make a name for himself as a dramatist. In 1904 one of Joyce's poems was published in *Dana*, a monthly magazine edited in Dublin by John Eglinton (aka W.K. Magee) and Fred Ryan. When an essay-cum-story on aesthetics, 'A Portrait of the Artist', was turned down by the same magazine, Joyce embarked on his semi-autobiographical novel *Stephen Hero*, which issued ten years later in *A Portrait of the Artist as a Young Man*. Then in the summer of 1904, as if in frustration at his lack of progress, he composed 'The Holy Office', a stinging attack in verse on the hypocrisy of his contemporaries and a reply in its own way to Yeats's more optimistic poem 'To Ireland in the Coming Times', which had appeared a decade earlier in *Poems* (1895). In 1904 Joyce was manifestly an aspiring writer who had something to show for his efforts, and most aspiring writers would have been happy with such an achievement at this stage of their career.

It's worth reflecting more on what being 22 is like, however. Forget for a minute the biographies of Joyce and give some attention to starting out in life. Many of us must have experienced a slight trepidation as the life so long prepared for becomes a reality, as the life of the mind gives way to decisions that affect the course of one's life. Joyce was in this sense no different from any of us, a combination of tension and contradiction, mixed with ambition and fear. All of us are different, and, in truth, when it comes to life narratives, we can only speak for ourselves. In my case I tend to indulge my sense of failure or draw attention to the negative spots. When I was 22 my life was shaping itself for me, but I wasn't shaping it. I was in my second year at university reading English and religious studies. I was awkward, slightly withdrawn, resisting the incursions and prying of others, worrying all the time, a smoker of untipped cigarettes. I look back on my photographs from that period and think uncomfortable thoughts about my sheer backwardness in clothes, fashion, glasses, shoes, and much else. 'Thoroughly un-modern and seemingly incapable of modernising himself' – if they ever thought about me, that I suspect must have been the verdict of my contemporaries. This is not an image of someone who had a career in front of him. The first time, I should add, I heard the word 'lifestyle' was in a seminar on the Romantics, and it impressed me. It seemed like a warning, an anticipation, when the 1960s dissolved, of our post-modern world, but I couldn't accept its implication, that you could change your life simply by changing your clothes or by dyeing your hair.

I almost never studied in the evening but took to going to bars, watching films and playing slot-machines. The evenings I recall with affection were singing folksongs in an out-of-the-way pub in Kirkby Lonsdale with a suitably odd group of 'folkies', led by Greg Stephens, who now has his own band The Boat Band, which I see from their website play a suitably wry mix of Creole, Caribbean, gospel, Cajun, Irish, zydeco and blues. Half-way through the evening, in an act of old-fashioned generosity in the quiet heart of the country in a pub that went by the name of The Highwayman, the landlady would make a fuss of us by serving up Lancashire hot-pot. Friends I must confess I treated like driftwood, for what they offered me amid the shifting currents was a temporary form of shelter but not destiny. I am sure I did nothing for them, and I have retained only two friendships from that period.

My directionless life came to resemble a parallel existence. In class, we studied the Romantics and the Victorians and, as if in sympathy, I became increasingly withdrawn. I heard nothing of the bard when we did Blake, only something about piping down the valleys wild from a blank-faced tutor with a thin voice who might or might not have been interested in what she was teaching. Whatever I was supposed to feel about Tennyson mourning his friend Arthur Hallam or Matthew Arnold on Dover Beach disconsolately gazing out across the English Channel, a sea of unfaith was swirling round me. And things improved little in my third year when we reached the moderns. *Ulysses* we 'did' in a week with a tutor whose mind was elsewhere. Indeed, that tutor's commercial instincts got the better of him, and the critic who used to insist that realism was the banner under which the middle class in history marched now runs his own company in the USA telling the world how to write business letters. The last fortnight of every ten-week term, as a mark of disaffection or perhaps of defiance, I would disappear home, 300 miles away.

During all my teenage years, until I was 19, I was convinced I was going to become a Catholic priest. Then the world changed. As student essays repeatedly confirm, such a change of direction in growing up is not unusual. The future points in one direction, and then all of a sudden the course shifts dramatically. New friendship groups, new musical tastes, new beliefs, and then, or indeed all the time, the pressure from others to conform to or revert to their image of you. The old and the new self in conflict, one not recognising the other. Break-up. Estrangement. The familiar no longer familiar. In retrospect, I could discern it had been on the horizon for some time. In my late teens I kept coming across other intellectual seams and I wanted to explore more outside the framework of the Church's jurisdiction. Unlike Joyce, an aspect I touch on again in Chapter 7 on *A Portrait*, I found I couldn't do anything with scholastic philosophy for, with its impossibly abstract concepts, it seemed to ill-equip me to understand the modern world. I have kept an essay from that period which I wrote in Latin, 'De Notitia et Explicatione Potentiae Operativae ad mentem Sancti Thomae' (on the idea and explication of operative potency according to St Thomas Aquinas), but, like a guilty secret I am ashamed of, I have shown it to no-one since. When Stephen in *A Portrait* outlines his theory of aesthetics, I must confess I am reminded not of a brilliant student but of someone with a certain perverse desperation to cling on to something, a student who refuses to consign to the past what is indeed past. Perhaps Joyce himself is to be distinguished from Stephen at this point, and he certainly has the qualification 'as a young man' in the novel's title to fall back on, but I suspect Joyce isn't so far removed from the line of continuity that links him with his fictional persona.

Detachment was what I sought, wholly fresh bracing air, an engagement with the many moods and meanings of modernity. I wanted no more of writing essays comparing the scientific notion of matter with the hylomorphism of Andreas Van Melsen, where I would be involved in ticking off the modern world as when I concluded that 'we cannot treat scientific definitions as if they were identifiable with science philosophy, and many errors proceed from neglecting that point'. I wanted no more abstract talk of matter or substance, potency or act, no more talk of what lies behind the world. Like the purged Stephen at the end of *A Portrait*, I, too, sought the 'reality of experience', whatever it meant. At the same time I must have been absorbing a critical perspective on what I was reading, for in one of my exercise books I see I posed the question 'Why isn't scholastic philosophy a greater influence on contemporary philosophy?'

The modern, the utterly new, where on earth was it I wondered? I was always in the wrong place. I couldn't have a vocation if I wanted to interrupt my studies and embark on a degree in philosophy or English at a university before returning to undertake the four-year programme in theology. This was the dramatic conclusion delivered by an impassive external Spiritual Director, Canon Arbuthnot, at St John's Seminary, Wonersh. It was a judgement with which my soft-spoken mentor and confessor, the theologian Peter Harris, felt obliged to concur. There was no ceremony when these two figures drew down the curtain effectively on the most impressionable stage of my life, and I've never forgotten the extraordinary ferocity and the utterly helpless charm of the Church in their passing looks. It was odd, but my mind had been made up for me, and I felt a certain freedom, which was not unlike a kind of defiance in the face of life.

When the English bishops returned in 1965 from the Vatican Council in Rome, their seminaries were uppermost in their minds. Pope John XXIII had opened a window on the Church and the winds were beginning to blow indiscriminately everywhere. In October 1966 I represented an early sign of the ravages to come. Cut such branches down and do it immediately, they must have thought. I was lopped off, cut adrift, with no shared life worth talking about except the one I would make for myself or otherwise. Within 48 hours I was gone from the seminary; within a decade I was gone from the Church. History in one sense I felt was against me but in another sense I was simply part of its flow. It's been a comfort of sorts to learn that since the 1960s over 100,000 priests around the world, including my confessor who taught for 30 years in a philosophy department at a Canadian university, have been laicised. I was, therefore, but part of a movement of the disenchanted and disaffected, of those who went away to lay claim to their life elsewhere. Today, when I read about the theological turn in contemporary criticism, I feel like a survivor from some earlier war.

At 22, you should be on top of things, but, like Joyce when he moved away from Catholicism, I discovered the ground had shifted under my feet. In abandoning a career in the Church, I had undergone some profound changes and these had sapped me of energy and direction. I was waiting again. With its appropriate motto 'Spes messis in semine' (the hope of the harvest is in the seed), life in a junior seminary on the edge of the Sussex Weald, where I spent my teenage years, had also been filled with waiting. I tried to convince myself that perhaps in time a university education would do something for me, not so much in terms of a career, because I wasn't interested in that and never have been, as in terms of a new intellectual reorientation and of a changed disposition towards the world. But the damage had been done, and I didn't really believe that salvation would come through a secular institution. I kept trying to look up, but, whichever way I turned, no new horizons appeared for me. Failure beckoned. In a darkly lit upper room we were informed by a supercilious university chaplain that ours was a special generation, that the moon was within our grasp. My generation. That seemed like the guff that it was.

Unlike Joyce, who was at the centre of something even if that was paralysis, I was at a new university in a northern English city, where the largest employer was a carpet manufacturer, where fish-and-chip shops stayed open until one in the morning, and where every other week hungry students had confrontations with their landladies. Geordies in donkey jackets drank you under the table, and at weekends the campus emptied with double-decker buses heading for London. I can still hear the clink of glasses and then the silence. It was an exceptionally bleak time for me, that second year, and I always respond to students when university disappoints them. At the end of my first year I thought of transferring to another university, but something held me back. Late at night, I would see my moral tutor cruising for pickups at the local bus station. Joyce's university education at the hands of the Jesuits resulted in isolation from community; my isolation stemmed from a search for community, which I never in fact found.

The mind obeys its own rules but the body will also have its way. At 22, Joyce had enjoyed lots of sexual experiences, but then suddenly something happened when he met a woman from Galway who was in Dublin working as a chambermaid in a hotel overlooking the railings of Trinity College. Nora Barnacle, too, had enjoyed lots of sexual experiences, but, unlike Joyce, she had also enjoyed several sexual relationships, including one with Michael Bodkin, who had died tragically young. At 22, Nora gave Joyce something to think about, and we shouldn't infer this was simply to do with sexual pleasure. He learnt to appreciate that if the mind is wayward and the intellect out on its own, the body sought stability and communion with another. What is more, in time, through stability, the homeless mind could find some sort of accommodation, one pulling the other clear of the wreckage we know as adolescence. The body, then, pursued its own needs, wants, desires, and some of these couldn't be satisfied by indulging in casual sex. That realisation must have been quite a moment for Joyce, an epiphany which threatened to put in place all his invented, self-regarding, little epiphanies. Almost immediately he turned to writing something more substantial, namely the stories that materialised in the collection we now know as *Dubliners*.

The summer of 1904 gives us in essence not only Joyce the man but also Joyce the writer. Joyce didn't begin as the great writer he became, so it's worth reflecting on what he might have been like at the moment when the world began to open up for him. Aspiration and defiance, these are the two buzz words I concentrate on in this chapter. In turning to the circumstances surrounding his first story in print, I want also to reflect on his adoption of Stephen Daedalus as a pseudonym. I am interested here in attitudes as much as in anything else, for attitudes are a form of radical exposure and often overshadow or at least precede everything else, including effectively second-order things such as the process of composition, styles of writing, and even choice of subject matter. How did Joyce cope with his given circumstances, and what motivated him to write, and where did his remarkable stamina come from? And by extension, what can he tell us about how we might embark on a writing career? Then as now, if you're 22 and want to become a writer, your options are limited and perhaps always involve you in false starts. There were no creative writing classes when Joyce was an undergraduate, and, for the most part, whatever he learnt about writing as such he taught himself. Was he a one-off, therefore, or are there lessons from his struggles for today's budding writers?

Stephen Daedalus

The first publication of 'The Sisters' was surrounded by farming adverts, and you can almost smell the milking parlours off these pages, but it's such an extraordinary context for the writer who was to emerge as the leading Modernist of his generation. Not one of the little magazines which acted as the midwife of Modernism but a newspaper for the farming community with the reassuring name *The Irish Homestead*. The city writer, the Dubliner, surrounded by a working agriculture and by country people, people that is who are often, even today, looked down upon by Dubliners. If the context is strange, what are we to make of the pseudonym, 'Stephen Dædalus'? There is often something contrived or slightly precious about a pseudonym, but especially this one. And is it Dædalus, Daedalus or Dedalus? It's uncertain

The first version of 'The Sisters' appeared in *The Irish Homestead* in August 1904 under the reassuring section heading 'Our weekly story'.

how much Joyce meant to convey in his choice of pseudonym. His brother Stanislaus thought he had used a pseudonym because he was writing for 'the pigs' paper' and didn't want to be recognised (Ellmann, 1982, 164). But, in June 1904, his head full of girls and innuendo, he signed a hollow-sounding letter to Oliver St John Gogarty (then at Oxford) 'Stephen Dedalus', the name he settled on for his fictional character. It's such a curious name to hide behind and indulge his mockery of the world, but at 22 Joyce was not unlike many people at that age, full of false starts and contradictions.

The desired or underlying identity can be real, however. Stephen was the first Christian martyr, an image perhaps of how the secular Joyce saw his own fate in 1904, someone who would have to suffer on behalf of his principles to art and conscience. Daedalus, as author of 'The Sisters' with the 'e' in the first syllable in his name, recalls the Greek myth of King Minos and the Minotaur on the island of Crete and how Daedalus and Icarus escaped from the labyrinth by fashioning wings for flight. 'Daedalus' has a stronger resonance and it must have appealed to a writer who repeatedly stressed the theme of escape from an island which threatened to imprison him with 'nets', as they are called in *A Portrait*. It's one of those nice ironies in cultural history that Joyce's first story in print should be consigned to the inside pages of a farming weekly and be composed by someone whose name suggested he shared precious little with his audience but would, instead, seek to fly above them. His aspiration seemed geared to becoming a different kind of writer, a writer who would invoke the classics as much by way of defiance as anything else and who seemed intent on complicating from the start the identity of the author.

Joyce's first story in print, then, was published on 13 August 1904 in a weekly newspaper for the Irish farming community. Associated with Yeats's friend, the practical visionary George Russell (A.E.), *The Irish Homestead* supported the ideals of Horace Plunkett's Irish Agricultural Organisation Society, which was founded in 1894 to share good practice and to promote among small farmers co-operative ventures such as creameries. 'The Sisters' was squeezed between a poem about the birds of 'beauteous' Ireland 'Making sweet music like the songs of the bards' and an advert for a 'Double Effective Milk Pump For Auxiliary Dairies'. It was in one sense an unlikely setting or outlet for the pretentious 'Stephen Dædalus', the pseudonymous city writer who scorned the language of the bards, who was not given to milking cows, and whose fictional persona in *A Portrait* was 'sickened' by a 'filthy cowyard', unable even to look at the milk the cows 'yielded' (*P* 63). But perhaps it wasn't so unlikely given that Ireland was an agricultural country, possessed a rich mythology to do with cattle raids and productive

> Three nights in succession I had found myself in Great Britain-street at that hour, as if by Providence. Three nights also I had raised my eyes to that lighted square of window and speculated. I seemed to understand that it would occur at night. But in spite of the Providence that had led my feet, and in spite of the reverent curiosity of my eyes, I had discovered nothing. Each night the square was lighted in the same way, faintly and evenly. It was not the light of candles, so far as I could see. Therefore, it had not yet occurred.

The first paragraph of the first version of 'The Sisters'. A promising start but not the knock-out punch of a great writer. It looks over-written and the work of someone trying hard to write. On display is a gulf between the narrator, who has an adult vocabulary, and a boy's consciousness. Bringing narrative and consciousness together, this is what Joyce became expert in, but it was not something in evidence at the start of his career.

cows, and, according to *Thom's Business Directory of Dublin and Suburbs for the Year 1906*, it was a country that could boast over 500 dairies in its capital city and surrounding area alone. Nevertheless, I suspect Joyce, who certainly had some sympathy with the plight of Irish agriculture, would have been clueless about the effectiveness or otherwise of Alfa-Laval's cream separators, Dr Gerber's tester or Hall's refrigerating machines.

Russell had asked Joyce for something 'simple, rural?, livemaking?, pathos?, which could be inserted so as not to shock the readers' (*Letters II*, 43). The series of question marks shaped themselves into a plea from someone who had a genuine wish to help a younger generation of Irish writers, but they were also a recognition that he was dealing with a person who had shown difficulty adjusting his remarks and who perhaps needed protecting from himself. What Russell received from the young would-be writer was a story far from simple, nothing if not city-based in its texture and scope, deathly from start to finish, uncertain in its pathos and, whatever else, designed not to reassure the reader. Indeed, while no pun was possibly intended by its author, 'The Sisters' was a story, as Cotter's tapping of his forehead reminds us, about a priest whose 'upper storey' had gone. Over the course of the next five months, two more stories appeared in Russell's paper – 'Eveline' on 10 September 1904 and 'After the Race' on 17 December 1904 – but then no more. The perplexed readers, one suspects, had had enough of their slightly off-tone, off-colour contents, and, in spite of persistent attempts to interest publishers in London and Dublin, the defiant Joyce would have to wait until 1914 before his other stories saw the light of day. Russell later paid tribute to Joyce's 'dark heroism of the imagination' (Russell, 1938, 139–40), but I doubt if the phrase came to his lips in 1904.

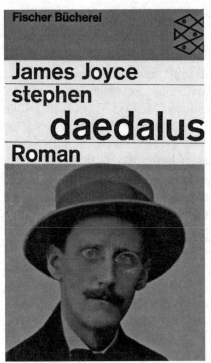

This German translation of *Stephen Hero* by Georg Goyert was published by Suhrkamp in 1965. The photograph used is one taken in 1915 soon after Joyce arrived in Zurich and the one he sent to Nora's uncle Michael Healy in Galway. The book's cover is arresting, with a nice balance between word and image. The eye notices each element in turn – author, title in lower case, and genre. James Joyce, stephen daedalus, novel. What also stands out for native English speakers is not only the word 'roman' (German for novel) but also the title 'Stephen Daedalus'. Unfortunately, the whole thing is quite confusing. The Greek-inspired Joyce used this pseudonym when writing the early stories of *Dubliners* but he dropped it almost at once. The protagonist in his unfinished novel is Stephen Hero. In *A Portrait of the Artist as a Young Man* he chooses the name Stephen Dedalus as his protagonist, turning the first syllable of the surname into something resembling 'dead'. The distinction is worth noting: Joyce was once Stephen Daedalus as an author but it should not be assumed he is identical with a character or with an author he called Stephen Dedalus. 'Joyce as' is an intriguing question. Joyce as character. Joyce as author. Joyce as narrator. Joyce as himself – behind everything he wrote, that's what everyone wants to know. What was he really like and where is he in his fiction? Unlike some writers, although we often feel the pressure, we should resist the temptation either to jump to conclusions with Joyce or to draw neat lines separating man and mask. Even defiance, for example, can be nothing more than self-promotion.

Myths and reality

When 'The Sisters' first appeared, the author had youth on his side and a future ahead of him. The biographer thinks s/he has a privileged access to a person, but a biography is always a rewriting of something that originally lay in the future. In one respect – and perhaps the only one that matters – Joyce's CV in 1904 was for the most part a private affair, available to a large extent only to himself. Jorge-Luis Borges, writing in an Argentine review in 1937, claimed that Joyce's 'historia personal, como la de ciertas naciones, se pierde en mitologías', that his personal history was, like that of certain countries, lost in mythology (Borges, 1986, 83). But such a view was itself a myth. The public face reveals something more ordinary. In 1902 Joyce graduated in modern languages from the National University of Ireland (now University College Dublin); in April 1903 he returned unexpectedly from Paris, where he had been for a time studying medicine, to be with his mother who was dying of cancer at the young age of 44; and in June 1904 he began seeing the woman who would become his partner for the rest of his life and with whom, four months later in October 1904, he would leave Ireland for work on the continent of Europe.

That in essence was his adult life until this point. Plenty of reality but no myths therefore – apart from the poem in praise of Parnell, which he composed as a nine-year-old boy and a printed copy of which his father apparently forwarded to the Vatican Library (where it has never been found). Myths did, however, accumulate round Joyce, some perpetrated by his biographers and some by Joyce himself. In his 1926 biography, Herbert Gorman, Joyce's first biographer, claimed that Joyce was married, when that didn't come until 1931 in London. In 1937, Borges could write that Nora's surname was Healy, the name of one of her uncles, and, following Gorman, he too believed that Joyce and Nora were married in 1904 (see Borges, 1986, 83). Another myth can be quickly dispelled. Joyce had entertained the thought at one time of becoming a professional singer but, as Gorman noted in his 'Brief outline of Joyce's life', 'a number of incidents put an end to his plans' (Gorman, 1926, 230). Again, what we have here is a good tenor voice but no myths. During the Great War, when he was living in Zurich, Joyce himself had to counter rumours that he was behind the Dada movement. In 1981, when I taught at Cabrillo College, a community college in Northern California, I had a student who believed Joyce was a member of some occult group such as the Order of the Golden Dawn, and he wondered if I too would come along to his own occult group and talk about *Finnegans Wake*. I didn't take him up on the offer, preferring instead jazz in the afternoon in the Cooper House in downtown Santa Cruz, sipping Anchor Steam on tap.

In 1904, with two years of experience since graduating behind him and the whole of his life in front of him, Joyce was in not unfamiliar no-man's land. Like many young people before and since, he was short on experience but anxious to succeed. He was known as an aspiring writer – in August 1904 the author of a short story but not yet 'an author', someone who was looking around for whatever opportunities might come along. Only with hindsight could his career as a writer be mapped, and that map was defined by a particular year and a particular month and a particular day, which we now know as Bloomsday, 16 June 1904. This in a sense is the real myth. Indeed, if Nora hadn't entered his life in so dramatic a fashion, Joyce might well have arranged that August to 'go away as a travelling actor' (*Letters II*, 48) or go busking along the English south coast picking up women. Man and mask, myths and reality. Nora enabled him to grow up fast. 'I made

JOYCE, James, Teacher of the Scuola Superiore di Commercio, Trieste, and writer; *b.* Dublin, 2 Feb. 1882, *s.* of John Joyce and Mary Murray; *m.* 1904, Nora, *d.* of Thomas and Ann Barnacle, Galway; one *s.* one *d. Educ.:* Clongowes Wood College and Belvedere College, Ireland; Royal University, Dublin, B.A. Has lived in Paris, Rome and Trieste. *Publications:* Chamber Music (verses); Dubliners (fiction); A Portrait of the Artist as a Young Man (fiction); Exiles (play); Contributions to Fortnightly Review, Saturday Review, Speaker, Smart Set (N.Y.), Egoist, Piccolo della Sera (Trieste). *Recreation:* Singing. *Address:* Seefeldstrasse 73, Zurich; Via Donato Bramante 4, ii, Trieste, Austria.

Entry in the 1918 Zurich *Who's Who*, clearly compiled by Joyce himself. Taken from Thomas Faerber and Markus Luchsinger, *Joyce in Zürich* (1988). By 1918 Joyce was nearly established as an author but he still needed to work as a teacher of English. Note what he writes: he was a teacher and writer in that order. Two addresses, one in Trieste, one in Zurich, available therefore for private classes in two different cities and countries. For recreation he puts down 'singing'. As for his being married, that might come as a surprise. He claims he married Nora, daughter of Thomas and Ann Barnacle of Galway, in 1904, when in fact he didn't marry her until 1931 and then in a registry office in London. It was a white lie presumably designed to stop people prying or to ensure he wouldn't be turned away by moralistic landladies when seeking accommodation for his family. Interestingly, he continued with the lie when he moved to Paris in the 1920s, even to the extent of keeping his biographer Herbert Gorman in the dark. Whatever Richard Rowan thinks in *Exiles* about telling the truth regardless, defiance, for Joyce, clearly had its limits.

him a man', declares Bertha in *Exiles* (*E* 128), and we don't doubt her. Equally, we should take seriously Sylvia Beach's later remark that Joyce's marriage to Nora was one of the happiest of any writer she knew (Beach, 1987, 42). But, until August 1904, as his previous four years suggest, there was nothing but promise as far as writing was concerned.

At a time when everyone was Gaelicising their names as part of an attempt to de-anglicise Ireland, Joyce quite deliberately chose Stephen Dedalus as a defiant pseudonym both to hide behind and at the same time to goad the world. 'Are you Irish at all?' (*P* 202) asks his nationalist undergraduate friend Davin accusingly in *A Portrait of the Artist as a Young Man*. If Joyce does belong to the 'New Irish School', it is only because we insist he belongs there, for he had no intention of being so defined. As for his relationship with Yeats, we should never forget that, in spite of early criticism of Yeats for playing to the 'rabblement', Joyce never wavered in his admiration for Yeats. Only someone completely moved by Yeats's verse would have sung without irony 'Who Goes With Fergus?' as we learn in the first episode of *Ulysses* Stephen did for his dying mother. Joyce, for whom inspiration was in large measure a question of memory, distanced himself from the Irish literary revival and the imagination-driven Yeats, but he always felt Yeats's towering presence on the poets' mythical Mount Parnassus. In 1938 Joyce confided in his Swiss friend and helper Jacques Mercanton that 'the immortality of his books is assured, which is hardly the case with mine' (Potts, 1977, 239); and, in 1939, when Yeats died, Joyce was happy to admit that Yeats was the greater writer. Memory had got the better of him.

Joyce, then, was an aspiring writer and protective of what he imagined was his own identity as a future writer. He took to knocking impolitely at the door of the literary establishment. Kick and kick again, and, if the door opened, kick again. That was the preferred line of attack, but as yet he had little to show for it. When John Eglinton, that is W.K. Magee, recalled the artist as a young man in 'The Beginnings of Joyce', an essay published in 1932, what struck him was Joyce's determination to succeed, for at the time 'no one took him at his own valuation' (Eglinton, 1932, 404). Joyce, who always managed to engineer the last word (or so he imagined), had his revenge when he put all these people – John Eglinton, George Russell, Yeats – into the Library episode of *Ulysses* and doubly taunted them with the view that 'He' (Stephen Dedalus) 'is going to write something in ten years' (1914 was the year he began *Ulysses*), and that he, James Joyce, and not George Moore, as George Sigerson opines, would go on to write the Irish 'national epic'. Among the books listed in Joyce's Paris library there is one by John Eglinton which carries the dedication 'To James Joyce with kind regards from the ex-author, W.K. Magee, Dec 11 1936' (Gheerbrant, 1949, 479). The tables had turned, and the fiercely competitive Joyce had won out over his former gatekeepers.

A young-looking Yeats on the front cover of the monthly magazine *The Bookman* in January 1905. By 1905 the Irish movement was already in full swing with Yeats at the helm. In what we might see as a symbolic move, Joyce, ever independent and semi-detached, left Ireland in October 1904; in December the same year the Abbey Theatre opened its doors for the first time.

Even when he was on the point of distinction and widespread acclaim, Joyce never let go, and he used the past to level with those he perceived in 1904 as his adversaries or rivals. Rewriting history so that it fell out as indeed it did is especially vindictive, but it was linked with something else in Joyce, 'a tendency to sombre, mystical brooding'. This is how an early commentator Charles Duff in *James Joyce and the Plain Reader* (1932) describes Joyce when reflecting on his Irishness and his Irish background. Brooding, a word and an emotion close to feuding, is an apt word to describe the person who constantly retreated to the high ground of art to launch further engagements with the enemy. Indeed, in what still remains a valuable introduction to Joyce for 'the plain reader', Duff insists that broodiness is among the most notable qualities of Joyce's mind, and he does so in a book that carries in its title that singularly odd-sounding, problematic term 'the plain reader' (Duff, 1932, 23–4). It wasn't just Joyce's character, then, that was charged with brooding but also his mind. People who brood have long memories and wait sometimes years to wreak their revenge, for brooding doesn't always impart an edge to memory, but in Joyce's case it did.

Moving back and forth is what the biographer of Joyce is forced to do constantly. Stanislaus Joyce knew this from the start when he described a brother in his *Dublin Diary* who, though he possessed a 'genius of character', also exhibited 'a proud, wilful, vicious selfishness' (Stanislaus Joyce, 1962, 14). The run of adjectives is precise: 'proud, wilful, vicious'. No wonder Stanislaus thought 'few people will love him'. Duff's use of 'sombre' in the phrase 'a tendency to sombre, mystical brooding' also recalls something else. Sunny Jim, as his father called him, preferred the shade – the sombre in one of its original meanings – to the sun. It wasn't the weather that attracted Joyce to Trieste and the Mediterranean, and when circumstances permitted he moved north in 1915 to the other side of the Alps. As he confessed to Stanislaus in September 1905 after enduring his first summer abroad, he hated 'a damn silly sun that makes men into butter' (*Letters II*, 109).

Defiance and displacement

As for the path of experience, in spite of what biographers might infer, this was anything but smooth. Joyce had suffered several knocks and reversals, most notably the loss of religion in his teenage years. At secondary school he was leader of the Sodality of the Blessed Virgin Mary. At 16, according to Stanislaus, Joyce had been approached by the Jesuits to join their Order, presumably because they saw in how he conducted himself that he was an ideal candidate for the priesthood (Stanislaus Joyce, 1954, 51). Within six years, however, he was confiding in Nora that he had rejected the whole social order and Christianity:

> My mind rejects the whole present social order and Christianity – home, the
> recognised virtues, classes of life, and religious doctrines. How could I like the
> idea of home? My home was simply a middle-class affair ruined by spendthrift
> habits which I have inherited. My mother was slowly killed, I think, by my fa-
> ther's ill-treatment, by years of trouble, and by my cynical frankness of conduct.
> When I looked on her face as she lay in her coffin – a face grey and wasted with
> cancer – I understood that I was looking on the face of a victim and I cursed the
> system which had made her a victim. We were seventeen in family. My brothers
> and sisters are nothing to me. One brother alone is capable of understanding me.
> (To Nora Barnacle, 29 August 1904, *Letters II*, 48)

Admirable or not, the defiance is that of youth on the point of departure
elsewhere. Joyce was especially fortunate in possessing a sympathetic audience, a woman, who within ten weeks of first meeting her on the streets of
Dublin had become effectively his church and refuge from the world. Everything, he informs Nora, that had made him the person he is – home, family,
religion, morality – he now rejects. To those of us who are outside observers, what Joyce signals in this letter is nothing less than the shift in alle-
giance from his own family to a 20-year-old chambermaid from Galway.
We might agree: that's what happens at 22.

Finn's Hotel in Dublin where Nora was
working as a chambermaid when she first
met Joyce. Photograph by David Pierce. The
sign is still there, as this photograph taken
in October 2006 shows, but the hotel has
long gone. For their first date, Nora agreed
to meet Joyce on the corner of Merrion
Square (outside Wilde's house), which was
just along the road from where she worked.
When she didn't turn up, Joyce found
himself inquiring after her at the hotel. The
second time, she kept her word, and they
met on Stephen's Green where they caught
a tram out of town. When she returned to
Ireland in July 1912, she stayed two nights
at her old hotel, and, in a letter to Joyce,
she expressed her dislike of Dublin and
agreed that she would soon tire of the city
if she had to live there again.

The Wilde house on the corner of Westland Row and Merrion Square where Oscar was born in 1854. Photograph by David Pierce. Joyce and Wilde have much in common, not least their Irishness, their sense of guilt and their acute insight into the nature of writing. Wilde believed that 'A work of art is useless as a flower is useless' (Wilde, 1962, 292). Joyce called his most famous character 'Bloom'. Whether useless or blooming alone, imaginative writing after Wilde and Joyce would never be the same again. Wilde, however, was dragged down by the English courts and died a broken man. Joyce behaved as if the reversal suffered by the aesthetic movement in the 1890s hadn't happened. In 1904, as he waited for Nora outside this house, it would be interesting to know whether Joyce gave any thought to the lessons or trials of his fellow Dubliner. Five years later, in his article on Wilde for the Triestine newspaper *Il Piccolo della Sera*, Joyce called him a 'court jester to the English' (along with Sheridan, Goldsmith and Shaw) (Joyce, 1959, 202). By contrast, in *Finnegans Wake*, Joyce went on to murder 'all the English he knew' (*FW* 93:2).

Joyce's belief in Nora was an extraordinary act of faith. As it transpired, their circumstances threw them together. She, too, shared something of his future fate as an exile, being in Dublin in part to escape from her uncle and her alcoholic father, a baker, who, in the words of the witty Joyce, 'drank all the loaves'. In the 1901 Census, her mother is entered as head of family, but there is no mention of her father. When Nora was five, she was sent to her grand-mother, and in time her parents separated and Nora's maternal uncles assumed responsibility for her. We learn from Joyce's biographer that following a beat-ing from her Uncle Tommy, she left Galway effectively for ever (Ellmann, 1982, 159). Whatever else, having made the break, the young woman with reddish-brown, curly hair and twinkling eyes had no intention of returning home. As she remarked in Paris 30 years later, with characteristic directness as if she had just been set free from something, 'A wretched country, dirty and dreary, where they eat cabbages, potatoes, and bacon all year round, where the women spend their days in church and the men in pubs' (Potts, 1977, 220). Joyce had by that stage softened, and, as Jacques Mercanton recalls, he simply smiled, praising Dublin as the seventh city of Christendom.

In fact, whatever his own family was, it was not 'simply a middle-class affair'. Joyce would have liked his family to be middle class, and to Nora he hid behind the label even as he dismissed it. The Sheehy family, who lived in a fine Georgian townhouse on Belvedere Place and who hosted social evenings which Joyce attended, was middle class, as was Charles Curran's family, and as were his contemporaries at Clongowes Wood College, the sons of magistrates and other members of the professional middle class. To Nasty Roche's inquiry about his father's occupation, Stephen in *A Portrait* replies 'A gentleman' (*P* 9), and the reader needs no additional commentary to sense the subject is touchy for the young boy. John Joyce a gentleman! Indeed, we might well retort 'a gentleman Oirish, mighty odd', as the author of the Irish-American ballad 'Finnegan's Wake' humorously puts it, where the reversal of the juxtaposition 'Irish' and 'gentleman' confirms its unnaturalness. The epithet is traditionally associated with the landed interests, not with the middle class, for a gentleman mixed in higher circles and was more decidedly allied with the gentry. Laurence Sterne's fictional character Tristram Shandy was a gentleman, or at least his father was. So too was Mr Henry Dashwood, the owner of Norland Park, in Jane Austen's *Sense and Sensibility* (1811). As for Charles Dickens's Pip, he aspires to

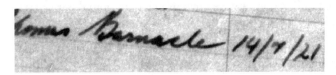

The entry in the record book at Rahoon Cemetery in Galway for Nora's father, Thomas Barnacle. It was an unmarked grave when I visited the site in October 1985 (Section G, Row 14, Number 11). Nearby, there is the grave of Michael Bodkin, Nora's teenage romance, whom Joyce writes about in 'The Dead'. In every cemetery there are hundreds of stories. Some of them are known within families, others lost to history. And in every family there is a skeleton. For Nora, the west of Ireland was a place to escape from and to return to in her memory. When she returned home in April 1922 it was to show off her children and to be with her mother who had nursed her husband through his last illness the previous summer. Present and past. Past and present. James Joyce and Nora Barnacle, two defiant children brought up in families destroyed by drink, found joy together in exile. Joy but not fusion. Together and apart. In turn Joyce exhibited the traits of both the archaeologist and the intruder. He spent a lifetime trying to recover the past but he never quite managed to possess Nora's past. In a letter he wrote to her when she was in Galway soon after the publication of *Ulysses*, more than anything he wished she would read 'that terrible book' (Ellmann, 1982, 534).

Grave of Michael Bodkin, Rahoon Cemetery, Galway. Photograph by David Pierce. A young man dead before his time. Bodkin is the model for Michael Furey in 'The Dead' and he was also the occasion for one of Joyce's most moving poems, 'She Weeps Over Rahoon'. The story of Michael rising from his sick bed and throwing stones up at the window to get Nora's attention, and then to die as a result – for love of her, as she imagines – has all the elements of a traditional folksong or a ballad. Joyce was in the presence of his theme, but perhaps it's not surprising that the city boy felt like an intruder.

become one and thereby achieve his great expectations. Or, if we were to move away from fiction and adopt a cricketing vocabulary, we might say that John Joyce and his son were players, not gentlemen, that is they had to earn their keep – or not, as the case might be.

Stephen's touchiness, then, is a classic example of deception by a new boy at boarding school. However, in case we are tempted to withhold our sympathy at this point or look down our noses, who is there who hasn't done this when mixing in higher social circles? With his six inherited properties scattered round the city of Cork, John Joyce could pose as a gentleman living off rents, but in reality his position was closer to a canvasser for advertisements (which he was for a time) and to the status of the lower-middle-class Bloom than to the gentry or to those members of the Anglo-Irish who frequented the Royal Dublin Horse Show or the Kildare Street Club. Yeats, the son of a lawyer on his father's side (who preferred the freedom of art to the pursuit of money and the law) and leading Sligo Town merchants on his mother's, was middle class with aspiration above his status. Joyce, the son of a Corkonian, was lower middle class with aspiration. Hence *Dubliners*, which is a collection of stories dominated by the mores, fears and anxieties of the lower middle class, some of whom have aspiration, some pretension, some hatred, some resentment, some socially on the way up, some on the way down, nearly all looking over their shoulder.

Joyce's childhood and early youth coincided with the family's increasing impoverishment, but it isn't true to say, as Peter Jones does in his potted biography of the writer in *Imagist Poetry*, that Joyce was '[o]ne of a large poor family' (Jones, 1972, 168). These things are worth getting right. Nora's family were poor, so poor in 1884 that she was born in the Union Workhouse in Galway. But this is a world away from Joyce's background. The lower middle class can experience poverty without themselves becoming part of 'the poor'. Behind Joyce's at times shabby exterior, there was a very stylish person who knew how to dress the part. Unlike his contemporary Sean O'Casey (1880–1964), Joyce never saw himself as a representative of the poor, but he did understand what it was like to be without money. Indeed, he spent years living in such a state. On learning via Maria Jolas of criticism voiced against him at the Soviet Writers Congress in 1934, he had a ready response: 'I don't see why they dislike me', adding with a smile, 'Nobody in my books has any money' (Aubert and Jolas, 1979, 115). This is the obverse side to the touchiness mentioned above, and it constitutes another way of outflanking his critics by playing with money, class and identity. When Dermot Freyer, the anonymous reader for the publisher Elkin Mathews, was asked to assess the stories of *Dubliners*, he was convinced they should be rejected, revealing in his report something of the prejudice of the time: 'Most of the stories treat of very lower-middle class Dublin life' (Freyer, 1973, 457). For Freyer, peering down at the world from a comfortable height, the 'lower' in 'lower-middle class' betrays more than simply a sociological category but constitutes indeed a class marker. As *Dubliners* constantly reminds us, within the lower middle class there are significant gradations and observable distinctions, but Joyce seems too involved in his characters for Freyer's accusation to come anywhere near its mark.

St Peter's Terrace was the final destination of the Joyce family decline before the children began to take flight. Joyce, however, retained a curious affection for northside Cabra and Drumcondra, where he perversely believed the best English was spoken. Living there for a while in 1902–4 also had certain advantages for the future writer, not least the proximity of St Peter's Terrace to Eccles Street. Only someone familiar with the edges of the city could understand the true character of Dublin, a remark as true today as it was then. After perusing the map for some time, I was struck by the streets named after four provinces of Ireland: Leinster, Munster, Connaught and Ulster. In 'Eveline' a different kind of ideology is on display: 'One time there used to be a field there in which they used to play every evening with other people's children. Then a man from Belfast bought the field and built houses in it' (*D* 36). Everywhere in 'Eveline' there is an invasion of space, as if Joyce was being reminded, whether consciously or unconsciously, of St Peter's Terrace when he came to write that story in August 1904.

In the 1880s and 1890s, father and son could inflate their standing in society, but by 1904 they could not in all honesty claim they were middle

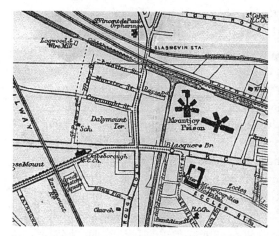

Map of St Peter's Terrace, Cabra and photograph of the house today. It was here that Joyce read his mother extracts from a manuscript which, if his sister Mary is right, was eventually to become *A Portrait* (see *Letters II*, 383). The street, which is just off the North Circular Road and presumably at that time surrounded by fields or spare ground, was on the perimeter of the city with the jagged lines of the municipal boundary running along it. It was situated between two railway lines, the Midland Great Western Railway and the Liffey Branch Railway, and the Royal Canal, and, as if to emphasise its abject status, St Peter's Terrace was within sight of Mountjoy Prison, Glasnevin Cemetery and a Vincent de Paul Orphanage. Photograph by David Pierce.

class. In 1908, when Joyce's younger brother Charlie – who wore James's cast-off suits, and who, according to his father, mixed with corner-boys – entered 'Gentleman' in the marriage register, we know the game is up for the Joyces (Jackson and Costello, 1997, 298). Debts, moonlit flits 'oft in the stilly night', chopping up banisters for firewood – this was hardly a 'middle-class affair', and hardly 'simply a middle-class affair'. Few of the jobs or positions John Joyce tried his hand at can be considered securely middle class. He started out in his home city of Cork as an accountant, but that was not the professional position we might associate with the term today, for what it involved, at least in part, was clerical work, going from shop to shop or business to business making receipts and returning to an office for filing. When he arrived in Dublin in the 1870s from Ireland's second city, John Joyce worked as secretary for a brewery in Chapelizod and then in the Collector-General's Office as a tax collector for rural districts outside the city boundary. In 1881 he inherited properties in Cork and took out mortgages on them. It could have been a middle-class affair if John Joyce had made something of his opportunities, but in the Index to his biography the 15 references under the entry marked 'financial difficulties' tell their own story. In the 1901 Census under the entry marked 'Rank, Profession, or Occupation', John Joyce inserted triumphantly 'Government Pensioner'.

He was still only 51 and went on to live for another 30 years. Only when he reached Paris in 1920 and the cheques from Harriet Shaw Weaver started flowing did his son feel financial security. He was then in his late thirties and had spent 20 years collecting debts and IOUs. In Norah Hoult's *Coming From The Fair* (1937), a novel which reconstructs the period leading up to the Easter Rising of 1916, we read that, according to one of his contemporaries at school, Joyce 'had the loveliest way of touching a pal' (159). 'Always odd sums he'd choose. "Lend me ninepence," he'd say. "If you have a shilling I can give you threepence."' I know it's only fiction, but it's a story that has a ring of truth about it.

Joyce's father was responsible for the household decline, but Joyce acknowledges in his letter to Nora that he himself was partly responsible for his mother's death. Indeed, as he looked on her face in her coffin, Joyce blames the 'system' for turning her into a victim. How Nora responded to the contents of this letter, we do not know. She must have been pleased by his implicit valuing of her in his rejection of the world, but, equally, she must have been puzzled by his attempt to explain his life not in terms of his own family and the luck of the draw in life but in more general abstract terms rooted in causes and determination. Moreover, she couldn't have known that the influential figure behind Joyce's critique was not a systematic political thinker or sociologist such as Karl Marx or Émile Durkheim, but a Norwegian dramatist who focused on the strained interface between the personal and the social or political.

Dust-wrapper of Bjørn Tysdahl's book on Joyce and Ibsen, published by the Norwegian Universities Press in 1968. Joyce looks across to Ibsen, Ibsen looks out to the world. When Ibsen died, a statue of a miner was placed above his grave.

Like Ibsen, Joyce too is a miner, digging under the surface of life. It was for the writer to expose the truth and to be fearless in confronting the majority, whom Joyce referred to as the 'rabblement'. Truth for both involved an exposure of social systems and inauthentic forms of human behaviour. In their advocacy of female liberation and the emerging women's movement, they are our contemporaries. Joyce's decision not to marry and 'enslave' Nora, as he called it, must have been in part because of Ibsen's female-centred plays. As Tysdahl points out, two of Joyce's epiphanies concern Ibsen, as if from the outset of his career the young poet was being drawn towards Ibsen's sense of realism. *Exiles*, a title which links both writers, is Joyce's most Ibsenesque work, but throughout the stories of *Dubliners* Ibsen's presence, particularly evident in the theme of paralysis, can be felt. In a famous passage in Joyce's final book, *Finnegans Wake*, Ibsen, who wrote in the language of his people, is celebrated as the champion of minority languages: 'no mouth has the might to set a mearbound to the march of a landsmaul' (*FW* 292:26–7). Just as 'no man has a right to fix the boundary to the march of a nation' – which was Parnell's famous slogan in regard to Irish nationalism – so no-one should be able to set a limit to the march of a rural dialect such as Landsmaal, which some Norwegians in the nineteenth century, including Ibsen, hoped would become the standard language of Norway.

Statue of Parnell at the top of O'Connell Street, with Parnell's slogan set in stone. Photograph by David Pierce.

In his searching for social explanations to medical conditions, in his choice of charged words such as 'system' and 'inherited', and in his elevated or dramatic mode of address, Joyce reveals to the educated person he had been reading plays such as *Ghosts* (1881) and *An Enemy of the People* (1882). Indeed, Ibsen's ideas must have been so persuasive that Joyce chose to imagine his own circumstances in the light of the plays, or he was influenced enough to be persuaded of such an identity. The system, however, was not going to get him. Against such a social background and a theatrical backdrop, the injunction he must have imbibed almost with his mother's milk was 'Save Yourself!'. As for Nora, she presumably struggled to understand the tragic reading on offer of Joyce and his family. A part of her would have understood only too well, but another part of her must have wondered, as Molly does in 'Penelope', about some of the unfamiliar words or concepts: 'he came out with some jawbreakers about the incarnation he never can explain a thing simply' (*U* 18:566–7).

The sociological explanation, together with his candid confession, therefore, betrays at once a picture of Joyce's inner soul and a form of evasiveness or of distancing. Explanation is never far away in the stories of *Dubliners*, especially regarding the motivation of characters, but, in real life, truth sometimes got the better of Joyce. Loss is loss is loss. It didn't help that the pious Catholic May Joyce endured so many pregnancies, but the one-time medical student must have realised it wasn't the system that killed her but cancer. In his moving elegy on Charles Péguy, the French Catholic socialist thinker who died in the trenches in the Great War, the English poet Geoffrey Hill writes with a characteristic mixture of brevity and profundity: 'Dying, your whole life / fell into place' (Hill, 1985, 184). No amount of theorising could alter the fact that, on dying, May Joyce's life did not in one sense fall into place.

It was at the Hôtel Corneille in Paris that Joyce received a telegram from his father on Good Friday 1903, bringing to an end his sojourn in Paris: 'Nother dying. Come home.' The announcement must have produced a profound shock. According to Gorman, recalling what sounds like Joyce's voice, he was 'dumbfounded' (Gorman, 1948, 108). His feelings for his mother, however, are deflected by the letter 'n' in 'nother', away from experience to language. And yet, nothing could transform her into 'another' or simply 'an other'. Or perhaps death could. What is the case is that her death brought home the decided otherness of the world, part of which included his own complicated feelings towards her. In the telegram, Joyce had something to pin this moment on, a form of emotional displacement which at the same time was to initiate a textual conundrum in *Ulysses* that has continued to excite editors and critics to this day. In the original manuscript to *Ulysses*, Joyce retained John Joyce's misspelling (or perhaps the mistake

Hôtel Corneille at 4 rue des Moulines in Paris. Now the Paris Louvre Opera, a Best Western Hotel. Photograph by David Pierce.

had been introduced by someone typing the message), but when it emerged in the Shakespeare and Company edition in 1922 the mistake had been silently corrected as it were. In the Gabler edition, published in 1984, the 'mistake' has been restored: 'Nother dying come home father' (*U* 3:199). It remains for critics and readers to decide on the respective merits of the misspelling, the correction for the 1922 edition, and then the restoration in the 1984 edition of the misspelling. But such pursuits, in the way they implicitly side with Joyce, shifting the accent at the announcement of his mother's illness from experience to textuality, are also a continuation of the displacement prompted by Joyce himself. His mental distraction is remembered, but the 21-year-old penniless young man descending into this street late at night to secure a loan for a ticket home from one of his wealthy students has been well and truly forgotten. From experience to writing, from Dublin to Paris, the umbilical cord took many twists and turns for Joyce and it prompted several more for his readers. Dumbfounded, at a loss as to what he should do, was perhaps one twist we shouldn't forget.

Family details invariably complicate the picture, and such details are not always consistent with the story given to us in the first episode of *Ulysses*. Like most of us, Joyce was an expert at putting truth and untruth together. May Joyce died of liver or abdominal cancer, and, if she is a victim of 'the system', it's not clear what that system is. John Joyce's ill-treatment of her is mentioned by Joyce, but it is not within a framework of patriarchy and power. Indeed, John Joyce was utterly distraught by her death, weeping openly in front of his children, hoping like Simon Dedalus in *Ulysses* that God would 'take him whenever He likes' (*U* 6:646). The 'system' may have killed her but the children couldn't let go, and they still wanted direct contact with the figure they thought was haunting them. One night after her death, Joyce joined his sister 'Poppie' (Margaret) and the rest of the family in a vigil at the top of the stairs in their home at 7 St Peter's Terrace, Cabra. They were hoping she might give them a sign. Whatever he thought later, this is not, we might properly conclude, the dismissive attitude or disturbing mood we encounter in 'Telemachus' when Stephen cries out:

Ghoul! Chewer of corpses!
No, mother! Let me be and let me live.
(*U* 1:278–9)

Sixty years later, 'Poppie', who spent her life as a nun in New Zealand, did indeed believe she saw her mother that night, dressed in the brown habit she wore in her coffin (Jackson and Costello, 1997, 259).

As for the 'years of trouble' in the letter to Nora, this sounds like a conventional portrait of a woman worn out with caring for a large family, himself the eldest son included. Joyce makes nothing of the 17 pregnancies or so, and yet this is the best example of a system at work here, the Catholic system that is, a Church that was not given to questioning large families. May Joyce spent nearly all her twenties and thirties literally carrying someone else. There's something sweeping and contradictory, limited and impersonal in Joyce's attitude, as if, like Ibsen's protagonists, he was distancing himself from personal involvement in order to discover the ground or vantage-point from which he could launch an attack on the world. In this respect, only his spendthrift habits and a measure of guilt is he prepared to admit into his new life; everything else, including the warmth of affection for his mother and her solicitousness for him, belongs to the file marked 'reject'. They may exist, but I've never come across any group photographs of the eldest son with his brothers and sisters in Dublin.

The cards in life had been stacked against him, but the defiant Joyce was determined not to show anyone his vulnerable side. On meeting Yeats in the street one day in April 1903, the aspiring writer, just ordered home from Paris, told the poet that it was uncertain if his mother would live or die. Joyce then added 'but these things really don't matter' (Yeats, 1954, 399). It's an odd thing to say and, in his letter to Lady Gregory, Yeats puts the phrase in inverted commas, as if the poet too thought it odd and difficult to know what to do with. How do you respond to a remark like that? Writing in 1939 just after the publication of *Finnegans Wake*, one of his earliest commentators, Edmund Wilson, the critic who in *Axel's Castle* (1931) did more than anyone to introduce Joyce to American readers, noticed a peculiar characteristic about Joyce, which he defined as 'a curious shrinking solicitude to conceal from the reader his real subjects' (Wilson, 1941, 239). If Wilson had at his disposal all the biographical information we now have, he might well have been able to discern the psychological roots to a characteristic pattern in his writing. Defiance, we might concede, is brilliant at betraying and revealing forms of concealment.

How far can you travel on defiance? A long way if your name is James Joyce and you have a sympathetic travelling companion. Defiance drove him to leave Ireland and sustained him through years of self-imposed exile. By the time he reached Paris in the 1920s, he had achieved what T.S. Eliot

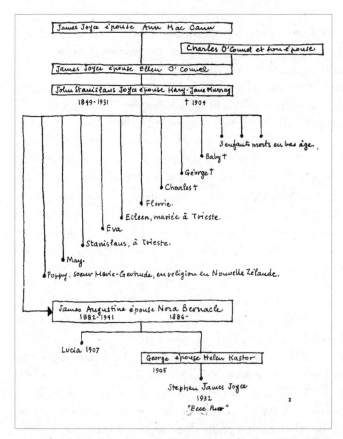

Joyce's family tree as it appears in the catalogue for the 1949 exhibition at La Hune Gallery in Paris (see Gheerbrant, 1949). Next in age to Joyce is 'Poppy', Sister Marie-Gertrude, 'in religion' in New Zealand. Notice all the deaths of his siblings and his mother, with no birth year indicated, dead by 1904 (actually she died in 1903), never knowing how much fame her son would bring her. In saving himself, Joyce saved his family from obscurity.

Joyce with hands in pocket outside the greenhouse at Constantine Curran's house in Dublin. This is my favourite photograph of Joyce. When asked what he was thinking when it was being taken, Joyce replied something about borrowing five shillings from the photographer. It's a photograph of Joyce at 22 with attitude, the head to one side, the chin square and resolute, the eyes looking out at the world resisting its gaze. *Dubliners, A Portrait of the Artist as a Young Man* and *Ulysses* are a long way down the line when this photograph was taken. The corollary also causes one to pause, for it's impossible to imagine the modern world without these books. A century later, we have no option but to adopt the backward look, but everything in the photograph is geared to the future, and you can almost hear Joyce, protected by his waistcoat and clean detachable collar, saying to us 'What do you think an aspiring writer looks like? Forget about the greenhouse; it's not mine anyway. I may have nothing to my name, but in the centuries to come when you regard me you'll see my achievement in this pose. See it all worked out and all by my own efforts.' Only one letter in English separates pose from prose.

in a letter to Robert McAlmon, dated 2 May 1921, was to commend in him, namely independence of 'outside stimulus' (McAlmon, 1970, 8). 'As stubborn as a mule or an Irishman,' was how Ezra Pound quipped to John Quinn after first meeting Joyce in person in June 1920 (Pound, 1971, 177).

But in Joyce's youth, it wasn't just stubbornness but defiance. Defiance furnished him with a theory of the artist as a lonely individual in a struggle against convention, against those in the publishing industry, against his contemporaries, the courts and what he termed 'the rabblement'. The minority, as Ibsen had argued, was always right, never the majority. On his first stay in Paris between December 1902 and April 1903, Joyce surprised people in the street and in cafés by roaring out loud laughing. What he was expressing was scorn, defiance, a marker on the way to his own vision of the world.

Every sentence Joyce penned is in some way governed by this youthful and by then ingrained defiance. He deferred to no one. In 1906 Grant Richards wanted him to rewrite or cut pieces of *Dubliners*, but Joyce realised he would merely find again 'the Holy Ghost sitting in the ink-bottle and the perverse devil of my literary conscience sitting on the hump of my pen' (*Letters II*, 166). It's as if he knew that without the distance he imagined for himself as a young man, without the spirit of perversity, there would be no writer. He was after all, as Gorman rightly conceded, 'possibly the most arrogant writer that Ireland has produced' (Gorman, 1926, 6). Later in life came independence and the search for an accommodation with the present order, an accommodation that issued in his delight in the ordinariness of Bloom and in the universality of the figure in *Finnegans Wake* he called HCE or Here Comes Everybody. The trajectory is not dissimilar to the one followed by his country in this sense, independence followed by a search for a new state without the Crown. But as a young man, Joyce was on a different tack, the isolated artist who obtained great comfort, as he tells his mother in March 1903, from a passing remark made about him by John Eglinton, one of the leading cultural figures in Dublin at the time: 'There is something sublime in Joyce's standing alone' (*Letters II*, 38). His mother and Nora notwithstanding (and it is a big notwithstanding), 'standing alone' is in fact what the fiercely competitive Joyce did throughout his life, and, if it stemmed from anything beyond his genes, it was the acute sense of reversal that he underwent in the six years between 16 and 22.

At 22, Joyce was marking out his identity. He identified with Ibsen in cultural politics, and with Parnell, the lost leader, in Irish politics. He was also identifying himself with a fictional persona he called Stephen Dedalus. He distanced himself from the Irish Literary Revival and from the Church. He also distanced himself from his family, and at the earliest opportunity he formed an attachment with a woman whom he imagined would be his ally through the long years of physical and mental exile which lay ahead of him. It was a lot to ask of her, as *Exiles* reminds us, but the battle lines were being drawn in his own mind. An end to one kind of life

Standing alone was also the position forced on Joyce's hero in Irish politics, the patrician landlord Charles Stewart Parnell. In the 1880s Parnell nearly managed to win Home Rule for Ireland when, as leader of the Irish Parliamentary Party, he forged an alliance with the Liberal Party under Gladstone. But his career was brought to an end in Committee Room 15 of the House of Commons in December 1890 when it was discovered he had been having an affair with the wife of one of his colleagues. Here is a vicious cartoon by Tom Merry, which appeared in *St Stephen's Review* in that same month, showing the adulterer Parnell, in his pursuit of 'Home Rule' and by implication the break-up of the British Empire, taming not only Gladstone and the Liberal Party but also members of his own Irish Parliamentary Party. Defiance in Joyce found both ammunition and succour in the idea of betrayal, and in the fall of Parnell he had a compelling example of how the Irish people turned on their leaders in history and betrayed them.

PROFESSOR PARNELL
IN HIS
GREAT WOLF TAMING ACT.
WITH ASSEMBLAGEMENTS TO THE LIBERAL ASSEMBLAGE

and the start of another, but, as I have been attempting to suggest here, it's what linked the two that intrigues me. Unlike others in a similar position, Joyce doesn't simply draw a line under the past, but he brings all the past along with him, including his double sense of rejection, rejection of others and rejection by others. The students who came into my office wanted just a job, not to take on the system. Joyce wanted a job but only so that he could take on the system. Culture, politics, the Church, his family, all had let him down. Now he was on the point of turning his weapons on them all. But what weapons did he possess? Not so much a political programme but rather an attitude, or more specifically two attitudes: aspiration and defiance.

Defiance is an attitude formed in the crucible of circumstance and experience. At the same time, it constitutes a line of continuity between past and present, self and world. Defiance is an attitude, a gesture, something that frequently makes itself felt through some other means such as a smirk or a smile or an aside. Defiance is about disobedience, standing up for oneself, denying power, a refusal to accept norms or conventions or cultural codes. It's also wilful, or it can be. Frequently among the young – and Joyce, like the rebellious Shelley, is essentially a young writer – it belongs to a personal statement and the determination to set down a marker. What seems to be the most natural thing in the world is being prevented by a school rule for example. In itself, wearing an item of jewellery is not an act of defiance, but it will become so if the school has a policy of forbidding jewellery. Once challenged, the individual resorts to natural justice by way of defence. What's wrong with including a mild swear word like 'bloody' in a story or using real names of shops or people? Why should I as an author and my name is James Joyce alter anything I have seen and heard? Why shouldn't I deploy the actual names of 'restaurants, cake-shops, railway-stations, public houses, laundries, bars, and other places of business' (Gorman, 1926, 37)? Why should I, Percy Byshe Shelley, be sent down from Oxford because I had a pamphlet printed on *The Necessity of Atheism* (1811)? Why shouldn't I, if I have the force of personality, not secure a job as a fashion journalist in London? What's to stop me? Aspiration and defiance, there's a lot to be said for them.

Dubliners, the collection we are now going to turn our attention to, has its origins in this moment of isolation and defiance. As I suggested in my opening remarks to this chapter, such attitudes in Joyce connect to the wider issue of colonialism and can indeed be read in terms of a larger de-colonising process. Defiance is a form of defence, and defence can assume the attitude of defiance. In this way defiance can constitute a means of engaging or provoking those in positions of power to defend their position or articulate their assumptions, which are then often exposed as mere prejudices. So defiance is also a form of exposure, exposure which in this case involves both parties digging in against each other, a rejection of common ground or the possibility of negotiation or compromise. It's as good a place as any to start with Joyce.

CHAPTER 3

The unfinished sentences of 'The Sisters'

Unfinished sentences

Joyce's defiance, as we saw in the last chapter, is open in his letter to Nora, but in 'The Sisters' it is folded inside a narrative that refuses to say what it means. The boy, who is nameless, is surrounded by two displaced father figures, the priest and old Cotter, and two maiden aunts. The title can apply perhaps equally to the aunts as to the boy and the disgraced, effeminate priest. Fr Flynn has an 'egoistic contempt for all women-folk' but he is himself identified as effeminate, most noticeably when he smiled, for then he 'let his tongue lie on his lower lip'. Old Cotter's insistence in the revised version on the boy playing with lads his own age rather than spending his time learning Latin with the priest hints at something not entirely wholesome. Throughout the story the boy repeatedly sides with the priest against the insinuations of old Cotter and the coldness of the sisters, as if to remind us of a defiant, sisterly, unconscious or suppressed gay embrace between a boy and an old man. When Nannie tempts him with a cream cracker, the boy declines. In the coffin he sees not, as the sisters do, a disappointed man or the figure of failure whose mind had gone, but someone 'truculent in death'.

From today's perspective, we are more ready to recognise and talk about things that would have been repressed a century ago, so we might well agree that there is what amounts to a gay undercurrent to the story. Or perhaps with Ibsen's *Ghosts* in mind and that play's theme of sexual disease and its transmission, we might be willing to concede that 'The Sisters' is a story about a priest who has contracted syphilis which eventually attacks his mind, leaving him confined to the back room of the shop in front of a fire, reaching for his snuff. In 1904, in a newspaper for the Irish farming community, it would only be possible to hint at such things, but Joyce does enough to suggest all these possible meanings. However, there is a broader question. For myself, I doubt if this is what the story is about; it certainly includes such a theme but I don't believe such a theme constitutes the story. Critics have rightly puzzled over its meaning, but it must be more than a study of a boy's relationship with a syphilitic priest. After all, the author of the story is not the naturalist, single-issue Ibsen in mid-career, nor the Irish Zola, but the youthful proto-Modernist James Joyce, bent on a more general form of undermining or disturbance. What exactly is the story about and do we have the means to discover what that is? Is it, as Kevin Dettmar (1996) cheekily suggests, a whodunit with Cotter as a Sherlock Holmes figure? Did the sisters slowly kill their brother and could that be why the boy's mother asks them if he died peacefully?

We ask such questions because they're there to be asked and also because we haven't got the answer or haven't got all the answers. My advice is to enjoy the experience of not knowing everything when you embark on reading the stories of *Dubliners*. Share your ignorance, forget about displaying your knowledge. Enjoy the moment. If you've never been to Ireland, so what? If you've never been to a wake, who has these days? If you've never met a defrocked Catholic priest, perhaps, in a period of sexual abuse cases, you should count your blessings. Literature is about encountering things you're not familiar with, and if reading Joyce is about any single thing, it's extending one's pleasure in reading – or it should be. *Macbeth* is a tragedy; it's also concerned with the mind of a murderer, but for all that, it's unbelievably satisfying. Joyce opens the door to something else. He's a great teacher, and if you allow him time he will tell you nearly all you need to know about writing and a great deal about the history of English literature. From its classical origins to its medieval romances, from English madrigals to Edwardian popular songs, from Shakespeare's *Hamlet* to Victorian melodrama, from Byron's love poems to Eliot's *The Waste Land* – there's very little his hand hasn't brought to life again.

Before it was closed down, I lectured for many years at the Quaker-inspired St Mary's Settlement in York. Founded in 1909 by Joseph Rowntree's nephew Arnold Rowntree, the Settlement was one of the oldest independent adult education centres in Britain, and it was a sad loss to the city when it closed. When I taught there in the 1980s it was run for the most part by a group of enthusiasts who rallied round the warden, the historian and electrician Alf Peacock. The popular courses at that time were in modern languages and contemporary film. There was a buzz about the place, a refreshing, down-to-earth intimacy, and, after class, tutors would adjourn to the railway-workers' pub, The Fox, nearby. The teaching was, like much of the teaching I've been involved in, not far removed from missionary work, because you never knew who might enrol for your class.

Students came from all walks of life, and when numbers were short, as mine sometimes were, 'Sean O'Grady' would be added to the register to ensure the course wasn't pulled by the funding bodies.

Only once in my teaching career has someone fallen asleep in my class and started snoring. That was at an afternoon class at the Settlement in the days before Alf single-handedly installed central heating. I was droning on about Mrs Dalloway or some other character from the pages of a book, the electric fan heater was on full, the late-autumn sunshine was streaming in through the distant, rain-smeared windows, and the room was filling up with ever deeper tones from a woman who was, if I recall correctly, middle-aged and overweight, who had her arms folded over a brightly coloured cardigan and her pointy chin decidedly on the way down. I was impressed by her determination in a public place to work up a real head of steam. I was slightly embarrassed, however, as much for the class imagining I might be embarrassed as for anything about my ineffectual teaching (which it often was). In mid-career, it taught me a lesson: no matter how far away, always open the window, and modulate your voice.

One person I recall who regularly turned up for my modern literature class at the Settlement was a retired tax inspector, a position he had obtained after a career in the navy, where he had been a naval commander, I believe. Unlike the middle-aged woman in the cardigan, the retired tax inspector was always wide awake as he looked me over to ensure that I was up to the mark and that I wasn't fiddling my taxes or running down the country. There was never an occasion when he didn't have some comment to make about the authors we were studying, and more often than not it was always along the same line. With a barely concealed note of irony, which was accompanied by the merest hint of a twinkle in his eye, he would insist on dropping anchor: 'What exactly is Lawrence saying in this novel? Is there anything to be said for this modern literature? I mean, take Virginia Woolf or James Joyce or Malcolm Lowry. I couldn't exactly take their novels on holiday now could I? Is this the best you can offer? Nothing happens in any of them.'

I never took the bait. At the end of each session, I would turn to the class and innocently enquire if they had enjoyed the text that week. Mr B—— (I keep to the tradition of anonymity, for he might have family who've survived him reading this) would at this point always make the same gesture. Rubbing his index finger against his thumb and extending his arm, he would pretend to be dropping the book into a wastepaper basket: 'The bin', the dapper, retired naval commander would say. Followed by 'Enough said'. Hook, line and sinker. A formidable judgement worthy of sinking any enemy battleship on the western approaches. Toward the end of the course, his disdain could be expressed simply with the gesture. No words needed, only the semaphore. Modern literature? The bin. Or rather, modern literature? The index finger and thumb. But, like that elusive Irishman Sean O'Grady, he always signed up for more modern literature classes with me. Mr B——. The bin. All at sea, I thought at the time, but who was I to tell him? I was hearing again my primary school teacher bawling me out: 'Get in the corner and stay there!' When you're young, explore; when you're old, the bin. I think that's right. Reading Joyce keeps us young but you need to give a little and not close down your options as Mr B——was wont to do with modern writers. In old age, you can throw the lot in the bin and settle down to a diet of biographies, but who wants that when you're young?

To return to 'The Sisters', my own view is in keeping with the tone of the story, more literary and downbeat. The boy we learn searches in vain to 'extract meaning from [Cotter's] unfinished sentences'. This is the sentence that intrigues me most in this story, linking as it does with the word 'gnomon' in the first paragraph of the final version. How might those unfinished sentences apply to the story as a whole? In other words, could the 'gnomic' story be as much about style as about discourse, as much about how the absences inform the story as about what the story says? It would then provide another kind of defiance to accompany all that discussion in the previous chapter. 'The Sisters' seems to defy conventional interpretations, and by conventional I mean not only cultural conventions but also conventions of reading. It's a story that seems to outflank the reader, constantly undermining or, what amounts to the same thing in Joyce, extending reading expectations. As I suggest in Chapter 1, most readers when they arrive at the end of the story must be puzzled. 'What was that about? Did I miss something?' Or, conversely, 'Am I reading too much into this?' Such questions shouldn't defeat us, but the reverse; they should encourage us. That's what I seem to be saying repeatedly in this book. Enjoy the challenge and resist the temptation to say 'This isn't for me'.

Every time anyone – and I include myself in this – is tempted to write 'The story is about . . .', there should be a short pause, a moment of hesitation before the sentence is finished. Better always to say 'The story is also about . . .'. One of my students takes this a stage further, linking it with Joyce's use of realism in the stories, and I let it stand as it is:

> Dubliners gives the reader much to think about. The reader is presented with hurt, poverty and suffering with no easy answers to the problems shown, if there is any answer at all. Being a realist text, Joyce tinges each story with sadness and suffering that rings true throughout. Although Joyce moves away from realism later in his career, he shows a great understanding of how realism can be one of the most moving ways to tell a story.

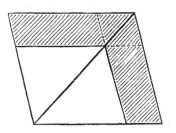

This diagram of a gnomon in Euclidian geometry appeared in *Euclid: Books I–IV*, a textbook edited by Rupert Deakin (1897) at a time when Joyce was still at secondary school.

The conventional reading of a gnomon in Joyce studies can be found in the Viking Critical Edition of *Dubliners*: 'a gnomon is that part of a parallelogram which remains when a similar parallelogram is taken away from one of its corners' (D 463). The French edition by Jacques Aubert says much the same thing: 'la partie d'un parallélogramme qui reste après qu'un parallélogramme analogue a été retranché d'un de ses coins' (the part of a parallelogram that remains after a similar or analogous parallelogram has been removed from one of its corners) (Joyce/Aubert, 1974, 33). This isn't quite what is stated in Euclid. In Book Two of Euclid's *Elements*, we encounter the following definition: 'And in any parallelogrammic area let any one whatever of the parallelograms about its diameter with the two complements be called a gnomon'. In the figure reproduced above, the gnomon is shown as the shaded area and the diagram includes a diameter. The explanation below, from an 1898 textbook, makes more sense in this regard, since it refers to two gnomons. If you're anything like me, you might already be finding this slightly confusing. Joyceans, who are better at what the term signifies, tend to skip over all this, but in the notes to this word in *Dubliners* there should be entered a certain doubt as to what exactly gnomon means. Some interpreters have assumed that what remains in the

3. In any parallelogram the figure formed by either of the parallelograms about a diagonal together with the two complements is called a gnomon.

Thus the shaded portion of the annexed figure, consisting of the parallelogram EH together with the complements AK, KC is the *gnomon* AHF.

The other gnomon in the figure is that which is made up of AK, GF and FH, namely the gnomon AFH.

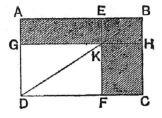

Gnomon and explanation in Hall and Stevens, *A Text-Book of Euclid's Elements For the Use of Schools* (1898), a textbook that Joyce had in his Trieste Library.

diagram is the white area. In a curious way, the idea of what 'remains' is not inappropriate, but equally there's something to be said for thinking of the gnomon as the shaded area. The boy and the priest are on parallel lines which meet, and where they meet there is a gnomon, a shaded area. In this sense, 'The Sisters' is a story full of parallel lines but it is also shaped around something missing.

From the outset of his career as a writer, Joyce seemed to have absorbed where our culture was heading. Who any longer wanted the whole picture when a few sketched-in or distorted lines by a Brancusi or a Picasso or a Motherwell would do the trick and in effect give us the whole portrait? What was missing or unfinished was precisely the new mode of inquiry and expectation, and Joyce had this in abundance. It was an extraordinary turnround from the era stretching from the Enlightenment to the Victorian period, when the whole world had been systematically put into boxes, joined up, sealed or colonised. Equally, only Joyce among the moderns could have noticed the potential of an ancient Greek geometrical sign of an absence or a shaded area for a principle underlying his new theory of art. We can alter the image and at the same time take this further: more than most modern writers, Joyce writes between the lines as it were, and he shows us how to discern presence in absence and absence in presence.

Great Britain Street wasn't such a dingy back-street as might be supposed when reading the story. According to *Thom's Business Directory of Dublin and Suburbs for the Year 1906*, five hairdressers and perfumers had

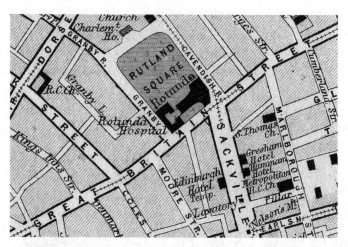

Great Britain Street on Bartholomew's 1900 map of Dublin. It is now Parnell Street, a replacement that won't be lost on those attuned to nationalist politics: Charles Stewart Parnell replacing Great Britain on the streets of Dublin.

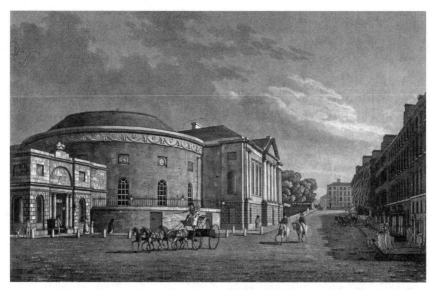

James Malton's contemporary view of the Rotunda, from *A Picturesque and Descriptive View of Dublin* (1792–9).

businesses on this street, and the Shamrock Dining Rooms and Hotel stood at number 81, the Parnell Restaurant at 158. The Rotunda Hospital, a lying-in hospital built in the eighteenth century, is on this street or just back from it, as is the Rotunda itself, a building much loved by the Ascendancy for its masked balls and other forms of entertainment. By 1904 those stylish days had gone, replaced on the map by the Victorian world of temperance hotels and public lavatories (see Sackville Street, now O'Connell Street). However, the facades of the buildings and the layout of the streets remain. Equally, as can be discerned from the broken lines representing electric tram routes, Great Britain Street was part of the new Dublin transport system. Fittingly, it was only five minutes away from the upmarket Gresham Hotel where Gabriel and Gretta Conroy spend an unhappy night at the end of 'The Dead', the last story of *Dubliners*. The Easter Rising leader Thomas J. Clarke owned a newspaper and tobacconist shop on Great Britain Street, where 'the Irish fellows', as Stephen notices in *A Portrait of the Artist as a Young Man*, would gather (see P 210). It's a street, in other words, full of things to notice.

The note 'The Sisters' strikes throughout is consciously restrained, as if the defiant Joyce were countering something in the culture or something more upbeat in story-telling conventions. The family lives on 'Great Britain-street' (the hyphen is Joyce's), but, for Joyce, there's nothing great about the street.

The drapery shop the sisters own has an 'unassuming name' (which in the first version in *The Irish Homestead* we're not told, and in the revised version the adjective 'unassuming' is transformed to 'vague' and accompanied by the word 'Drapery' in italics). In the window there is a note on 'ordinary days' advertising 'Umbrellas Recovered', but this is an exceptional day and the blinds are down, so the note cannot be seen by passers-by (who in the first version are described as 'three women of the people and a telegram boy'). As we read the note today, we sense it is a cruel reminder not only of Edwardian pinched circumstances but also of a family with precious few marketing skills, for we're never told if the sisters recover umbrellas with new material, are in possession of lost umbrellas, or, indeed, go hunting round the streets of Dublin on behalf of clients in search of lost umbrellas. The death of their brother means the blinds are down and a crape bouquet of flowers tied to the door knocker with white ribbons. Pinned to the crape is a card giving details of the dead priest, Fr James Flynn, and the date 'July 2nd 189–' and then the simple wish 'R.I.P.'.

Wherever we look in 'The Sisters', we encounter something 'unfinished'. The priest's age is given, as is the day and month but in the first version not the year. More importantly, the sisters expected so much from their brother, especially as he had been selected to train for the priesthood in Rome. A seven-year Rome training was the normal fast track to promotion in the Church, but Fr Flynn ends his days in the back of the family shop, never having attained the higher status of a monsignor, say, or a canon or, higher still, a bishop. This would presumably explain why throughout the story the sisters can barely contain their disappointment that he hadn't raised them out of their pinched circumstances.

On the edge of Europe, Irish Catholics, in common with Roman Catholics elsewhere, looked to the Vatican for their interior life and keys to the kingdom. The Pope meant more to them than the British monarchy ever could. Indeed, their religion, which was nothing if not universal in scope and ambition and had nothing peripheral about it, always retained the potential to outflank the jurisdiction of the State. Every Sunday at Mass, Catholics recited the Credo, insisting on their belief in 'unam, sanctam, catholicam et apostolicam Ecclesiam' (one, holy, catholic and apostolic Church). Their creed, then, was not in a United Kingdom but in a universal Church. Interestingly, in his first story, Joyce brings together the two most powerful institutions in Ireland, focusing on a Rome-educated priest who lives on Great Britain-street. In doing so we catch an early glimpse of the two masters the defiant Stephen Dedalus confronts more directly in the opening episode of *Ulysses*.

Leo XIII, who was Pope from 1878 until his death in 1903, spent his Papacy issuing encyclicals and decrees. Some of these were on topical themes, such as *Rerum Novarum*, his anti-socialist encyclical on labour and labour relations published in 1891. He was, according to Mr Cunningham in 'Grace', 'one of the lights of the age', but he was also the person who strengthened the Vatican's office for censorship known as the *Index*, banning books by among others Milton, Defoe, Sterne, Voltaire, Zola and Renan. Here, on this contemporary, ghostly, embossed postcard, posted from Cork in July 1903, Leo raises his right hand in a traditional gesture of papal authority. Shades of things to come, we might find ourselves thinking as we look on.

Ritual and folklore

'The Sisters' is also about ritual or rituals, not only the ritual surrounding death in Catholic Ireland but also the ritual in what is denied and what isn't said – in the unfinished sentences, as it were. The first version begins not with God but with the more pagan word 'Providence'; later, there is a reference to another form of ritual as deception, how the priest 'used to make believe to read his Prayer Book'. Equally, the wake is a sombre one. It is not like Tim Finnegan's wake in the Irish-American ballad, where the whiskey rouses the dead man from his slumber, or Irish wakes in history, which were sometimes so lively that the Church hierarchy had to intervene to remind their flock of the sombre nature of the occasion. No whiskey or snuff is offered at this wake, and it is only in the revised version of the story that Joyce, touched perhaps by a more generous instinct, introduces sherry and cream crackers.

The boy's aunt is anxious to learn from the sisters if Fr Flynn died a peaceful death. The phrase she uses is 'Did he . . . peacefully?' The elliptical points reflect her concern not to utter the word 'die', precisely why she is in the house with the two sisters. It's a story about unfinished sentences, about what isn't said, about the appropriateness of not saying anything inappropriate. Passing on, passing away – our culture is full of such 'passing' phrases at such times, for emotional moments require restraint in language. But in this story there's something else that isn't said. 'Did he die peacefully?' is the kind of question sometimes asked about a person who has been ill with cancer or some other painful condition. (On hearing of Oscar Wilde's death-bed conversion to Catholicism, Joyce expressed the hope that it had not been sincere.) But the boy's aunt seems to be alluding to something else.

Given that Fr Flynn was a fallen priest or a priest who no longer said Mass, the question seems to allude to his soul at the last moment. 'Did he . . . peacefully?' Did he, in other words, go to meet his Maker with a clear conscience? 'O, quite peacefully, ma'am', replies one of the sisters, and the reply to this is immediate: 'He had a beautiful death, God be praised.' And, in case we didn't know what a beautiful death was, we are told: 'You couldn't tell when the breath went out of him' (D 15). It's as if the priest's last moment was also unfinished in that you couldn't tell when he was alive and when he passed on. The calming effect of the dead is continued into Joyce's last work. When Joyce imagines Finnegan coming to in present-day Dublin, the figure of Tutankhamen, whose tomb was being excavated when Joyce was starting on *Finnegans Wake*, exerts a totally calming, totemic influence: 'Totumcalmum' (FW 26:18).

There's something wicked or wickedly funny about 'The Sisters', as if Joyce is exploiting the long-sustained commerce with the dead in Ireland. 'Clay', to take another story in *Dubliners* involving ritual, can be read humorously or tragically. Maria works in the Dublin by Lamplight Laundry, which happens to be a charitable institution where rescued fallen women were put to work. This is Joyce putting us on our guard and arming us against a sentimental reading, for Maria seems too innocent to have had such a past. It is a Halloween story, a story that is set on the eve of All Saints, 1 November. The following day in the Church's calendar is All Souls. If you don't make it to sainthood, the Church seems to be saying, there's a chance you will get to heaven anyway. Hence All Souls. These feasts were inserted into the autumn of the year partly to counter the ancient Celtic festival of Samhain, a feast that marked not only the end of summer but also a heightened moment in the struggle between summer and winter. On the other side of the world, in Mexico, All Saints' and All Souls' Day, the Day of the Dead, is the time when coffins are carried through the streets to remind the living that the dead are among them, that there is a line of continuity between the living and the dead. Pagan rituals in the English-speaking world continue in the gothic convention of children dressing up as ghosts and spirits.

'Clay' has its own peculiar ritual taken from Irish folklore. Maria, who has already had her gift probably stolen from her on the tram across the city by a kind of male Lamia figure, is blindfolded and shepherded to a table on which are placed a prayer book and a saucer of water. One signifies the religious life, a nun say; the other the water of life, life that is or in this case marriage. But one of the neighbours' children has mischievously added a third saucer with a clump of earth fetched in from the garden. The joke is not lost on the reader, for I suspect most of us connect the earth with the title of the story. Clay signifies death, the earth, the destination of all the dead who are buried. Indeed, the lifeless body sometimes resembles its utterly inert, resistant quality. But clay is a material that also reminds us of life. The sculptor creates life from it, and in this sense Maria has the look of someone waiting to be moulded like a piece of sculpture. At the same time, she inadvertently anticipates or moulds her own destiny. So, both meanings, both fulfilment and death, inhere in this story and are kept alive until the end.

In the fifteenth-century ballad, 'The Unquiet Grave', the ghost of the dead man tells his former lover that 'if you kiss my cold clay lips, / Your days they won't be long'. The traditions of gothic and folklore and ritual here meet in a powerful embrace, but it is more, for 'cold clay lips' is such

Halloween ritual: Maurice Curtin's photograph of an Irish divination game, taken in 1935.
Source: The Department of Irish Folklore, University College, Dublin

an evocative phrase that we can almost touch the clay. 'Clay', too, is a story about the unquiet grave, only now the grave is part of life, constantly intruding on Maria's self-enclosed space. The option for Maria as she pauses in front of the objects on the table should be either the religious life or marriage, but, instead, she finds neither of these but death. She doesn't even get as far as choosing celibacy. Without looking, as if she were blind, she chooses her fate, or, with Providence in mind, she acts in accordance with her fate. In the face of interfering with ritual, those present are uncomfortable, and Maria is asked to choose again. The saucer of earth is removed and Maria touches the prayer book. Later, when asked to sing she embarks on 'I Dreamt That I Dwelt in Marble Halls', Michael Balfe's dreamy song from *The Bohemian Girl* (1843), but, instead of the second stanza about suitors seeking her hand in marriage, she repeats the first stanza. The narrator, either cruelly or in keeping with the way Maria might portray her own psyche to herself, then adds a sentence that an English teacher might feel obliged to correct for its awkwardness: 'But no one tried to show her her mistake' (*D* 106).

Rituals associated with death are Joyce's forte. He understood the role of ritual in family life and how it simultaneously brings together and divides families and the wider community. Shaping a narrative around a ritual allowed him scope to tackle his material accordingly, especially through the use of free indirect speech. Maria's self-enclosed mind is best captured when she thinks about her body: 'In spite of its years she found it a nice tidy little body' (*D* 101). You can almost hear her in front of a mirror saying to herself 'Yes, I do have a nice tidy little body'. No dark declivities there. The boy in 'The Sisters' is also distanced from events, but this time the mind perceiving the world, like Blake's Tyger, burns bright. Gabriel in 'The Dead' should be at the centre of family and community at the annual dinner of his aunts, but he keeps being reminded of his isolation and of his lack of incisiveness or appeal to women. In each case, like ritual itself, the narrative continues almost of its own accord, reminding us all the time of the claustrophobia of Irish life and of the nets or ideology at work restraining the individual. But as we read the stories, we are also impressed or surprised by the powerful sense of community on which Joyce is drawing, as if the nets also form part of a support system or community template or image of solidarity for the individual.

If you're asked as a writer to draw water from the well of Irish life, you'll find like Joyce that what you return with again and again is ritual. Yeats begins with the ritual of storytelling in *The Celtic Twilight* (1893), Synge with the ritual of weddings and wakes in his plays, Roddy Doyle with the ritual of abuse, John McGahern with the ritual connected with the seasons. Rituals give us a culture, and, in Ireland particularly, culture, whether urban or rural, gives us rituals. Thirty-five years ago in the west of Ireland, I remember visiting a funeral parlour in the county town of Ennis where one of our neighbours was lying in her open casket the night before her funeral in the parish church in Liscannor. After a short painful illness, which was the result of a blood clot if my memory serves me right, she had died in hospital. Although I never particularly took to her, she was a 'good woman' as the expression has it, and ran the local shop at the crossroads to which the family gave its name. The year was 1972. I was then in my mid-twenties, a few years older than Joyce was when he composed 'The Sisters'. My mind turned over all her acts of kindness, especially towards my favourite aunt and uncle when money was short. I recalled the times as a child I had entered her slate-roofed, two-storied solid block of a house, which was both her shop and her home. It always intrigued me, all that home-shop-pub hybrid-business-thing in rural Ireland, where standing at one end of the counter you could buy a pound of butter or a newspaper, move down the counter and order a pint of Guinness or a glass of orangeade, and then watch family members coming and going into the back room for a cup of tea or to stoke the fire – and all before noon if the mood took you. I never got to see into the private quarters of her house (my aunt did because she would do domestic chores for her), but scattered in all the rooms there seemed to be more than her fair share of hundredweight bags of meal and flour on untreated wooden floorboards. A hoarder, I must have half-thought at the time. Not a usurer, though, not a gombeen person, that scourge of the Irish country people in the nineteenth century whom William Carleton (1794–1869) excoriates in novels such as *Fardorougha the Miser* (1837) and *The Black Prophet, a Tale of Famine* (1846).

There was something mythical about her, as if she were like one of the poet John Montague's 'dolmens round my childhood' (Montague, 1982, 26). She was never young, always ancient, and an habitual inquirer in that country, nosy, off-putting way. She somehow gave the impression that she was a member of the shop-keeping class (which she was) and that I, in spite of only being home on holidays, was an associate member of the Irish poor awaiting full enrolment (which I was determined to prove otherwise). Her husband, Johnny, had returned home with money from the USA in the 1930s and he eventually took over the family store on the bend of a main road overlooking the ruins of Kilmacreehy Church and its crowded graveyard beside the restless Atlantic Ocean where my own grandmother is buried. The store itself, which was like the one in Joyce's story 'unassuming' but needed no sign to advertise itself, was well patronised, and throughout the morning a steady stream of local farmers on their way home from the creamery would pull into its low-walled, cream-coloured forecourt. The slow-speaking, deliberative Johnny was one of the first in that part of the country, along with teachers and priests, to own a car, but, well into the 1970s, he never mastered the art of driving at speeds above 20 mph. They had no children and, when he died a decade after her, their house fell temporarily into disrepair, passed daily by buses and tourist coaches on their way from the Cliffs of Moher back to Shannon Airport and the indifference of the wider world.

What impressed me, however, as I peered into the coffin of Nora O'Dea (née Cooney) on that spring evening was how young she looked, for, instead of ageing with rigor mortis, she had become ten years younger. All the lines of anxiety had drained away from her face and she looked radiant in her Marian blue, printed cotton dress. I felt closer to her in death than when she was alive, as if I was no longer challenged by her looking through me or at me. Such pious, indeed excessive, thoughts accompanied me on my way outside into the night sky, but they were as soon interrupted by a distant relative who had also been in the parlour with me. Tom Haugh (pronounced Ock or Hock), then in his sixties, had had a tough life struggling like everyone else in that part of the country to make a living on a smallholding as a subsistence farmer. In his later years he worked as a migrant labourer in a sugar-beet factory in the market town of Brigg in Lincolnshire, and every autumn he would wait for the 'call', put his 50cc Honda moped into store, and then disappear for three months 'across the water' to earn his keep for the rest of the year on the 'campaign'. 'Well', without prompting, the impertinent Tom exclaimed to me, looking up at the young clouds scudding across the March sky, 'she didn't put up much of a fight.' It was a perfectly formed, wicked thought and took me aback for a moment. I should have been on my guard, for you never knew with Tom what would come out of his mouth. And didn't my giggling grandmother have some delightful, rigor mortis stories from her time laying out bodies of neighbours in the parish? Tom, though, was the country version of Joyce's father, someone in complete command of the language, who delighted in the well-honed remark, but who used language provocatively, all the time waiting to see if he had stimulated a response in his listener. And, like John Joyce, he was rarely stuck for a word, transforming everyone from his auditor into his audience. So much, then, for my idea that death had made her beautiful or that she, like Fr Flynn, had died a beautiful death.

When Tom's brother, my uncle Jack, died some years later, he was laid out in an open casket in a funeral parlour in Ennistymon. Droves of people came to bid him farewell, some of the mourners reaching down into the casket to kiss him, for he was well liked throughout that part of the country and I never

Dan Harper's photograph of my uncle and aunt, Jack and Mary Haugh (née Kilmartin), sparring in the garden of their agricultural labourer's cottage, the ruins of Kilmacreehy Church and the Atlantic Ocean in the background, October 1985.
Source: Dan Harper

heard a bad word said about him. He was one of the last thatchers in the west, and had worked for years for the County Council repairing roads and watching the world go by. There were few who could match him at cards for he seemed to know what was in everyone's hand and, indeed, what card you would play next, but his real understanding of the future lay in his ability to forecast the weather simply by noticing changes in wind direction. When the wind veered round so that it was coming, say, from the direction of the Cliffs of Moher, you knew there was trouble brewing. Then he'd reach for a packet of Woodbines on the cluttered mantelpiece high above the turf fire.

Jack's brother, Tom, faced his own death alone. When I shook his hand the last time to say goodbye on returning to England some years later, I didn't know what he knew – that it would indeed be the last time, for he was dying of cancer but he told no-one. Indeed, his death took everyone by surprise. The look he gave me was as much as to say 'Good luck with your future'. Followed by another look: 'Remember me with kindness in the years to come'. I do. I wish I could remember all his other sayings. Some of those I do recall are unprintable, but that's another story. When I get to the other side, he'll make his way across some incense-filled room, ignoring the service that's going on, shake my hand, and want to know what kept me.

A free spirit. His other brother will then insist on me playing a game of 45 and thump the table in triumph with the ace of hearts which was secretly placed in the top pocket of his suit jacket when he was buried. 'Bate that!' From the devil's card playing to dutifully attending the funerals of others, there's no-one more conscientious than the Irish at adhering to rituals whether in life or death. Indeed, they live as if they are always on the way to becoming 'faithful departed'.

Joyce couldn't have chosen a more suggestive introduction to his work than a story concerned with the ritual of death. Clear the ground, establish a marker, draw a line, but also show your understanding of the culture and how it deals with the intercourse between this world and the next, how it lays to rest its ghosts. Begin with the past as a young author, with the dead hand of those who have gone before, and with 'Providence', move on to destiny, as is the case with Maria in 'Clay', and then conclude your collection of stories with one entitled simply 'The Dead'. Insist, that is, on the theme throughout. 'The Sisters', 'Clay', 'The Dead'. Throw in a suicide in 'A Painful Case' and a dead hero in 'Ivy Day in the Committee Room'. Hear the calling card, the order in which they appear in the collection: 1, 10, 11, 12, 15. What persistence! The sign of a covenant. Thereafter, in your major novel, *Ulysses*, devote a whole episode to 'Hades', the underworld and show how the Irish, like the ancient Greeks and Romans, also have a special way of burying their dead, full of humour, gossip and, at times, salacious talk. And, finally, wait for 15 years before announcing to the world in 1938 that the work you have been in progress on has the word 'wake' in its title.

Humour

Which brings us by a circuitous route to the humour of *Dubliners*. Like the sharp-witted Tom Haugh, Joyce reminds us that funerals are also about life, how to face death, and finishing sentences. Not for nothing is 'Hades' one of the funniest episodes in *Ulysses*. 'The Sisters', on the other hand, plays with language in a way that some readers might find disrespectful. Malapropism, where language comes off the rails as it were, is integrated into the story, as when we learn that instead of *The Freeman's Journal* Eliza calls the Dublin daily newspaper *The Freeman's General*. But other forms of humour suggest a mind at work elsewhere. Fr Flynn sits by the fire in his great coat 'almost stupefied' by the heat. It's the image of someone getting roasted, or perhaps we might say, with puns in mind, 'toasted', for every time the boy's aunt visited the house she brought him snuff that went by the brand name High Toast. Once started, especially in company, the humour

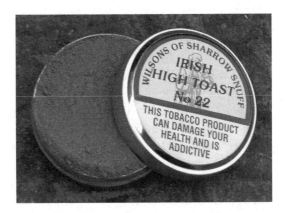

Irish High Toast, with a government warning prominently displayed. Photograph by David Pierce. I bought this tin of snuff from a tobacconists on the Headrow in Leeds in August 2006 and it cost me all of £1.26.

accepts no limits or propriety. Joyce makes much of the priest 'pushing huge pinches of snuff up each nostril alternately', and we could be forgiven for wishing to see some reference to chimney stacks to enforce the connection between the toast he was becoming and the High Toast he was consuming.

Irish High Toast (which may or may not be the same as High Toast) has a musty smell, sharp and tangy, reminiscent not so much of toast or indeed of Ireland as of a fine, specially sifted past long gone. In an intriguing reference in *A Portrait*, we learn that Stephen refuses to exchange his snuff box for a conker. According to his biographer, Herbert Gorman, when he was at Clongowes Wood College as a boy, Joyce had his own black, coffin-shaped snuff box, which had been given him by his godfather Philip McCann. He also had 'a larger one to fill it from' (Gorman, 1941, 280). Nineteenth-century public schools were often peculiar places, and Clongowes Wood was no exception. We learn from *A Portrait* that a Spanish boy was given permission to smoke cigars, and that a generation earlier boys had been allowed to drink beer and keep greyhounds. But Stephen as a six or seven-year-old taking snuff must have been an odd sight. Gorman could have elicited more from Joyce one suspects. The reference occurs in connection with a dream Joyce had about Molly throwing a snuff box at Bloom and then at Joyce himself, the snuff box being the one he had at school. The story would be easier for us to understand if it was an empty snuff box his godfather had given him, possibly for storing pen-nibs in.

What I do know is that my English grandfather, Alfred Pierce, who worked all his life in the gasworks in Brighton, was an intrepid snuff-taker, and, in his last years in the early 1960s, when he came to live with us, he would send out for threepenny worth of a brand I think was called either Wilkins or Wilkinsons, which was decanted carefully from a large jar into a conical bag and transported home. The snuff stained everything it came into contact with, including handkerchiefs, pockets and furniture, but smokeless tobacco was a great comfort to the addict taking it. Snuff sniff. Sniff snuff. That sound must have echoed throughout the home of the sisters on Great Britain Street before the priest did indeed snuff it. I took precautions with the tin above, taking it outside to photograph on a wormy flagstone I had brought back years ago from the quarries in Doolin, County Clare. Irish snuff on an Irish flagstone. The wind blew some of the remains down the garden.

When the boy in 'The Sisters' enters the room where the body is laid out, the narrator observes: 'There was a heavy odour in the room—the flowers'. The explanation is in one respect quite inappropriate since it resembles an afterthought: how it wasn't the corpse that gave the room a heavy odour (which the reader might naturally assume) but the flowers. However, the qualification takes us out of the room and into the boy's thoughts in composing the story. This is how a boy's mind might work, frequently juxtaposing, qualifying, explaining things that shouldn't be juxtaposed, qualified or explained. The qualification also has a humorous aspect to it, partly because it raises expectations only to deflate them, for, even though it might seem obvious, the last thing one expects in a sentence beginning with 'heavy odour' about a room with a corpse in it is 'flowers'.

Such dashes also belong to the unfinished sentences motif, and they afford a reminder of death or perhaps of the awkward space over which something is hastily draped. In Joyce their use is at times comic. In Chapter 2 we commented on Cotter's '—gone' in *The Irish Homestead* version. But Nannie too has her dash when the narrator explains what caused the silence to be broken: 'Nannie's mutterings—for she prays noisily'. Some old people do, and in a story about language and silence it is an appropriate kind of observation, complete with an em dash, an appropriate form of punctuation. The boy's aunt also has a dash, only in this case it reminds us that 'The Sisters' in the first version is the work of an apprentice: 'my aunt spoke a good deal, for she is a bit of a gossip—quite harmless'. Cotter's dash contains a gesture and is entirely fitting therefore, but the other two reflect an uncertain register as if Joyce was learning narrative economy and consistency. In the revised version, we read how 'I could not gather my thoughts because the old woman's mutterings distracted me'. This has a more consistent tone and is closer to the schoolroom exercise in writing that the story in fact occasionally betrays. The reference to his aunt being a gossip is dropped in the final version, as if Joyce realised that such an attitude lay outside the legitimate scope or confines of the story.

There is a deathly seriousness about the stories of *Dubliners*, so much so that humour is at a premium. For me, one of the funniest sentences in the collection, and again it is connected with death, occurs in 'Grace'. After his fall from grace when he collapses down the stairs in a city-centre pub, Mr Kernan spends time at home convalescing. There he is visited by his friends including Mr M'Coy. Joyce mischievously provides a thumbnail sketch of Mr M'Coy, including the various jobs he had held as if it were giving us a CV. Mr M'Coy 'had been a clerk in the Midland Railway, a canvasser for advertisements for the *Irish Times* and for *The Freeman's Journal*, a town traveller for a coal firm on commission, a private inquiry agent, a clerk in the office of the Sub-Sheriff, and he had recently become secretary to the City Coroner. His new office made him professionally interested in Mr. Kernan's case' (*D* 158). It's that last sentence I like, coming after what we might recognise as M'Coy's inflated listing of his achievements: a clerk, a canvasser for advertisements or 'space-hound' as they were known, a town traveller 'on commission', an inquiry agent (a private detective), a secretary. It's a long list of fairly menial jobs, and, in contrast with Mr Kernan, the commercial traveller of the old school and given to wearing silk hats, • M'Coy, compared with his friend, is the slightly anxious clerk, conscious of his inferior status, who has trouble holding down a job for any length of time. Interestingly, without realising it, Joyce in this little vignette of Mr M'Coy steals upon the territory he would later exploit in *Ulysses*, a novel that would afford a full-blooded, humorous portrait of his city through the eyes of a canvasser for advertisements.

Matching character and situation was essential for Joyce's kind of humour, and quite often it's for the reader to fill in or supplement what we're given on the page. Humour in that sense supplies another example of the unfinished sentence. Working in the city coroner's office, Mr M'Coy has a professional interest in the case of his friend. Joyce's use of indirect free speech at this point in the story reminds us of Dickens and his ability to nip pretension, or whatever it is, in the bud, for this is a story about a group of lower-middle-class, Pickwickian friends who never let go of their surnames. Mister Men. It's the story that most closely anticipates '*Mr* Bloom', the hero of *Ulysses*. Mr Power, who worked for the Royal Irish Constabulary, Mr Cunningham, an elder colleague, Mr M'Coy and Mr Kernan. A story about surnames, about 'mister' and 'mister-less', and how people are addressed by each other and by their clergy – remember that the text Father Purdon chooses for his sermon is for 'business men and professional men' (*D* 174). You couldn't imagine Mr Kernan without his title and surname. Equally, you couldn't imagine Mr M'Coy actually saying that his 'new office made him professionally interested in Mr. Kernan's case'. Or perhaps you could. So, we might hear him saying something like this: 'Sorry, to see you like this, Mr Kernan. I do hope you pull through. I have a professional interest in your case.' This sounds stilted and not very appropriate to address to someone convalescing, but then M'Coy does appear stilted as a person, and *Dubliners* is full of inappropriate remarks. I get the impression that the sentence Joyce uses sounds like something Mr M'Coy might have half-thought to himself, giving him a hook on his friend, but at the same time allowing him a role, a crossover from the world of work to his social life. Analysing the situation makes it sound less funny than it is, however, and constitutes yet another aspect of what we might term Joyce's defiant style. As I say, humour is at a premium in these stories, and while *Dubliners* is not the 'funferall' on offer in *Finnegans Wake*, for all that, there are funny moments.

CHAPTER 4

Saying goodbye in 'Eveline'

Emigration

'Eveline' is an emigration story with a difference. It opens: 'She sat at the window watching the evening invade the avenue'. And it closes: 'Her eyes gave him no sign of love or farewell or recognition'. It begins therefore on a depressing note and it ends for some readers on an equally depressing note. The evening *invades* the avenue and at the end the invasion is complete. Eveline spends her time dusting, but dust continues to hang in the dusky air. Dusty and dusky, letters that separate and unite in a single embrace, dance their way through this story. 'Eveline' ends where it began with Eveline presumably returning home to sit at the window and watch again the evening invade her avenue. Some readers and critics no doubt conclude that 'Eveline' offers yet another example of the city's paralysis. In *The Cambridge Introduction to James Joyce* (2006), Ed Bulson insists:

> Everyone in *Dubliners* seems to be caught up in an endless web of despair. Even when they want to escape, Joyce's Dubliners are unable to. The young woman in 'Eveline' is a perfect example. Instead of choosing a new life in Buenos Aires (where many have suspected her beau will turn her into a prostitute) she stays put in Dublin.
>
> (Bulson, 2006, 33)

That she stays put tells in her favour I would have thought, especially if Frank was out to deceive her or turn her into a prostitute. The view Bulson espouses, however, has been afforded quite an airing in recent years. Jeri Johnson, for example, in her edition of *Dubliners* (2000), cites Jonathon Green's claim in *The Cassell Dictionary of Slang* (1998) that 'to go to Buenos Aires' in the nineteenth century meant 'to start working as a prostitute'. This, to my mind, is to reduce the story to a private joke on Joyce's part. If it was a well-known saying in Dublin at the time, then the joke would have been at the expense of whom? The Irish farming community where the story first appeared? If the saying wasn't well-known, then the joke must be on later readers unfamiliar with its hidden meaning, unfamiliar that is until *The Cassell Dictionary of Slang* was published nearly a century later. Even if it were a well-known saying at the time, I would still resist making too much of it. After all, in one sense there's nothing metaphoric about going to Buenos Aires, and the story turns on Eveline not boarding the ship.

What one looks for in reading is an interpretation that has the most, not the least, resonance – an interpretation that takes off rather than tracks back. Floating over Joyce's stories is what he called a 'special odour of corruption' (*Letters II*, 123), but, as I try and argue throughout these chapters on *Dubliners*, the stories are 'about' more than corruption or paralysis or sexual disease. Joyce's discourse is invariably polysemic, and, even when we detect what we think is a source, however wicked, it's worth remembering all the other so-called or potential sources and, more importantly, how such sources function in the story as a whole. What intrigues me perhaps most about Joyce is that his mind appears to be constantly elsewhere. One of the implications of this is that, as I suggest elsewhere in relation to Joyce and context: 'Try and move from context to text, from text to context, and you will never stop playing the game' (Pierce, 2006, 148).

'Eveline', then, is an emigration story with a difference. Eveline could alter her entire circumstances – which might include a father with sexual designs on her – but she decides against it. Indeed, there's something to be said for seeing this as a story about the fate of a woman caught between two men. But the passivity Eveline adopts in the face of her fate is very special, so special that we never hear one of her own sentences or indeed catch a flavour of her spoken voice. Until its closing moments, the plot is nicely balanced and could be resolved either way. Her passage booked, Eveline arrives at the quayside still presumably intent on emigrating with Frank. It's a moment of choice. Eveline, who is 'over nineteen', has innocence and family duties on one side; on the other side, she has escape – 'Escape!' – from family care and life, with a relatively unknown stranger who has seen the world.

I am reminded of a thoughtful if somewhat conventional Canadian-Irish immigration novel by Edward MacCourt called *Home is the Stranger* (1950). The story centres on an Irish couple from County Antrim and their coming to terms with the empty spaces of the Canadian midwest. In this story, unlike in Joyce's, landscape plays a significant role as Jim and Norah bid farewell to the hills of home for prairie life where their outlook will be unencumbered by trees and hills; 'space-crazy', as Norah puts it when imagining what such a life might mean for those driven west. By way of contrast, in opting not to follow the emigrant's well-travelled path, Eveline reminds us of the call of home, that for some people home is the known and

Front cover of the catalogue of the James
Joyce Exhibition at La Hune Gallery in Paris in
1949. The signpost points in one direction
to Drumcondra, where Joyce was living
in 1902–4, and in the other direction to
the North Wall, where Joyce and Nora
embarked for the continent in October
1904. Signposts tell us nothing about those
reading them. Indeed, it can be argued that
it is narratives not signposts that make most
sense of the world. The day Joyce departed
he was accompanied to the North Wall by
his father, but John Joyce didn't know
his son had a travelling companion. At
the North Wall, Eveline bids no sign of
recognition to her would-be partner Frank.
Actually, this particular signpost carries
within it a story of exile, and it was fitting
that such an image should adorn the front

cover of an exhibition catalogue in Paris to mark Joyce's recuperation in Europe after the
Second World War. Where, we might well ask, is an exile's home? Does it belong to the
past or the future or is it always attached to the signpost pointing in both directions? In
one sense, there was no direction home for either Eveline or Joyce.

never the stranger, moored for ever to the past and never to the future, and
that while she can feel 'All the seas of the world tumble[] about her heart'
she is not emboldened. It begins with Eveline at the window watching the
evening invade the avenue, but it ends with some kind of resolution that
Frank is not going to invade her life and make her a stranger.

To my mind, there is an exquisite poignancy about 'Eveline' which no
amount of cheap air travel or talk of pimping can destroy. Emigration from
Ireland until the 1960s was a profoundly dislocating experience both for
the individual and for the family. Forget forever the possibility of return. In
the nineteenth century, if you emigrated to Australia, letters alone might
take three months to arrive, and the chances of you ever returning home
were remote. *Oceans of Consolation: Personal Accounts of Irish Migration
to Australia* (1994), edited by David Fitzpatrick, is the title of an anthology
of letters from that period, the title appearing in one of the letters cited.
'Eveline', which speaks of all the seas of the world tumbling about her
heart, is overshadowed by a passage to oblivion or, rather, it has the capacity to become a story in which the only consolation is through letter writing
and the family left behind periodically noticing a yellowing photograph on
the mantelpiece. The narrative builds to a climax with extraordinary economy and internal power. While Eveline – 'Evvy!' – grips the iron railings on
the quayside and prays to God for guidance, Frank is beyond the barrier

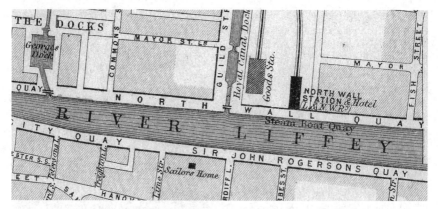

The North Wall on Bartholomew's 1900 map, with the train terminal marked and room for a steam boat beside the quay. As she got off the train and stood among the swaying crowd in the station, through the shed doors Eveline would have caught sight of the steam ship. On the opposite side of the Liffey there is a sailors' home, as well as Sir John Rogerson's Quay, along which Bloom walks at the beginning of the 'Lotus-eaters' episode of *Ulysses*. In Joyce's world, almost everything could have happened. What we're not told is if Eveline's father accompanied her, or where Eveline caught the train that brought her to the North Wall. If, as I suggested in Chapter 2, Joyce had St Peter's Terrace, Cabra in some part of his mind when he composed the story, then Eveline might have boarded the train at Glasnevin Station.

and shouted at (presumably by harbour officials or other passengers) to go on. Perhaps it's because today's emigrants can return home on a whim across thousands of miles for holidays or indeed for weekends that the story allows us an opportunity to reconsider what's involved or what's been lost in balancing such wrenching lifestyle choices. After all, nostalgia isn't always about the past but can be the articulation of continuing concerns. 'Eveline', a daughter's story, gives us enough to set our minds working.

MacCourt's *Home is the Stranger* is more straightforward in this respect, a canvas in which we might plot almost beforehand the various tension points and unfolding motifs. Throughout the novel, we are presented with the contrast between the new life and 'the old country'. There are no ghosts in the new country, only ghosts from the past to trouble you. On the other hand, because you are on your own, no room exists for compromise. Equally, in contrast with the intimacy of home in Ireland, living on the prairies is a constant reminder that no man is an island. MacCourt is alert to the human cost and to the inside story of the first settlers and their take on things. Place names in the new country often exhibit an unimaginative quality about them. On the other hand, the imagination itself is given too much rein and becomes a prey to obsessions and groundless fears. 'Eveline' works differently. Joyce doesn't need the whole canvas to give us a powerful insight into the emigrant's predicament and how the mind finds itself moving between past and future, future and present, a reality of dust and dreams of something else, for 'Eveline' is a story that is also about 'reviewing' 'familiar objects':

> Home! She looked round the room, reviewing all its familiar objects which she had dusted once a week for so many years, wondering where on earth all the dust came from. Perhaps she would never see again those familiar objects from which she had never dreamed of being divided. (D 37)

Some time in the 1950s I attended an 'American Wake' in the house now owned by the famous uillean piper Davy Spillane. The memories have stayed with me in part because even as a child I sensed the finality of the young man's departure for the USA and how he, like Eveline in the story, might never ever return. All my nascent sympathies were aroused and on edge as the drama unfolded. The house in Knockeven was a stone's throw from the Cliffs of Moher and the limestone slate quarries mentioned in the last chapter. It enjoyed an open aspect and looked south over the picturesque Liscannor Bay, with the sandy golf links at Lahinch to the left and O'Brien's Tower to the right, and then in the distance the moody Mount Callan where in pre-Christian times bonfires used to be lit in summer to celebrate the ancient feast of Lughnasa. The house itself was, as Spillane rightly entitles one of his albums, a place among the stones. I went up that evening through the boggy, reed-strewn, treeless fields from my grandmother's house in Caherbarna with a neighbour Denis Guerin (who later emigrated to New York where he became a 'liftman' or security guard in an apartment block). The 'wake' was for Tommy MacNamara's nephew, whose name I've temporarily forgotten, but he would have been a Carroll (another of his aunts celebrated her 104th birthday in 2006). The following day he was emigrating to the USA, hence the term 'American Wake'.

I must have been about eight or nine at the time. Perhaps younger, for I see in a letter dated 20 December 1955 to my mother from her brother John Kilmartin, who lived with my grandmother, that 'T. Mac always asks for David'. Into the night, there was the murmur of voices in my ears as well as music and singing with periodic breaks for tea and sandwiches in the 'room'. The 'room' I should add is how, traditionally, the bedroom was described adjacent to the main kitchen/living room where the singing and dancing took place, a room that was often situated on the western side of the house, closer that is to the setting sun and the dying of the light. The mood I recall was both strained and strange. It wasn't a night for jollification, just the going-through-the-motion of some kind of ritual. No shouts of 'round the house and mind the dresser' to accompany their movements, but couples did take care in that small kitchen to click their heels and dance their way through the Clare half-set of reels, jigs and hornpipes.

As hosts, Tommy and his wife Bridget made little fuss of me that night, for I could see they were preoccupied with their departing guest, with someone that is who was bidding farewell to his family perhaps for ever. I couldn't quite dislodge that thought from my mind, and yet, until the final farewell, the family and the young man had somehow to keep themselves emotionally in check, together for one last time together. Tommy himself, I should add, was the first adult I had ever met who couldn't read, and I remember the rather awkward moment – it must have been about that time – when I showed him something from the newspaper. 'You'll have to read that for me, son,' he said. 'I'm afraid I never mastered the art of reading.' But people don't need to be literate to understand the language of loneliness or feel the oceans of consolation.

As the first three stories of *Dubliners* remind us, all these things happen to a child, a kind of over-layering of impressions, which then become with the passage of time part of a single event or memory. Only with writing does a structure or scaffolding really unfold or reveal itself, however. The songs must have included one or two from the repertoire for that part of the country at that time – emigration songs such as 'The Cliffs of Doneen', 'Lovely Old Miltown', 'Lovely Derry on the Banks of the Foyle', sung with perfect pitch and characteristic restraint by Mary Haugh (née Kelly), 'The Shores of America', or the gothic ballad about death by drowning, 'The Waves of the Silvery Tide', sung by the bright-eyed Dan Considine. Or perhaps this was where I first heard 'Erin's Lovely Lee', the nineteenth-century ballad about the Fenians driven out of Ireland and about their final journey to America, their heads filled with the thought that one day they might see their country free, the harp without the crown that is. How majestically the raven-haired Michael Malone, clutching his hands and looking down at the flagstones at his feet, would sing that century-old song of defiance, his sinewy tenor voice rising into the smoke-filled thatch above our heads and out into the night air.

> *Farewell, slán, adieu. Farewell, slán, adieu. Farewell, slán, adieu.*
> *God speed.*
> *Sailing, sailing, sailing.*
> *Land of my youth, homes that I loved so well, mountains grand.*
> *My own native land.*
> *The big ship is sailing, lovely Nancy is wailing.* ('Lovely Nancy')
> *No finer harbour anywhere to be found.* ('The Maid of Coolmore')

O I know a sweet spot, 'tis a place of great fame. ('Lovely Derry on the Banks of the Foyle')
You'll see the high rocky mountains to the west coast of Clare. ('The Cliffs of Doneen')
To seek a home o'er the dark raging foam. ('Shores of America')
Deep in the heart of London town or over on Broadway. ('Boys of Barr na Sráide')
I'll forsake friends and relations and quit this Irish nation. ('Craigie Hill')
Don't be afraid of the storm or the sea. ('Green Fields of America')
And as I leave my heart did grieve for lovely old Miltown. ('Lovely Old Miltown')
For ever true it flies to you, my own dear Galway Bay. ('Galway Bay')
Aroon, aroon, O come back soon
To the one who will always love you. ('A Stór Mo Chroí')
Farewell, slán, adieu. Farewell, slán, adieu. Farewell, slán, adieu.

Sailing/wailing, home/foam, relations/nation, leave/grieve, true/you, aroon/soon – those wrenching internal rhymes the Irish emigrants took with them to the ends of the earth. From the River Foyle in the north of Ireland to the River Lee in the south, seemingly not one mountain or mossy river bank, not one blade of grass or watery meadow in Ireland, had escaped the grieving songwriter's notice. The whole world had been fashioned into rhyme, scored with emotion; a world, too, evoked in a process of naming, at once local and therefore, by extension, national. An imagined and a real community called up and gathered again in each departure and every passing moment. How we all got through that evening I don't recall, but we did and, what's more, everyone bade goodbye and took their formal leave outside the house on the road that led in one direction to the turf-bogs of Ireland and in the other to the 700-feet drop into the Atlantic and the shores of America. Away.

Among those people among the stones there was nothing like endurance, testing limits, and ringing the last emotional drop. Bracing themselves, they embraced the departing guest. Head bowed, the sprinkle of holy water nearby inside the door, they would say goodbye a hundred times if they could. By rights, in addition to *cead mile failte*, a hundred thousand welcomes, there should an Irish expression meaning a hundred thousand goodbyes, *cead mile slán*. That too would be appropriate. Today's New Irish, as the new immigrants are sometimes called in the USA, are a different breed, flying in and out of Dublin Airport with neatly compact, carry-on hand-luggage and

"Sweet Innisfallen, fare thee well." p. 3.

Sweet Inisfallen fare thee well. This sketch by Marianne Nicholson graced the title page of the ninth edition of Tom Moore's *Irish Melodies*, published in 1834. Inishfallen is an island in the Lake of Killarney, and it seems to be this scene the sketch artist has in mind, for what we observe are some early tourists or day-trippers leaving the island with umbrellas up. Moore's song, however, concerns the fate of the Irish and how 'No more along thy shores to come, / But, on the world's dim ocean tost, / Dream of thee sometimes, as a home / Of sunshine he had seen and lost!' Why anyone would want to leave such an idyllic setting as depicted in the sketch never seems to have crossed the mind of the publisher. In the next decade, however, the Hungry Forties that is, emigration began in earnest and destroyed in the process such romantic scenes, as emigrants lined the quaysides of ports and harbours all over Ireland to escape the Famine. In the modern period, lyricism returned again, but this time under the guise of quotation. When Sean O'Casey in his autobiography writes about the period he took the emigrant ship to England, he calls his volume *Inishfallen Fare Thee Well* (1949). It would be interesting to know how many emigrants left Ireland with this beautiful phrase on their lips. Sweet Inisfallen fare thee well.

portable lifestyles. Instead of the long goodbye, all you hear is 'Catch you soon'. But the country people in the 1950s were at the end of something, people who held a house dance to celebrate someone's passing and wish him or her God speed for the last time. Possibly for ever.

For it was a death in its own way, an RIP for a way of life. *Away* (1995) is what the Canadian writer Jane Urquhart calls her Irish immigration novel, while for the New York Irish-Jewish novelist Mary Gordon the phrase she alights on is *The Other Side* (1989). 'Out there' is how my uncle John Kilmartin in the letter quoted above refers to the place where those who emigrated now lived. One of the local priests had spent some time in America on holiday, and John continues: 'Travelled Boston Chicago New York and met nearly everyone out there from the parish'. 'Out there.' The parish tied them all together like stooks of corn, and it was natural for the priest to spend his holidays visiting former parishioners. In all kinds of ways, that world has gone for ever. Away.

England was different, for you could return more easily, even for Christmas. Christmas 1955 was quiet: 'There are not many at home yet but this week is the week if they are coming'. John, who never married until late in life and almost never travelled outside the parish, was particularly anxious because he was hoping one of his sweethearts would return, especially after they'd had such fun the previous summer under the August moon: 'no cloud on the horizon and a lover's moon sailing slowly across the sky'. John preferred reading to farm work, and, although he didn't know Synge's work, he possessed a lyricism that could have come out of one of his plays. The last time I visited Caherbarna, in the 1990s, he was in the cow cabin milking, anxious to greet me with a clean pair of hands. As if that mattered. He was a slow riser, but his mother never let up, and every morning her words would echo round the house as she bellowed at him in the coffin-shaped settle bed: 'John, John. Wake up. You'll be late for the creamery.' He was, though, a good teacher, the son who never emigrated, unconscious that, a half century ago, he was laying the cross-channel foundations for my lifelong interest in Irish music and culture. On one occasion he was indeed late for the creamery and returned home with no payment and with three large cans still full of warm unpasteurised milk, and then he had to face a different kind of music to the one he played with verve and grace on his unpretentious instrument of choice, the lowly tinwhistle.

Emigration, as I say, found its way into every aspect of the culture, and no statistics can ever do it justice. 'Whatever he'll do. Stay probably', is how John refers to another neighbour who wasn't 'pulling too good at home', that is not getting on too well with his family. Weighing up the balance, two lifestyles, family commitments and emotional attachments. Mother–son, father–daughter relations. 'Not pulling too good at home' is a phrase that wouldn't be out of place somewhere in Eveline's thoughts, and it cautions us against being too sentimental about emigration. Equally, even if at the time he didn't realise it, there is something very Irish about Joyce immediately following 'The Sisters' with an emigration story. Imagine if Nora hadn't become his travelling companion, how would I then be reading the story I wonder.

When the 'wake' was over, I was obliged to wait for some time outside the house for Denis Guerin to whisper a few words to some girl who had taken his fancy. The sterile blue moonlight, I remember, was transforming the familiar world into a landscape of shapes and shadows, but I delicately held back from overhearing what he had to say for himself. All evening I had felt an outsider. Over my shoulder a two-pronged hay-fork, which I had been asked to bring home, dangled, and somehow it slipped from my grasp, and, on its clumsy way down to the ground, it pierced the soft skin surrounding my ankle. I thought nothing of it at the time and we traipsed home in silence across the patchwork of fields and tumbled gaps, which, by night, I tried to convince myself, were nothing more than the haunt of foxes and a gathering place of restless ghosts. My companion provided little protection from my fears, being in a world of his own.

Joyce, it transpires, was petrified of walking along country roads at night, but there's nothing like getting off the beaten track in the west of Ireland to confront the Irish dark. In retrospect, the word that comes to me across the years is phthisis, but the fear itself was essentially nameless or indeterminate. It was like a smell, the breath in the nostrils and the lungs mixed with something that felt crushed or in the process of yielding. Phthisis, a good word to spell and to pronounce and to be reminded of but not to have, for tuberculosis was the killer disease in that part of the country for generations. Phthisis, so many Greek letters to clog up the English-speaking mouth. Pulmonary. Panting. Breathless. Phth. Every second, every minute on that journey home I was at the mercy of bog holes, cow pats and shifting, alarming shadows from the constantly moving gorse bushes and clouds overhead. We need people to teach us how to avoid obstacles, but we need no one to teach us panic. In the early morning, I awoke in some pain and emerged from the back bedroom next to the cow cabin, a room where you could hear the tied animals breathing contentedly through the dividing wall, to discover my own family still up and ready to comfort me with that universal panacea from the period – a hug, a bowl of hot water, and the threat of a bread poultice to draw the sting.

When I read 'Eveline', the mixed strains of all these memories and associations accompany me. When Joyce himself was writing this story in the late summer 1904, emigration with Nora was in his mind, and hovering somewhere over this story to my mind is this moment. It's Joyce inventing a story in which he can play with a putative identity and mix together truth and fiction, what might or what might not transpire. It's in that sense a 'what if' story. Elsewhere, as in 'The Dead', you can hear him asking: 'What if I had stayed in Dublin? What if I married a woman who had a past or a past lover? Would I have been like Gabriel?' Here in 'Eveline' there is a mixture of concerns, including how he as Frank might appear to Nora as Eveline. Perhaps it's for this reason above all that I resist the temptation to view this as a story about a pimp. That seems too mean by far, though it has to be admitted that Joyce was concerned about not enslaving Nora, which is how he viewed marriage.

I used the word 'emigration' above but this isn't quite the right word, for Joyce never anticipated in 1904 that his departure would be effectively for ever. At that time, as he had done in December 1902 after graduating, he was simply departing for the continent in search of temporary work for a few years. Indeed, until 1912, Joyce always entertained the idea that he would return home. But, like most of his fellow countrymen and women, Joyce, although he never attended an American Wake as far as I know, understood the emotional cost of emigrating, and part of the story's poignancy stems from the pressure of a felt life among the huge numbers of emigrants departing from the North Wall. We perhaps shouldn't forget that of the ten Joyce children, five were to emigrate: Joyce himself, Stanislaus, Charlie, 'Poppie' and Eileen. And in case you were to think that's excessive or a higher than average proportion for an individual family, recall that there are now 70 million people around the world who claim Irish decent. Closer to home, my Irish grandmother bore ten children, five of whom died in infancy, and three of whom in the 1930s, a decade or so after Irish independence, emigrated to England for work, never to return. Make of that what you will, but for me it's a painful but unexceptional story – like Joyce's. The thing that must have offset the sadness of departure for Joyce

Caherbarna, October 1985, the road home. Photograph by Dan Harper. The new Kilmartin house, with cow cabin attached, is just beyond Pat Dunleavy's thatched house in the foreground. Denis Guerin lived behind the Kilmartin house, near the ruins of a house that once belonged to Pat 'Cormac' Dunleavy. To the right can be seen a stack of turf and beyond that ricks of hay, ready for the slow days and long nights of winter. The tarred road was relatively new when this photograph was taken.
Source: Dan Harper

The itch to live not in London, Buenos Aires, Melbourne or Boston but in continental Europe. This was the route Joyce took for the continent in 1902 and then again in 1904. The steam train from London Victoria to Newhaven would have been like this one, and then there would have been a 3¼-hour crossing by the new 21-knot steamers from Newhaven to Dieppe. 'Real adventures,' as the narrator of 'An Encounter' also recognised, 'must be sought abroad' (D 21). It would be interesting to know what the young couple spoke about on that first journey into exile and what kinds of signs they gave off to each other. On arriving in Paris, Joyce had arranged to meet Charles Curran and a former benefactor Jacques Rivière, but he was anxious for them not to see his travelling companion, so, before resuming their journey to Switzerland, he left Nora in a public park for a few hours tending a blister from tight-fitting shoes. Almost straight away, space was piling up behind them. When John Joyce was later told about Nora Barnacle, he hid his disappointment behind a humorous quip: 'Well, with a name like that she'll never leave him'.

was the thought of intimacy with a woman without the anxiety of being seen fondling in some public space down by the River Dodder or playing with seedcake high up on the Hill of Howth among the rhododendrons, as Bloom and Molly do or did in *Ulysses*.

As Bulson (2006) serves also to remind us, most critics when discussing the stories of *Dubliners* have recourse at some point to the theme of paralysis. Joyce himself inadvertently prompted this line of interpretation when, in a letter to the English publisher Grant Richards in May 1906, he declared: 'My intention was to write a chapter of the moral history of my country and I chose Dublin for the scene because that city seemed to me the centre of paralysis' (*Letters II*, 134). When you're defending a project to a potential publisher and answering particular charges raised by a printer about the use of a word like 'bloody' or a phrase such as 'a man with two establishments', you tend to overdo things. But, as we can discern with the two stories we've been discussing so far, 'The Sisters' and 'Eveline', paralysis isn't the word that necessarily or automatically springs to mind. Not everything points to paralysis. There are other things going on in the narrative and inside the characters. Indeed, both the boy and Eveline represent something other than paralysis. The boy sees truculence on the face of the dead priest, and Eveline, though she shows Frank no sign of recognition, registers one of the most lyrical moments in *Dubliners* when 'all the seas of the world tumbled about her heart'.

Sometimes when a person is unable to move it is for good reasons. Eveline is tempted to leave Ireland, but she gets hopelessly confused and freezes. Counsellors no doubt have a term for this. At the last minute something holds her back, a kind of emotional seizure. Perhaps it was something in Frank that cautioned her to think again. Perhaps she caught a glimpse of something else, that the exotic would soon be invaded by the familiar. Perhaps with 'his peaked cap pushed back on his head', he as Adam to her Eve was the tempter, and he as Frank, with his hair 'tumbled forward over a face of bronze', was less than frank with her. Perhaps she realised just how far away Buenos Aires is from Dublin (around 7,000 miles and some three weeks or more by sea). Perhaps she foresaw her own fate as an exile and that she too would become like the yellowing photograph of the priest in Melbourne and referred to by the family in similarly automatic, unemotional, distant terms: 'She's in Buenos Aires now'.

In Joyce's story, Frank told Eveline 'stories of the terrible Patagonians', but in 1904 Argentina was more sophisticated and settled than that. Indeed, within a few years of Joyce composing this story, Argentina had produced a young writer who was to become the master of spell-binding and lyrical prose and who was one of the first to absorb the lessons of Joyce and promote him in Latin America. In his essay 'El "Ulises" de Joyce', published in Buenos Aires in 1925, Jorge-Luis Borges (1899–1986) announced to the world that he was the first 'aventurero hispánico que has arribado al libro de Joyce', the first Spanish adventurer to come across Joyce's book and bring it into port. According to Borges, 'Joyce es audaz como una proa y universal como la rosa de los vientos' (Borges, 1925, 25). That is, Joyce,

Recuerdo de la Rep. Argentina

Grupo de Gauchos

Recuerdo de la Rep. Argentina Un Payador

The Buenos Aires reference can be given a different gloss: Argentinian *gauchos*, together with an Argentinian *payador* (a wandering minstrel associated with the *gauchos* who sang *payadas*). Two postcards sent in June and September 1905 from Buenos Aires to the same address in France. Both postcards provide *recuerdos* (memories) for the person sending the postcards and for the person receiving them. The subject matter reminds us that it's an exchange designed not only to be enjoyed but also to strengthen solidarity among the civilised against the exotic world of the travelling cowboys of the South American plains.

like a modern Odysseus, is audacious as a prow cutting through the waves, and universal as the compass rose – both a driving force and a navigator. Interestingly, *Proa* was the name of the Argentinian journal founded by Borges in 1922, so Joyce is accorded a particular honour in the phrase 'como una proa'. Cultural difference lies elsewhere, for Joyce and Borges were at the cutting edge of a movement that embraced both Europe and Latin America. As Beatriz Vegh has recently suggested, both were tolerant, humorous, cosmopolitan, semi-colonial Modernists and Postmodernists (Vegh, 2002, 92–3).

The language of 'Eveline'

The language of 'Eveline' is intense and impossible to ignore. Indeed, its full effect comes about largely because it is focalised through the consciousness of Eveline. I've commented on the seas tumbling about her heart, but there is another sentence that draws attention to itself because of its poetry and lyricism. 'Through the wide doors of the sheds she caught a glimpse of the black mass of the boat, lying in beside the quay wall, with illumined portholes.' Perhaps she felt something devilish in Frank – that he resembled a celebrant in a black Mass in which she was not about to participate. Perhaps she imagined not herself lying in of a morning beside Frank but the ship lying on its side foundering in the ocean. Equally, the wide doors, the sheds, the glimpse, the boat beside the wall, the illumined portholes – did she imagine she was caught up in a ghost story like the ones her father would tell her? More worryingly, from today's perspective, such a sentence can provoke all kinds of other things which are independent of the story, as if the reader is responding to the way Joyce's mind is also frequently at work elsewhere. I am reminded of the stories of the survivors of the death camps told in Claude Lanzmann's extraordinary film *Shoah* (1985), and how some of the victims must have momentarily glimpsed their fate on arriving at the station in Auschwitz or Treblinka; how, when the wagon doors were flung open wide, immediately they were hurried along by the guards toward the sheds with most not realising that the illumined portholes of death were directly ahead of them. Was it worse to know or worse not to know your fate at that moment?

'Illumined portholes' is a phrase that plays on the mind. An illumined porthole is strikingly evocative and yet allusive and symbolic, both itself and suggestive of something else. The illumined portholes that Eveline glimpses mean that the night is drawing in, that the ship will be sailing into the dark. 'Illumined' also carries its own gothic charge, and what she glimpses is not therefore a passenger ship but a ship of death, more foreboding than inviting. There's a terrible image in Gerard Manley Hopkins's poem 'The Loss of the Eurydice', his lament for a frigate which in 1878 foundered in shallow waters off the Isle of Wight with the loss of over 360 souls. The phrase Hopkins uses to convey this is 'Death teeming in by her portholes'. Portholes provide light for those on board, but when a ship is listing they help it on its downward path, the pitiless water of death 'teeming in' as Hopkins puts it.

My mind races on. I think of human history as a whole. Was this Eve's fate, the 'Eve line' to play on Eveline's name, on exiting Eden? 'Her hands clutched the iron in frenzy. Amid the seas she sent a cry of anguish.' Joyce allows us space to imagine things for ourselves, and not all of those associations will be shared by others. Joyce himself knew nothing about the camps until his Jewish friends were seized by the Gestapo in Paris in 1940, but he knew enough about the cry of the heart and how this gets expressed or otherwise in our culture. In this light, although it is expressed in terms of non-expression, in terms, that is, of an emotion that can't get into language or formulate itself as a sentence, Eveline's defiance of Frank seems a not wholly inappropriate response.

There is merit in speculating how Eveline, trudging home that evening from the North Wall, would have rationalised to herself all that had happened. Of course, that would issue in a different story, and the implications of that are worth pondering, especially in the light of the unfinished sentences mentioned above. Arguably the strangest sentence in 'Eveline' is uttered by her mother on her death-bed: 'Derevaun Seraun! Derevaun Seraun!' Whatever else it is, the phrase looks unfinished, as if the woman was trying to make a last wish or plea but only managed the first part, which she repeats. Jacques Aubert, in a note in his French translation, is quite definite as to what he hears: 'Très probablement un dicton (déformé) du dialecte de la region de Galway, "deireadh amhá in saráin", dont le sens est à peu près "La fin n'est que vers!"' (Joyce/Aubert, 1974, 69). That is, the phrase is very probably a saying (corrupted or deformed) of the dialect of the Galway area, meaning something like 'The end is only towards (something else)'. This is nothing but speculation on the editor's part. When Joyce wrote the story he'd only just met Nora, and Galway speech or dialect was only just entering his consciousness. But I like the suggestion that the translated sentence ends on the word 'vers', towards. Unfinished in other words. Like the mother's dying words, the story is a journey towards. The editors of the standard edition of *Dubliners* dating from 1969 are more tentative: '[A]lthough it appears to be Gaelic, this mysterious explanation has never been satisfactorily explained. Joyce may have intended it as delirious gibberish' (*D* 472). In the most recent edition published by W.W. Norton in 2006, we read: 'Meaning unknown. Speculations include suggestions may be corrupt Gaelic for "the end of pleasure is pain" or "the end of song is madness"' (Joyce/Norris, 2006, 31). Would it help, I wonder, if we could translate in this way? If we knew that she says 'the end of pleasure is pain'? Is that why Eveline 'stood up in a sudden impulse of terror', hearing her 'mother's voice saying constantly with foolish insistence' these words? I doubt it. Surely that would in an instant transform the story into melodrama and pure sentimentality? Surrounded by the Cyrillic alphabet, the Bulgarian translation leaves the phrase sensibly untouched.

Even if she were to understand it as the fate of women in the modern world, you just can't imagine Eveline telling her friends that what made her consider leaving home was listening to her mother repeatedly claiming 'the end of pleasure is pain'. You could imagine her sounding off about her parents: 'I've had enough of all her raving and all his nonsense'. Joyce knew from the final months attending his own mother's last illness that there is something awful about the mind going: 'She calls the doctor sir Peter Teazle and picks buttercups off the quilt' (*U* 1:211–2). 'Derevaun Seraun! Derevaun Seraun!' With their rhythmic pattern and incorporation of Gaelic vowels and diphthongs, the phrases afford a certain comfort for the speaker, as if some memory (or, more lyrically, some memory of a lost language) was being accessed or activated. In 'The Sisters' the boy notices the 'mutterings' of his aunts; in this story it is another form of comfort born of repetition. For the family, the mother's 'gibberish' is the reverse. No memory is activated except the memory of the person with her full faculties. Instead, the family confronts the physical presence of their mother but, as Cotter might say, with 'the upper storey' gone.

The stories of *Dubliners* are rightly unfinished or rightly contain unfinished things in them. Relish those defiant and defining moments and take care with how you regard annotations, no matter how much status they may have by way of being included in an 'authoritative' edition. It's for the reader to exercise judgement in these matters. Let me conclude with a final example. Consider the way the following sentence is glossed in the 2006 edition: '–He is in Melbourne now.' 'Melbourne, Australia was a common destination for Irish emigrants in the nineteenth century' (Joyce/Norris, 2006, 28). Does such a note add anything to our understanding of 'Eveline'? You might as well gloss the reference to Buenos Aires as 'The capital city of Argentina where Irish emigrants went in the nineteenth century (but not as many went there as to Australia) and where they founded a newspaper entitled *The Southern Cross*. Patagonia is in the south of the country.' 'Eveline' is an emigration story but it is an emigration story with a difference. The reference to Melbourne (where actually the Irish didn't settle in such numbers as compared with other parts of Australia) is presumably meant to be interpreted in terms other than displacement in geographical terms. Indeed, in the first version in *The Irish Homestead*, Joyce includes the country, which later editors of notes feel obliged to mention as if it were some kind of explanation: 'In Australia now–Melbourne'.

There are nine sentences in this story where we hear actual dialogue:

—He is in Melbourne now.
—Miss Hill, don't you see the ladies are waiting?
—Look lively, Miss Hill, please.
—I know these sailor chaps.
—Damned Italians! coming over here!
—Derevaun Seraun! Derevaun Seraun!
—Come!
—Come!
—Eveline! Evvy!

If dialogue conventionally carries significance in fiction, 'Eveline' reveals something else. We might have guessed as much from the French use of dashes to introduce dialogue. With just the opening and closing sentences, it is possible to reconstruct the story, but it would be more difficult to do something similar with these nine spoken sentences. The first is a factual observation or rather one posing as a factual observation; the second two are workplace commands; the fourth is a father's worldly-wise warning to his innocent daughter; the fifth is an anti-immigrant remark; the sixth is possibly gibberish; and the next three are Frank's pleas to Eveline. The world is too much with Eveline. In these spoken sentences, Eveline is being hemmed in by her family, by work and by her boyfriend. Every sentence implies obligation or is a taunt in some way or other. Even the anti-immigrant sentiment expressed by her father is a reminder that she too might face such prejudice if she were to decide to live abroad.

Conversely, imagine if we filled in what Joyce omits. Imagine Eveline saying to herself the following:

'If I emigrate, will I become to my father like the photograph on the wall?'
'Every hour of every day that photograph has accompanied my life. Why should it have any meaning for me?'
'Why can't I accept without any deep, emotional soul-searching the fate that befell the priest, and just emigrate?'
'Why can't I become one of the fixtures, and accept passively the fate that awaits me?'

It doesn't work, does it? Eveline couldn't formulate her thoughts in such a way, but, to risk repeating myself, the point to notice is how dialogue in this story is used by Joyce. First, it contributes to the ventriloquial effect, whereby the story is told from the viewpoint of one character while treating that character as a third person. Dialogue is therefore like an invasion or a threat. Second, and following on from this, in the context of the theme of paralysis, the dialogue shows us the language of a paralysed world invading the privacy of consciousness, a privacy that such a world only recognises in Eveline's case as absence. Third, the dialogue, none of which is spoken by her and in which her response is never given, gives us a sharp insight into Eveline's psychology. Fourth, we might also recognise through the injunctions directed at her how Joyce wanted to show the way power relations in Ireland work effectively to paralyse and silence women, whether in the workplace or at home.

So the actual dialogue comes at a premium. Whereas most of the other sentences are injunctions or expressions of emotion, '—He is in Melbourne now' has a lifeless quality to it. If there was any humour in Eveline's family, the remark, because it accompanied every allusion to the photograph, would have become a catchphrase. 'Oh, here we go again.' And they could have expanded it to include any relative or friend who was away from home, in mental hospital, for example, or prison, or in the armed services, or simply working abroad '—He is in Melbourne now'. Instead, the repetition reminds us of Flaubert and of his interest in the idea of dead language – in language that lacks life or urgency, language that is overused as in clichés and in what Flaubert castigated as 'received ideas'. Some forms of observation belong therefore not to the world of facts but to the world of objects. And as with 'The Sisters' and the other stories of *Dubliners*, there is a subtle tension or interplay in 'Eveline' between language and silence. If Eveline could deaden her feelings, she might have been able to emigrate like the priest in the photograph and fade into a future existence. She can't, and that's what makes the story until the end particularly rich and inviting for us both as readers and, hopefully from all that has been said here, as sympathisers with her plight.

CHAPTER 5

Blinds and railings in 'Araby' and 'Two Gallants'

'Araby'

As is evident from the previous chapters, my own fascination reading Joyce is in part with details, with words and their associations, with delay. 'Araby' begins:

> North Richmond Street being blind, was a quiet street except at the hour when the Christian Brothers' School set the boys free. An uninhabited house of two storeys stood at the blind end, detached from its neighbours in a square ground. The other houses of the street, conscious of decent lives within them, gazed at one another with brown imperturbable faces. (*D* 29)

In 1954 William York Tindall took a black-and-white photograph of this street. The photograph, which is reproduced in *The Joyce Country* (1960), is itself a period photograph, a half-way point between 1905 when the story was written and today's date. Somehow, Tindall in a single shutter movement managed to capture something of the feeling and atmosphere of Joyce's story and to hold it in place for later generations. A woman with a shopping bag walks toward the camera and on the other side of the road another woman attends to a child in a pram. The rows of imperturbable houses, flanked by an impressive display of heavily ornate black railings, face each other as they did in Joyce's time. The Christian Brothers' School on the left of the photograph, whose foundation stone was laid by Daniel O'Connell in 1828 and which Joyce perhaps attended for a short while before going to Belvedere College in 1894, betrays no sign of the home-time rush when the poorer class of boys would be set free. Meanwhile, the lamp-post, in splendid isolation, stands guard over the proceedings, keeping its own counsel from Joyce's time to the time when this photograph was taken.

The words I warm to in this opening to 'Araby' are the adjectives, and in particular 'blind', 'uninhabited', 'decent', 'brown' and 'imperturbable'. What exactly is a 'blind' street? The French translation begins 'North Richmond

William York Tindall's photograph of North Richmond Street, 1954. From early 1896 until autumn of that year, the Joyce family lived here on the right, opposite the school (see Costello, 1992, 134). The street, which lies just off the North Circular Road, backs on to the Royal Canal. The 'North' in its name invites the inquirer to seek its counterpart, but such a quest leads only into a cul-de-sac as it were, for you will look in vain for South Richmond Street in this area north of the river. The detached house, no longer uninhabited, has become the office of Thos. Pearson and Co. Ltd, Dublin Wireworks, and parked outside, with no sign of their drivers, are an array of small pickup trucks and boxes of containers. That company, together with its dated name 'Wireworks', has now gone; in my copy of *Thom's Commercial Directory 1979/80* the firm had relocated to Jamestown Road, Finglas. *Thom's Dublin and County Street Directory 1979/80* shows that the three houses adjacent to the school have been demolished to make way for an opening and that only one house remains as owner-occupier; the rest have been turned into flats, tenements or offices, with one now a boarding house. Someone in particular had an entrepreneurial eye on the future because the uninhabited house in Joyce's story was in 1981/2 occupied by a computer office. If those ironies weren't enough, one other thing strikes me about the changing fortunes of this blind street. The houses, which were built in the nineteenth century as homes, may have been 'imperturbable', but that was never the case with the occupants, who seem to have always been on the move. A street for those without homes to call their own. That's also something worth writing about, in case we were misled into thinking paralysis was the whole story. We can ratchet this up another notch, for Joyce's view of the city reminds us, or it should do, that there are other ways of imagining the city.

Street, se terminant en cul-de-sac' (Joyce/Aubert, 1974, 71), signifying that the street ends in a cul-de-sac. That's true, as can be observed from the photograph, which is why a tradesman's office and depot is not very clever planning. But 'cul-de-sac' completely misses the metaphoric meaning of 'blind'. The street is blind, its houses have imperturbable faces. In the French translation, the two-storied house stands 'au fond de l'impasse', at the end of a cul-de-sac. Joyce repeats the word 'blind', but the busy French translator invokes yet another street word. The street is effectively an impasse, but the meaning or effect of this word is different in French and English. In English we don't normally refer to a street cul-de-sac as an impasse. On the other hand, to say North Richmond Street had an impasse encourages a metaphoric way of thinking about the street, but that would be for English readers to appreciate. Where there is a linguistic crossover is in the phrase 'blind alley'; an 'impasse' in French can mean blind alley, and similarly in English where an impasse is also a blind alley. However, Joyce doesn't say this. North Richmond Street is not a blind alley. It's blind.

At times a knowledge of Dublin is assumed by Joyce. We can think what we like about this, whether or not it's deliberate, a form of resentment perhaps by the colonised against the coloniser, or part of Joyce's unconscious peripheral vision. But the upshot is that there is an onus on readers and commentators alike to make explicit some of those assumptions or contexts. On the map above, for example, you may find it interesting to track

Location of North Richmond Street on Bartholomew's 1900 map of Dublin. If you need help with its location, find Richmond Place, which is an extension of the North Circular Road, and then you will soon discover North Richmond Street stretching up to the canal and railway line. In the story, when the boy eventually gets to go to the bazaar, we are told he 'strode down Buckingham Street' to catch the train. This is one of those moments when those not familiar with Dublin will have to resort to a map, for the station is in fact Amiens Street Station (now Connolly Station), from where the boy will catch a train to Westland Row Station (now Pearse Station).

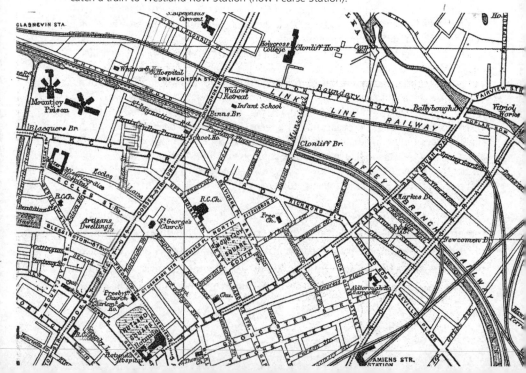

down Great Denmark Street. This is where Belvedere College is located, the prestigious Jesuit school where Joyce was educated from 1894 to 1898. As you can see, it's only five minutes from the Christian Brothers' School in North Richmond Street, and yet in terms of wealth and opportunity they were miles apart. Just above Great Denmark Street is Hardwicke Street, the setting for 'The Boarding House', a street which according to *Thom's Business Directory of Dublin and Suburbs for the Year 1906* did indeed have such a house at number 75, run by a Mrs Flook. Just above Hardwicke Street is St George's Church, where the bells peal out in *Ulysses* to remind Leopold Bloom that he is about to be or is being cuckolded. Notice, too, the Vitriol Works at the upper right corner. This is the direction the boys walk in 'An Encounter' along North Strand Road (also marked). Theirs is an excursion to the city limits, an adventure that turns if not vitriolic then sour. It's uncanny and can defy our normal understanding of things, but in the end it seems everything in Joyce's world contributes, in the end everything contributes to Joyce's world. Begin a paragraph with North Richmond Street, a blind endstop of a street on Dublin's north side, and you end with the world.

Like many other visitors to Paris, Joyce during his first stay there in 1902–3 must have registered the not uncommon sight of 'impasse' in street names, and perhaps it was this that set him thinking about a street being 'blind'. But a blind street is not quite the same as a street with a cul-de-sac. Rather, it is a street that is likened to a person who is blind (in that there is an obstacle at one end of the street preventing a longer view, as it were). It's also blind in the sense that it can't see. From the start of this story we are involved in a metaphoric reading, which is not quite what Colin McCabe, at the height of the post-structuralist movement, had in mind when he claimed that 'these are not stories "about" Dublin in the sense that Dublin is an entity understood and referred to outside the text' (McCabe, 1979, 28–9). For me, metaphor implies place but it is not destroyed by contact with the so-called entity 'outside the text'. Hence my insistence on the particular features and landscape of the city and then broadening out from there. 'Araby' is a story about blindness, about an adult world blind to a child's worldview, about a boy's blindness in the face of an early awakening to sexual desire, and perhaps about the blindness of Europe toward Araby and the exotic East, transforming the Orient into a trading bazaar and the exchange of coins.

'Araby' is also a story about blinds in a house, and peeping through them or under them; it's about a street that lacks bright lights to shed on the world. The French translation has 'le store' for a window 'blind', and therefore manages to miss again all the compression of meaning that the story

Araby House today. Photograph by David Pierce. 8 North Richmond Street, the uninhabited house at the blind end in 'Araby', is now occupied by the Irish National Organisation of the Unemployed. Blind, unoccupied, unemployed – eventually, and appropriately, the Joycean inheritance returns to its material base in Dublin. Eventually, we realise that Joyce is a writer on deprivation. Indeed, he thrives on deprivation. What is 'Araby' but a story about a boy's deprivation and the close proximity of pocket-money and the fulfilment of desire? No money, no gift, no encounter, no exchange of values, no joy. Opposite 7 Eccles Street, where Joyce imagined the Blooms lived, a house that was demolished some years ago, someone has stepped into the breach and ingeniously called their house 'Bloom House'. Araby House is much more appropriate, a house that dominates a whole street and which quite legitimately has supplanted a whole story of Joyce's. There is no plaque outside to remind us of its Joycean inheritance and neither is it mentioned on most Joycean itineraries round the city. Perhaps that's as it should be. Look at the house of desire, and then notice the emblem of the unemployed. Eastern promise and western values – it's another way of thinking about Joyce's story.

deliberately seeks to exploit. Blinds and blindness, lanterns that are dull, houses that remain imperturbable, streets that are 'blind', old books that are yellowing with age, a priest who has (as in 'The Sisters') died in the house – and all under the romantic title of 'Araby'. Yes, 'blind' invokes a memory of 'The Sisters' and the blinds in that story, how the blinds were drawn as a mark of respect and to show the neighbours that someone in the house had died. The image also anticipates the final story of the collection when, the blinds drawn, Gabriel imagines sitting with Aunt Kate to mourn the death of Aunt Julia. Later, in *Ulysses*, through a drawn blind on Eccles Street, a woman with a 'plump bare generous arm' throws down a coin from a window to a one-legged sailor who is begging in the street outside – but that's another story. Once activated, certain images can be seen as recurring in Joyce's writing.

Restriction and escape, or escape and a return to restriction, which is it? Again, as elsewhere in *Dubliners*, the story of 'Araby' is nicely balanced. The other adjectives also invite comment. The 'uninhabited' house at the end is intriguing. An uninhabited house whether in the city or the country is a reminder of death. A warning sign. It stands there with the privative prefix 'un-' on display for the whole world to see. A minus, a without, not within. No curtains, no lights, no open windows, no sound, no arguments. Push in my windows, blot out my eyes, it dares would-be vandals. When a person dies, s/he leaves the house, and this in both a physical and a spiritual sense. In some cultures, and traditional Irish culture was one such, a window is opened to allow the spirit to escape. When people visit a funeral parlour to see a relative or a friend for the last time, they often sense that, wherever the dead person is, it is no longer in the body. The body is in this sense uninhabited. Throughout Joyce's collection of stories, he repeatedly invokes the intercourse between the living and the world of the dead. At one level we are made aware of the separation of the real and the unreal, but at another level there is something else at play. If we mistype one letter and change 'inhabited' to 'inhibited', we are back to Ibsen, Freud, and the speech community that first coined these two words and took care to restrict their semantic fields. The dead, the real, the no longer inhabited or any longer inhibited. The boy's immediate environment is described in detail for us, but, if asked, what would he have made of 'uninhabited'? He is about to enter the world beyond the given, the world of desire and attraction. Will he find the world a place of habitation or will he learn, like Gabriel in 'The Dead', that the heart is inhabited or inhibited by figures from the past?

'Decent', 'brown', 'imperturbable'. 'Decent lives.' The effect here is in fact its opposite. People on this street lead decent lives where 'decent' means respectable, bourgeois, conventional. It's difficult to admire people who lead 'decent lives'. You can see what Joyce is getting at, but it's not something I feel inclined to go along with. It's the kind of phrase used by a boy at school writing a story for his weekly composition class. People on this street would have been presumably aspiring lower middle class. Their houses were not two-up, two-down, but built on three floors. They were large family houses and their occupants presumably wanted an education for their children above that offered by the Christian Brothers. Perhaps they kept themselves to themselves, but so what? If the neighbours are letting down the tone of the street by the father coming home drunk, or the children are dressed in hand-me-down clothes or observed visiting pawn shops, or if the previous occupant, an old priest who died, was thoroughly untidy and allowed the house to fall into disrepair, perhaps the neighbours would insist on keeping their own children at a respectable distance. At times in *Dubliners*, there is a lazy observer at work where Joyce seems to slip a gear, as if he was pressing his case without having to argue for it, or condemning without real cause, or not allowing us access to his real motivation or peripheral vision. Snobbery of course can work both ways, and it's in keeping that early biographers were uncertain whether Joyce did attend the Christian Brothers School opposite before going to the upmarket Jesuit College of Belvedere.

North Richmond Street today. Photograph by David Pierce. A still afternoon in October, the secondary school children, with rucksacks and school uniform, and some in trainers, have just been released from school. It's 2006, a century and more after Joyce penned 'Araby'. The street is still blind, but the Victorian street lamps have gone, and a grotesque extension has been added to Araby House. A building contractor's delivery van, loaded up with a square gutter, noses its way towards the camera and the North Circular Road. The character of the street has changed. You don't have to know much about vernacular architecture to recognise that the railings look especially sad. Most of the gates have gone, as have the original finials, and, except for one of the two renovated houses, the upright stunted rails have been painted black and the railheads white. Partly because the frontage to the row is no longer uniform and partly because parked cars interfere with the wide-angle perspective, the houses no longer gaze 'at one another with brown imperturbable faces'. Today's street reminds me of an unloved street waiting to be put back together, which is not quite what Joyce had in mind when he set the story here a hundred years ago.

'Brown' in the story I like. It stares you in the face. 'I'm all brown', Mr Browne quips in front of the aunts in 'The Dead', roguishly playing on his name and their sense of propriety. I assume the red bricks have turned a shade of brown with the city's pollution, and bricks that have become discoloured in this way can be depressing and therefore in keeping with the story's opening. Today, the frontage on two houses near the Joyce former home has been restored to the original red colour, suggesting what the street must have looked like when first constructed. In the story the colour Joyce alights on is brown, not the colour grey of eighteenth-century Dublin which Yeats uses in 'Easter 1916' to contrast with the green of Ireland. The effect would be different again if Joyce had written 'red imperturbable faces'. Colour symbolism. Before he came to write *Ulysses*, Joyce was learning all the time about this in *Dubliners*. 'Yellow' is a colour worth tracing in the stories, from the 'yellow teeth' of the paedophile in 'An Encounter', to the yellow pages of *The Memoirs of Vidocq* in this story, to the 'yellow streaks of egg' confronting Mr Doran at breakfast in 'The Boarding-House', to the way the 'dull, yellow light brooded over the houses and the river' as the Conroys make their way back to the Gresham Hotel at the end of 'The Dead'. In each case colour defines a mood, advances the narrative, or seals a character's fate. For another example, 'Two Gallants', which is discussed in more detail below, furnishes a 'blue' story and it's worth noticing how colour functions in that story. A writer with poor eyesight sees the world in colour, and Joyce was no different. The photographs we have from the period are all in black and white, but imagine a world in colour and everything comes to life. That is what reading *Dubliners* can be like – the awakening to colour.

As for 'imperturbable', again I warm to the privative 'im-'. Not perturbable. No response. And the sound of the word is suggestive also, as if there was a babble going on or a struggle to maintain pretension. In this sense we might see a connection between 'imperturbable' and 'uninhabited'. Both contain a negative syllable to begin with, 'im-' and 'un-'. But then we realise that in this case the other houses on North Richmond Street are inhabited – it's just their faces that give off an air of imperturbability. Living, not living. Decent lives surround him, but the young boy has caught a glimpse of passion outside the house. Joyce plays a descant on all these themes in this opening to 'Araby', the confrontation between something that doesn't move with something that does, between waiting and action, between the harp of romance and the impossibility of its setting. But, as we have noticed, North Richmond Street did change through time and so, too, did Joyce's city. Arguably, its constant feature was that it never remained the same, and in an important sense it is this quality that tends to escape

Title page of the French edition of *The Memoirs of Vidocq*, suitably foxed and menacing. Eugène Vincent Vidocq (1775–1857) was a French criminal who became one of the first private investigators. In turn, he became the inspiration for two characters in Victor Hugo's *Les Misérables* (1862). His multi-volume memoirs, first published in 1828–9, were very popular, as this new single-volume edition published in Brussels in 1829 suggests. Vidocq made the first plaster cast of shoe impressions and is credited with inventing indelible ink. The reference to Vidocq in 'Araby' and the reading matter therefore of a former occupant, who was himself a priest, adds a certain mustiness and perhaps intrigue to the story.

Joyce. As *Ulysses* reminds us, the myth of 1904, a year frozen for Joyce in time, was never to release its grip. Not imperturbable but changing should have been his motto here. The boys set free from the Christian Brothers' School in the 1890s included Éamonn Ceannt, Con Colbert and Sean Heuston, boys who in 1916 took to the streets to free Ireland from the Crown. Not everyone was leading decent lives at this time; some were dreaming of revolution. Blinds often defy meaning and sometimes tell us nothing about the occupants.

Like his snobbish father, Joyce seems to have had little sympathy with working-class boys who were educated by the Christian Brothers, but what he did understand was something in a sense more inclusive, namely boyhood itself. And, as *A Portrait* reminds us, he also knew how to write about it in retrospect, how to put it in perspective that is, as when he writes: 'All through his boyhood he had mused upon that which he had so often thought to be his destiny and when the moment had come for him to obey the call he had turned aside, obeying a wayward instinct' (*P* 165). For Joyce, as it was for Dickens, boyhood was a state or condition separate from the adult world. Parallel to the adult world, the world of boyhood exists charged with its own electricity and atmosphere. Its unmarked borders are constantly crossed or pierced by inquisitive or insensitive adults, but boyhood, even, as is the case in *Dubliners*, when there is no mention of the boy's actual father, still retained a sense of itself as different. In the confrontation between the boy in these early stories of *Dubliners* and the various adults, none of the adults gets the better of him. The stories of boyhood are given to us as little scenes, complete in themselves, but they are all utterly blind, uncompromising, and in their different ways defiant. Adolescence, as we will now turn our attention to, is a different thing, being a state that one passes through along a corridor of mirrors.

'Two Gallants'

With the preying of boys from the North Circular Road on girls from the South Circular Road, 'Two Gallants' constitutes a Northsider's revenge on Dublin south of the river, or, to give the story a contemporary ring, we might imagine it as the revenge of the Northside and the working-class estates on Dublin 4. See the two heroes, the two soldiers, or, if we pronounce gallants with the accent on the second syllable, the two dashing ladies' men, swaggering down the hill of Rutland Square (now Parnell Square), down what is now O'Connell Street, across the river, then glancing up at the clock at Trinity College, passing a busker on Kildare Street, and then into Stephen's Green and on to Merrion Square. The route is rich in association of Dublin's past and present glories, but in this story the two gallants are like ignorant tourists roaming through a city that doesn't belong to them. In turn, as we retrace their steps, we too are like today's tourists who would studiously avoid visiting blind streets on the Northside or the huge working-class estates to the south, confining ourselves to the safety of 'touristy' areas and buses in between. There's another form of revenge at work in this story, then, the exposure of the worldview of the have-nots on a society that would prefer not to know about such a coarse world. A clever move on Joyce's part, we might add. Following the walks in this respect is almost a distraction for, as ever, Joyce's mind is also elsewhere.

After Corley catches the tram, Lenehan retreats back across the river, up Sackville Street, then presumably makes a left along Great Britain Street to Capel Steet, where he turns down towards the river again. Across the bridge takes him past Dublin Castle, which was at that time, as already

James Joyce

DUBLINERS

Verhalen

De Bezige Bij

On the cover of Rein Bloem's Dutch translation of *Dubliners*, published by Van Gennep in Amsterdam in 1987, there is a graphic image of the soles of shoes on a city map. 'Two Gallants' reminds us that Joyce is a topographical writer who insists on noticing where and how people traverse a city. In *Dubliners* he was learning all the time, so by the time he came to *Ulysses* he had honed the technique to perfection. Hence all the Joycean walks now around his native city, providing a potentially never-ending stream of revenue for the city and the Irish Tourist Board. My students sometimes ask me how much they should know about the layout of Dublin, to which I reply 'A lot'. As I suggest above, I have found little in Joyce that might be described as 'background', for at some level, frequently difficult to predict, nearly everything contributes to what Fredric Jameson (1999) has called the process of cognitive mapping.

mentioned, the administrative headquarters of British rule in Ireland. Then along Dame Street. It's a circular tour of some 2–3 miles, and it takes him eventually back to Stephen's Green and Merrion Square. Some critics have discerned a question mark in his route, which is possible, but, to me, it's Lenehan going round in circles that impresses. Without his friend, Lenehan is footloose, killing time, condemned for ever to musing on missing out.

In the Edwardian period, the central district was much as it is today. During the day, as contemporary photographs from the Lawrence Collection in the National Library of Ireland remind us, the area round Grafton Street was buzzing, full of shoppers, tradesmen, office workers, chambermaids, domestic servants, delivery boys, accountants, solicitors, surgeons, cyclists, draymen and drivers of every description of vehicle. Sunday evenings were also buzzing, but it was a different kind of buzzing. Sober and expectant. A dry time. Ireland sober is Ireland free, as the saying goes. Joyce informs us the shops have their shutters pulled down; he doesn't need to tell us the pubs are shut, for when the story was composed everyone knew the Sunday licensing hours. Presumably, this is in part why Lenehan, who always manages to get himself counted into a round of drinks in Dublin's bars, is at a loss where to go for refreshment: 'He paused at last before the window of a poor-looking shop over which the words *Refreshment Bar* were printed in white letters. On the glass of the window were two flying inscriptions: *Ginger Beer* and *Ginger Ale*' (*D* 57). It's a shop, not a café, appropriately not far from Great Britain Street and the cold house of the sisters in Joyce's first story. The shop is near Rutland Square, a mile or so from the excitement of Stephen's Green. It's an unrefreshing, unwelcoming, unshuttered 'shop', complete with flying inscriptions to be read slowly by passers-by (and readers of the story). A bar in name only. By contrast, crowds in a city, as Joyce well knew, can warm the heart, and he was always tuning into the heart of the city.

It's an evening in August so there will be light in the sky until around nine o'clock (today it would be an hour later, but British Summer Time wasn't introduced until May 1916, and remember Dublin is in terms of

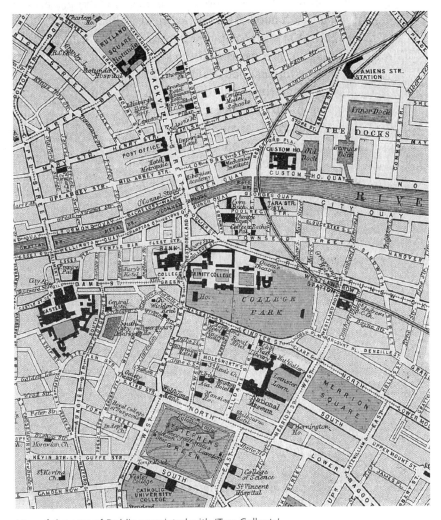

Map of the area of Dublin associated with 'Two Gallants'.

longitude 6 degrees or so west of Greenwich and 25 minutes therefore behind GMT). The young woman has a sunshade, which at the end of story is
transformed into an umbrella. She has a sunshade not only to swing but,
presumably, just in case it rains, as happens on her return. In the photograph from the Lawrence Collection reproduced on the front cover of my
James Joyce's Ireland (1992), there is a woman in a long white dress holding a parasol or sunshade as if it were a fashion accessory, and another
woman on the same, shady, sombre side of Grafton Street has her parasol
up. The photograph shows men in jackets rather than overcoats, and the
sun, high in the sky, coming in from the west. A sunny afternoon in summer. In *Ulysses* we learn something about the Blooms and umbrellas that's
also potentially relevant here: 'She disliked umbrella with rain, he liked
woman with umbrella, she disliked new hat with rain, he liked woman with
new hat, he bought new hat with rain, she carried umbrella with new hat'
(*U* 17:706–8). A woman with an umbrella takes Bloom's fancy, and I think
there's a suggestion of this in 'Two Gallants'. The young woman meets
Corley with an umbrella and proceeds to swing it as if she knows what she's
doing. It's a small detail that resonates against the period in part because
such an accessory functions differently in today's sexual economy. By way
of contrast, the image of umbrellas in 'The Sisters' is more understandable,
in part because it's closer to penury and the real economy – in *Thom's Business Directory of Dublin and Suburbs for the Year 1906* 14 'umbrella,
parasol, and walkingstick makers' are listed.

Railings protect Trinity College, but there's nothing to protect the railings from Lenehan's
wandering fingers. Photograph by David Pierce.

The inviting grounds of Trinity College. Photograph by David Pierce. In the heart of the city, round which the crowds are forced to flow, Trinity College, founded in the reign of Elizabeth I, was for most of its 400-year history off-limits to most Dubliners. It's reputed that Joyce only once darkened its doors and that was to watch a cricket match. All over the city, Dubliners must have glimpsed through railings and half-opened doors and shutters an exclusive world that excluded them for, perhaps more than anywhere else in Europe at the turn of the twentieth century, it was a city famous for its haves and have-nots. For most of the last years he lived in Dublin, Joyce, too, shared an outsider's view of his city, and he understood precisely the predicament of being forced out, of finding himself kicking his heels, walking at times aimlessly round the streets. Even when he passed the 'sentries' of his youth and entered what is now University College Dublin, he would have been conscious of the much older and more prestigious university half a mile away, an 'English' university which had the luxury of parading its spatial wealth, playing cricket in the middle of a colonial city full of the shouts of real deprivation. Howzatt? How's that? How do you say that?

The crowds, then, in their brightly coloured clothes are out enjoying the last bit of the weekend before the drudgery of Monday comes round again. As Corley and Lenehan turn into Stephen's Green, 'the noise of trams, the lights and the crowd released them from their silence' (*D* 54). It's true, Kildare Street is quiet, but once you reach the top of the street the mood changes. And perhaps we shouldn't forget – though Joyce doesn't tell us this – that it was here in the shaded walk round Stephen's Green that prostitutes plied their trade (see Costello, 1992, 226). Joyce understood the mood not only of the city but also of the various districts, streets and pavements of the city, and, contrary to what I sometimes read in commentaries on Joyce, he didn't need *Thom's Official Dublin Directory* or any guide book to tell him any of this. North Richmond Street is blind, but this area is humming. Interestingly, when commenting on the Irish landscape to this story in a letter to Stanislaus, Joyce did so by reference to Lenehan, the harp and the Sunday crowds (see *Letters II*, 166). That's a slightly strange observation. The harp is obvious, and Lenehan one can accept is Irish through and through (and the same can be said of nearly all of Joyce's characters). But Sunday crowds? An Irish phenomenon? Surely the cities of Catholic Europe were also buzzing. And it dates Joyce, for it's not something that particularly strikes us today – Temple Bar throbs every night. Perhaps Joyce meant it in comparison with desperate English Sundays during the late-Victorian and Edwardian period.

'Two Gallants' is also a story about cultural tourism, with the reader doing all the work. The two young men pass many of the main attractions in Dublin without identifying any of them for the reader. Little is appreciated. Trinity College Dublin, where Lenehan, like a distracted little boy, runs his fingers along the railings, has a clock with a moonlike face, as does the College of Surgeons, and Lenehan employs both to tell the time. What the young men betray is a functional attitude towards their city. They can

Stephen's Green in the autumn, blessed with falling leaves and the morning light. Photograph by David Pierce.

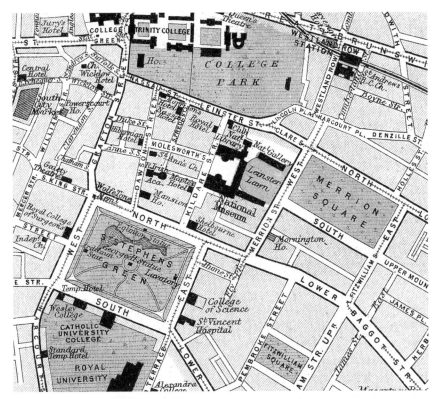

Close-up map of places where Corley and Lenehan meet the young woman.

make nothing of the city's remarkable buildings and historical institutions, nor of the larger symbols that hold the world in place. The story is in this sense about betrayal. The harp, the symbol of Ireland, is being played 'heedlessly' outside the Kildare Street Club on Kildare Street, the club where the Anglo-Irish – the Horse Protestants, as Brendan Behan, another Dubliner once famously called them – would meet for lunch, read about themselves in *The Irish Times*, never imagining they were living on borrowed time. The tune being played is a melody by Ireland's national poet Thomas Moore about the exiled state of Ireland. The cultural tourist, that is the reader, listens to the words and picks up on their significance, but not the characters themselves. They pass without comment, continuing on to the Shelbourne Hotel on Stephen's Green, a hotel that was once known as the best address in Ireland, where members of the Anglo-Irish such as the novelist Elizabeth Bowen stayed in transit between their estates in Ireland and their homes in England. But for those on the other side of the tracks in hot pursuit of a quarry, all these sites are essentially unheard, unseen and unnoticed. Victorian ornate lamps are simply for shining gold coins under.

Coarseness, too, is a form of betrayal, and, re-reading the story, I find myself noticing how these particular terms keep switching back and forth. One minute I think 'coarseness', the next a terrible betrayal, not least a betrayal of the body and the course of its natural desires. Dublin coarseness. In a class of its own. Corley's 'crudeness' is commented on by the narrator, but this refers to the way his stride and swagger along the pavement ensures Lenehan has constantly to step out into the road. Complementing their triumphal parade across the city is the suitably low, racy language of the gutter:

> where did you pick her up
> I spotted a fine tart
> squeezed her a bit that night
> I was afraid, man, she'd get in the family way. But she's up to the dodge
> I suppose you'll be able to pull it off all right, eh?
> There's nothing to touch a good slavey
> damn the thing I ever got out of it
> Only off of one of them
> She's on the turf now
> There was others at her before me
> are you sure you can bring it off all right?
> a fine decent tart
> Work it all right now
> Did it come off?
> Did you try her?
> A small gold coin shone in the palm.

I assume there will be few people reading this story who are unfamiliar with this kind of talk. We are surrounded by it. It's an example of male predators conversing, and worth seeing or rather hearing in print, for it is the language of the street brought home to us with some force in (or as) the language of fiction in our hands. It's the kind of thing the boys in 'The Sisters' and 'Araby' will have to counter if they are to carry their chalice safely though life. Shocking, but, if it helps and I don't know if it does, we might see such language as belonging to the theme of paralysis in that boys and young men keep repeating it as if it were newly minted or as if their solidarity stood in need of constant renewal. This, too, is Joyce's city, where young men sometimes never get beyond the view of sexual relations as a battlefield. In the companion story, 'The Boarding House', we encounter the female predators at work, but here it is the young men who, though well into their twenties, are still in adolescent mood, wrapping everything in the language of innuendo, abuse and denigration.

However, as Sean O'Faolain pointed out a half century ago, we should also register a qualification, for the tongue in this case escapes paralysis

(O'Faolain, 1956). There isn't a single phrase out of place, for this was a world that Joyce for a time clearly inhabited and knew intimately. Indeed, his first night out with Nora started with them catching a tram at Merrion Square and alighting at Lansdowne Road, followed by a stroll down by the banks of the River Dodder and Nora, apparently, reaching in to undo the buttons of his flies and pleasure him. As if she too wanted in on the act, it's a scene that finds an echo in Molly Bloom's soliloquy: 'he hasnt such a tremendous amount of spunk in him when I made him pull out and do it on me considering how big it is' (*U* 18:154–5). One of the best moments for me in Pat Murphy's film *Nora* (2000) is when the chambermaid, played by Susan Lynch, asks Joyce, played by Ewan McGregor, if he's got a hankie. Only a woman who knew about such things could be so practical. And there must have been a lot of Noras walking the streets of Dublin at that time, most, one suspects, quite capable of dealing with those who would want to 'try' them.

It sometimes surprises readers that what Corley is angling for is to have sex with the young woman and get her to pay for it. Most young men would be happy to enjoy the former without ever expecting the latter. But, to continue in the style of this story, Corley wants to have his cake and eat it. Joyce, the well-travelled observer, tells us how Corley's name would be pronounced by Italians living in Florence, and we don't miss the double irony about the fruits of travel and a university education. Corley, then, is 'whorely', whoring after women, and then getting them to pay him for services rendered. Life (and fictional accounts of it) is full of the unexpected, and most commentators seem to think it works, that the young woman does pay him. But I wonder if she does so, at least for services rendered. Wouldn't it be in keeping that this is the impression Corley wants Lenehan to have? All we are told is that she disappears into her employer's house and returns some time later with what we assume is the coin that Corley produces for Lenehan. When defending this incident in a letter to Grant Richards against objections by the publisher's printer, Joyce observes: 'Is it the small gold coin . . . or the code of honour which the two gallants live by which shocks him?' (*Letters II*, 122–3). And Joyce continues by going on about conventional ideas concerning gallantry and those who receive an education from reading the novels of Alexandre Dumas and others. In the real world, Joyce the Ibsenite is saying, life is other than we find it in books. I think we might all agree with this, and how important it was for Joyce and his generation, in the name of a more honest view of the world, to resist propriety, but it still leaves open the question of whether or not Corley succeeds.

Invoking my theme of defiance, I like to think this young woman is well able to match Corley blow for blow, including his delusion that he is 'up to all their little tricks'. In her blue dress and white sailor hat, she knows how to play the part. She is also more wised-up than Eveline, and, to reverse the image of Frank and sailor boys in general, she is dressed as a sailor girl. A woman who's as blue and as daring as he is. Perhaps for ease of access, as one of my female students once proposed, she was wearing no knickers. As suggested, there's a hint of Nora Barnacle in her, the woman who in all kinds of ways made a man of Joyce. Indeed, when Nora first met Joyce on these self-same streets, she too thought, with his blue eyes and sailor cap, he might be a sailor, from Scandinavia or somewhere. Like the Joycean narrator, Lenehan sees the woman in the story from a distance. She turns on her heels, swings her umbrella, and, perhaps out of feigned innocence, bends her head to the conqueror's suggestive talk. From a further distance at the corner of Hume Street, Lenehan turns back and he has more time to take her in. He notices her blue serge skirt, the black leather belt, the silver buckle, the white blouse, the black jacket with mother-of-pearl buttons. She comes accessorised with a 'ragged black boa' and a 'big bunch of red flowers . . . pinned in her bosom stems upwards' (D 55). Less flattering to Lenehan (who's hardly anything himself) is her 'short stout muscular body' and two projecting teeth. Well, you can't have everything, someone should have told him.

Does she need a makeover? Perhaps, but some things you can't cover up, and would you want her to be any different? Like Corley, she is out to have a good time and has dressed to catch his eye. The red flowers with stems facing upward she thinks are a come-on, as are the belt and buckle and black jacket. To anticipate a (masculine) syntactic structure and phrase from 'The Dead' when Gretta is described in reflective mood on the landing, what is a woman wearing red flowers at her bosom with stems pointing upward a sign of? 'Wouldn't you like to know what I'm like underneath', she's saying to him. 'Well, what's it worth? You see my red flowers, but let's

The corner of Stephen's Green and Hume Street, a meeting place for those hoping to catch a tram, now accompanied by a surveillance camera. The joke used to concern the possibility of walking across Dublin without passing a pub. Today, the question shapes itself differently: is it possible to walk 50 metres without being caught on CCTV? Secret trysts must be a thing of the past. Photograph by David Pierce.

see what you've got, what your stem looks like? Your stem joined to my fine red flower pointing downward.' A fair exchange. The worm in the bud. Perhaps the evening was fun, nothing more. Perhaps, as once happened to Molly Bloom with a man, Corley got as far as her petticoat, the layer underneath all her other, outer clothes, not mentioned by Joyce. The last line of defence, to adopt a military image in a story about two gallants. Perhaps Corley put it to her that he was short of cash and she agreed to help him out by stealing a gold coin from her employer. Perhaps she gives him the money on account, for she'd like some more where that came from. That Lenehan interprets the coin as sex-plus-financial-recompense doesn't mean it happened. Corley, no doubt, will continue striding out and 'unbosoming' to his disciple on the theme of how he goes about conquering the fair sex, but I wonder if the epiphany at the end is not so much proof of all the story is saying as thoroughly ambiguous (as gender itself is). Indeed, we might well agree, especially with Nora also in mind, there's nothing to touch a good slavey.

CHAPTER 6

Teaching *Dubliners*

Handouts

We've spent the last three chapters considering individual stories in *Dubliners*, but we need also to reflect on the structure and coherence of the collection as a whole. Most of us coming to Joyce for the first time will experience not only difficulty but also recognition. The boy in the first three episodes is unnamed but he seems to be the same boy, and perhaps we read the stories accordingly. Images, too, recur, and I remember on first reading *Dubliners* connecting the word 'chalice' in various stories and thinking there was perhaps a purpose on the author's part, but at the same time not being sure. This kind of tentativeness I always enjoyed when teaching those new to Joyce, for I felt I was in touch again with the journey that had a beginning for me but at this juncture no end. I also learnt from my students about reading things I hadn't thought about or noticed. It must have occurred to many readers of the previous chapters, for example, that mental illness in *Dubliners* is another topic worth exploring. That said, Table 6.1 shows a simple matrix of *Dubliners*, divided into theme and setting, which I used to give my students.

For seminar discussion, I would then get them to prepare one of the following topics:

Epiphany.
Unity or otherwise of collection.
Joyce's 'style of scrupulous meanness'.
Humour, social realism, use of symbols.
Nothing happens – how would you defend Joyce against this charge?
Joyce's topographical imagination. Dublin as capital city.
Church and State, colonialism, postcolonialism.
Dubliners as a critique of modern Ireland.
Relationships, sexuality, ethics, morality, upbringing, punishment.
Suppressed or expressed lyricism in the stories.

Table 6.1 Analysing *Dubliners*

Title of story	Theme	Setting
The Sisters	Paralysis, death	Inside house/shop
An Encounter	Corruption, disappointed adventure	North Wall/Ringsend
Araby	Child's disappointment	Home/train/bazaar
Eveline	Emigration	Home/North Wall
After the Race	Unequal competition	Streets/Kingstown/ yacht
Two Gallants	Corrupt lives, betrayal, male predators	Streets/café/central area
The Boarding House	Female predators	Inside house
A Little Cloud	Contrast between home and abroad	Pub/home
Counterparts	Frustration at work	Office/pub/home
Clay	Death, waiting	Laundry/tram/shops/ home
A Painful Case	Failure in sexual relationship	Home/concert hall/ railway line
Ivy Day in the Committee Room	Failure in politics	Local committee room
A Mother	Ugly face of Irish Revival	Concert hall
Grace	Ugly face of Church	Pub/home/church
The Dead	The dead hand of the past	Home/hotel room

Use of songs, reading material, photographs, English literature.
Images of Europe.
Clothes, eyes, looks, accent.
Domesticity, home life, marriage, family.

And if the collection is part of a course on Modernism, I would ask them to consider *Dubliners* with that in mind.

All this material shows how much there is when we reflect on Joyce's achievement in his early collection of stories. My remarks in the preceding chapters stem from my own particular concerns but I am equally attentive to the concerns of my students. When fresh to Joyce I would devote special attention to the unity of the collection and to the idea of an epiphany. In recent years, I find myself fascinated more by other things, such as the delay that seems built into the writing and how Joyce's mind, especially apparent here and in *Ulysses*, seems to be constantly, almost defiantly, at work elsewhere.

Student responses

My students bring their own interpretation and I want to work with some of these here. One student writes:

> Throughout *Dubliners*, and especially in the stories concerning maturity and public life, Joyce displays the effects of alcohol. It is a stifling thing which hinders the growth of Dublin. In 'A Painful Case' Mrs Sinico gets into the habit of 'going out at night to buy spirits', and as a result her drinking leads to her death. A similar thing can be seen in 'Grace' where a man has drunkenly fallen down some stairs in a pub and is described lying at the bottom of them 'smeared with the filth and ooze of the floor'. It is a disgusting, degrading image and Joyce is trying to show the effects of alcohol and the damaging effects it was having upon Dublin life. Alcohol is evident in every story and in some way or another it has a damaging effect upon the protagonist's future.

This is a not untypical kind of response. It's an example less of the levelling muse and more of the destructive muse, a form of trampling. I never know how to respond to such plainness. Clearly, there is a moral note being struck throughout *Dubliners*. After all, Joyce believed he was writing a chapter in the moral history of his country. But what he preaches has precious little in common with an address you might hear at a Salvation Army Citadel on a Sunday evening. Sometimes, by way of a response to the moralising viewpoint, I recall the repeated acts of kindness by Robert McAlmon and others when Joyce was in Paris in the 1920s and how the prone writer would be carried home after bouts of drinking in clubs and bars. Joyce, I tell my students, is Irish, and most of them, especially if they're Geordies or Scousers, understand immediately what I'm saying. According to Peter Costello, Joyce began drinking after the death of his brother George from peritonitis in May 1902, and, from that point on, alcohol was an active presence in his life (Costello, 1992, 177). Joyce was not a saint and he loved his father in spite of all his drinking. He loved his characters, too, whether they were 'screwed' like Freddie Mallins in 'The Dead' or falling down the steps of a city centre pub as happens in 'Grace' to Mr Kernan. Don't miss the humour: it is claimed that Mr Kernan has only had 'a small rum'. In their annotated edition of *Dubliners*, Jackson and McGinley (1993) take particular delight in noticing that 'a drop taken' is an Irish form of litotes or understatement. No, we can confidently say, Joyce shares little with his fellow Dubliner Matt Talbot (1856–1925), the reformed alcoholic who, in the words on his dedicated website, 'found sobriety through prayer and self-sacrifice' and who today is on course to becoming canonised by the Church, which Joyce isn't.

It would be difficult to read *Dubliners* as various tirades against drink. Well, it would be possible, but only by someone who had got hold of the

All over Dublin people tread on these street signs. *Uisce*: Irish for water. But pronounce it properly and you can hear the roar of whiskey. Uisce, hwoosh, woosh. Whiskey comes from the Gaelic for water. *Uisce beatha*. Water of life, to be precise. This water stop-tap lid is on Kildare Street, opposite Leinster House, where the Irish Parliament meets. Dublin is a thirsty city; it's also a very watery city. Indeed, because it is an *aqua* city, it possesses 'aquacity', a special kind of quality associated with the water of life. Photograph by David Pierce.

wrong end of the stick, someone who couldn't see Joyce's own defiance in such matters. 'Lookut', as the traditional concertina player Packie Russell in the 1960s would scowl when he caught German tourists and others, in their hopeless attempts to dance, destroying the music he was playing for them at Gus Connors's pub in Doolin, County Clare. 'Lookut, will you sit down and just listen.' That was one of his more polite responses, for Packie, who was in terms of personality almost the exact opposite of his brother the angelic tinwhistle player Micho who would play all night at our house dances without a break, could as easily take off out of the pub altogether until a different crowd had emerged later in the evening. Sit down and listen is sometimes good advice for literature students, too. Listen to the music of Joyce, the mood music. He never stayed a single night in one of those temperance hotels indicated on the 1900 map of his native city.

Trieste, Joyce candidly laments and at the same time enthuses with a sigh in *Finnegans Wake*, 'ah trieste ate I my liver!' (*FW* 301:16). Only a shortage of money held him back. 'Liverpoor? Sot a bit of it!', he asserts elsewhere (*FW* 74:13). Sot. Not a bit of it. Only at night. Joyce was well acquainted with all the various stages of alcoholic fog and enjoyed writing about the experience, especially the crossover or linked passage between drunkenness and sleep. After the reference to 'liverpoor', he proceeds to describe the HCE figure – one of whose incarnations goes by the appropriate name of Mr Porter – losing consciousness: 'Words weigh no no more to him than raindrips to Rethfernhim. Which we all like. Rain. When we sleep. Drops. But wait until our sleeping. Drain. Sdops' (*FW* 74:16–9). Underlying *Finnegans Wake* is the ballad of 'Finnegan's Wake', a ballad that features Tim Finnegan reviving at his wake after some whiskey is accidentally splashed over him. To my mind, only someone with lots of drink around him could have composed Joyce's last, almost impenetrable work, drilling for years in the dark into the two sides of a mountain, all the while hoping that at some point the tunnels would meet.

'We rescue thee, O Baass, from the damp earth and honour thee' (*FW* 312:17–18). Bass beer mat in shape of a delta, the female delta. Maths and geography and the body. One definition, one image of life. A triangle, a river. 'Tell me all', begins the famous chapter on Anna Livia Plurabelle in *Finnegans Wake*. Flow on gentle river.

Source: Courtesy of InBev

During its composition, drink was both a source of comfort in the evening and also heady subject matter for writing about during the day. Indeed, fog not only in part constitutes the medium of *Finnegans Wake*, it is also one of the most *potent* metaphors for the reading experience. Needless to say, Joyce put everything to use. The provincial that he was, his friends in Paris in the interwar years remembered him singing repeatedly in praise of Fendant de Sion, a little-known Swiss white wine he had become attached to in Zurich. When he had guests round for dinner, the drink was always plentiful, and, for his party piece, before he collapsed into an armchair, he demonstrated his dancing skills, his body swaying to music, his legs kicking high. Thereafter came the 'bedtick' and sleep. Drips. Drops. Sdops.

Mrs Sinico takes to drink in reaction to a man who has withdrawn his affection from her. Mr Duffy is the kind of person who cannot cope with an emotional relationship and at a crucial moment holds back. The whole story of 'A Painful Case' is given to us in the opening sentence, complete with another telling example of free indirect speech: 'Mr James Duffy lived in Chapelizod because he wished to live as far as possible from the city of which he was a citizen and because he found all the other suburbs of Dublin mean, modern and pretentious' (*D* 107). What you see in one sense is what you get, but in another sense the voice we hear behind the opening sentence is that of someone aspiring to be a writer, to put his life into words. 'Mean, modern and pretentious' – there's a nice ring to that triplet. It trips off the tongue, but it issues from someone trying to be a writer and thinking writing's to do with pronouncements and what we might call sealants. How do I capture that feeling I have about living here away from the city centre? Yes, 'mean, modern and pretentious'. That sounds good. Let me get that down.

In real life, without a label pinned to the lapel, it's not always easy to read such people, but language has a habit of betraying a person even as they speak and of doubling back on itself to reveal all, for 'pretentious' is indeed an apt word also to apply to Mr Duffy. In today's kind of parlance, we might say he is a tragedy waiting to happen, but, as sometimes happens in life, he is the occasion for someone else's tragedy. We never get to see Mr Duffy walking round the city; he pops up in various points but he is not given to traversing the city, and he lives in Chapelizod, some 4 miles or so from the city centre. This is another way Joyce has of showing how removed he is from the world, for, except at a concert, Mr Duffy rarely bumps into people. Unlike Leopold Bloom, the cultured Mr Duffy is a 'citizen' who fails to connect with his city.

It's not her drinking, then, that leads to Mrs Sinico's death, but something in her troubled relationships with men which leads her to throw herself under a train. The clinical report of the coroner's inquest in the newspaper is designed to maximise the sense of impersonality: 'The evidence showed that the deceased lady, while attempting to cross the line, was knocked down by the engine of the ten o'clock slow train from Kingstown, thereby sustaining injuries of the head and right side which led to her death' (*D* 113). A slow train, but it was a quick end for Mrs Sinico, who endured a slow death over years of failed relationships with her husband and then Mr Duffy. The extinguishing of hope for the 43-year-old mother. In one sense it's a story about a suicide, but it's also about something else. We read

Mrs Sinico, her daughter and Mr Duffy in a pencil sketch by Charles Bardet; from *Gens de Dublin* (1941), a French translation. There's almost nothing in the story about Mrs Sinico's daughter, and yet sometimes a sketch artist can capture something about a story by coming at it from a different perspective. The story exploits how people are locked inside their own heads. Mrs Sinico's headgear tells its own story, as does Mr Duffy's raised hat and almost featureless face. They could be promenading in the Tuileries in Paris in the 1890s. I must confess it's not really my idea of the story.

the newspaper report through the eyes of Mr Duffy and when he puts down the paper we continue reading: 'Mr. Duffy raised his eyes from the paper and gazed out of his window on the cheerless evening landscape'. The denial of responsibility is beautifully rendered by Joyce, whereby Mr Duffy, the would-be intellectual or writer, assumes that the unpunctuated 'cheerless evening landscape' is somewhere out there and that he has no part in it. Cheerless, something one reads in the evening newspaper, a sad case. Put down the paper and gaze out the window. If we hadn't already guessed it, we might well conclude at this point that it is Mr Duffy, not Mrs Sinico, who is the painful case. He attends classical concerts in Earlsfort Terrace, but you could never imagine him in an audience at a Bob Dylan concert and listening to the words 'May you stay forever young'.

'A Painful Case', based on a deputy coroner's report, is one of those fabulous stories where the private and the public worlds collide with such dramatic effect. Mrs Sinico's death was so public, yet her motivation was so private. In one respect, Mrs Sinico doesn't want the world to know of her

The DART train. DART: Dublin Area Rapid Transport. Photograph by David Pierce. An example of Irish plagiarism, for what is DART but BART, the Bay Area Rapid Transport round the Bay Area in California. East, west. New, second-hand. The train system is aspirational: rapid, no longer slow, steaming along the same tracks as in Joyce's day but now 'steamless'. The train in this photograph is approaching Sandymount Station from Sydney Parade, where Mrs Sinico was killed, and it's on its way round the picturesque Dublin Bay from Bray to Howth. Keep behind the line we're told. No Exit.

suffering; in another respect, she does. That is an example of real anguish. As is more often the way, the newspaper report misses the real story. It's merely a painful case, with which Mr Duffy can concur, for it is nothing to do with him. After the suicide, the track is cleared, reopened and the world goes on as if nothing has happened. The coroner's court has another case to deal with, the newspaper another story to report. But this is where Joyce picks up the pieces, as it were, for 'A Painful Case' is another such story, this time about the story behind a story reported in the newspaper. An interruption in the circulation of the transport system, of coroner's courts, of newspaper reports, of life itself. And it is another *Dubliners* story where the woman's viewpoint is upheld.

Why would a student assume it's essentially a story about the effects of alcohol? That worries me more than anything – a failure at a basic level to grasp what Joyce is getting at. Thinking of trains, we should look out for the points along the tracks of a Joyce story. Without risking simply paraphrasing what he was doing – paraphrasing was a no-no for Modernists – I don't believe he could have signalled more clearly than he does when the reader is traversing such points. Take note of the points as you cross them. They are not all hidden or difficult to perceive. Indeed, some of them are designed to create confidence in the reading experience. When the doctor who examined Mrs Sinico concludes that death was 'probably due to shock and sudden failure of the heart's action', we should concur. Heart failure. The doctor is referring to the physical body, but the reader knows more than the medic. Failures in relationships can lead people to take to drink and some to commit suicide. There's nothing exceptional about that. What is exceptional is Joyce's maturity when he composed this story, for in July 1905 he was all of 23. What an astonishing achievement.

Detail of map of Trieste, 1900.

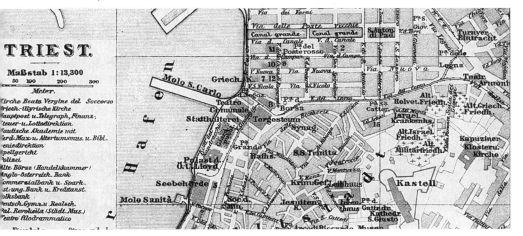

A postcard of via Donota in Trieste, posted in 1910. This street leads up from the centre of town to the cathedral of San Giusto. It is close to via S. Nicolò where the Joyce family were living when 'A Painful Case' was composed. After spending hours devoted to creating Dublin situations and characters, what must Joyce have thought on exiting his flat to encounter such lively street scenes? Long-skirted Oriental women carrying trays on their heads, children standing around with hands in their pockets like little old men, a man on the right, his hat pushed back, with what looks like a bucket of white paint and a piece of wood, the tools of his trade. The attention of everyone in the photograph, including people from upstairs windows, seems focused either on the camera or on something that has just happened. Perhaps the woman under the Pistoria sign has just said something to the man with his hands in his pockets in the centre of the street, possibly an arresting put-down in Triestine dialect. Recording reality. This, too, is what Joyce was doing, a thousand miles away from the scenes of his youth. *Giacomo Joyce* is the only text which features a non-Irish setting throughout, and yet the scene in this photograph reminds us that life was going on much the same in the Austro-Hungarian port city as in his own native city. Continental city life appealed to Joyce, and it formed the backdrop to his own life as a writer. Sitting in cafés, people watching, sipping something. An escape from the isolation of composition and contact with home.

Another student comes at all this from a different angle and in the process enters a more nuanced response:

Whereas many other writers may have wanted to add tantalising facets to their stories to intrigue the reader, Joyce presents a stark, real perspective of his home town. One may think that in doing this Joyce has surrendered his imagination to a bleak portrayal of everyday life. But if this were so why is Joyce hailed as one of the greatest writers of all time and his stories as 'brilliant'? He may be relaying normal life but it is what is not said and done that provides intrigue for the reader. The dark undercurrents that are not overtly referred to are common among family, friends and indeed everyday life, so why not encompass these realities into fiction? What is the man's motivation for speaking to the boys in 'An Encounter'? Why does Mr Duffy stop seeing Mrs Sinico in 'A Painful Case'?

The word that seems to propel this student forward is 'intrigue', the 'not said'. Intrigue tracks back to Aristotle and his formulation of the 'desire to know' as marking a characteristic of human beings. 'All men by nature desire to know', as he puts it at the beginning of his *Metaphysics*. With intrigue you can go a long way in reading the Aristotelian Joyce. The converse is equally true: if you are never intrigued by Joyce's writing, then you won't get very far. To this end, I sometimes ask my students to focus on something intriguing about a story and share their findings with the group. The 'shaping imagination' to which Coleridge called attention can then be seen as operating also in the critical response. Indeed, a critical imagination is often necessary in shaping our reading of Joyce. This student is intrigued not only by what takes place in particular stories but also by the whole concept of paralysis. I agree – there must be more to these stories than simply the portrayal of bleakness.

Another student latches on to the misery of *Dubliners* and offers a comparison with the mood of Beckett's plays:

> Although we are never truly allowed to feel thoroughly miserable for Joyce or Beckett's characters – Joyce's economic measure in his descriptions or the sheer absurdity and often slapstick comedy in Beckett put paid to this – we still notice their effect. Rather, we notice these things more simply because we are not bogged down in emotional narrative. We begin to realise the far-reaching effects of an unfulfilled and wasted life and relate this to our own existence.

Some students I taught, perhaps most, could only get into a story through identifying with the characters. It's as if the purpose of reading literature is to encounter individuals who share their own experience of life. Equally, anything that smacks of something depressing is put down. 'I went through that phase when I was 14,' one student candidly let slip to her neighbour, 'and I don't want to go through it again.' A little bit of misery can be accepted, especially if the reader isn't 'bogged down in emotional narrative'. 'The Boarding House', a wink-wink, nudge-nudge sort of story, is something you might come across in the contemporary columns of *Tit-Bits*, or at least its title and subject matter would suggest as much. But almost at once we are taken up into its language and into the character who is certain to dominate the proceedings. It opens thus: 'Mrs Mooney was a butcher's daughter'. The sentence is in one sense unfinished, and we wait for some time but we sense that the corollary will come, and we are not disappointed: 'She dealt with moral problems as a cleaver deals with meat'. Cleavers slice, cut, chop, cleave. The point is made, and the points over the tracks can be felt. Trifling with her daughter's affection is not to be tolerated. Or rather it is to be tolerated (and encouraged), but, if you do trifle or – God forbid – dip your wick on Hardwicke Street, beware, for you might be trapped into marriage. It's part of the wider theme on display in this story of 'catching'. Mrs Mooney *catches* 'short twelve' Mass, but there's no cut and run for Mr Doran, whether in the boarding house or at work. He's been had and catches it. Our sympathies, then, are engaged, but, interestingly, the question puts itself: who or what are we sympathising with here?

This leads me to the larger issue of consumption. 'Consuming' Joyce and Beckett in a consumer culture is always going to prove difficult. The writers in question have some disturbing news; a consumer culture is resolutely upbeat. Downbeat, upbeat. Pessimistic, optimistic. Take it or leave it, could be the answer. The conveyor belt is running. I don't press the point. The sympathetic imagination works differently for me. I try and notice everything that is going on in a story. In that sense the story resembles a stage production. I notice the lights, the stage props, the entrances, the colour, the music if there is any. Each of the characters, how they make their entrances and their exits. How the theme of the play is introduced. Who or what carries significance. The dialogue, or, in the case of *Dubliners*, the narrative voice, the use of free indirect speech, the silences, the unfinished sentences. When teaching Beckett I would show the class part of a production and get them to relish the words. 'Spool', hear how that word from *Krapp's Last Tape* is pronounced by Patrick Magee or Jack MacGowran. It would get me going, and I would become excited. I would keep pronouncing the word out loud with different effects into the four corners of the classroom. That long vowel sound deserves plenty of resonance. Coin it. Give it some welly. Detach the word from its meaning, and then reinsert it back into a world of meaning and begin talking about repetition in modern life.

Writing and politics

Another student is intrigued by something else:

> While Joyce was Irish he did not identify himself as suffering from paralysis. He had gone away from it both spiritually and geographically. However, Joyce liked Ireland enough to want to do something about the situation as he saw it – hence his writing.

Even if it is not fully formed, I think this is a worthwhile comment. In exile, Joyce developed the art of close observation, but it was from a distance. This is another way of saying that from the Austro-Hungarian port of Trieste on the Adriatic Coast, Joyce was observing his native city as if he was living there. Ironically, distance gave him intensity and single-mindedness. As already mentioned, in a letter to the publisher Grant Richards in May 1906, he declared, 'My intention was to write a chapter of the moral history of my country and I chose Dublin for the scene because that city seemed to be the centre of paralysis' (*Letters II*, 134). Joyce is intent on castigating what he sees as the whole life of a small country: culture, ideology, sexual morality, religion, politics. However, with the possible exception of 'Grace' and its damning critique of Irish Catholicism, or the running commentary throughout the stories on the colonial encounter between Britain and Ireland, what exactly is the moral history of a country? Not the social history or cultural history or intellectual history or Church history, all of which are understandable and traceable, but moral history.

I've often puzzled over that phrase and how it might relate to a political history, to, say, Thatcherism and Reaganism in the 1980s, or to the bleak Bush years after 2000, or to the cash-for-honours scandal that overshadowed the last months of Tony Blair's premiership. Did Joyce have any inkling that the Irish would take to money-making with such relish in the 1990s or that Irish public life would become disfigured by the widespread corruption of its leading politicians? Maybe, but, as the persistently self-seeking and materialistic contents of his letters suggest, Joyce would have liked to have joined the party himself. He certainly understood the idea of betrayal, and, with the fall of Parnell in mind, perhaps it was this that energised him most. In 1900 he wouldn't have been alone in seeing paralysis and hypocrisy all around him in Dublin. He would surely have watched with interest a campaign for honesty in public life, and perhaps he genuinely felt he was contributing to 'the moral history of my country'. But I doubt if Brecht or Gramsci, say, or those who confronted directly the rise of fascism in the 1920s and 1930s would have understood that phrase, and it does seem in retrospect somewhat precious. On the other hand, when you think of the link between the Thatcherism of the 1980s and early 1990s and the New Labour project which followed, when you think of that chapter in the moral history of a country, perhaps the term has some meaning. The 'managerialisation' of all sectors of the culture, the dispiriting loss of a shared language, especially in higher education and the public sector, the sense of betrayal and the wholesale transvaluation of values were felt by many at the time. Perhaps, Joyce was on to something.

Doubtless, 'moral history' and 'chapter' and 'my country' sounded impressive to the Edwardian young man, and the phrase was presumably designed to influence a potential publisher who might be wavering about the merits of the manuscript he had in his hands. But I'm slightly sceptical as to how much of this really stacks up. It would be difficult to read the ending of 'The Dead', which is so intensely personal, as part of 'the moral history of my country'. Indeed, that story was composed after Joyce's letter to Grant Richards. Joyce certainly identified with his city and his country, and this continued sentimentally to the end of his life. On the occasion of his fifty-sixth birthday in 1938, for example, Maria Jolas hosted a party and decorated her table with a plaster model of Dublin, through which, Peggy Guggenheim recalls, ran 'a green ribbon representing Joyce's beloved Liffey' (Guggenheim, 1980, 168). How much he really wanted to change his country remains an open question. Writing against the grain is what he did best; defiance gave birth to *Dubliners*. 'A gorgeous blasphemer' is how he is recalled by one of his fellow-pupils at Clongowes Wood in Norah Hoult's historical novel *Coming From The Fair* (1937). However, without any real commitment to common causes, such a disposition and such an attitude can simply feed off the thing it is attacking, with the system of inequality and hypocrisy and the culture of money-grubbing remaining effectively untouched. I suppose this is another way of saying James Joyce is not James Connolly, the revolutionary socialist, or Jim Larkin, the Irish labour leader.

Or to put this yet another way, *Dubliners* constitutes Joyce's judgement on Ireland in the wake of Parnell. Yeats thought the fall of Parnell in 1890 presented Ireland with an opportunity. 'Mourn—and Then Onward!' is the title of a poem he wrote at the time of Parnell's death for *United Ireland*. United and onward. But Joyce's head was elsewhere, and in some respects the fact that he wasn't looking forward helped with his writing. The opening sentence of 'Ivy Day in the Committee Room' provides an unforgettable image of a paralysed politics: 'Old Jack raked the cinders together with a piece of cardboard and spread them judiciously over the whitening dome of coals' (D 118). No longer Committee Room 15 of the House of Commons at Westminster, where Parnell's colleagues in the Irish Parliamentary Party turned against him in December 1890, but the seedy committee room of an impoverished political party in Dublin ten years or so later. The word that stands out in this opening sentence is 'judiciously'. A judicious comment is one that weighs up a situation and shows insight into all its many sides. A judgement. We are impressed with someone capable of acting judiciously. The Houyhnhnms in *Gulliver's Travels* act judiciously. Raking cinders is not something that needs to be done judiciously, and yet someone who performs it judiciously can convey better than anyone else the paralysed nature of politics after Parnell.

Joyce took his politics essentially from his father. Indeed, Yeats (mistakenly) thought Joyce was the son of a Parnellite organiser. At the end of the Christmas dinner scene in *A Portrait of the Artist as a Young Man*, Simon Dedalus's friend Mr Casey sobs rather pathetically 'My dead king' in reference to Parnell, and Simon's eyes fill up with tears. In 'Ivy Day in the Committee Room', the king is still dead, the fire has gone, and all that is left on 'Ivy Day', the anniversary of his death in October 1891, is to rake among the ashes for warmth or signs of life. The fall of Parnell was a powerful myth which held sway for a generation or more. In Joyce's case it was compelling, not least because over everything there could now be draped an image of betrayal. In a sense it stopped further thinking about history and politics. But, as ever, things unfreeze, and Joyce was not terribly good at unfreezing his view of things. He always sought an issue with Ireland. By contrast, in the years when most of the stories of *Dubliners* were being composed, Yeats was detecting that there might be no place for him in the new Ireland that was then beginning to emerge in the thinking of advanced nationalists.

Series

In a letter to Grant Richards in October 1905, Joyce suggests that 'the expression "Dubliner" seems to me to have some meaning and I doubt whether the same can be said for such words as "Londoner" or "Parisian" both of which have been used by writers as titles' (*Letters II*, 122). He's

Tom Merry's vicious political cartoon 'The Home Rule Coach and its Destination' from *St Stephen's Review*, 12 March 1887. Parnell and Tim Healy edge close to the sheer drop of the Devil's Dyke, driven on by Gladstone and the Home Rule coach. According to the Joyce family, it was Healy who was to betray Parnell three years later by turning on him. Joyce's lost poem 'Et, Tu Healy', written when he was only nine, commemorates this moment. But in this cartoon he is still pulling with Parnell.

wrong of course about Londoner and Parisian, for these terms have as much meaning as Dubliner. However, as an aspiring author, writing from the other side of the Alps, the claim was worth floating with a potential publisher in London. At that stage Joyce had written 12 stories, a number he surmised constituted the full complement. That Dublin is at the centre of his collection cannot be questioned. The city breathes through its pages. But in stressing the unity of the collection, perhaps without fully realising it, Joyce invites a certain doubt about the nature of his undertaking.

4 Ely Place, Dublin. Photograph by David Pierce. Home to George Moore from 1901 until 1911. It's not often noticed but Moore is a key figure immediately behind Joyce. At first glance the number of parallels between their work suggests a significant debt on Joyce's part to Moore. Even in the very titles to their works there are parallels: *Confessions of a Young Man* (1888) and *A Portrait of the Artist as a Young Man*. Two stories from Moore's collection of short stories *The Untilled Field* (1903) are entitled 'In the Clay' and 'The Exile', the latter being a story about emigration which concludes the volume. Some stories are remarkably cognate, as for example 'The Clerk's Quest' and 'A Painful Case', where a contrast is drawn between the humdrum existence of white-collar workers and the buried life of their emotions, between working in Dublin and living on the outskirts, between the body and the mind. In Joyce's story, Mrs Sinico suffers the fate of the clerk in Moore's story. 'In the Clay' deals with the relationship in Ireland between art and life, focusing on an Irish sculptor. Joyce's attention is restricted to the model, but reading *Dubliners* in the light of *The Untilled Field* can cast a fresh light on Joyce's themes and on what he was attempting in his collection.

Essentially, the problem with a series of portraits is twofold. First, unless it comes under some unifying heading, the collection can lack coherence or direction. *The Untilled Field* (1903), the title George Moore chose for his collection of Irish stories, offers an immediate comprehensive umbrella, at once striking and suggestive. The title recalls a period of heightened agitation in English history as well as Shelley's poem 'England in 1819', one line of which reads 'A people starved and stabbed in the untilled field'. By comparison, *Dubliners* as a title lacks not so much coherence as cutting edge. It carries inside it a phrase like 'scenes of Dublin life' and a reminder of a nineteenth-century fictional world of, say, Balzac, Trollope and George Eliot, with their scenes of provincial and clerical life. On its own, *Dubliners* (just) manages to separate itself from 'Scenes of Dublin Life'. Second, if everything can contribute, if all the stories come under the heading 'Gente di Dublino', people of Dublin as the Italian translation has it, there is potentially no end to the number of stories that might be included. Where do you stop, therefore? There's not even a definite article to limit matters; it's not *The Dubliners* but *Dubliners*. As ever, events overtook Joyce. In October 1905 he thought he had stopped, but then another three dropped on to the table in front of him.

One author Grant Richards 'discovered', and whom he published in the same year as *Dubliners*, was Robert Tressell (1870–1911), author of the popular working-class novel *The Ragged Trousered Philanthropists*. Tressell's novel, which also took some time to complete, is centred on a group of housepainters in 'Mugsborough' (Tressell's name for the south coast town of Hastings). When presented with the manuscript by Tressell's daughter after his death, Richards knew that Tressell was a pseudonym (and an appropriate pseudonym for a decorator), but what he possibly didn't know was that the author was a Dubliner and that his real name was Robert Noonan. Joyce and Noonan, subversive Dubliners – that's a pairing Richards might have made something of, especially when we recall that the dust-jacket of *Dubliners* contained a series of puffs for *The Ragged Trousered Philanthropists*. Indeed, what Richards wrote about that novel could well be applied to Joyce's collection of stories: 'The book was damnably subversive, but it was extraordinarily real, and rather than let it go I was quite willing to drop a few score of pounds on it' (Richards, 1934, 280).

Interestingly, in a subsequent letter to Richards in May 1906, Joyce in part gets round the serial problem by grouping the stories under four headings: 'childhood, adolescence, maturity and public life' (*Letters II*, 134). By that stage, two more stories had been added, 'Two Gallants' and 'A Little Cloud', stories which in turn added weight to the adolescence and maturity sections. The tussle between series and what we might call latent, organic

(left) 7 Carlton Street, Regent Street, London. From a sepia painting by Hester Frood.

(right) Grant Richards. Pencil drawing by Henry Lamb, reproduced in Grant Richards, *Author Hunting: By an Old Literary Sportsman* (1934). In this engaging book of 'memories of years spent mainly in publishing 1897–1925', there is not a single mention by Richards of Joyce, and yet he published both *Dubliners* and *Exiles* in 1914 and 1918. Indeed, *Dubliners* was arguably Richards's baby, even if it took nine years to materialise. With 278 pages, sized 7½ × 5 inches, reddish cloth, lettered in gilt, new endpapers, custom cloth clamshell, priced at three shillings and sixpence, it had a first print run of 1,250 copies, 746 copies of which were bound by Richards, the other 504 being sent to the USA for the American issue. In his memoirs, Richards spends not a little time discussing books that didn't make money for him, but, today, a single copy of a first edition of *Dubliners* will set you back over £4,000. Richards's big success story was A.E. Housman's *A Shropshire Lad*, published by him in 1898. That edition is scarce but copies can still be obtained for around £400. The best advice for those with a pecuniary instinct is: stick around long enough and see the world come back to you. Bibliophiles and others, on the other hand, will appreciate the work of independent publishers like Richards in the period that saw the birth of Modernism.

form, however, continued. I don't think this is ever quite resolved by Joyce. Are the stories simply a series, like days of the week, or are they like an individual maturing through time? Students enjoy slotting the stories into a larger structure and I help them to do this. They agree with Joyce: some men do act like adolescents and never grow up. Maturity has its own pitfalls, both literal and metaphoric. Public life is more problematic as a category, but on reflection one can see what Joyce is getting at. Politics, music, the Church, and so on. If he had identified the boys in the first three stories as the same boy who later appears in 'The Dead' as Gabriel Conroy, Joyce could have made more of the idea of organic form. But he was at that stage still waiting to see where the series took him. Equally, he carried around inside him pent-up emotions against Dubliners who had crossed him, and such feelings could be best discharged through writing a series rather than a carefully thought-out sequence as a whole.

What the idea of a series did yield in practical terms was the character of Leopold Bloom. When Joyce was in Rome in 1906 he gave serious thought to another story for *Dubliners*, one that would focus on a married man named Alfred Hunter whose wife was reported to be unfaithful. It was to be called 'Ulysses' but, as he told his brother in February 1907, it 'never got any forrader than the title' (*Letters II*, 209). In the same letter, Joyce also suggested he had a number of other titles for stories, including 'The Last Supper', 'The Dead', 'The Street', 'Vengeance' and 'At Bay', all of which he could write 'if circumstances were favourable'. Mr Duffy, Mr Kernan, Mr Hunter, you can perhaps discern how such a series might shape up both as single stories and also as part of a larger structure grouped under a heading such as 'modern marriage'. The germ of *Ulysses* begins, then, in Rome as a story for a collection of short stories he had been working on for three years in Dublin, Pola and Trieste. The various rejections and delays he had received from publishers proved in the end of real value to world literature, for they allowed Joyce time to write more stories and to stumble on an idea that 15 years later issued in the novel that now sells a huge number of copies every year round the world. With difficulty, the classics and much else had returned in triumph.

All the living and the dead

'The Dead' is such a morbid title for such a fabulous story. In that sense it's like Tolstoy's *The Death of Ivan Illych* (1886), another fabulous story about the interpenetration of life and death. I wonder if 'The Dead' was an alternative to 'The Last Supper', or perhaps the two stories were always separate in Joyce's mind. 'The Dead' is certainly more appropriate for the story we have than 'The Last Supper'. The Christmas-time setting is a nice touch and would have provided Joyce with a more appealing title. *Tit-Bits*, the weekly that formed part of the general education and culture for the Joyce household, always ran a Christmas story for their Christmas number, which was sometimes won by Philip Beaufoy, the writer who, as we will see in Chapter 9, turns up in the pages of *Ulysses*. It's true the set-piece is the annual supper thrown at Christmas time by the Morkan sisters at their upstairs rented accommodation on Usher's Island, but the heart of the story lies buried elsewhere. The ritual of 'The Dead' takes up into it, therefore, not only the Christmas story but also the Easter story and, with that, all the various myths, classical and pagan, Catholic and Irish, about the dead and their place among the living.

'The Dead' is a marvellously ambitious story, spacious, tense, and, in spite of its title, thoroughly satisfying. John Huston, who was in the last months of his life, didn't need to travel to Ireland to make his film of 'The Dead'. With the rushes in his studio in California, the film made itself, for this story has a simplicity that needs only the softest of hands to reveal. Indeed, as soon as he put pen to paper, Joyce seemed to come upon something with a much stronger resonance, so much so that we tend to forget it belongs to a series of stories and stands there in the glare of its own publicity, 20,000 words all contributing to the single title, 'The Dead'. It was indeed a story that Joyce thought embodied a more generous portrait of his native country than was the case with the other stories.

The structure of 'The Dead' resembles a triptych. Open up one panel on the left and there is anticipation, rush, arrival. In the central panel there is the main event, a supper party and a dance. Bustle and talk and eating at life's feast. In the panel on the right, there is departure, the gathering gloom, the dark that awaits us all, and the snow falling over all the living and the dead. Birth, life and death. A familiar triptych which every funeral worth its salt draws attention to. 'They lived und laughed ant loved end left' as Joyce memorably observes in *Finnegans Wake* (FW 18:20–1), the 'and' dissolved into und, ant, end. No more ands. An end to and. Hello comma goodbye. Joyce never saw Hieronymus Bosch's *Garden of Delights* (1500) at the Prado in Madrid, but if he had he might have used some of its grotesque motifs. At regular intervals throughout the day, the attendants in the Prado would unfasten the hinges on the globe to reveal all the panels in turn. It

The first thing to notice about a map showing Usher's Island is that Usher's Island is not today an island. It's a continuation of the various quays that run along the Liffey on the south side. And 'Usher' is not the usher one finds at church or at a funeral but is named after the Ussher family, whose fame today rests on James Ussher (1581–1656), who was Archbishop of Armagh and who donated his impressive collection of books to the library of his alma mater, Trinity College Dublin.

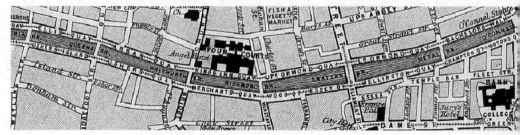

Entrance hall and stairwell of the house on Usher's Island. Photograph by David Pierce. A glassy perspective. It's a house that invites you upstairs, but to what? Only to return downstairs. A temporary respite from the cold outside.

was a dignified moment with no language but only gesture on display. And then came the utterly unexpected, with so much allegorical and symbolic detail and life flying at you after the simplicity of the globe on its creation. Everything is held in place by the three panels and a deathly silence: Eden, the garden of delights and hell.

'The Dead', too, is visually alive from start to finish, and everything contributes to its single-minded focus. But, unlike the Bosch painting, it works by sound and allusion. The reference to 'gasworks' is one of the few Bosch-like moments that is almost out of place in the story. The word is inserted matter-of-factly into the canvas to describe where Michael Furey worked, but with its potential association of a hell-like fuel and of how we describe garrulous people (such as Freddy Mallins and Gabriel Conroy's 'gasbag' attempt at oratory), it threatens to destroy the serious tone of the story. Fortunately, when we learn that Mr Browne 'has been laid on here like the gas', our minds, if they wander at all, do so only as far as recent municipal developments by Dublin Corporation in connecting up the city with heat and light and the 30 or so gas fitters listed in *Thom's Business Directory of Dublin and Suburbs for the Year 1906*. If we leave aside the meaning of 'gas' as empty talk, which I discuss below in connection with 'palaver', 'The Dead' is not strictly a story about gas, but it is a story that contains a gas (and electricity) motif. Historically, 'gas' came into the language in the seventeenth century when it was coined by a Dutch chemist to describe the occult principle contained in living bodies. By the late nineteenth century it had lost nearly all this occult meaning, but in a story about the dead and

The house on Usher's Island with the ghostly figure of Joyce at the window. When I took this photograph in October 2006, the house was being restored and someone had ingeniously inserted this image into an upstairs window. It is a ghostly house in more ways than one. Photograph by David Pierce.

the power struggle between the Archangels Michael and Gabriel, we can still feel some of these original associations. In this respect, 'gas' reminds us of the risks Joyce sometimes took in these stories, as if beyond a certain point in the layering process he was tempted to double-back on a story and reveal its composition or funny side.

The structure of 'The Dead' is relatively simple, but running through it are currents and surges designed to quicken the pulse. All the details contribute, but at the same time everything hangs on the final scene. It is not the story of creation to be found in triptychs by Bosch or his medieval predecessors but is a product of a more secular age, where everything is set out and weighed in the scales as it proceeds and where meaning accumulates until the end. The tension is increased because all the characters appear as in a canvas, with their gaze away from the viewer. We see and hear them in turn, and what we see – which they don't – is the ghostly presence that accompanies them. Living and dead. Not so much shadow selves as an extraordinary evocation of the present as past, the here as elsewhere, and back again. Tolstoy's interpenetration. The story, then, is too realistic to be an allegory. Indeed, the sense of realism is tangible, but at each stage the real is probed and subjected to another light, sometimes ghastly, sometimes ghostly. In his Irish melody 'Oh, Ye Dead', Tom Moore directly addresses the dead and wants to know 'Why leave you thus your graves' to haunt the living. Joyce's story gains by indirection, and we find ourselves saying without irony that it has a life of its own. At the same time, 'The Dead' also belongs to something wider that was happening in European culture, for in its intensity and sense of personal break-up, we might see it as belonging also with Ibsen's *When We Dead Awaken* (1899) and Chekhov's *The Seagull* (1895), dramas in which the lives of the central characters are sucked out of them from within.

'The Dead' begins with Lily, a caretaker's daughter on Usher's Island. She is the flower of death and related to Charon in classical mythology, the person responsible for ferrying the dead across the sacred river Styx to Hades, the underworld. Like an undertaker, a caretaker takes care of things, as old Jack also does in 'Ivy Day in the Committee Room'. Being an usher on an island surrounded by a river, she also steps out of (or into) the pages of a gothic novel. Literally, Lily is run off her feet, which, as most tutors remind us, means its opposite, for she is not literally but metaphorically run off her feet. If she were literally run off her feet she might be dead, which in another sense, as her name suggests, she is. A flower of death. But the author's indirect use of 'literally' and 'run off her feet' reminds us of the living texture of popular speech, speech that is full of clichés and misplaced words and phrases, of malapropisms as we saw with the 'The Sisters'. But, while such use shares something of the deathly motif, it isn't always to be castigated as dead language.

We might notice something else, for while 'literally' is invariably misused by people today, the word calls attention not so much to uneducated or sloppy speech as to the opposition between literal and figurative readings of this story, between the letters of the alphabet, as it were, and what you can do with them. Throughout this story, the literal activates the symbolic, the symbolic the literal. Indeed, the movement of the story is from the literal to the symbolic and back to the literal (and symbolic) again. At the beginning, the scene for the party is set for us with guests coming in from the cold, and at one level we learn to connect everything, including small details such as

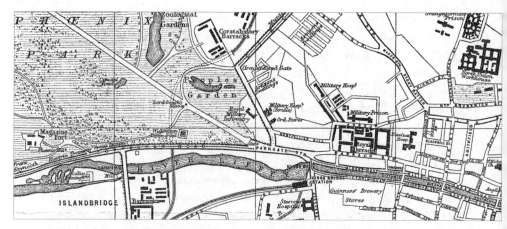

1900 map showing the Wellington Monument in the Phoenix Park.

the observation that the monks at Mount Melleray sleep in their own coffins, with the theme of death and protection against it. At the end, while Gretta falls asleep on the bed in the hotel after telling her husband about a romance with a boy who died for love of her, Gabriel, whose attention has been drawn to the 'ghastly light from the street lamp', finds himself looking outside the window and imagining snow falling all over Ireland. Literally snowing outside and metaphorically snowing inside. Another form of inter-penetration. If we're familiar with Moore's 'Oh, Ye Dead', we might discover an echo in the line: 'It is true – it is true – we are shadows cold and wan'. This

View towards the Wellington Monument in the Phoenix Park from outside the house on Usher's Island. Photograph by David Pierce.

The Bank of Ireland, opposite Trinity College, in the snow. An Edwardian hand-coloured postcard, processed as black and white.

is no longer an address to the dead, but a statement of fact and an acceptance by Gabriel of his own fate.

One of my students writes: 'In learning of his wife's past identity Gabriel sees that all of his memories and beliefs have been altered by the presence of something that is no longer part of the real world'. There is merit in drawing such a distinction, but to my mind 'The Dead' is a story that constantly involves the movement or passage between literal and figurative, between present and past. The 'real world' is shot through with the past. 'The Lass of Aughrim' is, therefore, present for Gretta in a way she hadn't realised until that evening. Like the lass in the song, her babe, too, in the guise of Michael, is now dead, and she holds him metaphorically in her arms to present to the world. The dead have this habit of constantly tripping us up. Just when we thought we had dealt with that person, got it behind us, that death, that relationship, that affair, gosh it all comes flooding back. Not dreaming back in the Yeatsian, occult sense but flooding back. Helpless, not restless. To my mind, the relentless momentum of this story – and it is relentless, at least for Gabriel, though he doesn't recognise this – is towards the confinement of the literal conceived in symbolic terms. Gretta is overcome literally by the thought of her past lover, and Gabriel learns the truth of the heart, that he is not at the heart of his wife's affections.

Another student mistakenly observes: 'Gabriel's decision to go "westward" can be seen as the bringing of a new dawn and is symbolic of a move away from the paralysis of the city west to the vast openness of Ireland'. The issue of the west of Ireland in 'The Dead' is an important one, which I discuss in more detail in my *James Joyce's Ireland* (1992), but of all the characters in *Dubliners* Gabriel is perhaps the most paralysed because he thought he was most free. To return to the literal and the figurative, what impresses me is how the adverb that Lily misuses at the beginning of the story comes to serve as a suggestive description of what happens to both Gretta and Gabriel. Literally silent. One reduced to tears, the other to numbness. All passion spent. You can't get into language when you only have letters of the alphabet to play with and no way of making words. Literally, no way out.

There are other moments in 'The Dead' when the living history of a language is invoked, as when Lily rasps at Gabriel, 'The men that is now is only all palaver and what they can get out of you' (D 178). 'The Dead', we might agree, is another story where the female viewpoint tends to be upheld against the male. 'Palaver', a common word in everyday speech, seems to have entered English via the encounter in the eighteenth century between indigenous people in West Africa and Portuguese traders, where it meant talk or parley. But, inevitably we might say, through time, talk became mere talk, and in turn it crossed over into the underworld where it was used to describe someone with slick talk, the feature of a trickster or a conman. 'Palaver' is in this sense a *palavra* or *palabra*, a 'word' in Portuguese or Spanish that becomes 'just a word' in English. From its nautical to its underworld associations, 'only all palaver' is precisely right for a story about a person whose language and identity come under pressure and whose name contains the syllable 'con'. Conroy. King con. Is Gabriel only all palaver, too, we wonder, and once that thought is released we find it difficult to dislodge. Equally, in the encounter between native and coloniser, another aspect comes into view: when you're waiting to be ferried across the Styx, it matters not a jot what register or dialect or language you once used, or what social class you belonged to, or whether you are or are not a West Briton, or which gender you thought inferior or superior. Only all palaver, as Lily might say.

You almost never see people wearing galoshes these days, but, with the exception of places in Lancashire and elsewhere, where galoshes was often simply another word for pumps or plimsoles, they always seem to have had a certain exotic appeal. The only time I ever remember seeing anybody wearing them was when my distant relations, the Kilmartin sisters, arrived home in County Clare on holiday from working in the USA. Katherine and Lizzie had been away long enough to be considered 'Yanks', but they weren't really posh, more practical, and always beautifully turned out and generous to the core. They never married, and neither did their two brothers or one of their other two sisters, Mary Ann. Six of them – and there were I

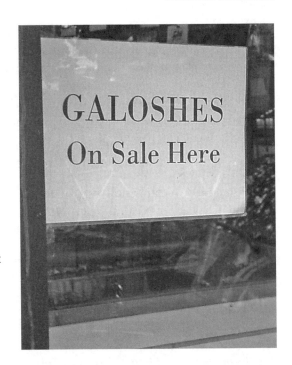

In October 2006 I walked past this notice on a window of a shoe-repair shop in the fashionable suburb of Sandymount and immediately thought of Gretta Conroy. Photograph by David Pierce.

think two more sisters who emigrated, but I never knew them – and only wedding bells for Maggie, who married our neighbour Pat Dunleavy, and not a single heir among them. In time, when they retired, the sisters took a house on the road from the seaside resort of Lahinch to the local market town of Ennistymon. By the sea or in town, they could walk to their hearts' content on the pavements with or without their galoshes. They had been in service to a shoe manufacturer in Boston, I think, and, when there, they must have decided that they needed protection from the country roads round St Bridget's Well and Caherbarna.

In a highly stratified society such as Ireland, which was, until recently, full of time-lags, Dubliners were at least a couple of generations ahead of the west. When Gretta arrives at the sisters' party, her rubber galoshes don't go unnoticed, as was the case with the see-through plastic galoshes of the Kilmartin sisters when they would turn up to our house dances in the 1950s. 'This is what everyone in Boston wears when the snow comes in winter', they would say. 'Outdoor shoes need protection'. That was an odd thought to most of my side of the family, slightly effete. And precious, given that nothing could be protected from the weather in that part of the world. After all, like her neighbours, my mother spent most her childhood barefoot and didn't own a new pair of shoes until she was into her teens. Joyce has caught something of all this in what we might call light-heartedly his 'footwear story', 'The Dead', but, as ever, he takes it a step further. When it comes to protection against the things in life that matter, galoshes, whether made of see-through plastic or guttapercha, won't quite do.

A final thought. There is something deathly about Joyce, always peering into coffins and the like. More than the tragic English novelist Malcolm Lowry, in part because it shines through everything he wrote, Joyce is the author above all others who has composed the modern equivalent of the Egyptian Book of the Dead. It's as if in search of immortality he thought he might discover it by writing about the topic. However, you will look in vain for the existential or metaphysical view of death in his work. As he languishes in prison in Shakespeare's *Measure for Measure*, Claudio is forced to confront the existential truth which is himself and an utterly unknown future:

> Ay, but to die, and go we know not where;
> To lie in cold obstruction and to rot;
> This sensible warm motion to become
> A kneaded clod; and the delighted spirit
> To bathe in fiery floods, or to reside
> In thrilling region of thick-ribbed ice;
> To be imprison'd in the viewless winds,
> And blown with restless violence round about
> The pendent world; or to be worse than worst
> Of those that lawless and incertain thought
> Imagine howling: 'tis too horrible!

At the end of 'The Dead', Gabriel faces up to something but it is not to my mind his existential self. Through the windows of his bedroom in the Gresham Hotel, he imagines the snow falling all over Ireland, but, even if such a thought does lie outside the confines of the story, we could not imagine him saying to himself 'Ay, but to die, and go we know not where'. That isn't the Joyce country. The philosophical Stephen Dedalus in *Ulysses* is arrested somewhere in space between the outer world and his interior consciousness, between solipsism and the 'ineluctable' or unavoidable nature of external reality, but in all his various acts of meditation and mediation he never seems to confront Claudio's void or indeed feel the pressure or the whirling after-effects of a phrase such as the 'pendent world'. The point's worth making here at the end of this discussion on *Dubliners*: Joyce's interest in the dead lies elsewhere, and, as in so much else, what we confront are the unfinished sentences and a certain reticence, perhaps defiance, in the face of the larger questions. As the references to paralysis, gnomon and simony suggest, no-one is better, swifter, or more slippery than Joyce at changing the subject.

Texts read us as much as we read them. As soon as students begin writing about Joyce – and we'll see more of this in Chapter 10 on *Ulysses* – what they reveal is an insight not only into their own background but also into the culture as a whole. In that moment of disturbance, of doubt and resolution in the face of tackling arguably the greatest writer in the modern period, all kinds of things tumble out. When as an awkward, fresh-faced graduate in 1970 I was employed by the British Council in Madrid to teach English as a foreign language, one of the comprehension activities I was fond of doing with my Spanish students was to read them wry little Sufi stories about Nasruddin. If, when we reached the end of a story, their faces lit up, it gave me confidence about their progress and my teaching, for they had been able to follow the story and, by implication, had understood what it was saying. The proverbial penny had dropped, and I was pleased as much for myself and my early struggles to become a teacher as for them. Even an unteachable Mexican priest, who would insist on greeting me every class with '¿Cómo va esta hermosa vida?' (how goes this beautiful life), managed to listen through to the end of the story, get the point, and still keep smiling. Inside the institutional setting of the classroom on Calle Almagro, in the centre of a polluted city on a central plain 2,000 feet above sea-level, with a legless amputee patiently guarding the Institute's entrance and exit and waiting for his own form of recompense from passers-by, it was real contact and quietly satisfying.

Getting in touch with students reading Joyce also requires a patient touch. At one level, the stories of *Dubliners* are like those of Nasruddin. Here is a narrative, there is the conclusion, you the reader make the connection. If the meaning in Joyce is denser, in part this is because of the complex ways narrative and discourse are folded into each other. Another reason is because Joyce's stories lack not so much definition as the clear outlines and logic of Nasruddin's stories. Constantly, there is the suspicion that something else is going on, that a part of Joyce's mind lies elsewhere, defying us to draw near.

Let me end these chapters on *Dubliners* with a comment by a student, this time comparing the 'moment' in Woolf's fiction with the idea of an epiphany in *Dubliners*: 'The whole of *Mrs Dalloway* is punctuated with "moments" and Joyce has epiphanies when people stop saying something and it's left to the reader to decide what's happened.' We're back with the unfinished sentences that we started with in 'The Sisters'. Intrigue, not said. The language of gesture and silence. And further back, defiance. It's a good place to pause and draw breath before we move on to *A Portrait of the Artist as a Young Man*.

CHAPTER 7

On *A Portrait of the Artist as a Young Man*

It might not be true for other readers, but for me the going gets distinctly tough as we cross over from *Dubliners* to *A Portrait*. In part this is to do with making sense of a novel that keeps shifting focus, a novel that at one and the same time invites and resists interpretation. In part it's to do with figuring out the relationship between the main protagonist Stephen Dedalus and the author James Joyce. In part it stems from our having to invoke often abstract ideas that the novel itself is exploring, such as child language acquisition and development, theological questions involving the soul and damnation, the theory of beauty as propounded by St Thomas Aquinas, and the idea of writing and exile from the self. I try not to shrink from confronting such difficulty here but, as before, I tend to rely on the concept of delay in the hope that this will intrigue or help the reader. I get delayed in the first part of this chapter on approach work to the novel, whether as context or initial exposition, and some of this is fairly abstract, but the movement of the chapter is towards seeing *A Portrait* as an extraordinary novel about language. Let me say at the outset, however, that Joyce, I think, had to write his way through this autobiographical phase before he could come upon a different kind of terrain, but if we want to understand Bloom in *Ulysses* we have first to understand Stephen in *A Portrait*.

Title, epigraph, orientation

Am I the only one to find several things odd about the title to *A Portrait of the Artist as a Young Man*? In the first place, most of the novel is not about a young man but about a boy and an adolescent. Only in the last chapter, when Stephen becomes a student at university, do we observe a young man emerging as such. The novel affords a retrospective account, but a retrospective account from much later in life, after the artist has become presumably an established figure. Somewhat impatiently, Dámoso Alonso in his Spanish translation throws his hands in the air and takes for his title *Retrato del*

Artista Adolescente (1978) (portrait of the adolescent artist). This is not right either, for Stephen is only for a short time an adolescent and, moreover, Alonso misses the effect of the qualification 'as a young man', a phrase which Joyce took care to insist on. And neither is the issue of the indefinite article in the title addressed.

The nine words in the title look like a tease or a hurdle to be negotiated and, I suspect, when first called upon to do so, there are few readers who manage to transcribe them accurately. Among the essays of any cohort of students I have taught, there is the usual crop of 'The Portrait of an Artist as a Young Man', 'The Portrait of the Artist as the Young Man', 'A Portrait of an Artist as a Young Man', 'A Portrait of an Artist as the Young Man', and 'Portrait of the Artist as a Young Man'. As if blindfolded, most of us regularly find ourselves tripping up. Is it an indefinite or a definite article I'm looking for, and is it that important if I get it confused? *Dubliners* is less problematic in this respect, being subject to fewer pitfalls in English, just the usual one when students add a definite article to make 'The Dubliners', the group associated with the modern folksong revival in the 1960s.

'Artist', too, in this context, shouldn't be overlooked. Not 'writer' but the more general term 'artist'. In Dublin, the word sometimes had or has an idiomatic or slang meaning, an 'artist' being a 'character'. According to Oliver St John Gogarty in a passage about Joyce in his autobiography *As I Was Going Down Sackville Street* (1937), an 'artist' was a 'quaint fellow or a great cod: a pleasant and unhypocritical poseur, one who sacrifices his own dignity for his friends' diversion' (Gogarty, 1954, 299). This is the

The French translation by Ludmila Savitzky, whose family had made available a neighbouring flat in Paris for the Joyce family in the 1920s, avoided all the traps and all the wordiness of Joyce's English title when she called the book simply *Dedalus* (1924), adding as a subtitle in small print *Portrait de L'Artiste Jeune Par Lui-Même* (portrait of the young artist by himself). It was a title she tells us in this 1943 fifth edition that met with Joyce's approval. 'D'accord avec Joyce', as she takes care to note (Joyce/Savitzky, 1943, 12). She must have caught him at a busy time or on a good day, for a 'young artist' is not the same as 'artist as a young man'.

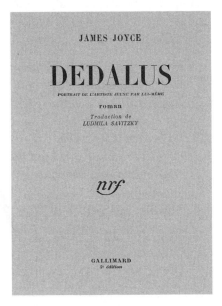

innocent artist, but there is the other 'artist' who is close to 'artful' as in Dickens's 'Artful Dodger', or to more ambivalent earlier uses. Consider, for example, how the word 'artful' is used in Jane Austen's *Sense and Sensibility* (1811). Marianne Dashwood is accused by Willoughby of being 'artful': 'You shall find me as stubborn as you can be artful' (Austen, 2004, 40). 'Artful' is a word, then, that shifts about, being close to deceptive, deceitful and wily, but it's also about being resourceful. Much depends on how you look at it, or rather, as here with Willoughby, much depends on who is making the observation or accusation. If the wily Joyce is using 'artist' in Gogarty's sense, then he is taking on board the charge against him, only to turn it against his former friends and enemies. A portrait of an artful poseur where the prose resembles a weapon in the cause of truth.

The title, then, contains more than its fair share of material to delay us. In typically perverse fashion, there is no mention of an artist's studio in Joyce's novel, no paint brush falls across the page, no discussion of any classical painting heard, and the only reference to a nude statue is when we learn from Lynch that he had once scrawled his name 'in pencil on the backside of the Venus of Praxiteles in the Museum' (*P* 205). In what must be a send-up of the convention or indeed of the reader's expectation, this life story of an artist begins with a father peering into a boy's face talking baby-talk. That, we might well deduce, is not where the artist begins. Or, conversely, on reflection, that is precisely where the artist begins.

To complicate matters, as soon as the title page is turned, we encounter an epigraph in Latin: 'Et ignotas animum dimittit in artes', and he lost himself in unknown arts, or in George Sandys's much-admired 1632 translation 'to Arts unknown he bends his wits'. The context needs a little glossing. The quotation is from Book 8 of Ovid's *Metamorphosis* where we read of Daedalus's resolve to escape from his imprisonment by Minos on the island of Crete:

> The Sea-impris'ned Daedalus, *meane-while*,
> Weary of Creet, *and of his long exile*;
> Toucht with his countries love, and place of birth;
> Thus said: Though Minos *bar both sea and earth*;
> Yet heaven is free. That course attempt I dare:
> Held he the world, he could not hold the ayre.
> This said; to Arts unknown he bends his wits
> And alters nature.
> (Ovidius, 1632, Book 8)

In *Finnegans Wake*, Joyce notices a peculiar characteristic of epigraphs: 'Epigraph: who guesses his title grabs his deeds' (*FW* 137:10). Often overlooked, the epigraph from Ovid is actually quite informative. Indeed, from its inception, the signs are that *A Portrait* is to be a novel of liberation and a discourse on freedom. Weary of exile, Stephen, too, embarks on a course to free himself from imprisonment. The epigraph we might then read as an announcement or a commentary in this case by a narrator from another text, and, like the recurring imagery of flight in the novel itself, it is inserted for a purpose and designed, therefore, not to be missed. That much is true. However, the novel is also linked from the outset, both in the title and in the epigraph, with art. 'Artes', arts, art, artist. So, while the epigraph to *A Portrait* consciously weaves together art and liberation, it's only on reading the novel to the end can we decide if such an aim is successful.

What arts, pursuits or skills does Stephen lose himself in, or apply himself to? Without knowing something of the context, this is a question to which most of us will have difficulty supplying an answer. The Ovidian context reminds us of the art of Daedalus in constructing wings to escape from the clutches of the Minotaur on the island of Crete, and we might also find ourselves conjuring with the occult arts in which the young Joyce expressed an interest. But for my part I also like to think of the 'artes', the arts, as to do with the philosophy of St Thomas Aquinas (1225–74) and the medieval schoolmen who made available the thinking of Aristotle for the Church. '[A]pplied Aquinas' (*P* 209) is how Stephen helpfully describes what he is doing. This is certainly the sense we receive from Stephen's discourse on aesthetics in Chapter 5 of the novel. With his deliberately provocative comments about eating cow dung and writing graffiti on statues in museums, Lynch draws attention to the isolation of Stephen in his attempt to apply Aquinas to the philosophy of art. The arts, that is, are unknown or secret to those who surround the adept Stephen, thus underlining the gulf between his embattled intellect and their ignorance.

Unknown they may be but, through 'the reality of experience' and through all its mazy twists and turns, the 'arts', now closer in meaning to 'pursuits', nevertheless proved efficacious in enabling the Daedalian figure to escape from his contemporaries and to fly by the nets thrown at him by his country. After all, heaven was free. As for the Latin word *animum* in the epigraph, I find myself associating this initially with *anima*, its feminine form in Church Latin, and translate it as 'soul'. From the Church's perspective, Stephen sins mortally with a prostitute and eventually loses his soul, aligning himself with Lucifer against his Creator in his famous declaration 'Non serviam' (I will not serve). But in leaving the Church, Stephen/Joyce has recourse to and is 'saved' by the classics, by a world that precedes the Church, and also by a philosophy of aesthetics which he elevates above belief and morality. 'Animum' then becomes the mind that saves the soul or 'animam'.

We can take this a stage further. *A Portrait* furnishes arguably the most intense inquiry into the relationship between the mind and the soul that we have in our literature, for, in flying by the nets of religion, Joyce, like Icarus, risked everything, not least, as his Jesuit masters would have never stopped reminding him, his eternal soul. The novel, then, constitutes a modern *Pilgrim's Progress*, except that now the progress is that of an exile, away from God towards something less clearly defined. It's not 'the life of things', as the more serene Wordsworth on his return to Tintern Abbey simply puts it, but 'the reality of experience', the searching phrase at the end of *A Portrait* which resonates against the whole novel even as it gestures towards an unknown future.

In *Reveries over Childhood and Youth* (1916), the first volume of Yeats's autobiography, we learn of the poet's interest in art and of his various meetings with his father's artistic friends, but there is none of this in *A Portrait*. When Stephen accompanies his father back to Cork, the only piece of 'art' he encounters is the word *Fœtus* carved into the desk in the anatomy theatre of Simon's alma mater, Queen's College (now University College Cork). Unless it's the skill in carving a diphthong in wood, which one suspects is an error on Joyce's part, for in schools I attended I never knew anyone that skilled in cursive script, there's little that is artistic or redemptive about that smutty inscription; its crudeness, especially when juxtaposed with the development of the child, one of the themes in the novel, stops us in our polite tracks. At this stage in the novel Stephen is not yet ready for flight, but he is arming himself with the necessary emotional detachment and defiance that will eventually lead him towards an Ignatian realisation that the world stands over against him. Later, when stirred, Stephen's natural inclination is refusal. He refuses to sign a peace petition and, the heretic that he is himself, he refuses to condemn Yeats's 'heretical' play *The Countess Cathleen* over the protagonist selling her soul to the Devil in return for bread for her people. In *Finnegans Wake*, Joyce imagines that he and Yeats represent a 'daintical pair of accomplasses' (*FW* 295:27). *A Portrait*, which was published in the same year as the Macmillan edition of Yeats's *Reveries*, reminds us that, before entering the major phase of their respective careers as writers, the towering Irish authors turned to quarry their own lives. But, while George Russell thought the person in Yeats's autobiography could have become a grocer as much as a poet, there is ample evidence in *A Portrait* to suggest a distinguished future for Stephen Dedalus.

I find myself circling round the title of *A Portrait* all the time looking for clues to the novel's meaning. I know this is obsessive, but we need to keep so much in play with Joyce – the context of his life as an exile, his relationship with other Irish writers and Yeats in particular, the tradition of writing

The National Library of Ireland on Kildare Street in Dublin. Photograph by David Pierce. It was here, near the Library entrance, that the bookish Stephen engages the worldly wise Lynch in conversation about aesthetics. In October 2006, when I took this photograph, the Library was mounting a major exhibition on Yeats. It was similar in design to the one devoted to Joyce's *Ulysses* in the centennial year of 2004, wide-ranging and evocative of all the stages of the poet's colourful life. The high-points were the documents and regalia from Yeats's membership of the Order of the Golden Dawn, as well as the large piece of lapis lazuli described in his poem of that name in the 1930s, which I reproduce in my *Yeats's Worlds* (1995) but which I had always assumed was a miniature and not the 2-feet-high object it in fact is. The memorable things for me in the Joyce exhibition were the recently acquired notebook in which we catch Joyce faithfully copying out sentences from St Thomas Aquinas, and the detailed recreation of a room where Joyce worked, complete with card files, coloured pencils and books on the shelves. With its delightfully secure Victorian plumbing down below and its fine domed reading room above, the Library as a building has changed little since its construction in the 1880s. Its reputation as a research library, however, has been enhanced by contact with Irish writers, some of whom, like the young Joyce, consulted material in its holdings a century and more ago. In common with his contemporaries, many of whom were to run Ireland after independence in the 1920s, Joyce as an undergraduate would wander down here after classes at Newman's university on Stephen's Green. Yeats was more familiar with the adjacent building, the Kildare Street Club, where he would lunch with members of the Anglo-Irish. Since his death in 1939, the Yeats family have made frequent bequests to the Library, so that it is now a leading place for Yeats research. Joyce's archives are more scattered; the *Finnegans Wake* manuscripts, for example, were donated by Nora after his death to the British Library in London. Whatever the case, across the religious divide and from very different social backgrounds, Joyce and Yeats, both of whom were bent on unknown arts, now enjoy in their own capital city the cultural capital they once aspired to a century ago.

autobiographies and in particular the line back to Wordsworth and the Romantics, his debt to the most important theologian in the Catholic Church, namely St Thomas Aquinas, the fall of Parnell mentioned in an earlier chapter, his Modernist sensibility, and so on. When we listen to debates in *A Portrait* about what constitutes the nature of art or the aesthetic experience, debates that I must admit I find a little tedious, I remind myself that this is a young man thinking through such questions, and if he comes at this question from a metaphysical angle then that's only to be expected of someone with his education and religious upbringing. At times, whether consciously or otherwise, 'making allowance' is what we all do when encountering a certain resistance in our reading.

To return to the title of *A Portrait*, 'artist' also recalls abstract debates in aesthetics, debates which from the classical era until the modern period subsumed the painter, sculptor, writer and composer in an homogeneous grouping concerned with το καλον (to kalon) or the beautiful. Whatever Lessing and Goethe had to say on such matters in the eighteenth century, the thirteenth-century Catholic theologian is the one who most mattered to Joyce. Somewhat pedantically, his fictional counterpart insists on explicating Aquinas's umbrella use of the Latin term *visa* in the phrase 'Pulcra sunt quae visa placent' (those things are beautiful which are pleasing to the eye). 'He uses the word *visa*, said Stephen, to cover esthetic apprehensions of all kinds, whether through sight or hearing or through any other avenue of apprehension' (*P* 207). Interestingly, Joyce is so committed to Aquinas that we never sense the tension between the Jesuits and the great Dominican, or between Aquinas and the nineteenth-century neo-scholastics. It's as if 'applied Aquinas' had a wider resonance to counter the Jesuit stress on morality with the lightness of the Angelic Doctor, for, as the Jesuit heretic George Tyrrell also perceived, 'Aquinas was essentially liberal-minded and sympathetic' (Petre 1912, II, 45).

What Stephen and his creator absorbed from scholastic philosophy was a belief in the superiority of stasis over kinesis, of stillness over movement. Pornography excites, but the aesthetic emotion stills. It's a distinction that clearly excites Stephen and perhaps Joyce, but, outside the confines of scholasticism – a system rooted in antecedents, prime movers and the issue of *potentia* or potency as opposed to its materialisation in action – I wonder if it adds very much to our understanding of aesthetics as a whole. It certainly lacks the force of Rupert Birkin's formulation in Lawrence's *Women in Love* (1920) when, in response to Gerald Crich's query whether or not the African carving in Halliday's flat of the nude woman in labour is art, he replies: 'It conveys a complete truth. It contains the whole truth of that state, whatever you feel about it' (Lawrence, 1982, 133). Aesthetics aside,

This stylish photograph of Joyce in his mid-thirties was sent to *The Egoist* magazine for a design for a woodcut. Looking east or west or wherever there was a market for his work, Joyce rests his hand on a thinking chin, conscious that not a single hair on his head is out of place, that his moustache has been well groomed, and that his pince-nez is secure. Pose, prose again. Largely because of Pound's influence, in February 1914 extracts from *A Portrait* began to appear in *The Egoist*, the magazine edited by the English anarchist Dora Marsden and the socialist Harriet Shaw Weaver, and they continued until September 1915. 'Egoist' was a good choice of title for the egoistical Joyce to shelter under, for, as his fictional persona Shem confesses in *Finnegans Wake*, he was 'self exiled in upon his ego' (*FW* 184:6–7). After all the years of heartache and frustration when nothing he composed had found its way to market, suddenly in 1914, the first *annus mirabilis* for Joyce, the world opened its doors, first to *Dubliners* and then to *A Portrait of the Artist as a Young Man*. He would never look back. Or, rather, he would, but his reputation was more or less secure. If Joyce had died in his mid-thirties, I suspect we would still be hailing him as one of the select group of writers who helped usher in the period of High Modernism in the 1920s.

what I find extraordinary is that Stephen uses the Church's 'Angelic Doctor' in freeing himself from the Church. The renegades among us, especially if we have English and Jewish blood in us, simply cut and ran or fell by the wayside, but then you have to remember that in a Catholic country rebellion works differently.

In attempting to explain the scholastic theory of art to a sceptical Lynch, Stephen points to the three elements that define an object: *integritas*, *consonantia*, and *claritas*. Presumably with a modern readership in mind,

Stephen/Joyce then feels obliged to translate Aquinas's dictum, according it extra significance by the use of italics: '*Three things are needed for beauty, wholeness, harmony, and radiance*' (P 212). Again, the title of *A Portrait* allows for all these chords of identity and difference, of fusion and separation, of belief and scepticism. *Integritas* carries within it its own sense of integrity, or 'wholeness' as Stephen translates it, but the French translation *intégralité* reminds us of language intervening in our construction of the idea of beauty. For *integritas* is not really *intégralité*; it is not really full or unabridged, but concerned with the integrity of an object. Stephen translates *integritas* as wholeness, but to my mind the Latin word belongs as much to integrity as wholeness. Significantly, integrity carries a moral association, an association Stephen presumably wants to keep separate from the aesthetic emotion. Inevitably, we can't help reflecting on the novel we are reading, for 'wholeness' is not a word that springs naturally to mind when rehearsing its course. Integrity, on the other hand, is another matter, as is Birkin's 'a complete truth'.

'Artist' also conjures up the late-nineteenth-century interest in the predicament of the artist and the role of the arts, the image of artists living in garrets, the era of Montmartre and Paris salons, and perhaps, with Mallarmé and Yeats in mind, the sacred book of the arts. In terms of its immediate literary setting, Joyce's title belongs with Henry James's novel *The Portrait of a Lady* (1881), George Moore's *Confessions of a Young Man* (1888), Oscar Wilde's *The Picture of Dorian Gray* (1891) and 'The Critic as Artist' in *Intentions* (1891), other prose essays such as Hubert Crackanthorpe's *Vignettes* (1896), and with the hundreds of books published in the 1890s with 'sketches' in the title and with the select number of books with 'artist' in the title. *A Portrait of the Artist as a Young Man*. When he deployed them together in a single title, Joyce knew what he was doing, for 'portrait' and 'artist' serve to remind us of a particular history, which in retrospect we might loosely define as the break-up of the aesthetic movement and the emergence of the modern movement in the arts. It's as if in setting out on its own path, Modernism in the guise of one of its earliest proponents was bidding farewell politely but decisively to its immediate past.

If I hadn't stressed it enough, 'A Portrait' is another phrase to delay us, for what the novel portrays is not 'a portrait' but a series of portraits. It's at this point that we begin to realise we are not so much dealing with a problem as being presented with an invitation or a challenge. 'A Portrait' lifts the novel into a wholly different kind of reading experience, and what I find compelling is the attempt to capture movement in movement or rather to capture movement as movement. Joyce's 'portrait' is constantly on the move, perversely kinetic, so that we never have the luxury of asserting that this moment above all others captures the subject. Each moment, each

A PORTRAIT OF THE ARTIST AS A YOUNG MAN

By James Joyce

❖❖❖

THE EGOIST LTD.,
OAKLEY HOUSE, BLOOMSBURY ST.,
LONDON, W.C.

Price 6/-

The Egoist Press dust-wrapper for the first edition of *A Portrait of the Artist as a Young Man*. *Dubliners* sold for three shillings and sixpence when first published in 1914 by Grant Richards. Six shillings suggests Joyce could command nearly twice as much for his subsequent novel, three years later. As for monetary equivalents at various times in Joyce's life, we can note that when he received a gift of £7 from his father on his departure for the continent in October 1904, this was worth, according to Roger Norburn (2004), £440 in today's money, while Harriet Shaw Weaver's gift of £5,000 in May 1919 was equivalent to £137, 522. Handsome and princely.

episode, may carry the provisional quality that inheres in the indefinite article, but it has to be appreciated for what it is at the time. Moreover, the experience – whether it is the baby tuckoo initiation passage, the incident with his glasses in school, the Christmas dinner scene, the retreat sermon, the altercation with the English Jesuit over the word 'tundish', Stephen's various conversations with Davin and Lynch on nationalism and aesthetics – the experience is first and foremost up-close. Expressed grammatically if less grandly, the novel is an exploration of the tension and difference between the indefinite and the definite article in English.

Hugh Kenner makes the valuable suggestion that *A Portrait of the Artist as a Young Man* is the first Cubist novel in the language (Kenner, 1976). Walk round a piece of sculpture by, say, Henry Moore and what we observe is a changing perspective, one portrait after another. Or, alternatively, if we took as our example Marcel Duchamp's painting *Nude Descending the Staircase* (1912), one minute we observe nothing but the cubes, shadows and shapes which compose the canvas, the next possibly the figure of a nude, but never the two together. Cubist isn't quite the right word to describe *A Portrait of the Artist as a Young Man*, but it does alert us to something peculiar about the novel – how talk of a single perspective won't quite do with what is happening in this novel. Turn the page, turn the thing round, and what do you see? Another person, or is it the same person?

Interestingly, one of the essays set at Belvedere College in 1897 for the end-of-year examination in English was an invitation to discuss Tennyson's claim in *In Memoriam* (1850) 'That men may rise on stepping-stones / Of their dead selves to higher things'. It would be fitting if Joyce in one of his exams at high school attempted this question, for *A Portrait* reminds us less of the unitary or integrated self and more of the sequential self. However, expressing it thus highlights an important aspect of the novel but little of the anguish and discontinuity involved. The movement in *A Portrait* is towards overcoming adversity, but always it is at the expense of something. So, 'sequential', which is an improvement on 'Cubist', is neat but still not a tight fit. Tennyson's lines remind us of Joyce's Victorian heritage, not least the call to rise to higher things, but, unlike Tennyson, Joyce adopts a stance which from the outset refuses to establish a bond of intimacy between reader and narrator or, indeed, between narrator and his subject. This goes hand in hand with something else in Joyce. If there is to be any accommodation with the world after the fall, it will be because of a pact or covenant between author and protagonist, between author and his fictional persona, between the artist and his past. We the reader, the fabulous voyager that is, might feel legitimately aggrieved, especially if we concluded that we had been confined to the sidelines, but there is something heroic on display in the novel and it is this that we can respond to or admire.

Joyce as hero. Taken in Zurich 1919.

Yeats wanted to call the first volume of his autobiography *Memory Harbour*, but another author Filson Young (1909) had got there before him. *Memory Harbour* was also the title his brother Jack B. Yeats chose for one of his paintings about the harbour at Rosses Point in the west of Ireland, a canvas dominated by the ship at anchor, the metal man directing the boats, and the blue-coated, bearded fisherman in the foreground. This lively scene, where Sligo's folk imagination met the modern world without embarrassment, meant so much to the Yeats boys growing up and so much to both of them in memory. Joyce, too, enjoys inhabiting his past, but in *A Portrait* he deliberately sets his face against the image of 'memory harbour', 'reveries', or indeed conventional introductions to autobiographies or fictionalised autobiographies along the lines of 'When I reflect on how my life began, I recall my father looking into my pram and singing me a nursery rhyme and calling me all kinds of baby names. I remember also wetting the bed and how first it was warm and then it went cold.'

Wordsworth, one of the great poets of memory, portrays his own life as a spiral and the recovery of oneness with the world. Joyce, also a great writer of memory, comes at this differently. Recovery of the self for Joyce follows in the tracks of the sequential self, but there is nothing smooth about the course of any of this. In editing Eliot's *The Waste Land*, Pound tended to crop the narrative bits, partly to emphasise the poem's fragmentary nature and partly to prevent a descent on the part of the reader into character analysis. Joyce's novel, which is a classic example of Modernist fiction from the middle period, has an excised quality about it especially noticeable in the transitions from one scene to another. On the second page, for example, the novel has only just got going, but the narrative shifts from Stephen as a very young child playing with a Protestant girl Eileen Vance to a playground scene at boarding school, a shift that is accomplished without more ado than a run of asterisks across the page in some editions. We might be tempted to conclude that such shifts lead to something fragmentary, but the narrative isn't so much interrupted as enforced and constituted by such procedures, and, what is more, as the portrait unfolds before our eyes, we get used to skipping over months and indeed years.

In this ever-resourceful, didactic novel, Joyce is also telling us something about the relationship between writing and experience. He knows his predecessors and how they wrote about loss, but he also knows some other things: first, that writing is more than simply a reflection of or on a prior experience; second, that writing is itself experience; and, third, that writing ironically affords an encounter with unknown arts, some of which he has already identified. In this, as in so much else, he was years ahead of Roland Barthes, for he seemed to have absorbed almost from the outset that, when it comes to writing, unlike what the books tell us, 'post' is often ahead of or built into 'pre'. Joyce's semi-autobiographical fiction is not simply, therefore, 'one damned thing after another' – a not unfamiliar lament by the biographer – but more like a sequence composed of episodes and breaks in transmission. That is, it is more like a series with repeated frames than a serial with reassuring continuity from one episode to the next.

Once upon a time

There's always, then, something happening when the curtains open on a Joyce text. At the same time, amid all the noise, a characteristic low note is struck: 'Look at how I'm orientating you the reader to my text'. The opening to *A Portrait* is no different, but it is an opening which for various reasons, some of which I touched on in Chapter 1, retains a certain resistance to translation:

> Once upon a time and a very good time it was there was a moocow coming down along the road and this moocow that was coming down along the road met a nicens little boy named baby tuckoo . . .

Even though there are equivalents in other languages, 'once upon a time' is peculiar to English. Joyce begins then with a formula announcing a children's fairy story, and for this reason perhaps we don't delay too much on the first word 'once'. But *A Portrait* is also about 'once', the absolute uniqueness of an individual life, how it's impossible to recover once lost, how there is only one throw of the dice to quote an idiomatic expression, how only by retrospective arrangement can it be recovered. Folded into its unique *onceness* – not Wordsworth's oneness that is – is as much history as myth, or, expressed more simply, the novel begins with the child's entry into history surrounded by myth. It links therefore with the formulaic phrase 'in illo tempore' (in those days), which marks the opening of the Gospel reading at Mass. This is a phrase that Mircea Eliade has written about persuasively in *Cosmos and History: The Myth of the Eternal Return* (1959), where he contrasts the time of the gods and the fall or entry into history. As I say, 'once' should delay us, but it tends not to when it's inserted into the familiar phrase 'once upon a time'.

The next phrase 'and a very good time it was' ushers in something different, for the formulaic opening is immediately undercut or thrown off course by such an addition. The spoken voice treats it as an insertion as if it had brackets round it and reads it accordingly. 'Once upon a time and a very good time it was.' 'Whose voice is that?' we might well ask. I assume it's the father's and I assume he's not saying anything about the old days and how great they were or how God was with the auld times. Savitzky's French translation begins thus: 'Il y avait une fois, dans le bon vieux temps' (There was a time, in the good old days). But this isn't really what the phrase 'and a very good time it was' is saying. Joyce begins with child-speak, a way of settling the child as you launch into what is in this case a made-up story. It's the adult world surrounding the child, who here becomes the centre of the story. It's the cow that meets the child, not the other way round. This isn't easy to convey, but it clearly matters. 'Once upon a time' is designed to take you out of time, but 'a very good time it was' plays with the idea of historical time. 'Allá en otros tiempos (y bien buenos tiempos que era)' is how Dámaso Alonso translates the opening into Spanish. The bracket is right and 'otros tiempos' (those times) becomes 'buenos tiempos' (good times). OK, but perhaps this translation is too close to being a statement of fact – that those other days, in spite of what people think about them, were in fact good days. Such an emotional climate is closer to Tom Moore's Romantic, sepia-like song 'The Light of Other Days'. But there's no nostalgia in Joyce's opening passage. Nothing is remembered or recalled in that sense. The original experience is preserved. There are no feelings of 'unremembered pleasures', as Wordsworth puts it in 'Tintern Abbey'. Everything is up-close and dramatised.

In all his major texts, Joyce deploys a title that allows him to connect the general with the specific. Eventually, nothing in the title limits him. He is a writer of chords. As mentioned in Chapter 2, *A Portrait of the Artist as a Young Man* began life as *Stephen Hero* (1944). In this case, 'Hero' recalls a 'heroic' tradition rather than a person, even though there is a suggestion that Joyce borrowed the title from the ballad 'Turpin Hero', about the legendary highwayman Dick Turpin, who in his robbing exploits became a hero for the common people. In time, such a choice of title must have presented Joyce with a difficulty, for it was less chord-like than it seemed, and perhaps it was for this reason that Joyce was persuaded to abandon it (just as he did with his pseudonym Stephen Dedalus). Stephen, after all, reminds us not of a trickster but of someone bent on establishing his own credentials as a hero. *A Portrait* returns us more certainly to a world of the resonant eponymous hero, where the protagonist attracts and displays both individual and typological colourings. Stephen is both a person and a type, both Dedalus and an artist, both Dedalus and Daedalus, both Daedalus and Icarus. As readers, we find ourselves constantly checking the protagonist against the title and in particular against the phrase 'the artist'. The title in this sense is both resonant and resistant, and works in tandem with something else. If Stephen is a 'hero', he's also 'the artist' and the craftsman. It's a reminder that *A Portrait* is a much more challenging novel than the fragment Joyce abandoned and which never saw the light of day in Joyce's lifetime.

Keep looking, listen out for the chords, seems the best advice when we approach a Joyce text. *A Portrait* is no exception. Although rarely alluded to, the title runs through the whole novel, engaging us in a series of connections and suggestive comparisons as we seek to make sense of what we are reading. The novel begins like a fairy tale and it ends with entries in a personal diary. Like a traditional ballad it mixes first-person and third-person narrative, beginning in this case with 'he' and ending with 'I'. In this novel, conventions of writing meet styles of consciousness meet English punctuation. 'His father told him that story: his father looked at him through a glass: he had a hairy face.' Here the colon, a highly sophisticated punctuation mark in English, registers precisely one of the earliest stepping stones on the way to consciousness, where two impressions for the child are brought into active relationship by a single mark, one dot above another. The French translation by Ludmila Savitzky has one semi-colon followed by another: 'C'était son père qui lui racontait cette histoire; son père le regardait à travers un morceau de verre; il avait un visage poilu.' But this misses all the drama between his father's 'hairy face' and his father peering at him 'through a glass'.

The interior space

The stories of *Dubliners* possess such restraint that one would think that their author would never have difficulty writing and that he would always be able to write with economy. But *A Portrait of the Artist as a Young Man* serves to remind us of something else about Joyce. It's not that it's wordy, for it isn't, but the novel has the look of something that has been worked on and cut down to size, as if it had proved difficult to handle. Adjusting the space on the page for a book that was essentially about the interior space proved especially tough. With its unfinished sentences, *Dubliners* resembles the tip of an iceberg. But what do you do with a manuscript that at one stage had grown to 'a thousand pages' (*Letters II*, 132)? Autobiographies and biographies invariably require careful authorial handling. Or rather they should do. The temptation is to include more than you should in the mistaken belief that 'everything is more' or in the hope that adding 'just this' will go unnoticed. Everything in a life narrative is an illustration not so much of itself but of something else, and in Joyce's case that something else, even when it comes at us in direct, physical terms, is focused on an interior space which can be variously defined as consciousness, the soul, the mind, the will or the self.

If the moment of *Dubliners* is rendered by defiance, *A Portrait of the Artist as a Young Man* gives us the next stage, for Joyce seems to have been driven by something that is akin to defiance but is now issuing from a different source. When he put pen to paper, and as I say it may come as a surprise to those who think he was born to write, he discovered he had to spend a long time under the water before surfacing. It's as if Hermes, the messenger from the gods, or Minerva, the goddess of books, or the Muse herself, had unceremoniously told him, 'Drown first, and then come up for air'. Look at the years Joyce spent on *Ulysses* and *Finnegans Wake*, and it's clear the pattern of writing was more like *A Portrait* than *Dubliners*. *Dubliners* took a long time to get published but not to write. *A Portrait* required years to get into shape, partly I suspect because of the conditions under which it was written – holding down a full-time teaching job, domestic circumstances, a young family, living abroad, the instinct to socialise – and partly because Joyce was without an overriding template such as Homer's *Odyssey* to act as a guide. Handwriting and small exercise books didn't help either. If he was composing it today, he would have had the benefit of word-processing and been able to discern more quickly how to block the material and rearrange it on the screen. The composition of *A Portrait* has all the appearance of an unhappy experience for Joyce. Indeed, in everything but its name, *A Portrait* is the book of an exile, and it was in keeping that his next book was called by its proper name, *Exiles*. And all exiles carry round with them an interior space.

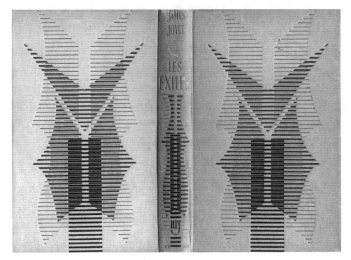

Les Exilés, the French translation of *Exiles*, published by Gallimard in Paris in 1950. The translation was by J.S. Bradley and the stylish cover design by Paul Bonet. *Exiles*, which translators have little difficulty with largely because every language understands the concept, affords another umbrella, another chord-like term, but it is centred not so much on a whole group of people nor on the plight of being an exile from one's homeland, as on the involvement and jealousies of three people with each other. As with *A Portrait*, though, throughout the work we can't help asking about the connection between the particular events of the play with the wider theme of exiles.

Source: Editions Gallimard

A Portrait of the Artist as a Young Man, then, threatened, perhaps repeatedly, to get out of control, and, before he could embark on what he seems to have enjoyed most, that is polishing a text, Joyce had to get it into shape. 'How do I get all this material to face in the same direction and to have a point or focus? Should I have headings or simply sections and leave it to the reader to fill in? How do I create a sense of the passage of time? Will the scenes I choose to focus on carry within them the course of the novel as a whole or will they threaten to dissolve that course into a series of mere incidents?' And all the time the nagging doubt wouldn't go away: 'Will this manuscript ever see the light of day?' In response to Nora's taunts about his lack of success as an author, the manuscript was once thrown into the fire, but, fortunately, it was as soon rescued by his sister Eileen. He was spurred on, but hard thinking remained. 'What do I need to sacrifice to get this thing into print?' Eventually, Joyce did get it into shape, arranging the material into five chapters and using layout and typography to divide those chapters into sections. But it's for readers to decide if it's finished or not, if its ending marked the natural conclusion to something or simply a moment to break off and have done with that which had taken him at least ten years to complete. 'Dublin 1904 Trieste 1914.' There was something disproportionate about it all. Ten years, perhaps more, spent on a fictionalised account of a life which up till that point was only some 20 years in duration. A third on two-thirds. Joyce must have felt at times that life was catching up on him or that writing, in both senses, was beyond him.

In the beginning was the word

Where to begin resolved itself for Joyce effectively as another question: how to begin? Sterne begins at the beginning in *Tristram Shandy* (1759–68) with the moment of the hero's conception, with the racy image of Tristram's mother wondering if her husband Walter Shandy had remembered to wind up the clock. Sterne is intent on mocking John Locke's *Essay on Human Understanding* (1694) and his theory that the mind begins life as a *tabula rasa* or blank sheet. Ever alert and intelligent, and never one to be satisfied with the familiar or what had been done before, Joyce begins not quite at the beginning but with the child's entry into language. His focus is not so much philosophy as the frame or window through which we see the world. Such a focus, we might notice in passing, is itself a philosophical position and close to a form of epistemological doubt about the nature of external reality. But if there is a pre-text, it comes perhaps from a source he would have heard every week in the Last Gospel at Mass.

IN princípio erat Verbum, et Verbum erat apud Deum, et Deus erat Verbum. Hoc erat in princípio apud Deum. Omnia per ipsum facta sunt : et sine ipso factum est nihil, quod factum est : in ipso vita erat, et vita erat lux hóminum : et lux in ténebris lucet, et ténebrae eam non comprehendérunt. Fuit homo missus a Deo, cui nomen erat Joánnes. Hic venit in testimónium, ut testimónium perhibéret de lúmine, ut omnes créderent per illum. Non erat ille lux, sed ut testimónium perhibéret de lúmine. Erat lux vera, quae illúminat omnem hóminem veniéntem in hunc mundum. In mundo erat, et mundus per ipsum factus est, et mundus eum non cognóvit. In própria venit, et sui eum non recepérunt. Quotquot autem recepérunt eum, dedit eis potestátem fílios Dei fíeri, his qui credunt in nómine ejus, qui non ex sanguínibus, neque ex voluntáte carnis, neque ex voluntáte viri, sed ex Deo nati sunt. ET VERBUM CARO FACTUM EST, et habitávit in nobis : et vídimus glóriam ejus, glóriam quasi Unigéniti a Patre, plenum grátiae et veritátis. ℞. Deo grátias.

The Last Gospel in Latin, with the phrase 'ET VERBUM CARO FACTUM EST' (and the Word was made flesh) in upper case. I have reproduced it from my plainchant book *Liber Usualis* (1932), an everyday book, which carries my signature and the date 1960. I had just turned 13.

The opening to St John's Gospel was so special to the Church that it was read at the end of every Mass. It clearly provided a fund of material that repaid study, and over the centuries there seemed to be no end to its spiritual sustenance. Even today, agnostic though I am, I find the sequence of sentences and the claims made quite riveting, as if the author was discovering as he went along what it was he wanted to say. In reading it again, I am struck first of all by a little word, the preposition *apud* (with). 'The Word was with God.' It's not the usual word in Latin for 'with', which is *cum*. *Apud* is used of places, as when you want to say that the Ponte Vecchio is *near* the Uffizzi Gallery in Florence. The preposition is also used to mean at the house of, so that to dine 'with you' is *apud te*. If we took the phrase 'Verbum erat apud Deum' and deployed these meanings, we would get 'the Word was in God's house', a looser, less enigmatic connection but easier in some respects to understand. In Greek, the preposition chosen is πρoς (*pros*), a word with an even wider distribution of meaning. When followed by an accusative case, as here with τoν θεoν (*ton theon*), it carries in classical Greek the idea of relation, 'with a view to', as in the phrase τα πρoς τoυς θεoυς (*ta pros tous theous*), 'our relations to the gods'. As I say, in that enigmatic opening to St John's Gospel, I get delayed by the first preposition, on the language used to express a mystery.

The early Church Fathers, too, in the second to the fifth centuries, wrestled with the problem of the Trinity and how they/it, the three persons in one, might be represented. And the problem didn't go away. The last verse of 'Pange Lingua', a hymn that was composed in the thirteenth century by St Thomas Aquinas, which is sung at Benediction when the host is 'exposed', and which provides the scurrilous backdrop to the 'Nausicaa' episode of *Ulysses*, contains an awkward phrase 'Genitori Genitoque' to describe the Father and Son. The former is clearly prior to the latter, one the active begetter, the other the begot *genito* (which the joined suffix *que*, and, can't quite conceal). Equally problematic in the same stanza is the phrase to describe the Holy Ghost 'procedenti ab utroque' (proceeding from the other two). Generation, procession, the only-begotten – seemingly, when thinking of the complex series of relationships that compose the Trinity, we're not in possession of a language that is not sexualised.

Latin inscription on the Jesuit Church of St Francis Xavier on Gardiner Street in Dublin, in which the theology of the Trinity is given public display. 'Deo Uni et Trino Sub Invoc S Francisci Xavierii' (to God One and Three under the invocation of St Francis Xavier). 'I.H.S.', initials on the back of a priest's chasuble when saying Mass, is the Greek monogram for Jesus. It is often thought, perhaps mistakenly, that the letters represent the first three letters of Jesus's name, Ιησ (or *Jes*). In *Ulysses*, Bloom, following Molly, thinks the inscription is English: 'I have sinned: or no: I have suffered, it is' (*U* 5:373). The word is out: Dublin may be only a thousand years old but it is a city full of Latin inscriptions. Photograph by David Pierce.

Bookplate for St John's Seminary library, dated 1891, with the opening to St John's Gospel: 'In principio erat Verbum' (In the beginning was the Word). John, the beloved disciple, in old age reflecting on what he had experienced as a young man.

I can't believe Joyce wasn't also fascinated by the opening to St John's Gospel, and he might have been tempted to follow his example. 'In the beginning was the Word.' The next claim is equally enigmatic and mystical: 'And the Word was with God, and the Word was God.' This is St John 'explaining' the Trinity to a Greek audience familiar with the philosophical idea of the *logos* or word. Jesus is the Word of God and He has been with God forever, since the beginning. Father and Son therefore are distinguishable, but belong, with the Holy Ghost, the third person, to the same being, the Trinity. A mystery waiting to be explained, or if not explained (for Catholics were always told at school that mysteries can't be explained) then symbolised or allegorised and put into words. St John, the beloved disciple, might have been the first to recognise that what he was articulating is a conceit, for words are uttered by someone, so there must be something or somebody that precedes the utterance. Moreover, the word, any word, belongs to a pre-existent language. It's for this reason that when Jesus is compared to the Word or the Word is identified as God, the analogy works only up to a point.

Interestingly, in the last chapter of *A Portrait* Stephen returns to the Last Gospel, and he offers a striking comparison, transforming the Evangelist's phrase 'The Word was made flesh' into a metaphor for the creative process: 'In the virgin womb of the imagination the word was made flesh' (*P* 217). Such a daring move, which in turn reminds us of the title of Ovid's *Metamorphosis*, is also a conceit, an inter-textual reply by Joyce across the centuries of belief to the most poetic evangelist of the foursome (Matthew, Mark, Luke and John), whom he affectionately calls 'mamalujo' in *Finnegans Wake*.

Ant.
1.

I -ste est Jo- ánnes, * qui supra péctus Dómi-

ni   in coéna recúbu- it : be- á-tus Apósto-   lus,

cú- i reve-lá-ta sunt secré-ta caelésti- a.

At the end of Vespers for St Stephen on 26 December, as part of the vigil for the following day, this Antiphon to St John the Evangelist, whose feast is on 27 December, is sung. The day after Jesus is born, the Church celebrates the first Christian martyr or witness, and this is followed in turn by a celebration of the beloved Apostle most associated with the mystery of the Eucharist and the continuing divine presence in creation. The translation of the Antiphon reads 'This is John who at supper rested his head on the Lord's breast: blessed Apostle through whom the secrets of the heavens are revealed'. *Sunt*, the present tense, 'are' revealed, not 'were' revealed. The plainchant makes much of St John's reclining on Jesus at the Last Supper, but the music really comes alive with several grouped notes when the evangelist is directly addressed as *beatus Apostolus* or 'blessed Apostle'. Once noticed, we might concede, the proximity of these two feast days also has something to contribute to our understanding *A Portrait*.

In contrast to St John, Joyce is intent on giving us language itself, not as an analogy for something else, but the thing, the sign, the frame itself. He begins in similarly enigmatic fashion to the Evangelist: 'Once upon a time', and in a way it's his version of 'In the beginning was the Word'. He continues with 'there was a moocow coming down along the road'. At a stroke, the otherworldly mysticism of the Evangelist has been replaced by something more down to earth or familiar, namely a boy encountering a moocow coming down along the road, or, rather, a children's story in which a boy meets a moocow coming down along the road. But, as if to remind us of something shared between the two worlds, Joyce retains the separation of father and son, as well as the hovering presence of a third person in the shape of the unknown narrator.

If there is a deliberate echo of a grand theological statement at the beginning of *A Portrait*, it is almost immediately undercut by something else, and we might read this either as an interruption or as another suggestive departure. The first note struck in the opening sentence of *A Portrait* sounds reassuring and familiar, the second slightly off-putting, as if it were doubling back on itself. St John has the capitalised Word but in *A Portrait* it is a child's word, or, rather, it's the way an adult speaks to a child. A moocow. The word possesses almost no status, but its two syllables ring alarm bells for those who are settling into a conventional retrospective style of storytelling. For immediately we are pitched into the consciousness of a child. A moocow. Or rather, the qualification needs repeating: it's not the consciousness of the child but how adults imagine a child learns a language. First take the object, then associate it with a sound. Cars brmm brmm, doggies wuff wuff, cats meow. Cows moo. Turn it round in this case, and you have the one word 'moocow'. Joyce clearly liked the word and the drop in register it afforded. In 'Tilly', a poem written at the start of his own career in 1904, cows 'moo and make brute music with their hoofs' (Joyce, *Pomes Penyeach*, 9).

But tell a story and see what happens to words and sounds, for now the object is no longer physically present except as it features in the story. This recalls something else about language, how it refers to objects that are absent from view, which can't be indicated in the room or pointed to in the world. A cow after all is the sound it makes. Moo. And moo signifies cow. Child language acquisition is to do with absence and non-attachment, with undemonstrative things, as much as with touch, the senses and association. Put the word in a sentence about coming down a road and meeting a baby in a pram and the complexity increases fourfold, especially when the baby in the story is identified with me the baby in the pram. 'In the beginning was the Word.' That's complicated enough, but how, we might readily agree, does anyone learn a language and through that an identity? 'Moocow', says Joyce. 'Can you hear that? It's me writing.'

The subject in language

Language, then, creates an interior space even as it seeks to describe the world before our eyes. This is especially evident in the scattering of sounds in the first chapter of *A Portrait*, some of which seem designed to insist on the sound as distinct from meaning. Most readers will have problems on first encountering this sentence on the second page: 'Uncle Charles and Dante clapped'. 'Dante' – is that a reference to the Italian poet and, if so, how could he be part of a child's viewpoint? And why would the author be invoking such a figure if the story is not concerned with the *Divine Comedy* or any of the various stages in the poet's journey through life and beyond? Only later do we realise 'Dante' is, presumably, what a child hears for 'aunty'. The reader is learning language just as the boy is, or at least this is one conclusion we might draw. Another is that words are not always properly anchored, and, at times, we have to live with sounds before we can tie them down to a particular meaning or referent – as happens all the time in *Finnegans Wake*. Alternatively, to fill the void of sense, we simply jump to wrong conclusions.

Words and things. As references to the word 'word' in the novel confirm, Stephen is learning all the time about the spaces that come between words and things. To list some of them as they appear in turn in the novel can be instructive. Stephen learns, for example, that God in French is *Dieu*; that 'suck' is a 'queer word'; that the words of the song Brigid taught him are 'beautiful'; that 'wine', too, was a beautiful word; that his fellow pupils don't know if the Latin word for sea, *mare*, has a plural; that, in his walks with his father and Uncle Charles, Stephen has difficulty understanding their words on politics and history; that he is unafraid of words uttered in banter; that a peculiar street name like *Lotts* (parallel to Bachelors Walk) on a wall near a morgue has a calming effect; that in Chapter 2 on the train journey to Cork at the end of reciting prayers to the rhythm of the train he finds himself uttering 'foolish words'; that his father's words in Cork sound like 'mere words'; that with the onset of puberty he finds the rush of 'unspoken brutal words'; that words from a poem by Shelley come back to him when he is approached by Fresh Nelly, a prostitute; that in Chapter 3 after his sin he is reminded of the contrast between the Virgin Mary and 'shameful words'; that the words of baptism uttered over an unbaptised child by a layman perhaps constitute a form of baptism; that he is reminded of the meaning of the word 'retreat' by the retreat father; that God insisted Adam and Eve obey His word; that at the retreat he feels every word is for him; that he is reassured by 'common words' on the weather and the like ('it might clear up'); that 'He had to confess, to speak out in words what he had done and thought, sin after sin'; that eternity is 'O, dread and dire word'; that the retreat father hopes his 'poor words' might prove efficacious; that Stephen 'had sinned in thought and word and deed' and that he will hear 'the grave words of absolution'; that during all the years with the Jesuits 'he had never heard from any of his masters a flippant word'; that, when asked if he had a vocation, he 'withheld the word suddenly'; that when he experienced a 'feverish quickening of his pulses . . . a din of meaningless words drove his reasoned thoughts hither and thither confusedly'; that a line of verse such as 'A day of dappled seaborne clouds' made him wonder about 'Words. Was it their colours?'; that when gazing at the woman on the seashore in Chapter 4 'no word had broken the holy silence of his ecstasy'; that 'His mind when wearied of its search for the essence of beauty amid the spectral words of Aristotle or Aquinas turned often for its pleasure to the dainty songs of the Elizabethans'; that in Chapter 5 in the office of the Director of Studies he realises 'How different are the words HOME, CHRIST,

ALE, MASTER, on his lips and on mine! I cannot speak or write these words without unrest of spirit'; that 'In the virgin womb of the imagination the word was made flesh'; that 'The soft beauty of the Latin word touched with an enchanting touch the dark of the evening'; that on 11 April, he 'Read what I wrote last night. Vague words for a vague emotion.'

What an extraordinary novel this is, a novel not only about bending our wits, to borrow Sandy's phrase in the Ovid translation above, but also about the subject in language. It's like a huge complex machine designed to illustrate the way the growth of an individual from childhood, through boyhood, to adulthood, is bound up with language. From start to finish it is in that sense a 'language novel' in which something else is happening, for, from all the varied and up-close details or 'artes', we try and establish or garner some underlying principles and concepts. So, if we were to rewrite the paragraph above in conceptual terms, it might go something like this. In *A Portrait*, we are presented with various examples of language in use: the language of difference linked to another language (*Dieu*), language as expressive (suck), the language of beauty, of the classroom and the playground, of adults not understood, of therapy, of inflation and self-importance and therefore character (his father), of enticement (prostitute), of shame, language as a performative utterance (baptism), as polysemic and in need of explanation (retreat). The novel contains the language of obedience (to God), of guilt (the arc lights trained on the self), of the everyday and its counter to the guilty self (it might clear up), of confession to a priest, of fear (eternity), of absolution, of never hearing certain words or tones (flippancy), the language of refusal or acts of refusal by silence, of words as meaningless but at the same time driving out rational thoughts, of poetry and its power and where that power derives from, the limits of language in the face of ecstasy, the language of past thinkers as spectral, of the coloniser, of metaphor, of Latin, of vagueness to capture vagueness.

Words do things. They express sounds, they make us afraid, they deceive us, they change things when used in a performative mode (I absolve you, I forgive you, I baptise you, God can condemn you to eternal damnation), they help us organise our responses to the world, they carry the past inside them. Words belong to the shaping of character, to the articulation of morality and to the strengthening of courage, to our understanding or otherwise of politics and religion. Not hearing things, not understanding someone, refusing to say things, or feeling the words someone is using in a general context refer to oneself – this, too, constitutes part of our experience of language. It's clear, then, that in one sense, as Ludwig Wittgenstein claimed, the limits of language constitute the limits of our world, but in another sense what Joyce shows us in *A Portrait* is the interior space that opens up when the individual confronts language. Put simply, *A Portrait* begins by describing the subject in language, a view that runs through the whole novel, but at the end, when we reflect on the novel we have been reading, another thought prompts itself: for all the control that language exerts, the individual is not entirely subject to language.

Joyce among the Jesuits

In 1888, Joyce entered the front doors of Clongowes Wood College, a square, castellated, imposing, big house in the heart of County Kildare, some 60 miles or so from Dublin, and took to walking down its dark corridors. He was six and a half, half past six, as the tiny boy was affectionately known. The Jesuit missionary St Francis Xavier is allegedly responsible for the motto we associate with the Jesuits: 'Give me a child until he is seven and I will give you the man'. Of no-one is this more true than it is of Joyce, the writer who in *A Portrait* returned with extraordinary courage to the formation of his intellect and character at the hands of the Jesuits. At the top of every piece of work, Joyce inscribed A.M.D.G, 'ad majorem Dei gloriam' (for the greater glory of God) the motto thought to have been coined by the Jesuits' founder in the sixteenth century, St Ignatius of Loyola. The Jesuits today might claim him, but nothing Joyce published in his lifetime shelters under their motto. On the other hand, the Jesuits were

Clongowes Wood College. A woodcut taken from *The Dublin Penny Journal*, 7 July 1832.

The class of Elements 1888–9 at Clongowes Wood. The six-year-old Joyce is sitting cross-legged in front of Fr William Power.

Source: Fr Bruce Bradley S.J.

responsible not for the deformation but for the formation of his intellect and character, a formation that was almost wholly masculine. In the wood-cut, only the branches of the tree in the foreground soften the image and give the scene a feminine touch. It's illness that reminds Stephen of his mother and home. When I went away to boarding school at the age of 11, the priests had to restrain my mother physically as I was wrenched away from her in the marble entrance-hall.

His Jesuit masters would have been pleased with Joyce, not at first but in time. A generation or so ago, when Maurice Craig wrote his architectural history of Dublin (1952), he ended his comments on Belvedere College by observing that, while Joyce was their most illustrious pupil, 'the visitors who enjoy the courtesy of the Fathers will do well to talk of other subjects' (Craig, 1952, 231). No-one had or has written so expertly and so power-fully about growing up among the Jesuits. Equally, the world had met its

The Jesuit priest, James Cullen (1841–1921); from *The Clongownian*, 1924. For five years from 1856 he was himself a pupil at Clongowes Wood College. Years later, after becoming a Jesuit, he was involved in establishing the Messenger of the Sacred Heart in Ireland, an Apostleship of Prayer for the laity with its own monthly publication. In 1898, he founded the Pioneer Total Abstinence movement. It is thought that he was Joyce's model for the retreat sermon priest.

match in their one-time pupil. Most of us writing about our religious up-bringing pretty soon abandon our attempts as lame or derivative or lacking something. Almost in desperation or in the hope that it will come good, we write a lot, pages of it, but in the end we are forced to abandon it. Joyce had done it better. Even the retreat sermon, which is Joyce simply lifting what he heard, has a power to move us by its originality. Yes, this was the way Catholic boys at an impressionable age were frequently addressed. Fear of eternity, fear of losing your eternal soul, fear of the body, fear of the imagination, fear of the world and its manifold temptations. And all leading to: confess, confess, confess. In childhood the pattern is established, and it is right that Stephen is told to apologise, apologise, apologise. It was true, wherever you looked in Catholic Ireland, the Jesuits, those mer-chants of fear, were seemingly lining you up – but only if you had money. In their quietly efficient drama of intimidation they knew how to dress the part, and they also knew how to create fear in their choice of steel-rimmed glasses or simply by opening the door of a classroom. Stephen seems to admire them for never uttering a flippant word. In England they would have faced a degree of contempt and a hostile environment, as when *Punch*, to take a small example from the 1880s when Joyce was growing up, refers to them as 'Loyola and Co' and Catholics in general as 'Romanesque' (12 May 1885).

At one of the retreats I attended in my teens, I recall the words of the retreat father: 'Try and develop an interior silence, so that all the time throughout the day the water of Christ flows over you. Interior silence is not the same as external silence. You are not called to a life of external silence. Rather, the secular priest is one who goes out into the world. He has to mix with people. But all the time you must have this interior silence, which is a sure contact with Our Lord.' And in the abandoned 'Portrait' I composed in my early twenties, I continue: 'Must pray harder. Spend more time in prayer if I'm to achieve this interior silence. Mary, help me. Can't do it alone. Two more days of silence and prayer. This time tomorrow I'll be here again. Will it never end?' Fortunately, it did. Interior monologue, which I explore in connection with the Molly Bloom soliloquy in Chapter 10, began long before Dujardin, Joyce and the Modernist novel. It was known in the Church as mental prayer and, crucially, it included the distractions that accompany mental prayer.

If *A Portrait* is anything to go by, what impressed Joyce about the Jesuits was not only the power of their personality but also how such power might be countered. The two went hand in hand: power and how to counter it (which in its own way was a tribute to that power). To illustrate this, Joyce focuses in particular on two incidents or portraits, one from his boyhood experience at Clongowes Wood College, his boarding school, and one from the later stages of his career as a day pupil at Belvedere College in Dublin. Against Fr Dolan's false accusation and the subsequent beating he received for not wearing his glasses, the young Stephen appeals to the Rector Fr Conmee, and wins a small victory against the prefect of studies, after which he is acclaimed in the playground by the other boys. Against the English

Belvedere College S.J. (Society of Jesus, or Jesuits as they are commonly known). The main door of the Jesuit School on Great Denmark Street, Dublin with polished brass nameplate and, nearby, an ornate Victorian street lamp. The sign is more temporary: 'Reception 30 metres →'. The public face of the Jesuits' main school in Dublin has a quietly impressive look, offering in its teaching and curriculum a 'belvedere' or raised outlook on the world. The real work was done behind closed doors. Photograph by David Pierce.

dean of studies, he wins another small, this time unseen, victory when he explains that 'tundish' is the word used in Ireland for 'funnel'. It happens that tundish was a word unknown to the Jesuit priest, and Stephen, in a further display of one-upmanship, continues by referring to the working-class area a stone's throw from Belvedere, an area Joyce got to know well when he lived at St Peter's Terrace in 1902–4: 'It is called a tundish in Lower Drumcondra, said Stephen laughing, where they speak the best English' (*P* 188). I like this scene, for it is a genuine moment where we catch a real glimpse of Joyce learning how to deal with the Jesuits.

Like Stephen, Joyce was invited to become a Jesuit. 'Stephen Dedalus S.J.' Perhaps Joyce himself saw his name in lights: 'James Joyce S.J.'. Joyce certainly possessed the necessary ferocity of mind and intellectual stamina to pursue such a career. But as he tells us in *A Portrait*, a 'wayward instinct' (*P* 165) got the better of him. The Jesuits presented Joyce with a stark choice, with a fork in the road, and he chose not the high road to the priesthood but the wayward path. Laughing was certainly part of that waywardness, for laughing constituted a means to deflect their power, but there were other ways. Learning how to put the world into boxes was another, for the Jesuits gave Joyce the most ordered mind of any modern writer. Making

Joyce as a student with his friends John Francis Byrne and George Clancy. Their gaze is directed at something but they don't seem too happy in their forced relaxed pose. Joyce is wearing boots (unlike his customary canvas shoes) and holding a check hat, but his jacket looks slightly too big for him. Clancy is the model for Davin in *A Portrait*, while Byrne, with his Dublin drawl, is the model for Cranly. When he returned to Dublin in 1909, Joyce stayed a night with Byrne at 7 Eccles Street. Byrne later wrote *Silent Years: An Autobiography with Memoirs of James Joyce and Our Ireland* (1953).

(left) In 2006 Newman's University celebrated its 150th anniversary. Photograph by David Pierce.

(right) Plaque outside St Patrick's House on Stephen's Green, Dublin. Favoured fathers and sons. An implausible trinity of two English converts and an Irish lapsed Catholic. Newman, the founder and first rector on University College, and, according to Stephen Dedalus, the best prose writer in English; Hopkins, the frail English poet who taught here in the 1880s and who is buried in an unmarked grave in the Jesuit plot at Glasnevin Cemetery; and Joyce, the student of three years, now welcomed back with open arms. In 2006 University College Dublin established the first chair anywhere in the world in James Joyce studies. Photograph by David Pierce.

sacred everyday life, which is how Joyce writes about what he is doing in *Dubliners*, was another. The Jesuits' power, however, could only be undermined, not overcome, and I think this is why Stephen resorts in the end to 'silence, exile and cunning'. Silence, the interior space, the mark of the rebel against his remarkable masters.

When we next see him at the beginning of *Ulysses*, Stephen has returned to Dublin after a brief sojourn in Paris. His mother has died, his wings have been clipped and his heroic stature undermined. His character is recognisably the same, slightly more morose and fatalistic, but, in the shadow of Bloom, he has lost a certain shine and appeal, and he seems lonelier than before he departed and less resourceful. Daedalus was the resourceful person who tried to escape the Minotaur; Telemachus is the slightly wooden son in search of his father. Joyce switches narrative templates, but the twin themes of exile and escape continued to preoccupy him. However, the myth of Daedalus and Icarus belongs to an early period of Greek culture and has limits in how it can be used by the modern novelist. Joyce does a fine job in *A Portrait* with the theme and with the imagery of flight and so on. But the story of Odysseus's adventures after the Trojan Wars is closer to history than myth, closer, that is, to a fictional representation, and it's for this reason we find ourselves responding all the time to how characters perceive their fate in Homer's story.

It can be admitted that Joyce's choice of *The Odyssey* was not especially original, but what he does with the story is. Stephen, the artistic, cerebral, courageous hero of one novel, opens the next novel and leads us through the first three episodes, but we are conscious almost from the start that the moody dispossessed son is not the hero of the new novel, just as Telemachus isn't in the orginal. Our attention is therefore delayed and we have to wait until the fourth episode and the Odyssey proper before coming upon the figure whom Homer describes in his opening line as 'polytropos', the many-sided, resourceful character, who is a hero but no saint, and whose humanity shines through everything he touches. In all kinds of ways we feel the gap therefore between the two novels, but to risk oversimplification we might say this: if the movement of *A Portrait* is towards catching the boat-train away from Ireland, the trajectory of *Ulysses* is return, and it's for this reason we listen politely to Stephen's complaints at the beginning of the novel, but we look forward to meeting the character of Bloom, the 'all-round' man, as Joyce calls him, who is earthy and sensuous but also intelligent and resourceful, the Jewish outsider whose thoughts never stray far from his wife and home.

CHAPTER 8

Approaching *Ulysses*

On reading *Ulysses* for the first time

When I first began teaching *Ulysses* in the late 1970s, I would give my students the following handout:

1. Don't panic.
2. Don't panic if after the first episode you haven't understood much.
3. Don't panic if you don't know if you've come to the end of the first episode.
4. Everything comes to those who wait.
5. Everything will be revealed by Linati and Gorman-Gilbert.
6. Everything comes in twos or threes.
7. If time permits, read Joyce's *A Portrait of the Artist as a Young Man*. There you will find a portrayal of Stephen Dedalus's childhood, adolescence, early manhood. The novel closes with Stephen as a recently qualified graduate about to go to Paris.
8. If further time permits, read Homer's *Odyssey*. This epic underlies Joyce's. Stephen Dedalus is Telemachus looking for his spiritual father (not his real father, who is Simon Dedalus). You may not recognise him in the bath but Leopold Bloom is our hero Ulysses, while his wife, Molly Bloom (ah, sweet Molly), who is being courted and bedded by suitor 'Blazes' Boylan, is Homer's Penelope, if a little more sensual and lascivious (Mother Earth in fact).
9. If further time permits (after time permitting and further time permitting), read Frank Budgen's *James Joyce and the Making of 'Ulysses'*. This book will fill in the gaps (or the gaping craters) in your early attempts at reading the novel.
10. Time is of the essence as it happens. All the events take place on one day, 16 June 1904: 'Bloomsday' to later devotees.
11. The novel begins twice, once with Stephen's early morning and once with Bloom's.

12. The novel ends twice, once with Stephen and Bloom having 'found' each other and once with Molly's soliloquy in bed.

13. The novel's space also matters. Dublin is the centre, though not the 'centre of paralysis' (as it is in *Dubliners*).

14. The Blooms live at number 7 Eccles Street on the north side of Dublin; Stephen is staying at the Martello Tower 9 miles south of Dublin on the coast at Sandycove (where the novel begins).

15. Bloom is an advertising agent, Stephen for the time being a school-teacher. Dublin is where they meet.

16. Consult the Linati schema and the Gorman-Gilbert plan. There are three episodes or chapters in Dawn, three in Morning, three at Noon, six in Day, three at Midnight. Eighteen episodes in all. This is enough to be going on with.

17. Begin now.

18. I will. Yes.

If there was an easy way of getting a handle on this novel, then it would have been discovered by now. One thing I did occasionally find beneficial was to get my students to learn by heart the Homeric titles to the 18 episodes. I'd take up time in class to do this, and then get them to write

TITLE	SCENE	HOUR	ORGAN	ART	COLOUR	SYMBOL	TECHNIC
1. Telemachus	The Tower	8 a.m.		Theology	White, gold	Heir	Narrative (young)
2. Nestor	The School	10 a.m.		History	Brown	Horse	Catechism (personal)
3. Proteus	The Strand	11 a.m.		Philology	Green	Tide	Monologue (male)
4. Calypso	The House	8 a.m.	Kidney	Economics	Orange	Nymph	Narrative (mature)
5. Lotus-eaters	The Bath	10 a.m.	Genitals	Botany, Chemistry		Eucharist	Narcissism
6. Hades	The Graveyard	11 a.m.	Heart	Religion	White, black	Caretaker	Incubism
7. Aeolus	The Newspaper	12 noon	Lungs	Rhetoric	Red	Editor	Enthymemic
8. Lestrygonians	The Lunch	1 p.m.	Esophagus	Architecture		Constables	Peristaltic
9. Scylla and Charybdis	The Library	2 p.m.	Brain	Literature		Stratford, London	Dialectic
10. Wandering Rocks	The Streets	3 p.m.	Blood	Mechanics		Citizens	Labyrinth
11. Sirens	The Concert Room	4 p.m.	Ear	Music		Barmaids	Fuga per canonem
12. Cyclops	The Tavern	5 p.m.	Muscle	Politics		Fenian	Gigantism
13. Nausicaa	The Rocks	8 p.m.	Eye, Nose	Painting	Grey, blue	Virgin	Tumescence, detumescence
14. Oxen of the Sun	The Hospital	10 p.m.	Womb	Medicine	White	Mothers	Embryonic development
15. Circe	The Brothel	12 midnight	Locomotor Apparatus	Magic		Whore	Hallucination
16. Eumaeus	The Shelter	1 a.m.	Nerves	Navigation		Sailors	Narrative (old)
17. Ithaca	The House	2 a.m.	Skeleton	Science		Comets	Catechism (impersonal)
18. Penelope	The Bed		Flesh			Earth	Monologue (female)

The plan of *Ulysses* that appeared in Stuart Gilbert's *James Joyce's Ulysses* (1930). Although less detailed than the schema Joyce had sent to Carlo Linati in 1920, Gilbert's plan, which is very similar to Gorman's plan, offers a broad overview of the novel. For a comparison between the various plans and Joyce's involvement in them, see the Appendix in Richard Ellmann's *Ulysses on the Liffey* (1984).

down 1 to 18 and fill in the various titles accordingly. Some such form of ownership over the novel helped give students confidence, and I'd repeat the exercise until they had got it right.

Structure

The structure of the novel is worth securing from the outset. The novel is composed of three sections (or four if you follow Linati): 1–3, the Telemachiad, episodes about about Telemachus; 4–15, the Odyssey proper; 16–18, the Nostos or Return. In the Shakespeare and Company first edition, three sections are marked thus: I, II, III. The chapters carry no titles. However, the convention has grown up to describe the chapters by their Homeric titles, but we should never forget that in the original there were no such titles. Joyce drew a line after episode 9, as if that marked one half of the novel. Or, if you want to emphasise the role of Penelope and the female-centred nature of the novel, you could perhaps imagine the structure as 17 plus 1. Alternatively, you could conceive the structure of the first half of the novel in terms of 3 plus 3, where Bloom's morning beginning at 7 Eccles Street runs parallel to Stephen's, which begins in the Martello Tower at Sandycove; then come another three episodes, 7–9, this time surrounding lunch: the Newspaper episode, Bloom's 'lestrygonian' lunch, and the Library episode.

Episode 10, 'Wandering Rocks', will always mark some kind of break or new direction, since it involves a cast of characters other than Stephen and Bloom. From that point on, particularly in terms of style, we seem to have one tour de force after another. 11 is 'Sirens', the Music episode which takes place in the afternoon in the Ormond Hotel; 12 is the 'Cyclops' episode, set in Barney Kiernan's pub on Little Britain Street, an episode full of lists focused in part on the issue of political and cultural nationalism. 13 is 'Nausicaa', an episode set on the beach at Sandymount, 4 miles south of Dublin, which features a famous encounter between Gerty McDowell and Bloom and which is written in part in the sickly style of a Victorian romance. 14 is 'Oxen of the Sun', a giving-birth episode set in a maternity hospital in which Joyce parallels the nine months of the foetus inside the womb with the history of the English language from Anglo-Saxon through all the different styles of writing English down to the Victorian period. 15 is the Night-town or 'Circe' episode, set in the red light area of Dublin, an episode when all the characters in the novel, whether dead or alive, such as Stephen's mother or Bloom's father, reappear in a series of comic tableaux or dramatic scenes inside a brothel. 16 is 'Eumaeus', an episode when Bloom and Stephen stop on their way home to Eccles Street for refreshments at a cabman's shelter; it is written in a deliberately tired and what for some is extraordinarily boring style. 17 is 'Ithaca', a question-and-answer episode in which Bloom and Stephen quiz each other over everything and nothing, an episode reminiscent of both the Catechism and Flaubert's last novel *Bouvard and Pécuchet* (1881). And finally we arrive at the Molly Bloom soliloquy, the chattiest and the most talked about episode of *Ulysses*.

Each episode has a distinct flavour therefore. This is important to grasp. An episode is more than just a label, for it tells us whose interior monologue we are hearing and whose head we are inside therefore. It also defines the parameters for the kinds of information that it contains. Some episodes belong to Stephen, some to Bloom, some to Bloom and Stephen, some to other characters. Stephen's interior monologue tends to be cerebral and more literary. In the first episode his mind is also trying to resist the verbal assault by his friend Mulligan, and inside his thoughts are the thoughts of Mulligan as it were. Stephen is a would-be writer. Hence at times his monologue is literary, as when he thinks of his mother's death and how she came to him after her death 'her breath a faint odour of wetted ashes' (*U* 1:106). Bloom, on the other hand, is more earthy and sensual, and more responsive in some respects to the world around him. The narrator's first introduction of him is memorable, for he is not only Mr, that is he is like a person we might meet in real life and worthy of addressing properly and not casually therefore, but we're told, almost in confidence, that he also enjoys for breakfast mutton kidneys 'which gave to his palate a fine tang of faintly scented urine' (*U* 4:4). In the second paragraph we find him 'righting her breakfast things', and we are already half-way between third-person narrator and interior monologue, for 'her' is not something a formal narrator would write before actually identifying who 'her' is, but issues from someone who has a more familiar relationship with the person. When the wily summer air is noted by the narrator, it is followed by the first occasion we hear Bloom's signature, his own thoughts that is, and marked by the absence of the first-person personal pronoun: 'Made him feel a bit peckish'.

This movement between third-person narrator and first-person character is one of the delights in reading the opening episodes of *Ulysses*, and most tutors will also enjoy drawing to the attention of a class such a procedure and where it kicks in and tunnels out. Share those moments, I would tell my students, and resist the temptation to panic when you stumble again into the void. If you have time for reflection as you turn the pages, make a note of any patterns or parallels, words or phrases that seem to constitute the common ground between Bloom and Stephen, between father and son, between citizen and artist, between religions and races. Stephen's mother's breath has a *faint* odour of wetted ashes; Bloom likes kidneys with a fine

JAMES JOYCE'S
ULYSSES *A study by Stuart Gilbert*

A VINTAGE BOOK   V-13
$1.95

Leo Lionni's twirling cover design for the 1955 Vintage edition of *James Joyce's Ulysses*, with faces of Bloom, Molly and Stephen coming at us from all directions.

tang of *faintly* scented urine. Yes, episode 1 and episode 4 are full of such parallels, some external and 'interesting', some more profound and revelatory. It's as if Joyce wants to distinguish his main protagonists not only in terms of the world but also in terms of each other. *Ulysses* is a novel full of correspondences for those with eyes to see.

Joyce tends to play fair with the reader – at least at first. Once you get attuned to the voices of Stephen and Bloom, you can accept them for what they are. Curious individuals, not terribly at ease with the world. Limited, like most of us I suspect, at the mercy of something. Equally, Joyce tends to play fair with the patterns in the novel, especially as they occur in a particular episode. Such-and-such takes place in 'Lotus-eaters', or is referred to in this episode, therefore it must be about time standing still, eating lotuses and forgetting the journey you're on. Horses munching in a bag of oats, boys smoking cigarettes, the faithful receiving Holy Communion, a tip for the Ascot Gold Cup, Bloom reading a letter from a woman with whom he hopes to initiate a relationship or an affair. Modern forms of lotus-eating. Most of the episodes follow this pattern, so that when you don't recognise a reference, say to yourself 'Oh, this must have something to do with dispossession if it's the first episode, with change or exile if it's the third, with intermediate things or "betweenness" if it's "Scylla and Charybdis", the rock and the whirlpool'. Then, if you're someone who wants to know everything, look it up; or, if you just want just the gist of something, read on. And don't miss the obvious. The cat meowing on the opening page of 'Calypso', 'the white button under the butt of her tail', her 'green, flashing eyes', her tail on high walking stiffly round the leg of Bloom's table, and the way Bloom calls her 'pussens', all alert us to the charms of Calypso and, more generally, to female genitalia and sexual attraction.

Getting help

It's worth building up a knowledge of *Ulysses* for yourself. Character and narrative voice, structure and theme, these are such delicate things to handle and come to us only once as new. 'How do you find living here?' was a question I would regularly face in my first weeks and months of living in California in 1981. What I realised was that it was not a question primarily addressed to me; it was my hosts wanting to relive the shock of the new which they had once felt for the lotus-eating country of sleepy hollow. Reading *Ulysses* is an experience best enjoyed as an experience. I delayed for six months before telling my California hosts what I thought about the land of the free. Experience, therefore, sometimes involves delay. I've never been keen on so-called idiots' guides, for they seem designed to foreclose on the experience and, in spite of promising so much in so short a space, effectively short-change the reader. Let readers claim the book for themselves and enjoy from the outset whatever the novel has to offer, to have in the one go as far as possible both the experience and the meaning. Schemas, notes, plot summaries and thumbnail sketches of characters, all these help, but, without making a fetish of the work of art, there's nothing quite like reading the thing itself.

   Ulysses in this respect is different from other Modernist novels such as Ford Madox Ford's *The Good Soldier* (1915), where reconstructing the chronology looks like a tease while an interpretation of the character of John Dowell the narrator will always remain a matter of opinion. With *Ulysses*, everything or nearly everything can be identified and known, and interpretation, therefore, is based largely on knowledge not speculation. With *Ulysses*, we can more or less determine what happens in each chapter; with *The Good Soldier*, as when Dowell recalls seeing out of the train window 'a brown cow hitch its horns under the stomach of a black and white animal' (Ford, 1995, 35), we're not certain what happens in the sense of what such an incident means or why Dowell chooses to tell us. But we know that if a piece of paper, a throwaway – the name as it happens of one

3.0—The GOLD CUP, value 1,000 sovs, with
3.000 sovs. in specie in addition, out of which
the second shall receive 700 sovs. and the third
300 sovs. added to a sweepstakes of 20 sovs.
each. h. ft., for entire colts and fillies.   Two
miles and a half.

		age	st	lb
M. J. de Bremond's Maximum II.				
	In France	5	9	4
Mr. W. Bass's Sceptre	A. Taylor	5	9	1
Lord Ellesmere's Kroonstad	J. Dawson	4	9	0
Lord Howard de Walden's Zinfandel				
	Beatty	4	9	0
Sir J. Miller's Rock Sand	Blackwell	4	9	0
Mr. W. Hall Walker's Jean's Folly				
	Robinson	3	7	4
(Above have arrived).				
Mr. F. Alexander's Throwaway	Braime	5	9	4
M. E. de Blaskovits's Beregvolgy				
	In France	4	9	0
Count H. de Pourtales's Ex Voto				
	In France	4	9	0
Count H. de Pourtales's Hebron II.				
	In France	4	9	0
M. J. de Soukozanette's Torquato Tasso				
	In France	4	9	0
Mr. Richard Croker's Clonmell	In Ireland	3	7	7

The runners for the Ascot Gold Cup in 1904 as they appeared in *The Freeman's Journal* for Bloomsday. Joyce made good use of 'Throwaway' and 'Sceptre' in *Ulysses*, adding to the realistic texture of the novel. Getting help: even throwaways can contribute.

of the runners at Ascot on 16 June 1904 – is dropped upstream into the River Liffey at a certain time it can be, or it will be, seen by another character, or remarked on by the narrator, downstream later in the day, mirroring in this respect the relation between a bet placed in the morning and winnings collected in the afternoon. Paths, too, cross, so that if a character is travelling in a certain direction between three and four in the afternoon, chances are s/he will encounter or pass another character coming from a different part of the city, as happens in 'Wandering Rocks', an episode that pays particular attention to space – time co-ordinates.

Having said all that, some guides and run-throughs, such as Harry Blamires's *The New Bloomsday Book: Guide Through 'Ulysses'* (1996), will prove especially valuable to students new to Joyce. A study I always have at my side when reading or writing about Joyce is Charles Peake's *James Joyce: The Citizen and the Artist* (1977). This is not only a guide but also a resource, which alerts the reader to the novel's richness in terms of structure and theme, and it does so within a larger framework of Joyce's concern with art and ordinary life. No-one studying *Ulysses* beyond a certain point will get far without consulting Don Gifford and Robert J. Seidman's *Ulysses Annotated: Notes for James Joyce's Ulysses* (1989). The notes are not always accurate, and will no doubt be updated in the years to come, but they are a first resort when something in the text needs elucidating. As for the Dublin walks tracing the footsteps of the characters in *Ulysses*, the book I'd recommend is Robert Nicholson's *The Ulysses*

Cover design by Max P. Kämpf, with photographs by A.T.P., H.P. Roth and Carola Giedion-Welcker, for an edition of *Ulysses* published by Rhein-Verlag in Zurich in 1956. Keep looking at this image and something interesting happens, for the faces in the crowd are not Irish faces but those you might see in New York or Chicago. Nelson's Pillar, the heart of Dublin, then becomes the centre of an American city, or, rather, *Ulysses* becomes a novel that has something to say about modern cities in general. History and modernity, faces in the crowd, bits and pieces of information, where 'cross here' is juxtaposed with 'costumes to hire' and a reversed image of an arrow pointing to hotel rooms, and over it all Joyce at Platzspitz in Zurich in 1937 smoking to his heart's content. This is perhaps my favourite dust-wrapper for a Joyce text where the 1950s style picks up on motifs and concerns expressed by American novelists such as John Dos Passos and James T. Farrell in the 1930s, encouraging us to broaden our conception of the novel beyond the reach of Dublin.

Guide: Tours Through Joyce's Dublin (2002). The internet is bulging with Joyce sites, but the one I'd recommend is Michael Groden's site at http://publish.uwo.ca/~mgroden/notes/index.html. For a comprehensive site reproducing images associated with the text, see Aida Yared's site at www.joyceimages.com.

Whatever guides readers have recourse to, whether in print or on the internet, they shouldn't neglect Frank Budgen's *James Joyce and the Making of 'Ulysses'*, a book first published in 1934, in which he reproduces his conversations with Joyce in Zurich and Paris. In a series of well-honed, almost casual reflections, Budgen presents us with the man and the author when he was in the middle of writing *Ulysses*, and the irony shouldn't be lost on us: it took an English artist to paint one of the best portraits we have of the Irish writer. Without Budgen there would be no intimate or sustained record of Joyce talking at the time about his method of working on *Ulysses*. One evening when they met up, Joyce informed Budgen he had been writing all day. Budgen imagined he had written a great deal. No, just two sentences came the reply. Budgen assumed Joyce had been looking for the *mot juste*, the exact word, which was Flaubert's method. No, retorted Joyce, he had the words: 'What I am seeking is the perfect order of words in the sentence' (Budgen, 1972, 20). In his review of *Dubliners* in *The Egoist* in June 1914, Pound observed that Joyce 'carefully avoids telling you a lot that you don't want to know' (cited in Benstock, 1985, 20). Budgen provides a companion insight when he recalls Joyce insisting that he wanted the reader to understand 'always through suggestion rather than direct statement' (Budgen, 1972, 21). A careful writer who typically communicated through suggestion. A guide book would tend to skip over such a remark as being too general, and yet I'd rather have Budgen on Joyce than reams of pages of commentary in the guide books.

Another day, while they were walking along Universitätstrasse in Zurich, Joyce remarked to Budgen that he wanted to provide a portrait of his native city 'so complete that if the city one day disappeared from the earth it could be reconstructed out of my book' (69). Such a remark has entered the Joyce canon and is quoted wherever *Ulysses* is talked about. What Joyce's comments to Budgen reveal is the mind and intention of the creator, and they

Frank Budgen's sketch of Joyce and Budgen in conversation, glasses to hand, legs like independent interlocutors.

help us whether we are readers new to Joyce or seasoned practitioners in the art of reading him. In turn, Budgen himself provides some sharp insights, as when, after recalling Joyce speaking about his native city of Dublin, he adds: 'Streets are named but never described' (69). It's something we might concur with as we think back to Great Britain Street in 'The Sisters' or Lotts in *A Portrait*. Again, it highlights the kind of city we have described in Joyce's fiction, and, if we care to, we can take the insight a step further, for Joyce's city is a city already named, a reminder that what we are dealing with here is a fabulous exercise in memory and faithfulness. In its own way we might see this as another example of Joyce's connection with the 'faithful departed' idea, mentioned in Chapter 3 when discussing my Irish relations, Tom and Jack Haugh.

Thalatta! Thalatta! – an epiphany

Budgen was lucky, for there's nothing quite like being close to the fire. The rest of us have to put up with the cold until something else comes along. This is why I enjoy learning how other Joyce critics go about teaching the novel. Several such collections have appeared in recent years, but the one that stands out for me is Kathleen McCormick and Erwin R. Steinberg's *Approaches to Teaching Joyce's Ulysses* (1993). Teachers sometimes give the impression that they were never neophytes or amateur readers of Joyce, but, to my mind, when *Ulysses* is under discussion, we are all in possession of 'owning-up' stories. My own first encounters with *Ulysses* were not terribly fruitful. To continue with the borrowed phrase from T.S. Eliot, I had the experience, or rather I had an experience, but I missed the meaning. Only some time after graduating did I return to the novel, and it took many years before I could say I genuinely enjoyed its company. At my first experience of the opening episode, I couldn't quite define the mood it created for me. The Bodley Head edition carries an initial 's' down the page, but I couldn't see what that detached letter was trying to achieve. That was the first thing that distracted me.

I kept looking at that initial letter and reflecting on its prominence. After noticing the bow on the spine of the Bodley Head green dust-jacket, I wondered if 's' was a play on the ubiquitous weapon on the pottery and ceramics of antiquity. *Ulysses* as a weapon, but against what? The Irish traditionally deployed the harp as a symbol, but why start an Irish novel with a Greek motif? And if it is a Greek novel, why not begin with a reference to the Muse, as is the case with Homer's *Odyssey*? These were the questions that began to edge their way into my thoughts, and still to some extent remain lodged there. As for the opening sentence, that doesn't sound

On the cover of the three-volume synoptic edition of *Ulysses*, published by Garland in 1984, there is a striking bow in gold-leaf. When Ulysses departed for the Trojan Wars, he left behind in his attic his bow. Any man who could bend the bow of Ulysses would win the hand of Penelope, his wife. On his return, incognito, Ulysses took part with other suitors in the competition, and on winning he turned his bow on his wife's chief suitor Antinous and shot him cleanly through the throat. The appropriateness of a bow as an emblem for Joyce's novel, however, needs weighing against this inconvenient truth: no suitors are slain in *Ulysses*.

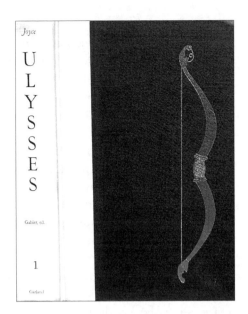

English at all, and it's a sentence I've never heard read properly, in part because it can't be. It's written English, flat, an 's' shape, designed to be scanned like Latin, but it's at war with spoken English and with the natural rhythms of English. In my *James Joyce's Ireland* (1992), I set it out like a hexameter, but here let me set it out like an 's', as if it were a three-line poem by William Carlos Williams or Denise Levertov:

> Stately,
>
> plump Buck Mulligan
>
> came from the stairhead,
>
> bearing a bowl of lather
>
> on which a mirror and a razor lay
>
> crossed.

Again, the opening seems designed to put us on our guard, to distance the reader from the world on display, to remind us from the outset of the peculiar nature of the novel's armoury. Bowed. Crossed. It's a long, long way from Molly's affirmative 'yes' that marks the end of the novel. For those with an eye to the significance of letters, *Ulysses* begins with an 'x', a cross, and ends with a 'y', a yes. 'Why?' you may well ask.

I felt, then, a sense of coldness, reminiscent of the atmosphere of paintings from Picasso's blue period. Expressing it thus, by way of a comparison, helps me communicate now what I vaguely felt at the time, but of course that is placing too much definition on something that refused such definiteness. The paintings I have in mind are those of the two adult figures and child in *Tragedy* (1903), and Picasso's *Self Portrait* (1901) with his long black coat, whitened forehead, blank expression and thick red lips. What intrigues me about this period in Picasso's career is not what Budgen calls his 'maudlin self-pity' (Budgen, 1972, 189) but the relationship between the figures and their background. How might we define that relationship? The background provides no comfort, being unbelievably, infinitely cold, designed seemingly to accentuate the lostness of the figures. But that doesn't seem right, either. It's less a mental landscape representing the mind and more an anonymous landscape in which humans are shown in adversity; and yet they betray no signs of struggle, unless it's a struggle against the paint or the uniformity of colour. Where the landscape is located is not really an appropriate question, and yet we feel impelled to ask. Nor are the figures inserted, as it were, into a landscape, for they seem part of it. The shore, the sea, the bare feet suggest a symbolic landscape and invite an interpretation along lines that might or might not give us comfort. The boy opens his hands in *Tragedy* as if he is trying to maintain or establish contact with the adult man and woman. In a world of resignation, the gesture seeks a response, but it looks forlorn in a painting that has tragedy written all over it.

Then, suddenly, in the midst of my blue mood, I discovered something in the first episode I could latch on to. It was the phrase '*Thalatta! Thalatta!*' (*U* 1:80) (the sea, the sea) a phrase that sprang out at me from schooldays poring over Xenophon in musty textbooks. In their journey home from the dusty Persian Wars, the Greek soldiers eventually reached the Black Sea. The maritime soldiers were so happy, according to the historian Xenophon, that they yelled for joy '*Thalatta! Thalatta!*'. I too felt like yelling as if in unison or by way of reply: 'Eureka'. At last, I had found something reassuring. My moment of recognition clearly didn't constitute a form of ownership, but it was a first step. Chrysostomos, another Greek word, on the first page of the novel, I also recognised, but had passed over. St John Chrysostom, Bishop of Antioch, was one of the Church Fathers, but I couldn't remember what he had written unless it had something to do with the importance of tradition. I knew that he had contributed to some aspect of Church doctrine and was nicknamed after his death by the name by which he is now known, which in English means golden-mouthed. On reflection and with the help of my Greek lexicon, I discovered what I had forgotten, that *stoma* in the second half of his name is Greek for mouth, or mouth of a river, or the edge or point of a sword. *Thalatta*, Chrysostomos, these Greek references I didn't connect at the time, and yet, with the title of the novel taken from Homer, I should have. Put simply, I couldn't see what I was supposed to be seeing.

That in essence was my first experience. Detachment in mood coupled with an untrained eye, the very worst combination for beginning to read Joyce's blue novel. I should have undertaken what I suggest above: study Joyce's earlier texts, read Homer's *Odyssey* again, get the guide books out. But I never heed instructions. I wasn't aware that theme itself was as important as character and narrative structure, and that the reader could run with theme almost the whole way round the track and never look back. What Stephen is recalling when he hears Mulligan calling to him is that Chrysostomos has 'white teeth' and 'gold points'. On first encountering the mention of Chrysostomos, what came into my mind was his contribution to Church doctrine, but that wasn't relevant at this juncture. I realise now that the first episode not only carries but also insists on a Greek theme and that such a theme uses a mix-and-match technique where all kinds of things can contribute, some utterly trivial, some profound, some arcane, some well-known. It's Joyce rearranging what we understand by surface and depth in reading. In this instance, teeth are as important as Church doctrine or tradition, being part of the Greek texture or theme. So much for it all being about Homer's *Odyssey*.

Something similar, with variation, is at work with Malachi Mulligan. This name contains two dactyls, that is, the Greek metre of one stressed

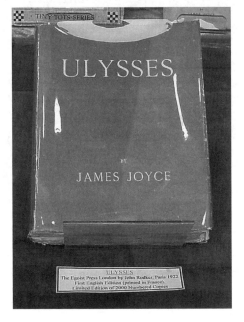

The Egoist Press edition of *Ulysses*, 'the bluest book in baile's annals' (*FW* 13:21–2). For sale in the window of Cathach Rare Books on Duke Street in Dublin for a four figure sum, October 2006. This edition was published in London in 1922 by Harriet Shaw Weaver. The blue cover with white lettering reminded Joyce of the Greek flag, and the Greeks always brought him luck, he believed. With their uncut pages, the editions of *Ulysses* printed in the 1920s in France have the look of a huge telephone directory, which in some ways it is, full of names and streets and dispersed lists in need of sorting. Stephen even imagines an imaginary phone number at the start of everything: 'Put me on to Edenville. Aleph, alpha: nought, nought, one' (*U* 3:39–40).

syllable followed by two unstressed syllables: / x x, / x x. Mulligan, too, therefore, is associated with the Greeks, an orator, compared – presumably ironically – with Chrysostomos. Like the Greeks, he is at home with his male body, plunging into the sea for his morning swim at the Forty Foot below the Martello Tower at Sandycove. Mulligan is modelled in part on Oliver St John Gogarty, the medical student Joyce was staying with in the Tower in September 1904. But if someone had informed me that Gogarty's name also contains a dactyl or a double dactyl if you bring in his first name, Oliver, I would have been impressed but slightly puzzled. Is this a game of parallels then, a supplementary exercise to contrast with the deconstruction of the gnomon where Joyce began in *Dubliners*? The last word of the first episode, 'Usurper', also shouted to me out of the void and I responded. I too felt usurped not really of a home, which is the fate of Telemachus in Homer, but, rather, of an experience that by rights I should have had. I perked up at mention of another usurper in 'Proteus', namely Perkin Warbeck, 'York's false scion, in breeches of silk of whiterose ivory' (*U* 3:315–16). A white rose in an episode whose colour symbolism is green. Thank God for a history of the world not dependent on a knowledge of a writer's family and his one-time friends and enemies.

In any novel where orientation can't be readily identified, questions multiply to fill the empty space, and some of these tend to be quite basic. Information overload I have already touched on, for there seemed to be too much of it, and, while Joyce eventually plays fair, not all the information was pointing in the same direction. Are we supposed to connect the phrase 'genuine Christine' on line 21, which refers to the Mass and the body of

Photograph of the Martello Tower at Sandycove, taken in 1904. From Weston St John Joyce, *The Neighbourhood of Dublin* (1913). 'The fort was, until a few years ago, occupied by the military, and at certain seasons of the year was utilised for artillery practice, the firing causing much havoc among the windows of the adjoining houses' (49). *Ulysses* begins in a former barracks where the previous night Stephen is awoken by shots ringing out. History, fiction – where does the one begin and the other end when it comes to Joyce? Worse, for he's a writer who defies limits, someone who constantly plays, for example, on the association of Dublin with doubling.

Interior of the Star of the Sea Church at Sandymount, where Mr and Mrs Kernan from Joyce's story 'Grace' were married. In the 'Nausicaa' episode of *Ulysses*, it is afternoon and Bloom is on the beach at Sandymount masturbating while Gerty McDowell is teasing him by gently hoisting her skirt. In the background, Benediction is taking place at this church. During the service, the Host, which has been consecrated at morning Mass, is temporarily taken out of the tabernacle on the altar and 'exposed' to the congregation. On the beach and in the church, there is therefore both an exposure and an elevation. The real presence, we might be tempted to add. Normally obscured from view. On the day I took this photograph it was Halloween, hence the pumpkin in front of the altar. As we saw when discussing 'Clay' or 'throwaway', all kinds of ritual, or simply parallels, could serve Joyce's purpose. A boxy sort of mind. Photograph by David Pierce.

Christ, with the name of Chrysostomos a few lines further down, and what are we to make of the word 'crossed' in the very first sentence? Christ and Chrys, 'i' and 'y' or *í* and υ in Greek, a similarity in consonants rather than vowels. And does the echo constitute anything more than a similarity in sound with no added significance? In the French translation overseen by Joyce, we read 'la fin-fine Eucharistine' for 'the genuine Christine', as if something more than sound is intended (Joyce/Morel, 1957, 1). Christine, Eucharistine. Female Christ, Eucharist. Eucharistine wouldn't work in English, but Christine does. But why would you start a 'Greek' novel with a satire on the Roman Mass?

Initial questions kept me at it as if I was trying to uncover the 'unknown arts' that might overshadow this novel too. After all the ink spilt over his name from discussions in my previous chapters, Stephen Dedalus finally reaches his explanatory moment or nadir in this episode, but what we learn is what we already suspected, that it is an 'absurd name, an ancient Greek!' (*U* 1:34). What's absurd according to Mulligan is not the Christian name, but only the Dedalus part. Absurd. Thank God someone had said it. Or does the absurdity lie in the way it attempts to yoke together the Christian and classical traditions? It must have occurred to many pupils in their teenage years at school: what's the connection between studying a classics text in the classroom and saying prayers in the chapel? Is the connection loose or disjunctive like the ablative absolute construction in Latin grammar or something more integrated? Is the attempt at a joined-up name absurd because in our culture the two, Homer and Christ, have never been satisfactorily united? We are back to the theological discussion in the previous chapter on St John's Gospel. Once upon a time. In the beginning. The Greek diaspora. The Trinity. I assume the link between Stephen and Dedalus is in name only, and that this is what we are to take from Joyce's pseudonym, namely Stephen the first Christian martyr, Daedalus the master craftsman and forger. Perhaps I'm wrong and that Joyce was more ambitious. Is this what he eventually believed, or is the joined-up name designed to confront Mulligan's insensitivity or show Stephen's sensitivity and his feeling of being usurped even of his name? Whatever the case, it's the attitude expressed in the exclamation mark I like: 'absurd name, an ancient Greek!' 'Make of that what you will', Joyce seems to be saying. 'I'm writing a novel, not telling you what I think.'

What I've been articulating is something that must be quite a common experience on coming to *Ulysses* for the first time. I'm not one for giving up, but I do understand signs of frustration and the value of human sympathy. It's sometimes encouraging for readers to see that even someone who now has a certain expertise in interpreting Joyce should have begun in similar fashion. Sounding off is common these days, especially over the airwaves, but to whom do you take your complaint when the person lies buried in a cemetery next to the lions in the zoo in Zurich? I've been stressing strategies for coping, but we might well agree that the first strategy is not so much a strategy as a cry. The first thing is to recognise a common reaction, that most people will find *Ulysses* tough going. You have to remember that the novel took some seven years to write, so it's been worked on again and again, polished, layered, added to, qualified, expanded, pored over, arranged, rearranged. It's like a well-tended garden in this respect, except that it requires us to get our hands dirty and do some work. Joyce wondered if he had over-systematised things, and I must confess I long at times for the casualness of, say, Forster's prose style, how for example he begins *Howards End* (1910) with 'One may as well begin with Helen's letters to her sister'. Nothing is casual in *Ulysses*, and every passing thought carries more than it should by way of authorial intention and meaning. It starts with an 'x' and ends with a 'y'.

Homer

When he published *James Joyce's Ulysses: A Study* in 1930, Stuart Gilbert did Joyce both a service and a disservice, for while the author's emphasis on the Homeric correspondences demonstrated to those who thought otherwise that there was an intricate pattern behind the novel, it also threatened to destroy its living texture and at the same time to reduce or collapse the distance between Dublin and ancient Greece. Joyce understood what Gilbert perhaps didn't: chords, whether consonant or dissonant, require different notes to be struck. The endearing Paddy Dignam might be the 'equivalent' of the endearing Elpenor in Homer's *Odyssey*, the figure who accidentally falls from a ladder and kills himself, but he is also the father of a boy who will now have to be cared for, the centre of attention in the Funeral episode, and the occasion for not a little humour when his surname is played on. Thus, when the Jesuit priest John Conmee alights from the presbytery of St Francis Xavier's Church on Upper Gardiner Street in Dublin and sets off for the orphanage in Artane on behalf of Paddy Dignam's son, he thinks to himself: 'What was that boy's name again? Dignam. Yes. Vere dignum' (*U* 10:3–4). 'Vere dignum et justum est' is the opening to one of the prayers at Latin Mass. It is right and proper . . . Dignam, dignum. It's a linguistic conceit, a play between languages and between feminine and masculine case endings in Latin, and it's also a reflection of Conmee's conceitedness. But we are a long way from the Homeric correspondences, and no amount of contrastive analysis will bring them together again under the youthful aegis of *consonantia*, the concept which, as we saw in the last chapter, Stephen makes much of in *A Portrait*.

Dignam is also a name that is confused by an increasingly agitated Bloom with Plumtree's Potted Meat: 'All up a plumtree. Dignam's potted meat' (*U* 8:744–5). 'What is home without Plumtree's Potted Meat' is one of the many jingles running through *Ulysses*, this time an advertising jingle. The answer to the question is the deflating 'Incomplete. With it an abode of bliss.' Dignam's death has robbed his home of completeness, and his meat is now coffined and potted in Glasnevin Cemetery. Meanwhile, Bloom is feeling the pressure, and his language begins to show signs of slippage, so that while Dignam may be up a plumtree, with four o'clock approaching and Boylan about to enter his wife's bed, he himself is up a gum tree. All up. Such a graphic phrase in the context. If *Ulysses* is a voyage tracing the course of Odysseus's wanderings after the Trojan Wars, it is also a voyage

A photograph I took in the early 1990s of the (restored) omphalos at Delphi in Greece. The ancient Greeks believed this stone was the centre or the navel of the world and was venerated as such. In *Ulysses*, Mulligan, in reference to the Martello Tower – one of many towers that were built to protect the coastline against the French at the time of the Napoleonic Wars – quips that 'Ours is the omphalos', meaning our defence, our navel, is Greek culture. Later, Stephen thinks about gazing at his omphalos and how Eve was the only person who didn't have a navel and how the human race is joined by the 'strandentwining cable of all flesh' (*U* 3:37). Following on from Stuart Gilbert's observations on the omphalos in *James Joyce's Ulysses* (1930), I have long thought that *Ulysses* constitutes a profound meditation on the idea of a centre to the world, with this proviso, that Joyce assumes there are many such centres. Homer's *Odyssey* and the Greeks provide one, and so does the body (especially the female body), and so does humour, and so does the area outside the General Post Office in the centre of Dublin where trams used to turn, and so does the colonised city of Dublin itself. Centres of the known world. Mythology, history, geography, human anatomy, the maternity hospital, culture and colonialism. Add the history of writing in 'Oxen of the Sun' and you arrive at Joyce in the centre. Photograph by David Pierce.

much closer to the Irish at home. There's something else about home. None of the characters in the novel know they have or that they are equivalents to characters in Homer, and, as I've been stressing throughout this book, it is the reader who is the fabulous voyager.

So, what am I saying here? Begin with the Greeks and with Homer's *Odyssey* is good advice, but take care how you proceed. *Ulysses* is a novel that moves ceaselessly and at times almost seamlessly back and forth: one minute we're in Dublin, the next in ancient Greece; one minute we're in the world of external reality, the next inside the heads of the various characters; one minute we're surrounded by realistic texture, the next by symbolic patterning and resonance. Sometimes myths are quickened from within and impress themselves accordingly; at other times we need to be reminded that a character has an equivalent in Homer. To recall an image used in discussing 'A Painful Case', chords or points sometimes click into place as we pass over them. Something that is major in Homer can be toned down by Joyce; conversely, something that receives only a few lines in Homer, as with the incident of the wandering rocks, becomes a full-blown chapter in Joyce. You think that 'Sirens', with its title, should be all about the sound of music, but then you discover it's as much about the visual as the aural, as much about writing as sounds, as much about expression as stopping up the ears, and it's an episode that features a deaf waiter and which contains a surprisingly heretical thought: 'Music. Gets on your nerves' (*U* 11:1182). The Night-town episode 'Circe' is the longest episode in *Ulysses* and is more like a phantasmagoria or Bosch's *Garden of Delights* than anything in the *Odyssey*. The final episode 'Penelope' is the star-turn, when Molly Bloom, whose maiden name Marion Tweedy evokes Penelope's characteristic domestic activity of weaving, recalls moments in her sexual past, but Odysseus remains throughout the primary focus of Homer's tale. On his return home after ten years away, the recognition scenes are some of the most memorable in Homer, but the Blooms know all about each other, all their little secrets and the ruses they deploy, so that any recognition scene would be either out of keeping or redundant or too explicit and confrontational by far.

Keep checking on the correspondences but don't become a slave to them. Early commentators on Joyce in the 1920s, as if they glimpsed where a certain line of inquiry might be heading, said something similar, and I think they were right. In Gorman's 1926 biography of Joyce we learn that Valery Larbaud, Joyce's chief advocate in France, also downplayed the Homeric parallels (Gorman, 1926, 122–3). The correspondences between Goethe's *Faust* and *Ulysses*, according to Mary Colum in one of the earliest reviews of the novel, are just as plausible as between Homer and *Ulysses* (Colum, 1922, 452). Joyce is such a creative thinker that he rarely does the expected. *Ulysses* grew from being the title to a possible story in *Dubliners* to the epic it is now considered to be. It takes up into it Homer's Greek epic and gestures towards something bigger than itself. If it had been called 'Leopold Bloom' or 'Mr and Mrs Bloom' or the 'The Love Song of Mr Leopold Bloom' or 'Affairs of the Heart', it would have been a less ambitious novel. Equally, although the Shakespearean theme is everywhere present, *Ulysses* would have been seriously diminished if it travelled round the world with 'Hamlet' round its neck, and tied too closely, therefore, to Stephen and the father–son motif.

As I suggested in previous chapters, Joyce was attracted toward the capacious resonance of a title. Nothing would tie him down unduly. With this novel he had an extraordinarily large framework, but he could also play little games with the name of Ulysses. In the Library episode, there is mention of 'another Ulysses' (*U* 9:403), namely Pericles, where 'another' has the look of a direct address or nod to the reader. In her soliloquy at the end,

Molly refers to 'general Ulysses Grant whoever he was or did supposed to be some great fellow landed off the ship' (*U* 18:682–3). Ulysses S Grant, the American Civil War hero, who went on to become the eighteenth President of the United States, is in one sense the person, 'whoever he was', with the largest claim on the titular name in this novel. The fact that the modern Penelope doesn't recognise her husband in his name reminds us that there are plenty of nods to the reader but precious few recognition scenes as such by the characters themselves in Joyce's novel.

Boul' Mich', Paris

Greek, Irish, French. *Ulysses* may be a Greek-sounding novel set in Dublin, but it was launched in Paris. In Chapter 10, I reflect more on Sylvia Beach's role in its publication, but here let me briefly touch on another aspect of the Parisian moment in *Ulysses*, for Paris, especially evident in the opening episodes of the novel, is the name for some of the earliest layering of this novel of exile and homecoming. On the defensive in the Library episode, Stephen wonders to himself where he, the hawklike man, flew to. And his answer is anti-romantic and precise: 'Paris and back' (*U* 9:953). In Chapter 2 in this book, I dwelt on Joyce at 22, but what was he like in the previous 18 months, that period between departing for the continent and meeting Nora in June 1904? What were some of the things that happened to him

Boul' Mich' café on the left bank of the Seine in Paris. Photograph by David Pierce. Welcome. 'Boul' Mich", a colloquial short-hand for Boulevard St Michel, also finds its way into Stephen's thoughts in *Ulysses*. Sporting a Latin Quarter hat, Joyce knew how to play the part or the 'character' as he puts it in *Ulysses*. Indeed, he knew all about being a tourist in Paris. Head for the left bank! Boul' Mich', how he would have enjoyed writing home and telling his friends and acquaintants how he was making out in the city that was to become his home for two decades between the wars.

Bibliothèque St Geneviève, Paris, designed by Henri Labrouste and built in the middle of the nineteenth century. Photograph by David Pierce. This view of the library has changed little since Joyce was here during his first stay in Paris in 1902–3. Etched into the walls are the names of Europe's leading philosophers, writers, artists and scientists, including Sterne, whose name accompanies the French astronomer Nicholas Louis de la Caille and the French mathematician Alexis Clairault. Perhaps, if he noticed it, the joke would not have been lost on Joyce either – Sterne, a co-opted Frenchman, who managed to ensure that he didn't die in France, a concern expressed by Yorick in the first paragraph in *A Sentimental Journey Through France and Italy* (1768), for dying in France meant all your belongings and property, if you were a foreigner, passed to the King. In the area surrounding the Bibliothèque St Geneviève are buildings of the University of Paris, the university where Joyce's mentor Aquinas studied and later taught in the second half of the thirteenth century, and where St Francis Xavier lectured in Aristotelian philosophy in the sixteenth century. Stephen, we learn in *Ulysses*, read nightly in this library 'sheltered from the sin of Paris' (*U* 2:70). He is the same person we discussed in the last chapter, only now he has taken flight from the nets that had been flung at him in his native city. In a nearby church, on the tomb of St Geneviève, the patron saint of Paris who flourished *c*. 500, there is inscribed the phrase 'Consolatrice des exilés' (consoler of exiles). In all kinds of ways, Joyce must have felt at home here.

during his stay in Paris between December 1902 and April 1903? And why did Joyce want to return to that period? Was it to ensure a line of continuity between *A Portrait* and *Ulysses*? Seemingly, he hadn't quite done with his past in *A Portrait*, as if he still had things to recuperate from his stay there, things that he wanted to incorporate into his celebration of 16 June 1904, shards from a past which in retrospect could be shaped by the novelist into a contribution to the theme and texture of the Telemachiad. As Victor Pritchett reminds us in a review of Ellmann's 1959 biography, Joyce was 'fanatically, superstitiously exhaustive' (Pritchett, 1960, 80). Until he arrived at his fortieth birthday, Joyce always seemed to feel the pressure to return to the experiences of his childhood and youth. That might be superstition, but it was now accompanied by something else, the fiction-writer's compulsion to see patterns in the connection between Paris and Dublin.

As suggested in the last chapter, Joyce, the Aristotelian, was fascinated by the figure who fascinated Aquinas, and Stephen, his head turned by reading in the beautiful Bibliothèque St Geneviève, quotes Aristotle on the 'actuality of the possible as possible' and continues by reflecting how 'Thought is the thought of thought' (U 2:74). This is the wisdom of the ancient world, as Telemachus, in search of his father, seeks information from Homer's old man Nestor. In one respect it's true, thought is the thought of thought, and if it seems profound that must be because the worldview it betrays still has some power or passing interest for us. But, as we can observe from Gilbert's plan, Stephen at this stage is someone without a body, and at the same time intrigued by procession, by the philosophical idea concerning the relationship between potency or potentiality and act or materialisation. For the medieval scholastic mind, getting from one state to another is fraught with a philosophical conundrum, for everything must come out of something. The image of caterpillars and moths wouldn't do, or rather it would, since it suggested that everything had to have a material cause. But in general, without resorting to analogy or the Prime Mover, how do you account for change? Thought comes out of thought – that neatly sidesteps one problem, and in 'Nestor' it's enough. In the next episode, 'Proteus', change is again on the agenda and it is announced in the very first sentence, as in the issue of the visible changing into the intellectual: 'Ineluctable modality of the visible: at least that if no more, thought through my eyes' (U 3:1–2). Most of us I suspect will get out of the library pretty smartly if we feel such thoughts or doubts about the nature of external reality coming on, and fortunately near the Bibliothèque St Geneviève are a host of little restaurants and, further afield, 'the sin of Paris'. This is Joyce before Bloom, before he met Nora, before the world opened up for him in 1904.

Wild Geese

'Proteus', as its name suggests, is all about change. From Dublin to Paris, Ireland to France. By way of showing something of what's going on in this episode and how important it is therefore to get on the inside of this novel, let's consider the snatch of a conversation Stephen has in a Paris bar with

A slightly blurred photograph of Joyce during his first stay in Paris in 1902–3. Long overcoat, thin body, wide-brimmed hat, patterned tie, clean-shaven, eyes looking somewhere far off. Not quite together, but then who is at 20 or 21? Joyce was composing epiphanies at this time, a route into writing that allowed him an opportunity to express his lyrical side and his understanding of the world with more emphasis on defining the artist than celebrating the citizen. In Paris he had little money, his teeth caused him problems (especially when he ate onion soup), and he gave up studying medicine, but his head was still full of defining the world in terms of essences.

Source: James Joyce Collections at Morris Library/Southern Illinois University

Kevin Egan. But first, some extra-textual historical background material is needed for the benefit of non-Irish readers. After the defeat at the Battle of the Boyne in 1689 and the Treaty of Limerick in 1690 and the consequent triumph of the Williamite cause in Ireland, many of the titled families fled Ireland for France and Spain and other parts of central Europe. Known to history as the Wild Geese, they kept the faith even as they inter-married and became assimilated within European society. In wars against the British, such as the Napoleonic Wars, they sacrificed their lives. The most inflated nationalist tribute to this group in the novel is paid by John Wyse Nolan in the 'Cyclops' episode: 'We gave our best blood to France and Spain, the wild geese' (*U* 12:1381–2). No Irish epic, a condition to which *Ulysses* aspired, could afford to neglect at least a brief mention of these famous, if inflated, exiles in Irish history, and it is appropriate that Stephen on his stay in Paris seeks out a meeting with Kevin Egan, whom Joyce associates with a modern version of the Wild Geese.

Joyce then adds to the mix another historical reference, this time to the Fenians, the group who in the 1867 attempted a rising to break by physical force the English connection with Ireland. In biographical terms, Egan is based on the Irish Fenian Joe Casey, whom Joyce met while in Paris in

1902–3 and who lent him money. Casey was a typesetter for the *New York Herald* in Paris and had fled to France after escaping from Clerkenwell Prison in London in 1867. He had been imprisoned there for attempting to free the captured Fenians, who became known as the Manchester Martyrs. In the brief conversation we will now look at, all this historical material has a bearing. The first episode of *Ulysses* ends, as already mentioned, with the one word 'Usurper!'. This theme is continued into this third episode, only now the emphasis is on Kevin Egan being usurped of a home.

Egan has fallen on hard times in Paris, and it is this aspect that Joyce chooses to highlight in an episode devoted to the shape-changer 'Proteus'. Stephen meets him and his son Patrice in a Paris bar with an Irish name. It's not MacMahon's but 'bar MacMahon', a bar that was named after a descendant of the Wild Geese, Marie Edmé Patrice Maurice de MacMahon, who became the second president of the Third Republic in the 1870s. (It's the world as much as Joyce that surprises us, or should surprise us, by its extraordinary sets of coincidence.) 'Patrice, home on furlough, lapped warm milk with me in the bar MacMahon. Son of the wild goose, Kevin Egan of Paris. My father's a bird, he lapped the sweet *lait chaud* with pink young tongue, plump bunny's face. Lap, *lapin*' (*U* 3:163–6). As a sign of assimilation, Patrick surfaces in France as Patrice, and he's 'home on furlough', that is he's on leave from military service with France.

Patrice is the son not of the Wild Geese but of the wild goose, and Joyce continues his mockery by putting words in Patrice's mouth about his father being a bird. The Wild Geese, we realise, is a metaphorical term and has an air of romance about it; 'wild goose' is just that, something you might shoot and have for supper. The French translation has 'canard sauvage' (Joyce/Morel, 1957, 45) or wild duck for 'wild goose' as if the species is of no importance. It also misses completely the historical allusion at this point. What Joyce made of such a translation we don't know, but perhaps he had other concerns in the late-1920s to occupy him and didn't have the patience to explain all the connections intended in using such phrases. In 'Cyclops', 'the wild geese', as quoted above, undergoes another inappropriate translation by Morel and becomes 'oiseaux migrateurs' or migratory birds (875), which the Wild Geese weren't, for they never returned. Earlier, in 'Aeolus', the windy episode, the same translation is used in a section that is followed by another section entitled 'Lost Causes' (149), which the Wild Geese were.

What intrigues me about this moment is that the historical allusions have become part of a much larger protean theme and could afford to be downgraded or lost therefore. Thus, the milk, too, experiences not only a linguistic and typographical change but also a temperature change, first as 'lait', then as '*lait chaud*', warm milk. 'Lap', too, suggests some kind of animal, a

Rue des Irlandais, Paris, adjacent to the Pantheon, where the Irish Cultural Centre, founded in 2002, is housed. Photograph by David Pierce. Ever since 1578 and the Elizabethan conquest of Ireland, Irish priests have been trained in Paris. In the Irish context, therefore, 'Paris and back' is a phrase that has a wider application. To bring the story up to date, in the modern period Paris has been a home for many Irish writers, including George Moore, Synge, Thomas MacGreevy, Beckett, Kathleen Coyle and John Montague. And we can never forget that Wilde is buried there. In the early years of his career, when he was absorbing the impact of French symbolism, Yeats was a frequent visitor. In the 1890s, he saw a production of *Axël*, a play by Villiers de l'Isle Adam (1838–89), which contained the supercilious line he enjoyed quoting: 'As for living, our servants will do that for us'.

cat lapping milk from a saucer, for example. In this way, the image of milk recalls the milk woman in the first episode who is herself an image of the Shan Van Vocht or Poor Old Woman in the Irish aisling or visionary tradition. In that tradition, an old woman is met on the roads and pours forth her tale of woe, speaking of the four green fields taken from her by the stranger. When she departs she has been transformed into a queen, for she is, as Yeats shows in his rousing play *Cathleen ni Houlihan* (1902), the sovereignty figure of Irish folklore, asserting her independence of Britain and inspiring her sons to take up arms in her cause. Milk and its associations in Ireland haven't quite been lost here in the 'Irish pub' scene. In the next episode, when Bloom puts down some 'warmbubbled' milk for his cat and listens to 'her licking lap' (*U* 4:43), he reminds us of domesticity and gender, as if politics and cultural nationalism could be countered by something less aggressive and more familial. In the scene with Egan, however, all such associations are held at bay, since 'lap' is followed at once by 'lapin', French for rabbit, and from there it is but a short squeak to 'bunny'. Kevin Egan of

Paris, lapping, a lapin. A one-time revolutionary, he 'rolls gunpowder cigarettes', but now he is 'Loveless, landless, wifeless'.

The passage is one of many in this episode that recall Joyce's early stay in
Paris. Its significance can be missed or skipped over, but what it reveals is
how the snatch of a conversation, a brief encounter with someone from
one's past, is transformed by the novelist into material that makes more
sense, or gains more resonance, in fiction than in real life. In 1902–3 Joyce's
meeting with Casey could not have carried anything like the importance
that Stephen's encounter with Egan carries in *Ulysses*. In this sense, 'Proteus' takes up into it the transforming effects of the novelist on the material
that precedes it. It's characteristic of Joyce that he should wrap some profound moments, whether in Irish history or in personal terms, in what we
might consider are pretty sentimental or fairly banal scenes or remarks. I
think that's right, for Joyce, after all, is the suppressed lyricist. We don't
know as readers if the encounter with Egan is supposed to be significant or
not. It could indeed be an example – God forbid – of a wild goose chase,
by us the reader or by Joyce during his stay in Paris. On the other hand,
in the Gorman-Gilbert plan Egan is identified with Menelaus, the figure in
Homer's *Odyssey* who was King of Sparta and husband of Helen. His connection with Odysseus/Bloom is also important but also underplayed by
Joyce. And one wonders if his fate as loveless and wifeless is meant to fore-
shadow some of our responses to Bloom's possible fate.

One part of me thinks Stephen's encounter with Egan is to be taken seriously, especially when Maud Gonne is also mentioned in these same pages.
I'm thinking here of Paris of the Irish exiles, plotting against the old enemy
in the name of La Patrie. Clusters in Joyce are designed to be noticed and
frequently remind us of a potential or underlying significance. Another part
of me thinks it's a send-up of the heroic or romantic tradition of the political exile and of sentimental songs about the Wild Geese (and by association
the Poor Old Woman). Egan remembers Ireland, but Ireland doesn't remember him. The Poor Old Woman doesn't even recognise the Irish language when the Englishman Haines speaks to her using it, and to make
matters worse she affirms pathetically: 'I'm told it's a grand language by
them that knows' (*U* 1:434). Stephen perhaps had some deluded idea
that he was 'going to do wonders' and become a '[m]issionary to Europe
after fiery Columbanus' (*U* 3:192–3). Paris and back. 'Telemachus' and
'Proteus', both episodes deal with forms of exile. Egan's must have been the
common fate of many exiles and one that Joyce in his early career – though
this is less true of Stephen in *Ulysses* – perhaps feared he might himself face.
But then I think of the ceaselessly transforming activity of this episode and
recall this sentence: 'In gay Paree, he hides, Egan of Paris, unsought by any

save by me' (*U* 3:249–50). Because he is sought out, Egan is *saved* by Stephen. This, too, constitutes the work of Proteus – to except, to transform the ordinary, the casual, the lost to history, the forgotten into the significant, the remembered, that is into the life, the very stuff, that is, of fiction.

All the discussion above issues from memory of a conversation. Yeats was impressed, as he tells us in 'Meditations in Time of Civil War' (1928), with the 'half read wisdom of daemonic images', but that would never do for Joyce. Elucidating just a small fragment so that it yields all that it has to offer involves the reader in quite a lot of research, in this case into Irish history and Joyce's stay in Paris in 1902–3. In fact, Stephen is walking along Sandymount Strand, 4 miles south of Dublin, but his mind is filling up with all kinds of memories from his Paris sojourn. 'In fact' isn't quite right, for it is Joyce's mind filling up with memories. The people he met there, the reading matter he enjoyed, the books he studied in libraries, the material he brought home with him in April 1903 on receiving the telegram from his father about his mother dying. All this finds its way into this Paris–Dublin, French–English moment, and, as we have just seen, Joyce enjoys punning between languages or playing with language as if he was already beginning the process that would eventually lead to *Finnegans Wake*.

A little further on, Stephen returns to the conversation with Egan. A waitress, who confuses Stephen with a Dutchman, is corrected by Egan: '*Il est irlandais. Hollandais? Non fromage. Deux irlandais, nous, Irlande, vous savez? Ah, oui!*' (*U* 3:220–1) (He's Irish. Dutch? Not cheese. Two Irishman we are. Ireland, you know? Ah, yes!). Morel's French translation has a comma: *Il est Irlandais, Hollandais?* This is one way of rendering this situation, where it is the waitress who is responsible for everything up to the question mark. So she says 'He's Irish, Dutch?' But to my mind it makes more sense if there's a period or full-stop after *irlandais*. I assume, translated, the original conversation went something like:

> Egan (speaking to the waitress but referring to Stephen): He's Irish.
> Waitress: Dutch?
> Egan: Not cheese. Two Irishmen, we are. Ireland, you know?
> Waitress: Ah, yes.

Because of the lack of sound similarity between 'Irish' and 'Dutch', the joke doesn't work in English. The sleight on the Dutch arises, I assume, from the waitress imagining she heard an order for 'cheese *hollandais*', Dutch cheese. I know what Edam is, but I'm not quite sure what 'cheese hollandais' is, for, if you search the internet for the phrase, nearly all the entries listed are to *Ulysses*, which is normally a sure sign that it's unique to Joyce. Perhaps the phrase affords another example of the protean theme.

'Cheese hollandaise' is different, for that is a well-established menu item, at least in something like hollandaise sauce. But 'hollandaise' has a feminine ending. Is that Joyce's point? Add an 'e' and you get it right; without the 'e' you get confusion and category mistakes. Perhaps Egan's French isn't terribly good and that he had dropped the 'e'. Perhaps the waitress was compensating for his mistake, or perhaps she was cleverer than Egan gives her credit for, gently pointing out his mistake by deliberately confusing Hollandais with Irlandais.

Throughout *Ulysses*, there are these intense moments when, as you set about trying to define or decipher what's going on, complex social relationships are unmasked. Sometimes one suspects that Joyce's peripheral vision, or 'near sight' as he calls it in *Finnegans Wake* (*FW* 628:2), especially when memory is involved, prevents him from supplying us with anything other than the minimum amount of information and that the rest remains locked away in his own head, uncalled upon or perhaps waiting to be called upon. Interestingly, this particular passage is one of the few I've come across in *Ulysses* where it works better in French throughout than it does in English and French. In English we read 'She thought you wanted a cheese *hollandais*'. In French: 'Elle pensait que vous demandiez du fromage *hollandais*' (Joyce/ Morel, 1957, 47). The switching back and forth between languages only works because we do some mental gymnastics, translating back into the

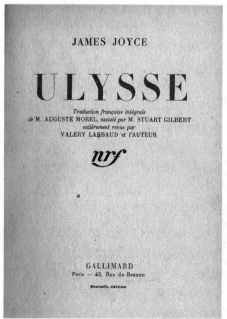

French translation of *Ulysses* 'de M. Auguste Morel, assisté par M. Stuart Gilbert entièrement revue par M. Valery Larbaud et l 'auteur' (entire translation reviewed by Larbaud and the author). Published by Gallimard in Paris. The stiff paper vellumised covers on my copy are cream-coloured and carry an attractive design in green, black and gold.
Source: Editions Gallimard

A copy of the slightly risqué French magazine *Le Tutu,* 18 February 1902. In 'Proteus', Stephen returned home from Paris with a copy of *Le Tutu* and the telegram about his mother's death from his father, part of what he terms 'rich booty'. 'Rich booty you brought back; *Le Tutu*, five tattered numbers of *Pantalon Blanc et Culotte Rouge*; a blue French telegram, curiosity to show: —Nother dying come home father' (*U* 3:196–9). That first stay in Paris was indeed 'rich booty' for Joyce. When he had worked his way through *Dubliners*, he could return to a period of his life that in terms of experience precedes the summer of 1904, but in terms of writing postdates it. In all kinds of way, it was appropriate that *Ulysses* was published in Paris in 1922.

original language and then returning to the sentence on the page in front of us. In French it makes more sense because it reflects what actually happened or what we assume happened. If the remark is by Egan to Stephen, then it's revealing, since he uses the more polite form of 'vous' to address Stephen, something that the English 'you' conceals. This clearly adds another dimension to the scene and, in case we thought the social relationship with Egan was all one way, it neatly puts Stephen in his place.

Anti-clericalism

Joyce needed an exposure to nineteenth-century French culture to write *Ulysses*. The 'sin of Paris' was clearly important to the young man, and that side of Paris – 'Gay Paree', with its cafés and bars and dancing girls – still attracted him when he returned there in the 1920s. But the note I want to end on here is to do with religion and French anti-clericalism. Anywhere you go in Ireland, even today when many of the young have stopped going to church, you hear people swearing on the name of 'Jesus'. 'By Jesus, I'll crown him, so I will.' 'Jesus wept!' 'Jesus, Mary and Holy Saint Joseph!' If Joyce had never ventured beyond Dublin, one suspects he would have succeeded in giving vent to – but nothing more than that – the residual fear of, or animosity against, Catholicism prevalent just below the surface of Irish life. Mr Casey screams at Dante in the Christmas dinner scene in *A Portrait*,

'No God for Ireland!' (*P* 39), but in general Irish Catholicism wasn't anti-clerical in the way continental Catholic Europe was, and, to take a small but telling example from something touched on above, on its own, one suspects, most Catholics in Ireland would not have been able to imagine a parallel between Benediction and Bloom masturbating on the beach. What the Fenians and advanced nationalists sought was the non-involvement of the Church in politics.

Ireland had developed differently, in part because the old religion offered a form of protection against the English Protestant stranger. Moreover, perhaps out of fear, its culture rarely strayed into something that Gabriel Conroy fears, namely 'thought-tormented' (*D* 203). To risk an over-simplification, the most the culture at the time of Joyce could produce by way of a contemporary critique of Catholicism was Michael McCarthy's rather leaden, sociological depiction of the gulf between the Irish poor and the well-endowed Church in *Priests and People in Ireland* (1902). But as the leading Catholic Modernist and one-time Jesuit priest George Tyrrell (1861–1909) understood, the strength of Irish Catholicism was its anti-intellectualism.[1] It was devotional, given to scruples, religious observances and the cult of inwardness. Its characteristic product in the period leading up to 1904 was *The Messenger of the Sacred Heart*, a monthly magazine founded in 1888 by the Irish Jesuit James Cullen, the same priest, as already noted, who in 1898 founded the Pioneer anti-drink association and who is probably the model for the retreat sermon priest in *A Portrait*. If its hierarchy was intent on anything by way of an ideological programme, it was to recuperate as much public space as it could from the State.

Nearly all the references to 'Jesus' in *Ulysses* are mild or strong forms of blasphemy. Mulligan announces the theme in 'The ballad of joking Jesus', and throughout the novel we hear repeatedly the name of Our Lord being taken in vain. 'Cyclops' is the episode with the most references to Jesus, and the funniest is when the Citizen declares in suitably ignorant terms: 'By Jesus, says he, I'll brain that bloody jewman for using the holy name. By Jesus, I'll crucify him so I will' (*U* 12:1811–12). In one sense, 'Jesus' didn't get much further in Irish culture than to be used or abused thus. The only reference to a debate that had begun to occupy continental Europe since the 1830s is when George Russell lumps it together with the identity of Shakespeare: 'Clergymen's discussions of the historicity of Jesus' (*U* 9:48). Both the Shakespeare debate and the issue concerning the historicity of Jesus were misplaced, according to the mystic who commissioned three stories

---

[1]For more by way of an introduction to Tyrrell, who was a prime mover behind the Modernist heresy, see my Cork *Reader*, and the titles in the Bibliography in this book.

from Joyce for *The Irish Homestead*, for art doesn't need to concern itself with such matters, only with the eternal.

Within six months of departing for the continent with Nora in October 1904, Joyce was reading David Friedrich Strauss's *Das Leben Jesus* (The Life of Jesus) (1835) and Ernest Renan's *La Vie de Jésus* (The Life of Jesus) (1863). George Bernard Shaw tells us that reading Karl Marx made a man of him. Only Nora made a man of Joyce, but what we can infer about his intellectual formation in his early twenties is that, following Marx, Joyce too felt that a critique of religion preceded a critique of society. Start with the Church and end up with the State. In Pola in early 1905, Joyce is reading Ferdinand Lassalle on socialism and Strauss and Renan on religion. Strauss's *Das Leben Jesus* gave fresh impetus to the philosophical critique of religion, and it was seized on by among others George Eliot who was among the first to translate it into English in 1846. Renan's *La Vie de Jésus* was equally influential, especially for the French reading public, and the book sold well for over 60 years. Within four years, the study entered its thirteenth edition, and by 1925 a forty-second edition had appeared. The issue of Jesus being nothing more than a historical figure, albeit a great reformer according to Renan, caused a real storm. In a Catholic country, a raw nerve had been exposed and Renan had to be answered. If you punch into the British Library catalogue the French title, you will be surprised at the number of 'answers' that appeared in the 1860s alone.

Sketch of Renan which appeared in the weekly newspaper *Le Petit Journal* in October 1892. When he died, Renan was accorded full honours and buried with other great French writers and thinkers in the Pantheon, opposite the Bibliothèque St Geneviève, Paris. In his religious and intellectual journey from seminary in Brittany to the centre of national life in Paris, Renan had managed to give expression to the wider tensions and contradictions in the culture in terms both of religion and of the re-emergence of political, cultural and ethnic nationalism. In 1924, when Joyce was on vacation in St Malo, he took time out to visit Renan's birthplace in St Tréguier. As Ellmann was quick to point out, both Renan and Joyce were 'disbeliever[s] fascinated by belief' (Ellmann, 1982, 567).

ERNEST RENAN

The separation of the historical Jesus from the theological figure of Christ worked to undermine religious belief in continental Europe, and one can see why Joyce, in his post-Catholic phase, might have spent time reading such material. *Ulysses*, too, is a novel that is ruthless not only in its pursuit of history, context and forms of determination but also in its campaign against the notion of heroes as above or beyond ordinary life. Renan is serious, but it's the author who wrote another life of Jesus with whom Joyce has most fun in *Ulysses*. Léo Taxil's *La Vie de Jésus*, first published in 1882 by the Librairie Anti-Clericale on rue des Écoles in Paris, and complete with Dessins Comiques or comic designs by Pépin, is a scurrilous account of the life of Jesus. The author's real name was Gabriel Jogand-Pagès (1854–1907), but as 'Léo Taxil' he made a name for himself first in attacking the Church, then in attacking the Freemasons from a Catholic viewpoint, for which he was rewarded with an audience with Pope Leo XIII. It's appropriate that Taxil should be mentioned in 'Proteus', the episode devoted to change and therefore to changing identities and changing beliefs and changing sides. Stephen himself in this episode is walking toward the Pigeon House along the coast from Sandymount. His mind returns to the scene in Paris with Patrice Egan and he recalls the illustration from Taxil's anti-clerical book where Mary is asked by Joseph for the identity of the person who made her pregnant: '*Qui vous a mis dans cette fichue position?*' (who put you in that awful position, i.e. pregnant?). And the reply is equally dramatic: '*C'est le pigeon, Joseph*' (U 3:161–2) (it's the pigeon/dove/Holy Ghost, Joseph).

Pigeon House, pigeon, Holy Ghost. A groping archangel, the virgin birth. The first Mass with a leg for Host. Once we have sight of all these illustrations – and there are many more in the book – we realise that Taxil's presence in 'Proteus' is more significant than the brief mention he is afforded. Joyce was obviously intrigued by all the material that came to him from continental Europe and his first stay in Paris in 1902–3, and you can see him working it all into the theme of 'Proteus'. In *La Vie de Jésus*, Marion (Mary) calls her husband Joseph by the affectionate term which Stephen uses when thinking about Patrice: 'mon gros lapin' (my big rabbit). Understanding the thoughts of Stephen at the beginning of *Ulysses* requires a certain patience and a certain flexibility in our reading.[2] Yes, this is what happens when we think about the world. One minute I'm walking along

---

[2] Other critics, such as Gregory Downing (2003) and Fritz Senn (1982), have made more of Taxil's presence in the novel.

LES SOUPÇONS DE JOSEPH

— C'est le pigeon, Joseph !
Pour le coup, le charpentier se fâcha tout rouge. (Chap. V.)

(Left) Shock, horror. Marion (Mary) tells Joseph the truth about who made her pregnant. An illustration from Léo Taxil's *La Vie de Jésus* (1882), with the caption lifted directly by Joyce.

(below left) The Annunciation scene as seen by Pépin/Taxil, with Gabriel groping Marion.

(below right) The Last Supper, by Taxil. Take and eat, Jesus tells his apostles. This is my body. Eat it all, leave not a morsel, as he forces a leg down the mouth of one of his chosen disciples.

the sand and observing the actions of the waves in transforming the shore-line and the sand itself. The next I notice the name of a landmark in the distance, and I start recalling something I've read. I'm back in Paris, hearing anti-clerical stories. I'll look up that book by Taxil. Well, that's as shocking as any pornographic image Bloom might show me. I'd never encountered anything like that in my own Catholic country. We know how to blaspheme in Dublin but not how to construct a systematic argument on the subject. I must make use of it. Where? Ah, yes, Proteus. Yes, and start the novel with the ballad of joking Jesus. See, it all makes sense.

Getting a handle on this novel – this is what I've been exploring in this chapter. The first three episodes constitute quite a challenge, and I sometimes recommend starting the novel with the fourth episode, which is where Bloom's day begins. Bloom himself is a much more attractive figure than Stephen and his thoughts are easier to grasp in part because he is not weighed down by all the autobiographical baggage that burdens his counterpart. Bloom has his own past, whereas Stephen has both a fictional past and Joyce's past. Here in this chapter I've made something of Joyce's stay in Paris and commented on how that surfaces in 'Proteus' particularly. Frequently, critics and guide books approach the novel in terms of Homer's *Odyssey*, but there is a fund of material in the opening episodes that lies outside the Hellenic reach. Needless to say, I've touched on only a small section of the Paris material, but enough to suggest something of the complexity and the characteristic method in how that material came to be there in the first place. Greek, French, Irish, all these strands have to be taken into account when we think about this great European novel. The problem is they confront us from the outset. Of course, anything we choose to comment on immediately reminds us that there's a whole bank of material we haven't even noticed, let alone addressed. To ensure we don't suffer any more at this stage from information overload or information deficit, we should draw a line here or leave things on one side for another occasion. In the next chapter I explore the fate of Bloom at home and at work. In a third chapter on *Ulysses* I look at how my students have written about the Molly Bloom soliloquy.

CHAPTER 9

Leopold Bloom at home and at work

7 Eccles Street

The house where Leopold and Molly live is worth more than the usual attention we might devote to a house in fiction. In a sense the house on Eccles Street, which was demolished in the 1960s, isn't so much fictional as factual, or, rather, historical. Indeed, its realistic texture casts a shadow over our reading of *Ulysses*. So becoming acquainted with the house can be rewarding not only in itself but also for the light it sheds on the characters themselves. Joyce we know delighted in playing with the relationship between reality and fiction, and as a result the more we know about the reality he's employing the more we know about the fiction he's creating. Of course, we have to pinch ourselves occasionally and remember that *Ulysses* is a work of fiction, that the Blooms never existed and that the house on Eccles Street was never occupied by them. But that, too, is part of the enjoyment in reading Joyce, a process of entanglement and disentanglement. There is something else, for in reconstructing the stage-set for *Ulysses* we can discern how the pieces fit together and relate to each other. Indeed, as we move ever further away from that period we can derive yet more pleasure from what might be called historical excavation work. Oh, so this is how people lived at that time, before the coming of the cinema, radio, television. Equally, the extraordinary attention to everyday life in *Ulysses* means that the novel can be used to reconstruct what life was like in the Edwardian period, so that in getting close to Bloom's immediate environment we are getting close to a whole world which, like the house itself, has now passed.

In 1965 a BBC film team accompanied Anthony Burgess to 7 Eccles Street in connection with a programme about Joyce entitled *Monitor: Silence, Exile and Cunning*. I have seen stills from this film by Christopher Burstall, a film which was made when the house was about to be demolished, but as far as I know there are no other extant interior photographs.

That's probably as it should be, because all of us remain therefore the strangers that we in fact are. After all, we haven't been invited inside by the Blooms, only invited inside by a narrator who positions us as visitors or co-opts us as companions or eavesdroppers or somewhere in between. Whatever view we gain of the interior is dependent for the most part, therefore, on what we are told in the novel. For their recent account of the lay-out of the house in *James Joyce's Dublin* (2004), Ian Gunn and Clive Hart rely in part on 77 Eccles Street, a surviving house opposite, which they claim is 'essentially similar' to number 7. They may be right. I once enjoyed a presentation at a Joyce conference in which Gunn, with the help of cameras zooming up the stairs and into all the various rooms, showed a computerised reconstruction of the interior of the house. It seemed a little intrusive, however, a kind of invasion of someone's privacy, as if it were one of those television programmes on selling a house or on guessing which-famous-person-lives-in-this-house. A home converted into a house. Bloom, of course,

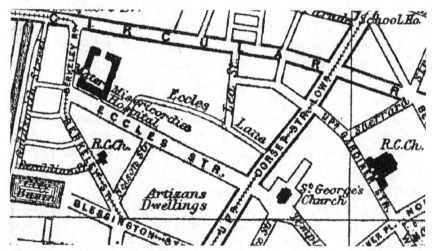

Detail of 1900 map of Eccles Street, parallel to the North Circular Road. The street, which was named after Sir John Eccles, Lord Mayor of Dublin in 1710, was built in the eighteenth century. Within a stone's throw of Bloom's house on Eccles Street, there were three churches (two Catholic), a Catholic chapel on Berkeley Road (unmarked), the Mater Misericordiae Hospital which opened in 1861, artisan dwellings for skilled workers, a small reservoir marked 'City Basin' at the end of Blessington Street, which supplied water to Powers and Jameson distilleries, and street names that recall, on the one hand, Bishop Berkeley and the Irish response to English empiricism and, on the other hand, Gibraltar and Nelson's victory at Trafalgar. Perhaps we might add that, as if in diplomatic or strategic sympathy with his English surroundings, in the front room of Bloom's house there is a neatly furled Union Jack. We might also notice that it's on Nelson Street that Milly plays out with 'those romps of Murray girls' (who I assume are Joyce's cousins and who were then living nearby on Drumcondra Road).

A photograph of 7 Eccles Street, which appears in Tindall's *The Joyce Country* (1960). Number 7 is the one which appears to be under the Sandeman Port sign, with a bicycle leaning against the railing and some children sitting on the 'dwarf' wall. Lucky 7.

Another photograph of 7 Eccles Street, from the Phil Phillips Collection in the Rosenbach Museum and Library in Philadelphia. Taken by Philip Phillips in 1950; gift of Sayre P. Sheldon and Lady Richard Davies. The grand entrance to the house has clearly seen better days. Young men are parked near the parked motorcycle, a young child perches against the area railing, a mother with two children is closing the front door of the next house, while a priest, Lowry-like with head down, presses on regardless. When Joyceans from North America began to take note of Joyce's city in the post-war period, Eccles Street must have seemed quite drab, but we should remember that it was less so in June 1904. In the nineteenth century Cardinal Cullen lived at number 59; Isaac Butt, the Irish political leader, at 64.

Source: Phil Phillips Collection/Rosenbach Museum & Library

Flora Mitchell's attractive, tawny sketch of 7 Eccles Street, made in the 1960s and reproduced in her book *Vanishing Dublin* (1966). The original is in the Croessman Collection at Southern Illinois University. Perhaps it's me, but the two figures in the doorway of the adjacent house look terribly small when placed against the height of the door. Whatever the case, Mitchell was prescient about 'vanishing'.

Source: James Joyce Collection at Morris Library/Southern Illinois University

when we first meet him, isn't famous, for it's only with 'Bloomsday' and his subsequent afterlife that he has earned this epithet. He deserves the space, the respect that is, we normally accord to strangers. It's for the Blooms to open the door to us or to pull aside or pull up the roller blinds at the front of the house on Eccles Street if they so wish.

As mentioned in the previous chapter, Bloom is introduced as *Mr* Bloom, a polite form of address for someone we don't know, which is then immediately undercut by the narrator when we learn what Bloom likes for breakfast. A positioning for the reader, followed almost at once by a shift in positioning for the reader. Stephen is simply Stephen, or his nickname to begin with, which is 'Kinch'. Similarly with Mulligan, whose nickname is the first name we encounter in *Ulysses*, 'Buck'. A male rabbit to accompany the discussion we had in the previous chapter about Kevin Egan and '*lapin*'. What's in a name, we might well ask? Buck, Kinch, Mr to you. Forms of address, which the novel is going to address. The novel starts with a bang, with a buck that is, and with all the eighteenth-century associations of that word including wild drinking parties, duelling, male rakes on the hunt, leppin' not 'lapin' in this case. As if the narrator can't let go, whenever it is mentioned in the first episode Mulligan's name is accompanied by Buck. Seventy-one times, to be precise. A little tiresome we might agree, but we get the message and, given that the episode is filtered through Stephen's consciousness, we can accept it. Mulligan, usurper. 'Telemachus' is dominated by moping and by bucking. Stephen mopes, Mulligan bucks. Bloom, by contrast, blooms, or should do. It's in keeping that when he throws off his trousers to plunge into the waters of Dublin Bay, Mulligan – correction, Buck Mulligan – informs the world that 'Redheaded women buck like goats' (U 1:706). Bucks are noisy, speak out of turn, and comment on everything.

When Bloom arrives on the scene, however, we encounter the quietness and the formality of a stranger, whose predicament the novel is going to explore. The Martello Tower at Sandycove, which is rented by Mulligan, is where panthers disturb the sleep of the occupants, but 7 Eccles Street, on the north side of the city, which is also rented, is quiet and ruminative. Cats purr and can be insistent, but there are no bucks and no shots ring out. This is where Bloom lives with his wife Molly and his teenage daughter Milly (who's currently away from home in Mullingar). Mulligan has an ego but he doesn't have a predicament – unless that is itself a predicament. Bloom doesn't have an assertive ego, and perhaps for that reason he can't escape his predicament. Expressed simply, or at least at one level, Bloom's predicament, which he might or might not collude in, is that of the cuckold, a condition that haunts him throughout the day and which the afternoon will confirm in the shape of Boylan.

Bloom's fate provides the focus of Joyce's comic rewriting of the Homeric story from the serious viewpoint of modern marriage, with the emphasis falling on the plight of Odysseus the married man, and on the realisation that his wife Penelope will surrender to one of the suitors. But it's not so much a tragedy as the pathos that stems from witnessing someone suffer amid the vestments of his passive self. Neither Bloom's name nor his title nor his familiar nickname Poldy will prove an adequate defence against another buck, who is foreshadowed in the novel's first usurper, Mulligan. The name of this second buck is Boylan, and his nickname is appropriately 'Blazes'. The word has a history. According to Sir Jonah Barrington, reminiscing in the 1820s about the 'fireaters', the young Irish gentry who fired up the country in the 1770s, the question often asked regarding a young man, especially when proposal of marriage was imminent, was 'Did he ever blaze?' (Barrington, 1997, 191). A young man's family was important but so was his attitude to life and living dangerously. Buck Mulligan, Blazes Boylan. Boylan, boiling. Bloom versus Boylan. Blooming versus boiling.

Colourful portrait of Blazes Boylan by the Canadian artist Saul Field, from Saul Field and Morton P. Levitt, *Bloomsday* (1972). A floral tribute in his mouth. Molly at his feet, as it were. Trophy time.

An eighteenth-century buck versus the Odyssean 'noman'. Mr Bloom carries his nameplate manfully through the novel, but with his wife sharing her bed with someone on fire we know it's all up for him. 'All up a plumtree' (*U* 8:744). His home is incomplete, and he himself suffers further ignominy when, on retiring for the night of 16 June 1904, he has to remove from the bedclothes the crumbs of potted meat presumably left by Molly and Boylan.

Plumtrees potted meat, Southport variety; courtesy of eBay. Photograph by David Pierce. When Joyce returned on a visit to Dublin in 1909, his one-time friend J.F. Byrne was renting 7 Eccles Street. In some distress, Joyce stayed a night pouring out his heart. During that same visit he discovered that Vincent Cosgrave, the model for Lynch in *A Portrait*, might have been seeing Nora in the summer of 1904. It turned out not to be true, but Joyce, now in exile again but this time away from Nora, was deeply affected by feelings of jealousy, insecurity and betrayal. In 1904, 7 Eccles Street wasn't just empty; like Nora, it also had a past.

Another view of 7 Eccles Street, looking toward St George's Church, which was built between 1802 and 1813. From Maurice Craig's *Dublin* (1952). Bloom's house, bathed in sunlight, is opposite the donkey and cart, with a drainpipe to the left of house. Throughout the day, 'Heigho, Heigho' ring out the bells of this Church of Ireland church, reminding us of Bloom's fate as a cuckold. All over the city they taunt him, as if they were ringing for him alone: 'Heigho! Heigho! Heigho! Heigho! Heigho! Heigho!' The bells, a gift by the church's architect Francis Johnston who was himself a keen bell-ringer, were first rung in 1829 (and last rung in 1990 when the church closed). Johnston, who had a house on Eccles Street, was a consultant architect for Nelson's Pillar (1808–9), and he was also responsible for designing the General Post Office (1814–18), among other landmarks in the city.

Source: Reproduced from *Dublin 1660–1860* by permission of Maurice Craig and Liberties Press

View today of Eccles Street looking toward St George's Church. The church was wrapped in scaffolding sheeting when I took this photograph in October 2006. Bloom's house, which was on the left, has gone, replaced by an extension to the Mater Hospital. Traffic's also a killer. Photograph by David Pierce.

The plaque on the wall outside the Mater Hospital is a pathetic reminder of modern literature's most hallowed shrine. Apart from the door, which is now in the James Joyce Centre on North Great George's Street, and various pieces of memorabilia in private hands round the world, 7 Eccles Street has vanished without a trace, gone up in smoke, part of the 1960s destruction of Dublin. Photograph by David Pierce.

The novel takes constant delight in showing us in the character of Bloom the many-sided encounter between the public face and the private reality, but the Odyssey proper begins chez Blooms. A house and a home. 7 Eccles Street, the starting-point for Odysseus's venture and site of betrayal, is a dwelling to dwell on, and 'Calypso', together with 'Ithaca' and 'Penelope', affords us such an opportunity. As the accompanying illustrations indicate, 7 Eccles Street is built on what I take to be four floors, a three-storied terraced house with a cellar or basement and with an apex perching on what would otherwise be a completely flat roof. As is often the way with Georgian buildings, the guttering shelters behind the front façade, and the one downspout visible is located outside number 7, which in turn serves several adjoining houses. As can be seen in Craig's photograph, a photograph taken around 1952, number 7 was slightly meaner than the houses on the same row towards the Mater Hospital end, but it was a much more substantial house than St Peter's Terrace in Cabra where Joyce's family was living in 1904. In estate agent's language, the Georgian terraced house was well-proportioned and boasted traditional features, including iron railings, an entrance with stone steps, a fanlight over an imposing front door, and two large sash windows on each floor.

As a boy, the Irish poet Austin Clarke (1895–1974), who came from a respectable lower-middle-class family, was impressed by the 'lofty Georgian houses' on Eccles Street and how it was 'too respectable to be of use to us' (he's thinking of children chalking on the pavement or swinging round lamp-posts) (Clarke, 1962, 38). When Tindall's photograph was taken in 1954, the house had been converted into flats, but in 1904 this row was still occupied by families, and for a small family like the Blooms the house must have been more than adequate. The rooms would have been square-shaped with fairly high ceilings on each of the three main floors, including the top floor. Whatever Joyce imagined about the coldness of the house or the 'gelid light' that reigned first thing in the morning, the south-facing windows would have admitted a considerable amount of light into the front rooms in the late morning and afternoon.

The Blooms seem to live on the ground floor or, as the Ithacan narrator tells us, 'the second storey', the same floor where there is the bedroom,

Mater Misericordiae Hospital today. Mother of Mercy. Photograph by David Pierce. A hospital run by the large-coifed Sisters of Mercy. The Mater Hospital is a major teaching hospital, now associated with Joyce's alma mater, the National University of Ireland. In 'Telemachus', Mulligan, the medical student, taunts Stephen: 'You saw only your mother die. I see them pop off every day in the Mater and Richmond and cut up into tripes in the dissectingroom' (U 1:204–6). Tripe. Sweet Mother of Mercy.

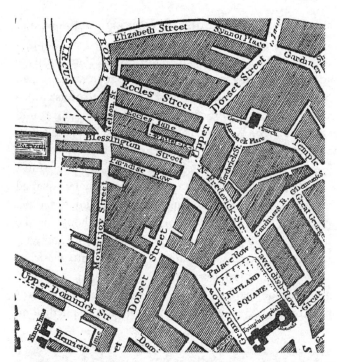

Inset of 1829 map of Dublin. Eccles Street is between what was then the Royal Circus and Rutland Square. A fashionable area of the city with fine streets. For those with an eye for such things, Eccles Lane on this map is south of Eccles Street. The Rotunda Hospital is listed as a lying-in hospital, a tradition in Ireland that Joyce exploits in the 'Oxen of the Sun' episode (which is set in the Catholic hospital on Holles Street). As ever, it took a long time to be born in Ireland.

together with the drawing room or living room at the front of the house. Again, the phrase 'second storey' is confusing, at least to Irish or British ears. The house has a basement, a ground floor, and then a first floor and a second floor. In American English, this would be different, with the ground floor the first floor. Leaving that aside, we learn from Molly in bed that one of the rooms 'upstairs' is empty, a room she imagines Stephen using to write poetry, and 'downstairs' is the kitchen. When I first began imagining the layout of the house, I thought the Blooms lived on the first floor, but yield to the judgement of others on this. I assume the 'front room' referred to in 'Ithaca' is the drawing room, where there is a piano, a 'prune plush sofa', a 'blue and white checker inlaid majolicatopped table', several types of chair including an easychair and a splayfoot chair, two bookshelves and a mirror. I also assume it's from a window of this room that in 'Wandering Rocks', the episode that takes place between three and four in the afternoon, we read that 'A woman's hand flung forth a coin over the area railings. It fell on the path' (*U* 10:252–3). Molly, readying herself for Boylan, is in her petticoat and has her 'shiftstraps' exposed, so, on hearing the blind stripling, rushes to the window, presumably from the bedroom at the back of the house, to throw him something and show the world what she's not got on. On the mantelpiece in this front room there is a clock, or as the narrator or Arranger[1] cruelly insists, a 'timepiece of striated Connemara marble, stopped at the hour of 4.46 a.m. on the 21 March 1896', a clock which we learn was a wedding present (*U* 17:1335–6).

In the bedroom, pride of place is given to a noisy double bed, whose history is faithfully recorded, belonging as it did to Molly's father, who bought it at auction on Gibraltar. Above the bed is an illustration *Birth of a Nymph*, a tasty fold-out from an issue of *Photo-Bits*; the chest of drawers contains various bits of memorabilia, policy documents and incriminating evidence, including a letter from Martha Clifford addressed to Henry Flower, two erotic photocards, an endowment policy with Scottish Widows, his father's suicide note, and a prospectus for 'The Wonderworker', 'the world's greatest remedy for rectal complaints' (*U* 17:1819–20). Elsewhere in the room we discover an orange-keyed chamber pot, a commode that has one leg fractured, and a washstand.

Downstairs is the kitchen where Bloom gets breakfast at an open fire, boils water, toasts bread, and fries, or rather burns, the kidneys. There is a range or stove in the kitchen, but I assume this would not have been lit for breakfast since it would take too long to heat up. When Bloom and Stephen return home in 'Ithaca', on the range there is a saucepan and a black iron kettle, and Bloom lights the fire. Also in the kitchen is a dresser, laden with crockery, a 'moustachecup' which was a present from Milly, Epps soluble cocoa, an empty container of Plumtrees potted meat, an empty bottle of invalid port, cloves, 'ribsteak', and much else. 'Subadjacent' to the kitchen is the scullery, which is where Bloom, without keys to the front door, enters the house in 'Ithaca'. The cellar is used as a scullery, and it is next to the kitchen, for when Stephen is waiting at the front door by the area railings (the railings that overlook a gap below), he observes Bloom in the kitchen lighting a candle. The layout here is slightly problematic, for, on entering

---

[1]This is a term that has become widespread among critics in discussing *Ulysses*. The anonymous Arranger intervenes not as a third person narrator but as a slightly unnerving, supra-personal figure, 'arranging' things, cautioning or advising the reader. David Hayman was the first critic to identify this figure as the Arranger. See his '*Ulysses*': *The Mechanics of Meaning* (1970). Hugh Kenner has many interesting observations on this figure in *Ulysses* (1980). No-one, as far as I know, has yet come up with an equally convincing term or, rather, series of terms to identify the various figures who compose the Arranger, for there are clearly many.

Jail Street, Ennis (now O'Connell Street), County Clare, c1900. It was in a nearby street that Bloom's father owned the Queen's Hotel and where he committed suicide in 1886. I have a hotel brochure from some years ago which contains the phrase 'mentioned in James Joyce's great masterpiece *Ulysses'*. That must be tongue-in-cheek, for who would want to draw attention to the place where Bloom's father committed suicide and composed his suicide note asking his son to be kind to Athos the family dog? On the other hand, the Queen's Hotel has survived, but 7 Eccles Street has gone. Fiction, non-fiction: there must be a moral in that somewhere. As a footnote, and these things never are, there were only 2,000 Jews in the whole of Ireland registered in the 1901 census, and almost certainly there would have been no more than a handful of Jews in Ennis in the late nineteenth century. It would, therefore, have been a lonely life for Bloom's father in that tight little town dominated by a statue of the Catholic leader Daniel O'Connell. You can get maudlin. I think of my own Jewish family, the Aarons and the Van Pragues, in the Jewish cemetery on the Sussex Downs overlooking the racecourse in Brighton and no Jewish heirs to join them.
Source: Courtesy of the National Library of Ireland

the house, they pass the lighted crevice of a doorway on the left, where presumably Molly has her lamp still lit, and they then descend a turning staircase of five steps into 'the kitchen of the house' (*U* 17:122), which is hardly as grand as that phrase suggests. The kitchen is at basement level, or below ground level, and the doorway on the left leads into the ground floor front room. The architectural drawing in Gunn and Hart (2004) helps clear up matters, for there is a landing half-way down into the kitchen and a back-door leading out into the garden, which stills from the 1965 BBC film confirm. From the landing you do indeed, I assume, have a view of 'the kitchen of the house'.

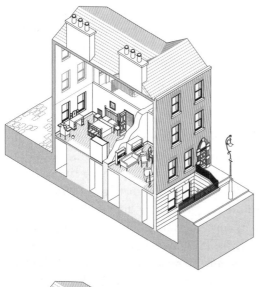

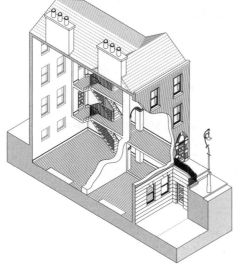

These drawings provide the most accurate reconstruction of the interior of 7 Eccles Street but, as Ian Gunn told me in August 2007, there are still some errors with regard to the internal chimney stack, the external back-wall chimney stack, the position of the internal staircase and what he assumes was an upstairs cantilevered toilet on the outside wall. See Hart and Gunn (2008).

Source: Ian Gunn & Clive Hart/James Joyce's Dublin/Thames & Hudson & Stephen Paterson/Napier University

In some informative remarks on *Ulysses* in *Dublin* (1979), Peter Somerville-Large claims there is a toilet upstairs on the landing. He makes this assumption on the basis of Bloom's thought in 'Calypso' when he is about to pay a visit to the toilet in the garden: 'Too much trouble to fag up the stairs to the landing' (*U* 4:453–4). Somerville-Large might be right, for the sentence allows for such a reading, but my own view is that Bloom is thinking about the cat's insistence on going out. The landing in question, as the drawing in Gunn and Hart indicates, is the landing half-way up the kitchen stairs. Bloom doesn't want to go up those stairs twice in the space of minutes to open the back door. Even though it's only a small flight of stairs, it's still too much 'fag', especially as his bowels are heavy with the pressure of waste matter. No, the cat can wait. Getting a purchase on the layout of the house – and the same applies to the layout of the city – often helps clarify things in our reading, or in, what often amounts to the same thing, our construction of *Ulysses*. I could be wrong of course.

Just when you think you have secured all the relevant details in this novel or you think you are in the process of getting them, the basics can escape you. The same is true of the Ormond Hotel, whose layout in the 'Sirens' episode constantly intrudes, but picturing that layout with any degree of certainty will defeat most readers. There are five house-bells in Bloom's kitchen, so we must assume the house had a servant, perhaps to live in or come in on a daily basis. Presumably in all the major rooms a family member could call the servant or maid or 'criada' (as Gibraltar-bred Molly calls her) in the kitchen. At one point the phrase 'kitchen stairs' is referred to, I take it that the phrase 'kitchen stairs', the most used stairs in this house, is employed by the Blooms to distinguish them from other flights of stairs in the house. The phrase betrays a history of the house as from within, and readers are reminded of their status as outsiders listening in to how the people who once lived there shaped their world. This is as it should be for the house belongs not to us but the Blooms. A private house subject to public gaze where details can escape us, therefore.

Gesabo

This takes us to something that will prove almost impossible to resolve and yet it is of some interest. Molly informs us that Bloom had an idea of taking in lodgers, which again supports the view that this is a fairly substantial house. In 1876 George Tyrrell and his mother took furnished lodgings with Miss Lynch at number 4 Eccles Street. Nearby in Dorset Street, the eighteenth-century houses were being converted into tenements, but Eccles Street retained a sense of itself. Taking in lodgers was more than an idea for Bloom, because when Molly is throwing the coin out of the window for the blind stripling, 'A card Unfurnished Apartments slipped from the sash and fell' (*U* 10:250–1). Molly is against such an idea, in part because the house is a 'gesabo'. This is a curious word and not in the *Oxford English Dictionary*. The sentence as such reads: 'Im not going to take in lodgers off the street for him if he takes a gesabo of a house like this' (*U* 18:1492–3).

Molly, I take it, is expressing her frustration, for Bloom has already decided to advertise for lodgers. According to Gifford and Seidman (1989), the word 'gesabo' means a show or a mess, and they base this on the appearance of a similar word used in 'Nausicaa' by Bloom when he's thinking about the interdependence of time and the universe: 'Then if one thing stopped the whole ghesabo would stop bit by bit' (*U* 13:989–90). 'Ghesabo' means here something like the whole shebang, the whole works, which is something like the whole show. Gifford and Seidman are probably right to notice the similarity between 'ghesabo' and 'gesabo', especially in a passage that finds an echo in 'Penelope'. But the two words are not the same, and neither is it quite accurate to say that 'ghesabo' is a 'variant' for 'gazebo'.

If we take 'gesabo' first, the recent Spanish translation by Francisco García Tortosa translates the phrase thus: 'Una pocilga de casa' (a pigsty of a house) (Joyce/Tortosa, 2003, 904). The Croatian translation by Zlatko Gorjan has *ropotarnica* or glory-hole, while the more recent translation by Luko Paljetak opts for *kasarna* or barracks. Molly actually uses this latter image when she calls the house 'a big barracks of a place' (*U* 18:978). We already know, therefore, in part how she pictures 7 Eccles Street, but 'gesabo' suggests something different. The French translation overseen by Joyce uses the word *caravansérail*: 'parcequ'il a loué un caravansérail comme celui-là' (Joyce/Morel, 1957, 866), because he rented a caravanserai (an inn for desert caravans in the Middle East) like this. The word then invites different perspectives on how Molly views her house. A mess, a pigsty, a glory-hole, a transit camp. It's fairly basic, the question of what Molly thinks about 7 Eccles Street, and yet there doesn't seem agreement on how we should interpret 'gesabo'. Molly is clearly worried about the dust that seems to collect in the house, though perhaps this is a form of psychological displacement, for Molly has a thing about the maid and Bloom. But a pigsty of a house would suggest more disorder than filth. The house in fact is not disordered. With four umbrellas, the hallstand is according to Bloom 'too full' (*U* 4:487) but the hallway itself is uncluttered, the bedroom has some of Molly's clothes strewn about, the careful Bloom takes care to right her breakfast things, and the front room has the furniture so positioned that Bloom can immediately discern when he arrives home after dark that it has been rearranged. In fact, the Blooms, who have always rented, have very few possessions, which is one reason why Joyce can list them. Dust and funny smells we can accept, but is this what she's alluding to in 'gesabo'?

As for the use of 'ghesabo', Morel translates this with *bazar*, another word entirely, 'tout le bazar s'arrêterait' (Joyce/Morel, 1957, 426) (literally, the whole bazaar would cease), while Tortosa deploys the image of a castle and it being torn down 'piedra a piedra' (stone by stone) (Joyce/Tortosa,

2003, 429). My own view is slightly different. 'Gesabo' is, one suspects, designed to echo 'ghesabo', and, even if we can't pin it down with any degree of certainty, worth dwelling on and speculating about. To my mind, it's Molly mishearing Bloom or misspelling a word Bloom uses. Presumably, she pronounces the word the same as Bloom but perhaps she doesn't quite understand it, and hence drops the 'h'. That's a nice touch on Joyce's part, and it's a trick that is missed by the French and Spanish translators. It's a word in the family therefore, like 'quoof' in the Paul Muldoon household, except that 'quoof' (a hot-water bottle) is more obviously a non-word and less pliable. Perhaps Bloom himself is responsible for Molly's error, mispronouncing the word 'gazebo' as 'ghesabo' (guess a bo). Joyce invites us to reconstruct this scene for ourselves. Imagine, for example, Bloom being asked to spell the word he coins. Would he insert 'h' after the 'g', and why would he do that? As I say, what we're dealing with here is quite simply indeterminate, and yet at the same time quite funny when invited to speculate as a reader in our construction of *Ulysses*.

But to continue, Molly imagines Stephen could write his poetry in the room upstairs, which is empty, and he could sleep in Milly's bed, which is in the back room. In French we read 'la chambre sur le jardin' for the back room (the room over the garden). Tortosa has 'cuarto trastero' (the junk room or lumber room), which fits in with the pigsty theme, but neither of which seems right here. 'Gesabo'. Yes, I think Molly is perhaps thinking of 'gazebo', a room with a view, but this isn't a variant of 'ghesabo'. Rather, it's Molly confusing two words, one she's heard Bloom using, and one she's got from somewhere else. Two kinds of error are therefore on display here, one when you apply a word wrongly, and one when you're searching for a word and get it wrong. Looking out across the backs, Stephen could invent great lines of verse to her, only, somehow, Bloom spoils the view. A house for potential lovers, but ruined by Bloom. Bloom, therefore, is the one small thing that threatens the ghesabo, that threatens the whole works. A gazebo which becomes a gesabo. In the BBC film there is an apex at the top of the house, which perhaps reminds Molly of a gazebo or possible skylight if opened up. Gesabo or not, however, there's nothing to view out the back, only outhouses, vegetable patches and next-door's chickens. Or an off-duty constable cuddling a woman in Eccles Lane (as Bloom imagines when queuing behind the woman in the pork-butcher for his breakfast in 'Calypso').

Having said all that, I warm to the French translation of 'gesabo' by itself, for this offers us a reminder that for Molly the house would never be really home, that like Bloom she would always feel it 'incomplete', in need of more potted meat. A final thought. Gazebo is a word with possibly oriental associations, as indeed are *caravansérail* and *bazar*. It recalls for us

German colony near Jaffa, with the Plain of Sharon and the Mountains of Ephraim in the distance. Bloom's attitude toward the Middle East is both hard-edged and soft-centred. He is interested in investing in the European colonisation of Palestine. At the same time, thinking about all its olives, cithers and crates of fruit lined up on the quayside at Jaffa, he is sentimental about oriental lushness. But then, as so often with Bloom, comes the counter-thought or extension. For it's a barren land, the land of Sodom and Gomorrah, and, in a move that anticipates his own patriarchal thoughts on his penis as 'the limp father of thousands' (*U* 5:571), he proceeds to compare the Dead Sea to 'the grey sunken cunt of the world' (*U* 4:227–8).

what we saw when discussing 'Araby', only now the relationship between eastern promise and western values is reversed and it is eastern metaphors that undermine and dissipate hopes for future dalliance with Stephen.

A regulated world

Gazebo, whether pronounced with an 'ee' or 'ay' before the 'bo', is a word full of light, for a gazebo lets in light into an otherwise dark interior. Before the coming of electricity, light was at a premium not only during the day but also at night. After dark, most houses were entirely dependent on candles, paraffin or oil lamps, and light from coal fires or gas taps. Such a world is a world away from that of most readers of *Ulysses* today. With power cuts, we occasionally face the predicament of a world without light, but the temporary nature of such interruptions protects us from confronting the real thing. Joyce's generation was just on the verge of this world of light, but they seem neither overawed by what was coming nor depressed by their own circumstances. Electricity was being generated for parts of the city in the Pigeon House at the mouth of the Liffey, and in this respect it's interesting to see an advert for the Shelbourne Hotel in the 1904–5 Ward Lock *Pictorial and Descriptive Guide to Paris* with the phrase 'Electric Light' prominently displayed alongside 'First Class' and 'Hydraulic Lift'. However, the houses on Eccles Street in June 1904 are without electricity. Stephen waits patiently outside the front door while Bloom lights a candle and lets him in. In Bloom's utopia there will be 'Electric dishscrubbers' (*U* 15:1689). You never hear anyone in *Ulysses* cursing the lack of light. Indeed, as if there were an excess of it, one of the nymphs in 'Circe' wickedly or innocently declares she eats the electric light (*U* 15:3393). And, as if they were participants in a philosophical seminar, Bloom and Stephen discuss 'The influence of gaslight or electric light on the growth of adjoining paraheliotropic trees' (*U* 17:44–5). When pressure mounts, they urinate in the garden under the stars.

In those dark and penumbral times it was wise to ensure things were in place, that furniture didn't move, that matches were where you last put them, that nothing blocked doorways, that stairs were free of objects. Otherwise, accidents would occur and people would bump their heads, as happens to Bloom in his rearranged front room. Without their realising it, people in *Ulysses* have a heightened proprioception, an acute sense of the self in space. They rarely put a foot wrong. It's a regulated world. Bloom's Plasto hat, which has lost the 't' through wear and becomes therefore 'ha' (*U* 4:70), has a place assigned for it on a peg in the hallway. Electric trams crisscross the city at regular intervals. Water flows round the city, supplied by the reservoir at Roundwood in County Wicklow, its pressure regulated by judiciously sited pumps. At the Ormond Hotel, customers' tankards are hanging in their customary place for their owners when they enter to imbibe. All the characters, except Stephen and Bloom, speak as if they belong to the same tribe. When Stephen shuts his eyes and walks along the strand in 'Proteus', he does so like an expert. When he closes his eyes he hears his boots crushing shells. 'Shut your eyes and see', the Jesuit-educated Luciferian has the audacity to observe, an observation that could well serve as a motto for the novel as a whole. Their dark lives light up their days.

Light and regulated lives. Indeed, both light and dark regulate their lives. 'Invent nothing' is the rule in a regulated world, no new streets, no new tram routes, no new tram timetables, and in a sense no new people. Work with what you've got or what there is, and wherever possible recycle characters. Joyce's world is so regulated that in *Thom's Official Dublin Directory* for 1904 7 Eccles Street was empty, and, in his assumed role as

A sketch of the dome of the south equatorial at Dunsink Observatory, County Dublin. From Robert Ball's *Story of the Heavens* (1897): Bloom has a copy of this title on his bookshelves. Telescopes remind us that the only way to view the heavens is through the dark. The Observatory, which is located some 5 miles north-west of Dublin at Castlerock, must have been regularly open to the public, for Bloom at one point thinks: 'Must go out there some first Saturday of the month' (*U* 8:572–3). The Dunsink Observatory is the oldest scientific institution in Ireland, dating from 1785, but because of the 25-minute time difference between Greenwich Mean Time and 'Dunsink Time', its scientific timepiece could be put to effective use in less scientific pursuits. Betting on horses, for example. Or so the theory goes when it is fancifully discussed by Bloom and Stephen in 'Ithaca'. In other words, you could, in theory, other things being unequal, put a bet on a race taking place in England already knowing the result in Dublin, and win hands down against the bookmakers, if, that is, time in Dublin were to be regulated according to 'Dunsink Time'.

absentee landlord, Joyce took the liberty of renting it to Mr Leopold Bloom. In *Dubliners*, Joyce is seemingly obsessed with the idea of paralysis, but by the time he came to write *Ulysses* 'paralysis' has given way to regulation. All the events take place on one day; so what, if I am an author, falls within my field of view? Nothing exceptional. Nothing that could not take place. Regular, regulation, regulated. As Joyce was no doubt often told at school: obey the rule. St Benedict did, and so did St Sulpice, whose rule governed my own schooling. Time-bound, and space-bound. Out of bounds. Beyond a boundary.

1 W.—Eccles-street.

From Dorset-street Lower, to Royal Circus,
P. St. George.—Inns-quay W.

A PILLAR LETTER-BOX *corner of*
Nelson street.

1 Clarke, Mrs.	25*l.*
2 Verdon, Mr. Christopher	27*l.*
3 Bermingham, William, stucco plasterer,	26*l.*
„ Dickie, James, esq. solicitor, and Seatown house, Swords	
„ M'Donnell & Brogan, house and land agents	
4 Lynch, Mrs.	27*l.*
5 Molloy, Mr. George F.	27*l.*
6 Smith, Miss Rose, music teacher	28*l.*
7 Vacant,	28*l.*
8 Woods, Mr. R.	30*l.*
9 Hayes, John, esq.	26*l.*

Page from *Thom's Official Dublin Directory* of 1904 with 7 Eccles Street empty. Next door lived a music teacher and nearby a solicitor and a stucco plasterer. Its rateable value at £28, which would presumably have been paid by Bloom's landlord, that is if Bloom had lived there as a tenant, confirms the impression that this street is respectable. In 1904 the pious Mrs Lynch, who provided furnished lodgings for George Tyrrell and his mother in 1876 and who helped Tyrrell when he was thinking of converting to Catholicism, is still there at number 4. It is never stated in the novel but one suspects it is unearned income, that is income from money in part inherited from his father, that enables Bloom to pay the rent and live respectably – but not so respectably when you consider he needs a lodger to supplement his income. As indicated, Molly is against taking in a lodger but she seems to be kept in the dark over the household finances, and assumes, for example, that all their money goes in 'food and rent' (*U* 18:467). We don't know the Blooms' tenancy agreement, so we don't know what their landlord, whether fictional or real, would say about subletting.

In a sense *Ulysses* is all about the regulated life. While it is based on the Homeric myth of a ten-year wandering, in reality it feels more settled and familiar than that. Indeed, it displays all the routine we associate with a modern city and modern clock time, confirming a view of life one gets from perusing something like *Thom's Business Directory of Dublin and Suburbs for the Year 1906*. To take a small example, the list of grocers in that directory comes to over ten pages, while wine and spirit merchants occupy over seven pages, and on each page there are two columns, each with some 30–40 names. Imagine all those people and all those premises supplying a city with its food and drink. Everywhere, the world is opening and closing at the same time to the same tune and, presumably, to the same kinds of actions and conversation. And in turn it must have been habit-forming. Quite simply, the Edwardian world was nothing if not routinised, reliable and saturated with identity and sameness. You could rely, for example, not only on an efficient tram system but also on five postal deliveries a day if you lived in Dublin. Routine, habit, reliance. You get a distinct impression that Joyce is drawing on a regulated life governed by clocks, routine and a Victorian inheritance – a life steeped in the expected.

Joyce in typical fashion takes this a step further. If you want to know what daily life is like, or, better, if you want to know how daily life is rendered in

PEN-AND-INK SKETCH OF THE LUCKY TIT-BITITE.

Three imaginary tongue-in-cheek portraits of lucky winners of prize-winning stories, from *Tit-Bits*, 22 December 1894. Bloom's consciousness, character and even his looks belong to the world of late-Victorian popular culture. We know from Stanislaus Joyce that *Tit-Bits* was avidly read by Joyce's father, and there's enough evidence to suggest it was absorbed like the ether by Joyce himself. *Tit-Bits* is fascinated by the great mass of humanity then beginning to drift into the major cities of the world in search of work (except Dublin), but while the tone running through many of the chosen items in *Tit-Bits* exhibits an invisible exclamation mark, such a tone is foreign to Bloom, who has a more even take on the things that strike him. Like *Tit-Bits*, however, Bloom is respectful of social and cultural differences, even as the imperial world was trampling on such things.

fiction, read *Ulysses*. Doing and being. First, doing. Rising, eating, thinking, waiting, talking, walking, thinking, bumping into people, stopping, acting innocent, thinking, defecating, reading, thinking of lying in a bath, drinking, noticing, observing, thinking, joking, praying, going to a funeral, speaking behind people's backs, thinking, coveting, scoffing, mocking, working, being shouted at, resorting to, eating, being repulsed, begging, calling, thinking, looking, seeing what you shouldn't see, flirting, masturbating, thinking, lying around and giving birth, singing, silently or out of earshot breaking wind, drinking, imagining, practising for a concert, making

BLOOMSDAY

16*th* June, 1904

'Bloomsday' by John Ryan, from *Envoy*, April 1951. A composition, a series of sketches, a collage, an arrangement, slices of agitated life held for a moment in space.

love, thinking, thinking of making love, thinking, worrying, thinking, talking to others, enjoying company, avoiding company, urinating, menstruating, wishing, slowing down, questioning, answering, calculating, all the time thinking, thinking. Doing and being. Being jovial, morose, tired, excited, bored, boring, meditative, angry, furtive, inquisitive, self-conscious and so on through the full spectrum of what makes us human. Or if we have a 'corresponding' mind, we might adapt this list accordingly, forget about the 10 miles or so distance between Eccles Street on the north side of Dublin and the Martello Tower at Sandycove, and begin: Rising, rising, eating, eating, thinking, thinking . . . What will 17 June bring I wonder? Shall we start again? But that would be repetition. Precisely. The regulated life. Repetition as routine. Repetition as boredom. Take your choice.

Speaking crudely, what could be more daily-like, more earthy and at the same time more heavenly, than an after-breakfast bowel movement? It's so much part of our lives and yet remains, perhaps still, off-limits for the fiction-writer. To describe that moment must have been one of the many jokes the scatalogical Joyce enjoyed contemplating. To borrow an image he had used to defend what he was attempting in *Dubliners*, here was a special kind of making sacred of everyday life. Here, too, was the meeting-point of the daily and the absurd. Absurd because it's what we all do everyday, a reminder by whoever designed us that we should never get above our station in life. Absurd, too, because even as Bloom is shown at stool he's only doing what everyone does, which prompts the thought not that it's obscene and should be censored but that it's so common as not to merit special attention. Like flossing or shaving or trimming eyebrows or looking hard in the mirror or getting wax out of the ear or clipping toe-nails or putting bleach round the toilet bowl or ironing the sheets or straightening the cushions or switching off the television when we retire to bed, or snoring, or involuntarily scratching ourselves when asleep. Sdop, to borrow a word from *Finnegans Wake*.

Bowel movements. Forget the why and ask yourself how. How would you describe such motions in a novel? Not for your clinician but in a novel? And how would you describe them to yourself? With full-on consciousness or with an accompanying consciousness? Oh, thinks Bloom a little later in the day when he's out of the house, did I remember to pull the chain? The remark, we can notice in passing, is an aside, but it enters our consciousness with some significance, for it reminds us that the toilet in Bloom's outhouse is plumbed to the city's sewerage system. Jonathan Swift, the confidence of the Enlightenment behind him, tried to face down his fears by writing about them. In a shockingly direct poem 'The Lady's Dressing Room', he eventually realises that, although she might be attractive, 'Celia, Celia, Celia shits'. It must have been such an effort for Swift to combine in the one thought Celia beautiful and Celia ugly; one uplifting, the other full of nasty things cascading down or trickling out. Coming from a large family, Joyce's sexuality was more realistic or turned from the start, and, as the title to his first collection of verse reminds us, he found Nora's chamber music more than a little suggestive.

Joyce, however, shared something of Swift's excremental vision, only he is more accepting, forcing us to confront not so much our squeamishness as taboos in writing. Indeed, if tackled, the defiant Joyce has a neat riposte, designed to put the other person on the defensive. When learning that his aunt Josephine thought the novel not fit to read, his response was immediate: 'If *Ulysses* isn't fit to read . . . life isn't fit to live' (Ellmann, 1982, 537). Such an attitude brooks of no discussion, and admits no morality issuing from the terrain of appropriateness. If Joyce is reprehensible, then so is the rest of the world. If Joyce can't move, then neither should the rest of us. At the same time, we are a long way from Swift. However, in the wider scheme of things, which we might discern as a theme with a peculiarly Irish inflection, Joyce occupies a position half-way on the road between his compatriots Swift and Beckett. Beckett in this regard is the more consciously reflective late Modernist, for whom the idea of crap, as in say *Krapp's Last*

Advert for Beecham's Pills, from *Tit-Bits*, Christmas 1886. Given the huge number of advertisements in this period designed to alleviate stomach upset and intestinal complaints, Bloom's contemporaries must have suffered all the time from stomach ache. Here Aesculapius, the demigod in Greek mythology responsible for healing, gives his approval to the efficacy of Thomas Beecham's Pills in putting out the internal fires and restoring a regulated life. Beecham's liked this kind of rhetoric. In *The Freeman's Journal* for 16 June 1904, the company advertises its pills as 'the Friend in Need of the Human Race', which in one sense at least is right, for Beecham's as a company was dependent on purchases by the human race and dependent, too, therefore, on stomach cramps. Stomach ache got everywhere. With Parnell in mind, the *Tit-Bits* issue for Christmas 1890 carried an advert for Eno's Salts under the heading 'The Home Rule Problem'. Even political upset had a medical cure.

Tape (1959), comes to represent something in the culture or the past, and it's partly for this reason easier to discuss 'Beckett and crap' than 'Joyce and crap'.

Speaking crudely, Joyce is physical and laid himself open to the charge of obscenity, more so in the past than today. In *Finnegans Wake*, Shem uses his own excreta to write with. *Ulysses* beckons us to accompany Bloom into the toilet and it can embarrass us. It's not something that one asks in polite company, but Bloom in the outhouse prompts such thoughts as the following. Do you read when you're at stool? And if you don't, what do you think of people who do? And do you leave a stack of magazines or books to read in the loo, and are they there for your benefit or in case you have visitors? And what sort of paper do you use? Soft tissue is the norm today but, in years gone by, most people applied something less kind to their tail. Hard toilet paper was the default kind, but there was a worse condition, for when you had no toilet, as was sometimes the case in rural Ireland until the 1960s, you had to resort to clumps of the green grass of God's holy island. Grass is plentiful, environmentally friendly and renewable, but in small hands it's a hit-and-miss affair and often incredibly messy therefore. And, never mind the sewerage system in the city in 1904, what about faecal matter in the green fields of Ireland in the 1960s? What kind of statement was

that? What kind of example was that to set to the neighbours by a new nation? When asked by passing tourists in the west of Ireland from the safety
of their rental cars whether or not there were any toilets in the vicinity, one
of my uncles, from the safety of the garden of his agricultural labourer's
cottage, would reply without a hint of irony: 'Anywhere from here to the
Cliffs of Moher'.

Think, too, about the contrast with our own en-suite times. Like Uncle
Charles in *A Portrait*, Bloom 'repairs' to an outside loo for all the world to
see. Joyce doesn't tell us how Bloom walked, and he gets distracted filling in
Bloom's thoughts with a passage about dung and lettuce and a file of
spearmint growing by the wall. But how would you walk down the garden
on your way to the loo? Without looking? Looking innocent? Nonchalantly?
Brazenly? With Boylan in mind, blazing a trail, jingle jangle here I come?
Once inside, Bloom is concerned about the state of his trousers: 'Better be
careful not to get these trousers dirty for the funeral' (*U* 4:494–5). What
does that tell us about the state of the outhouse? And the answer concerns
not the floor, which might have crossed our tidy or unclean minds, but the
walls: 'Mouldy limewash and stale cobwebs'. Equally, once inside, he's still
not safe, for the outhouse is, if not a communal one, not terribly private:
'Hope no ape comes knocking just as I'm.' (*U* 4:465–6). In a passage that is
nothing if not graphic, the omission at the end of that thought, represented
by the full-stop, is tactful, providing as it does a different kind of unfinished
sentence from the ones we encountered when discussing *Dubliners*.

In Bloom's case, for toilet paper he uses a past issue of *Tit-Bits*, a weekly
newspaper full of print. And while at stool, he thinks of 'Matcham's
Masterstroke', a prize story which supposedly appeared in *Tit-Bits* and which
was won by P. Beaufoy. As far as I know, the story has never been tracked
down, but it's a masterstroke on Joyce's part. Defecation, evacuation, all
mixed up with tit-bits, bricolage, cobwebs and the world of print. Enough,
I can see where that's going, you're saying. An issue that becomes a tissue.
All part of yesterday's news or titbits. What's left behind. Enough. Sdop, I
tell you. With Swift in mind, a tail for a Gulliver to attend to. Or perhaps
the title of an early soap: 'Daily life at 7 Eccles Street'. Enough. Sdop. 'Shite
and onions', as Joyce's father, the habitual curser, was wont to say habitually.
In *Finnegans Wake* Joyce takes such interest a stage further and injects an
ethical dimension when we read about Finnegan and the 'collupsus of his
back promises' (*FW* 5:27–8). Shite and ethics, to coin a phrase. Bowels and
promises. Are we talking about incontinence, doing a moony, or what?

Let's draw back a little from the outhouse. We were in there too long
anyway. You might imagine that intimacy is a word that springs to mind

MARCH 6, 1897.

THE PRIZE TIT-BIT.

THE following has been judged by the Arbitrators to be the best sent in, and has therefore gained the prize. As it is an original story, payment at the rate of One Guinea per column has been sent to the author,

Mr. PHILIP BEAUFOY,
Playgoers' Club,
Strand, W.C.

A READING-ROOM ROMANCE.

THE benevolent projectors of the Public Libraries Act probably never foresaw that their excellent libraries and reading-rooms would furnish extraordinarily good backgrounds for miscellaneous flirtations—else it is possible that in their philanthropic thoughtfulness they would not have been so energetic in counselling the Act as tending towards intellectual improvement. For although a grim notice hangs in the reading-room warning the readers that "Silence" must be preserved, yet young men and women can carry on violent flirtations in whispers, and even without whispers. It is the history of one of these flirtations which this brief record will endeavour to set forth.

This story by P. Beaufoy, 'A Reading-Room Romance', appeared in *Tit-Bits* in March 1897. Over the years, I have managed to track down most of the stories by Beaufoy that appeared in *Tit-Bits* between 1899 and 1904, but not 'Matcham's Masterstroke'. Whoever he was in real life, Beaufoy – a 'beautiful faith' name that resembles Purefoy, the woman of 'pure faith' who gives birth in the maternity hospital in the 'Oxen of the Sun' episode – had an enviable knack of regularly producing stories for a popular audience. His prize-winning stories printed in *Tit-Bits* included 'Dick Darrell's Victoria Cross' (23 December 1899), 'The Finale of Act 2: An Actor's Story' (9 February 1901), 'Wilfrid Mason's Engagement: A Story of the Stage' (17 August 1901), 'Billie Scott's Eva' (28 December 1901), 'Dick Armstrong's Sacrifice' (14 June 1902), 'A Mysterious Post-Card' (7 November 1903) (which begins like 'Calypso' with a breakfast scene and the delivery of an upsetting post-card on which is written 'Prepare to Die Before the End of the Year'), 'The Counsel for the Defence' (30 January 1904) and 'Mr Renshaw's Typist' (31 December 1904). In the 'Circe' episode, Beaufoy reappears to accuse Bloom of being a 'soapy sneak masquerading as a *littérateur*' (U 15:822–3).[2]

when we think of Joyce. But it's equally true to assert the opposite: intimacy is not really a word that springs to mind when we think of Joyce. He plays with the idea, but what he gives us is something else. Bloom is introduced as *Mr* Bloom, but, within a few pages of being introduced, we see him pulling down his trousers and gently easing his bowels. Whatever else that is, it isn't true to life. As I suggest elsewhere, Joyce 'tends not to distinguish but to elide privacy and intimacy, as if nothing more was needed for intimacy to be established than disclosure of private details' (Pierce, 2006, 78). Or, as Marilyn French, coming at this from another direction, rightly suggests: 'Joyce's approach to sexuality was primarily one of exposure' (French, 1982, 44). Towards the end of her soliloquy Molly acknowledges she knows every turn in Bloom: 'Ill tighten my bottom well and let out a few smutty words smellrump or lick my shit' (U 18:1530–2). Molly likes her

---

[2]For more on Beaufoy, see my *Joyce and Company* (2006), 39–43.

arse licked, and just by uttering the right word or phrase she perhaps gets Bloom to perform accordingly. Imagine the scene in the Bloom household at the onset of sexual arousal or when Molly turns over in the bed at night. Smellrump, you naughty boy! The joined-up word, which in its own way recalls 'ribsteak' in the previous episode, suggests a repeated command by Molly to Bloom: not small rump, but smellrump, not a description there-fore of one of her moving parts but a command. Head to tail, we might recall, is the way they sleep.¿?

Now the whole world knows, and it gives us, as students and readers, a certain licence, too. We now know how Molly gets her kicks, and we can write about it without censure. Smut. But there the licence stops. We can't normally, or we don't normally, say such things about our partners to oth-ers, whether family or friends or third parties. Joyce's so-called dirty letters, which he sent to Nora from Dublin in 1909, come under a similar kind of ethical restraint. We read them but perhaps we shouldn't. And this has nothing to do with prurience but with judgement about what constitutes appropriateness. The correspondence belongs to a couple's privacy, to that space marked 'intimate'; they don't belong to the world at large. Once pub-lished, however, as the dirty letters were in Ellmann's edition of *Selected Letters of James Joyce* in 1975, there was no going back. Smut will out, we might well concede. On the other hand, why didn't Joyce burn them? Or was he driven, like Richard Rowan in *Exiles*, by a repetition-compulsion syndrome always to tell the truth regardless? Regardless, that is, of what is appropriate, regardless of the line between intimacy and privacy, regardless of his family and what they might think or what they might have to endure as a consequence of his disclosure. After leaving the Church, Joyce took to confessing his sins in public, and therefore what should have been uttered in private and accompanied by repentance and shame was broadcast to the world. The world listens in, but, unlike the confessional, there's no-one to forgive him. 'Shame's choice' is how his name is sometimes rendered by Spanish speakers. An amazingly appropriate choice for a language to stum-ble upon.

Disclosing such details about Molly begs the question explored in more detail with my students in the next chapter: is this intimacy? I tend not to think so, if only because the reader shouldn't be hearing any of this. In Joyce's case it seems to concern not so much intimacy as the relationship between desire and absence, shrinking, that is, through masturbation the distance in 1909 between Dublin and Trieste. What seems to be happening in the novel is that Bloom and Molly occupy a site between being individu-als for themselves and being individuals for us the reader. The reader knows everything but they don't. In its own way it's shocking, but they don't even know they correspond to figures in Homer. How would they, since they're fictional characters? Molly doesn't know if, when she uses the word 'barracks' to describe 7 Eccles Street, she is recalling the barracks, built at the time of the Napoleonic Wars, where *Ulysses* begins. She doesn't know, that is, that she is contributing to the novel's cohesion or woven fabric. Joyce exploits this gap, this fictional convention, and he gives us a portrait of a marriage that has the look of intimacy, while allowing room for detachment and playful distance, and at the same time encouraging personal ownership on the part of the reader. Perhaps, in his defence, he also gives us a licence to talk about things like smut normally considered off-limits. He also does something else, for as Bonnie Kime Scott candidly confesses in *Joyce and Feminism* (1984), 'Joyce gets at my vulnerable places. I feel mocked for the feminine wiles I have occasionally practiced and the consumerist vanities I have indulged in' (Scott, 1984, 203).

The Freeman's Journal

As noted in a previous chapter, in the very first story of *Dubliners*, we encounter a reference to *The Freeman's Journal* when one of the sisters, Eliza, tells us that the notice of their brother's death appeared in the '*Freeman's General*' (D 16). The newspaper clearly performed a service, not least in the personal columns and death notices. Indeed, there's merit in Bloom's claim that it's adverts that sell newspapers. *The Freeman's Journal* was so familiar to Dubliners that Joyce can let Eliza's malapropism stand uncorrected, for, not unlike the snow at the end of 'The Dead', the 'journal' was indeed 'general' all over Ireland. In *Ulysses*, *The Freeman's Journal* occupies a more central position, not least because we get to see the inside offices where Bloom works, and I want to spend time reflecting on the significance of this for a reading of the novel.

As we turn from domestic intimacy to the public world that Bloom also inhabits, the focus shifts, but not the thread that weaves its way through the novel. As *Ulysses* constantly reminds us, consciousness recognises no limits, so whether at home or abroad Bloom is his delightful self, giving us constant cause to pause. From all that has been said, it will come as no surprise when I compare *Ulysses* to a huge linguistic workshop or distribution centre, with Bloom, Stephen and Molly as the leading officers or players. Joyce's image of Dublin is at once a city of words and a 'wordcity', and at the heart of his construction of the city is language. Winding its way through the streets of Dublin is a billboard with letters carried by five men (on 'three bob a day') advertising HELY'S, a wholesale stationer and printer, where Bloom was once employed to collect accounts. Everywhere you look

Tram advertising Hely's of Dame Street, Dublin. Complete with the apostrophe.

in *Ulysses* there is a print culture at work and on display. Indeed, when you think of a stationer's like Hely's with Bloom in mind, very quickly the image of blotting paper and ink erasers nudge their way into view. Bloom after all is disparagingly referred to at one point as a 'traveller for blotting-paper' (U 6:703). But what is *Ulysses* if not a quire of blotting paper containing the record of a whole culture, a record which is also full of smudges, inkstains, mirror-images, distortions, gigantisms and minor corrections? It's a book of scripts for us to read in this respect, a typescript that began life as a manuscript.

The idea of a 'wordcity' I have borrowed from Peter Fritzsche's persuasive study (1996) of Berlin at the turn of the twentieth century. It's a topic I've written about at length in *Joyce and Company* (2006), so I'm not going to repeat myself here, but let me just say this: not for nothing does language in *Ulysses* keep rebounding on us. As we also saw when discussing *A Portrait of the Artist as a Young Man*, Joyce writes nothing but 'language novels'. Nearly every street in Joyce has a name and nearly every shop is identified. Characters walk down particular streets and pass particular shops. The pork-butcher on Dorset Street where Bloom buys kidneys for breakfast has a name. It isn't the pork-butcher or some generic name, but in this case an invented name 'Dlugacz', which is a Jewish name, the name in fact of Joyce's Zionist teacher in Trieste. It's a substitute name and another example of recycling or satire on Joyce's part. Interestingly, in *Thom's Business Directory of Dublin and Suburbs for the Year 1906*, six pork-butchers

Among the many origins to Bloom's name are an Irish mountain, Slieve Bloom, a common Jewish surname, and 'bloomers', the new fashionable women's clothing particularly good for riding bicycles. We might also single out the reference to 'blooming alone' in Tom Moore's song 'The Last Rose of Summer'.

with middle-European or eastern European names•are listed, including Haffner, Koppinhoffer, Rŭhmann and Youkstetter, and there were in fact three pork-butchers on Dorset Street Lower.

One conclusion we might draw is that Joyce was spoilt for choice and that he was simply responding to the world around him. Sweny's is the chemist on Lincoln Place where Bloom buys some lotion for Molly. Davy Byrne's is the name of the pub on Duke Street where Bloom has a 'light snack', and it provides a welcome relief after the spit-and-sawdust experience of a Lestrygonian lunch on offer in the Burton Restaurant nearby. If Joyce tells us anything about identity it is that it has its roots in names and naming. The whole city is constituted thus by Joyce and so is the world of objects. When you don't know something or you lack education or you mishear something, you invent a word such as 'gesabo' or *Freeman's General* or 'met him pike hoses' (as Molly does for 'metempsychosis'). There's little which doesn't contribute in an arresting way to Joyce's wordcity.

At each turn in *Ulysses*, we confront language, choice and the wordcity. The first thing you need on entering a city for the first time is a map that will tell you how to get from A to B. Then you need to exercise choice. Where do I buy what I need and where shall I have lunch or something to eat? And all the time in Joyce there is thinking, thinking, consciousness of.

Sweny's in Lincoln place, in October 2006. Photograph by David Pierce. In one respect Joyce was right when he has Bloom think 'Chemists rarely move. Their green and gold beaconjars too heavy to stir' (*U* 5:463–4).

Davy Byrne's on Duke Street. Sunday morning early. Door shut for a change, the cursive script as inviting as ever. Photograph by David Pierce.

Some things we know, such as what Bloom is thinking as he's queuing in the pork-butcher. Some things we infer, such as how people think of Bloom as he traverses the city. Like the streets that compose the city, the house on Eccles Street is more than its material parts. The streets all belong to the wordcity, a reminder that Joyce himself belongs to a wider movement, to which in turn he gives expression. Reading the city – this is what the characters of *Ulysses* do in the novel, and this is what we as readers do. A joint exercise in interpretation.

It should come as no surprise that Dublin in 1904 was full of people involved in the construction of a wordcity. Take all the occupations in *Thom's Business Directory of Dublin and Suburbs for the Year 1906* concerned with the printed word and its dissemination. There are 85 letterpress printers, including Hely's on Dame Stret and Gibbs the printers for Trinity College; 20 typists are listed, a reflection of a new profession then beginning to establish itself; 20 advertising agents; and some 100 newsagents to sell papers. Over 80 newspapers and periodicals are listed, including *The Irish Homestead* published on Fridays, the *Daily Express* in bold letters (which Gabriel Conroy reviews for), *The Bee-Keeper*, a monthly that Joyce briefly worked for, and *The Freeman's Journal and National Press*, whose address is given as North Prince's Street, off Sackville Street. Over half the titles carry the word 'Irish' or 'Ireland', including Athur Griffith's *United Irishman* and Standish O'Grady's *All Ireland Review*. Print sellers and printer materials and roller manufacturers are further reminders of a material culture in the making of competing ideologies.

APPALLING AMERICAN DISASTER.

EXCURSION STEAMER ON FIRE.

500 LIVES LOST.

WILD SCENES OF PANIC

CHILDREN THROWN OVERBOARD.

WOMEN TRAMPLED TO DEATH.

Report in *The Freeman's Journal*, 16 June 1904. On newspaper hoardings throughout the city, Dubliners were given news of the disaster within hours of it happening in New York. *Ulysses* cuts through history to remind us that above all else a modern city is a text to be read.

DUBLIN UNIVERSITY v. COUNTY
KILDARE.
Owing to rain, there was no play in this match on
Tuesday in the College Park, but a commencement was
made yesterday shortly before 12 o'clock, in dull and
threatening weather. Meldon and Leeper started the
batting for Dublin University, on an easy wicket, to
the bowling of Harrington and Keys. The partner-
ship put on 17 runs. Leeper being then out to a
catch in slips by Harrington, off Keys, for seven,
whilst at 38 Meldon was out leg before to the same
trundler for 18, but he was missed previously in the
out field by Brown. This brought Fausett and

Another report in *The Freeman's Journal* for 16 June 1904, on a cricket match between Dublin University and County Kildare, poses a little problem for readers of *Ulysses*, and it concerns the weather on Bloomsday. In 'Lotus-eaters', Bloom is thinking about cricket and tells us 'Heatwave. Won't last' (*U* 5:563). The cricket report, however, tells us something different, how there was no play in the match on Tuesday (14 June) because of rain and play didn't resume until midday on Wednesday because of 'dull and threatening weather'. That's cricket for you, wholly dependent on the weather. On Thursday, Bloomsday, the weather might be muggy and hot, but nobody would describe that as a heatwave because such a term only comes into play after many days of hot weather, and you wouldn't know on Thursday if the same high pressure system was going to be around into the middle of the following week, when you might legitimately hear people talking about a heatwave stretching back to the previous week. It's possible that Bloom uses the phrase loosely, perhaps confusing it with the continuing drought; he's certainly right about 'Won't last', but then everyone in Britain and Ireland would know that. It's possible that Joyce deliberately throws a spanner into his perfectly designed work for critics like myself, 85 years or so later, to get excited over. I doubt if any of this is the case. I think it's an oversight on Joyce's part. It certainly doesn't do very much damage to the verisimilitude of the novel, and, given all the details he has accumulated for us, it's amazing there aren't more such errors.

Nothing could be more telling than Joyce's choice of a newspaper office for one of his chapters in *Ulysses*. *The Freeman's Journal*, the oldest nationalist newspaper in Ireland and one that had supported Parnell in the 1880s and 1890s, is the setting for 'Aeolus', and it affords perhaps the most graphic example we have of a language workshop. 'Aeolus', the Homeric image, is a windy one, and it insists on one aspect of the newspaper industry, namely its characteristic propensity to follow any wind that blows. In its own way, such a view contains a radical edge and it offers us a useful supplement to the contemporary analysis of Fleet Street in, say, George Gissing's *New Grub Street* (1891), whose focus is the struggling journalist in an unrewarding environment. It's true: we constantly need reminding that the news media is not so much biased as driven. Whatever we think about their ideology, the Murdoch press, Fox News, Sky News, the BBC, CNN, all of them are largely driven by events, tacking and veering in whatever winds are out there blowing. Driven but rarely blown off course or called to account. However, to my mind, the more radical side to what Joyce is doing in 'Aeolus' concerns the presentation of the world of work, his own included. Thomas Hardy gives us a working agriculture, especially evident in the descriptions of different kinds of farm work that the female protagonist turns her hand to in *Tess of the d'Urbervilles* (1891). But until *Ulysses*, the world of modern print workers remained largely hidden for readers of the novel. Joyce would have agreed: let's see what's happening before we start theorising, which, we might add, is good advice for the general reader and the student of literature and culture alike.

When Stephen and Bloom arrive at the offices of *The Freeman's Journal*, Joyce takes care to describe what they see and hear. It's a noisy place, and crowded with rooms and with people in movement. There's also a 'Heavy, greasy smell' in the air (*U* 7:223–4). Unlike 7 Eccles Street, however, the layout of the rooms and corridors and staircases remains, I think, almost impossible to visualise or reconstruct. Partly this is Joyce and partly it's because the newspaper offices were destroyed during the 1916 Easter Rising (in 1924 the newspaper merged with the *Irish Independent*). But this situation has now been partly rectified by two photographs that have recently come to light, for we can now see what the composing room and the foundry room were like.

Among the first things to strike us as we study the first photograph is the working environment. Ten typesetters or so are seated on fairly low chairs at work on Mergenthaler Linotype machines. These machines were invented by Ottmar Mergenthaler in Boston in 1884. They began to be used in the production of newspaper in New York in 1886 and were installed in *The Freeman's Journal* two years later. The Mergenthaler enabled operators to set type five times as fast as a human typesetter could previously. The operator of a Linotype sat fairly low down at a keyboard. Matrixes dropped into a line and were automatically pressed against molten lead, and a 'line of type' (hence Linotype) fell into a tray. The brass matrixes were then lifted to a bar and released into their original slots for reuse. 'Sllt' is the noise they make, Joyce informs us in 'Aeolus'. In the middle of the room there are various cases of type, printing equipment, and space for assembling the type into galleys. Electric lights and cables and pipes hang down from the ceiling all pell-mell, in what looks like the visual equivalent of a noisy environment. Everyone has stopped for the cameraman, who has clearly asked them to face him for a minute or two. No-one smiles and it's as if the printers are tolerating the outsider, oblivious of just how important this photograph will be for future readers of Joyce. At the back of the room a bowler hat is hanging, while near the door there is a wooden chair with a newspaper on it, perhaps one occupied by the foreman or overseer.

A view of the composing room at the offices of *The Freeman's Journal*, taken some time between the mid-1890s and 1904. Courtesy of eBay.

(*left*) Detail of Menotti Caprani seated. Behind him an older typesetter has a newspaper on an easel, presumably for copying purposes; beside him is the figure I take to be the foreman.

(*right*) Detail of the figure in the centre of the photograph. With his fine-cut suit, this person has the appearance of someone in a managerial position, someone who might indeed walk 'statelily'. I wonder if this is William Brayden, the editor of *The Freeman's Journal*. He doesn't look like Nannetti, whose sketch is reproduced on page 260.

A section of the stone room and foundry of *The Freeman's Journal*. The aprons, the ties, the collars, the men in waistcoats and jacketless, the boys who can't stand still, all convey in their different way a vivid impression of a print workshop at the turn of the twentieth century. The same figure as in the other photograph, with his jacket buttoned at the top, commands our attention in the middle of this photograph. He looks as though he might be the foreman – perhaps the person who preceded Nannetti. Galleys on the stone tables are awaiting type, there's a wooden mallet on the table, while overhead the electric light bulbs remind us that newspaper production was undertaken as much at night as during the day. 'By 1900,' according to the historian of Dublin Joseph V. O'Brien, 'only a very small part of the city was lighted by electricity' (O'Brien, 1982, 68). Perhaps this photograph is closer, then, to 1904 than the mid-1890s.

Walking round Dublin today are the grandchildren and great-grandchildren of these workers. I have identified only one person in this photograph – the fourth figure up from the left with a black clip on the left arm of his rolled-up white shirt – but it would be interesting if the photograph included other characters in *Ulysses* such as 'old Monks', for example, or Ruttledge the business manager. With the help of his grandson, Vincent Caprani, I have been able to identify Menotti Vincent Caprani, or 'Cuprani' as Joyce misspells his name in *Ulysses*. Prior to this discovery and my purchase on eBay early in 2007, the Caprani family possessed only a poor photograph of Menotti, so were naturally delighted to see such a clear image of one of their nineteenth-century forbears. As Bloom recalls in 'Aeolus', 'Double marriage of sisters celebrated. Two bridegrooms laughing heartily at each other. Cuprani too, printer. More Irish than the Irish' (*U* 7:98–100). Truth is even stranger than fiction because the Caprani family continued enjoying double marriages (Caprani, 1982, 20–1). For Joyce readers, the photograph has its own significance, for it is now possible to visualise part of Bloom's actual working environment, and in a way that is only half-realised by Joyce in 'Aeolus'.

The first person Bloom passes on entering the building on Prince's Street is Davy Stephens. Davy, who has a roll of papers under his cape, was a famous newspaper seller at the time. Indeed, he was once spoken to by King Edward VII when the king alighted at Kingstown Harbour on a visit to Ireland – hence the tag 'a king's courier', a courier, that is, who's entering a building on Prince's Street. Whose country is always a pertinent question running through *Ulysses*, and Joyce, not knowing when to stop, rarely misses an opportunity to insist. Word then passes that William Brayden, the editor, is making his way – not 'stately' like Mulligan but 'statelily' – into the building. Oblivious of rank, however, sounds continue. Doors creak and machines 'sllt', for it's true, as Bloom rightly observes in this articulate episode, 'everything speaks in its own way'. A telegram boy wanders

Davy Stephens in classic pose, selling a variety of papers including the *July Royal*, *Pall Mall Magazine*, *Answers*, and a comic with a front page about leprechauns. The date can just be made out: July 1905. From the Lawrence Collection in the National Library of Ireland.
Source: Courtesy of the National Library of Ireland

in, throws down an envelope, and disappears 'posthaste' with a shout of 'Freeman!' He has post for *The Freeman* (not for the *Evening Telegraph*, that is, which was also printed in these same offices), but he's also after delivering post. Hence 'posthaste'. The boy's also in a hurry and will do things not only in haste but quicker than that. Hence, also, 'posthaste'. Only a writer with a decidedly popular and ironic touch, only a writer with a political agenda intent on reversing centre and margin, would spend time on a wizened old newspaper seller, doors creaking, and a telegram boy.

Bloom realises that in such a noisy environment surrounded by hot type you need a 'cool head'. Such detailed and consequential work, where mistakes would prove costly, is done in an environment that seems to militate against concentration. Even if people have a cool head, however, newspapers are given almost as a matter of course to promulgating and propounding errors. In the report on Dignam's funeral in the *Evening Telegraph*, Bloom's name appears as 'L. Boom' (17:1260). Joyce also has fun with 'M'Intosh', the person at the funeral who is mistakenly identified thus when Bloom was simply telling a reporter about a man in a macintosh. There is also a 'line of bitched type' in the report, which Bloom feels he was partly responsible for: ')eatondph 1/8 ador dorador douradora* (must be where he called Monks the dayfather about Keyes's ad)' (*U* 16:1257–9). (I assume 'bitched type' is a bloomer for 'bastard type', which the 'bitched type' in this case isn't.) Newspapers go forth as an account of the world, but the situation is in many respects reversed, for it is the world that is auditing newspapers. A newspaper, therefore, is a place where mistakes are on display every day, and such mistakes, unlike Bloom's, stem from oversight by journalists, typesetters, or foremen and overseers. They also belong to happenstance, to speed, to a lack of cool heads, sheer sloppiness, or distraction. The earnestness on the faces of the typesetters in the offices of *The Freeman's Journal* above tells its own story.

Continuing past a side-door, where he hears machines and boards thumping and clanking, the modern Odysseus ends up in the 'reading closet' of Councillor Nannetti, who is the printers' foreman. Joe Hynes, whom we've already met in 'Ivy Day in the Committee Room' reciting a sentimental poem in support of Parnell, the uncrowned king of Ireland, is in with Nannetti. Later in the novel, we realise that Hynes is probably relaying details of the funeral for a report that will misspell Bloom's name and get other things wrong. Bloom waits patiently until the subheading informs us: 'WE SEE THE CANVASSER AT WORK'. The announcement is more than just description. 'Aeolus' is concerned to portray people 'at work'. Bloom's work as a canvasser for adverts in a newspaper means negotiation and living off his wits. He's paid a retainer by the newspaper, so needs commissions.

He seeks approval from a busy Nannetti for an advert for the tea merchant, Alexander Keyes. The design for the advert is a play on the Manx Parliament, the House of Keys, and the marketing intention is that it will catch the eye of summer visitors to Dublin from the Isle of Man. Bloom, who will return home that night without keys to his own house, lays the cutting on Nannetti's desk in front of him and takes care to allow the foreman an opportunity to absorb it all, inserting judicious and what he thinks are persuasive comments in time with the clanking machines. The alert reader notices everything: busy, business, Bloom characteristically waiting, never insisting, keys, Key(e)s – 'always **be** closing', to borrow a phrase from the film of David Mamet's *Glengarry Glen Ross* (1984), or hoping to. This is Bloom's 'work' and this is what it means to say he is 'at work'. Waiting and pausing are part of his work, and he is thinking all the time how to get hooks into people or follow up leads or, indeed with Hynes in mind, how to collect debts owed him. In among the pauses, somewhat ridiculously but in its own way part of the 'whose nation' theme, he thinks he might ask the 'Italian' foreman how to pronounce '*voglio*' (*U* 7:152), but he counsels against it because if Nannetti didn't know there would be embarrassment all round. As with Cuprani, Nannetti is 'More Irish than the Irish'.

In 'Cyclops', Nannetti is referred to as 'Nannan . . . The mimber' (*U* 12:825). In 'Aeolus', we learn that Bloom also calls him Nannan. So, this was presumably his nickname, perhaps a rather exaggerated abbreviation of Nannetti, which in a sense it isn't. Could this be a further indication of

House of Keys, the Manx Parliament, in an Edwardian postcard.

DUBLIN—COLLEGE GREEN.

Mr. J. P. Nanetti—Ind N... 2,467

---

*Mr. J. L. Carew—N 2,173
    Nationalist majority ...... —— 294

Electorate : 10,223.

1886 : T. D. Sullivan (N), unopposed.
1892 : Dr. J. E. Kenny (P), 2,568 ; Sir H.
Cochrane (LU), 1,441 ; T. D. Sullivan (AP), 1,116
—Parnellite majority, 1,127.
1895 : Kenny (P), unopposed.
    Mr. Joseph Patrick Nanetti, who challenged
Mr. Carew's right of succession because that
free and independent
member had dared to
attend a levée of the
Duke of York's in
London, was the fore-
man printer of the
Dublin *Evening Tele-*
graph, is a member of
the Dublin Corporation,
the Dublin Port and
Docks Board, and the
Dublin Trades Council.
He was one of the can-
didates nominated by
Mr. William O'Brien's
United Irish League,
and on the eve of his
selection he stated that
in 1887 he was a sworn
Fenian and trusted in
the inner ranks of that
organisation. He was
the Dublin correspon-   MR. J. P. NANETTI.
dent of the *Board of*
Trade Gazette. As his name indicates, he is of
Italian extraction.
19 Hardwicke Street, Dublin.

Sketch of Joseph Patrick Nannetti which appeared in the *Pall Mall Gazette* in 1900. Nannetti was a local councillor and in 1900 he was elected MP for the College Green constituency in Dublin. In 1906 he became Lord Mayor of the city, succeeding the Joyce family friend Timothy Harrington. With a name like that, he couldn't escape his Italian background, but Nannetti's father clearly identified with the cause of nationalist Ireland. Joseph Patrick, not Giuseppe Patrizio. Perhaps, like Caprani, a second-generation immigrant. The spiteful London-based *Pall Mall Gazette* finds it necessary to point out that 'As his name indicates, he is of Italian extraction'.

his foreignness, given that most native English speakers have to take care with double consonants in spelling Italian names? Or could it be that 'Nannan' is short for Nannygoat (see the reference to the nannygoat in 'Circe' at 3370), and therefore a reflection of his fussy stewardship in the offices of *The Freeman's Journal* and *Evening Telegraph*? Or is he like a godmother or an aunty in the family, a nannan? A female man, like Bloom, in contrast with the male buck Mulligan? As for 'mimber', this is presumably an echo of how Nannetti would have pronounced the word: not a 'member' of Parliament but a 'mimber' of Parliament. It's unclear if this betrays Nannetti's slightly effete way of speaking or is designed to emphasise his foreignness – that would almost certainly not have been ambiguous to contemporaries, who would have known one way or the other what Joyce was intending. Bloom wonders if he will know the English for *voglio*, which perhaps suggests that Nannetti's first language is English and that he has lost any Italian he might have known. Interestingly, on 16 June 1904, Councillor Nannetti asked the Chief Secretary of Ireland if it was right that polo should be allowed in the Phoenix Park and not Gaelic games, a pertinent question that Joyce might well have made use of.

Everyone needs Nannetti's approval, so he's in demand. Bloom is forced to wait again while one of the typesetters shows the foreman a galley page. Bloom in the pause notices the typesetters sitting silently at their 'cases'. Then, after getting the nod from the foreman on the understanding that he secures a three-month renewal from Keyes, Bloom wanders off through the 'caseroom'. (I assume the 'caseroom' is the composing room in the photograph.) Bloom stops to observe a typesetter distribute type: 'mangiD kcirtaP' (*U* 7:206), and he's impressed by his dexterity, but there's something odd about what he sees, because this isn't how Patrick Dignam's name would be set. What we witness in *Ulysses* is that the letters are in a reverse order; in practice, as the illustrative page from Horace Townsend's *The Mergenthaler Linotype Company* (1915) suggests, not only are the letters in reverse order but each letter is itself reversed. The error cannot be the typesetter's so it must be either Bloom's or Joyce's, and one suspects it's Bloom's, an example of a bloomer which, incidentally, many of us make.

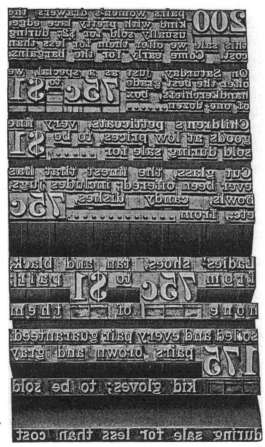

Page of typeset from *The Mergenthaler Linotype Company* (1915).

Until the advent of modern computerised print, typesetting meant whole sections of the printing industry spent their working lives reading from left to right and in reverse. The world in print, which looks so natural going forward, needed a well-practised eye to read. Bloom, once 'a traveller for blottingpaper' as we have seen, is now a 'spacehound', and his work involves him in filling empty spaces in a newspaper, but nothing would get sold without the skill of typesetters, who filled the empty space with a strange view of language and what Bloom imagines is 'backwards': 'mangiD kcirtaP'. In 'Hades' we reflect on Patrick Dignam in his coffin, a coffin that Bloom has followed that morning to Glasnevin Cemetery, but now we witness how poor Paddy gets into print almost without dignity, for he is nothing more than a name reversed. 'mangiD kcirtaP'. If you came across that name on a headstone, you'd quite properly think there was something wrong. 'Hades' and 'Aeolus', what's the connection? Empty spaces is one answer. From death to life is another, for printing is indeed a process of reversal and reversal is a process of revival. Come forth, Lazarus.

'Aeolus' is such an interesting episode and reminds us of something not often noticed about Joyce the consumer, namely his ability or his concern, as mentioned above, to portray the world of work that he had come into contact with at first hand. It's an episode that strains to dramatise working conditions and create a realistic atmosphere. Joyce was familiar with the processes of publishing and had obtained many impressions of newspaper offices and journals, including a visit to *The Freeman's Journal* when he returned to Dublin in 1909 (see Ellmann, 1982, 288–9). His interest in communications and reaching a mass audience resulted at one stage in his career in his involvement in a practical venture and a new technology. One of the reasons he returned to Dublin in 1909 was to set up and manage the first cinema in the city, the Volta, on Mary Street. Ironically, if the project had been successful, it's doubtful if we would now be reading a fictional account that draws on Joyce's experience of the mass media.

As a writer Joyce was always responding to the latest technological advances, presumably in order to give his writing an up-to-date look. In *Ulysses*, Bloom imagines fitting telephones into coffins, just in case, if the person was not dead, s/he would have the means to communicate with those above ground. More scurrilously, Boylan in the flower shop wants to say a word to the young assistant's telephone. In *Finnegans Wake*, Joyce evokes one of the earliest responses to watching television. In one sense, he was but part of his age. In the Christmas 1898 issue of *Tit-Bits* there is a burlesque of a telephone conversation which plays on the technical hiccups that first generation faced: 'Halloa! Whir-r-r-r-r-r-r-r-r'. If Joyce was writing today, he would have had a field day with all the new means of communication and text-messaging.

What I like about 'Aeolus' is that as soon as we enter the newspaper offices there is a question of payment being discussed. This is a nice touch on the part of the money-conscious Joyce. Get payment up-front. Good advice, for there's nothing airy about 'Aeolus', and, as ever, Joyce remains true to his non-conforming self. If you get an opportunity to hold *The Freeman's Journal* in your hands, you will recognise at once its unwieldy size and also the unwieldy size of the paper rolls needed to produce it. A newspaper that could only be read folded or at a desk or on the floor. It's right that when the newspaper is mentioned in 'Lotus-eaters' it is in a context where the public world impinges on the private. Bloom, on his way to the post office to see if Martha Clifford has replied to his saucy letter, 'took the folded *Freeman* from his sidepocket, unfolded it, rolled it lengthwise in a baton and tapped it at each sauntering step against his trouserleg' (*U* 5:48–50). For a single man, when it comes to looking natural in the street, a newspaper – any newspaper – is a great help, or at least so Bloom imagines. As we saw with *Tit-Bits*, printed matter serves many purposes, not all of which have to do with reading.

A final point before we conclude this chapter. In this episode Joyce comes closest to understanding culture in material terms and this had certain consequences, not least in altering his practices as a writer. One of the subheadings or crossheads is 'HOW A GREAT DAILY ORGAN IS TURNED OUT' (*U* 7:84). The words that stand out for me here are not simply 'ORGAN', which is

The Freeman's Journal carried this nationalist motif prominently on its front page. As Bloom notices in 'Calypso', 'Sunburst on the title page. He smiled, pleasing himself. Arthur Griffith also described the headpiece over the *Freeman* leader: "a homerule sun rising up in the northwest from the laneway behind the bank of Ireland" (*U* 4:100–3). The motif reminds us that in 1904 the paper's ideological viewpoint also served in part the interests of advanced nationalists like Griffith, who in 1905 went on to found Sinn Féin. In his novel of 1904, Joyce even has the audacity to suggest that Griffith, the author of *The Resurrection of Hungary: A Parallel for Ireland* (1904), might have got some of his ideas from Bloom, the son of a Hungarian Jew from Szombathely. Ikey Moses.

Richard Hamilton's *How A Great Daily Organ Is Turned Out*, 1990–8: a composite of 20 mixed intaglio plates. If the reader has got this far, it should be possible to identify several of these scenes from *Ulysses* and Joyce's life.

always potentially smutty in *Ulysses*, but also 'HOW'. 'Aeolus', as I say, sounds as if it might be simply full of wind offering a critique of the newspaper industry, but actually it is the most materialistic episode in *Ulysses*. In turn, the episode taught Joyce something about the novel he was writing, for the subheadings are not just an interesting addition or decoration but come to constitute something in themselves. Imagine the episode without those subheadings, and you have a narrative in miniature about Bloom (and Stephen) in a newspaper office. But insert the subheadings and you have interruption and the impossibility of reading it simply as narrative. The voice of the subheadings, if 'voice' is the right word that is, becomes increasingly dominant and satiric, so that by the time we reach 'K.M.A.' (kiss my arse) or 'CLEVER, VERY' we are clearly somewhere else in terms of the reading experience.

Subheadings in the tabloid press are normally skipped by most readers I suspect. They are there to break up the text and for ease of reading. But in 'Aeolus', and this is especially apparent in the large font size of early Shakespeare and Company editions of *Ulysses*, we can't help but notice them, and as we do so we can't quite integrate them into what's coming or what's just gone. Only after he had written the episode did Joyce stumble upon the idea of inserting the subheadings. It's as if in the process of writing that only then could he discern where the novel was heading. I think that's right. If you concentrate on how the world is constructed you discover something of its secrets, and in this particular case how effects in reading are altered by a simple device that appears in every newspaper around the world. It was a graphic lesson, and one that argues strongly not only for the importance of long periods of gestation time when writing but also for the view that at the heart of *Ulysses* is the printing press. The temporary and the spatial, one given to time, the other to space. After, before, insert, and then look again.

As Michael Groden underlines in *Ulysses in Progress* (1977), the novel begins with an 'initial style', particularly evident in the opening episodes, where characters are situated in realistic situations, and we follow their movements accordingly. In the second half of the novel, realistic treatment gives way to parody and imitation and different styles of writing. I tend to agree with this analysis, except that we witness it happening in dramatic terms as early as 'Aeolus' (and before). Once the subheadings are inserted, the second half of the novel is well and truly under way. With this episode, it becomes apparent that 'how' is always liable to take over in our reading experience. How do you write about a character in a newspaper office? Not naturalistically. Or, rather, naturalistically, but then introduce actual features from a newspaper and a style that resembles satire or parody. How do you write about someone masturbating on the beach, as happens in 'Nausicaa'? In the 'namby-pamby jammy marmalady drawersy (alto là!) style' (*Letters*, 135) of a Victorian romance, such as you might encounter in Miss Cummins's novel *The Lamplighter* (1854). How do you write about a brothel? Stage it as a dream or a play or a courtroom scene with prosecutors, women dressed as men, and the agitated Bloom in the dock again. How. After all that's been said about Bloom, it's a good place to end before we move on to the final episode of *Ulysses* and the Molly Bloom soliloquy. A *how* episode which becomes a *wow* for many readers.

CHAPTER 10

Student responses to Molly Bloom

A female gorilla or a slapper?

In one of the earliest reviews of *Ulysses*, published in *The Freeman* in New York on 19 July 1922, Mary Colum, a contemporary of Joyce at university and later a friend in Paris, made what seems now a quite extraordinary assertion that 'The revelation of the mind of Marion Bloom in the last section would doubtless interest the laboratory, but to normal people it would seem the exhibition of the mind of a female gorilla who has been corrupted by contact with humans'. Such a comment seems almost wholly foreign to us today, in part because Molly has been accepted as a major character in the novel on an equal footing with Stephen and Bloom, and in part because we now recognise Molly as one of our own, closer to our own psychology than to people in the 1920s, who still retained remnants of a late-Victorian, Darwinian sensibility. The remark, however, reminds us that while Molly has been on the receiving end of many insults – few stranger than Mary Colum's – she continues to survive her critics and face them down.

'Penelope', which is not so much Joyce's as Molly's episode, marks the end of a journey that began in the morning with Stephen Dedalus in the tower at Sandycove, and it is arguably as good a place as any to begin Joyce's novel. Indeed, unlike most novels, there's something to be said for starting at the end with 'Penelope', the unashamedly female episode. As the comments by my students below suggest, beginning with 'Penelope' is like entering a country without traditional markings or known signposts. It is in that sense a journey as much for me as for my students. What I particularly cherish about the episode is that the unexpected things that tumble out require something other than traditional forms of interpretation. Take any five lines and most people will struggle to describe what is going on in terms of language, psychology or narrative theory.

As I mentioned in Chapter 1, for his study of *Ulysses*, Richard Kain alighted on what is to my mind the most attractive of all Joycean titles,

It was here on rue de Lemoine, Paris, in a flat lent him by Valery Larbaud that Joyce completed 'Penelope' in 1921. He was a five-minute walk away from the Sorbonne and the Bibliothèque St Geneviève, the library where he had studied in 1903, sheltered from the sin of Paris. If Nora taught him anything, it was that the university of life is at least as interesting as anything going on in libraries. Photograph by David Pierce.

Fabulous Voyager (1947). According to Kain, Joyce 'guides the reader into the amazing microcosm of modern life which is *Ulysses*'. But Kain wants to convey something else by the term, how the fabulous voyager is not Joyce or the modern Odysseus but the reader. It is the reader who is on a journey constructed by Joyce's *fabula* or story, the reader who, in the blurb on the book's jacket, 'visits lunch-joint, library, newspaper office, hospital, bar and brothel'. Kain also invokes the meaning of 'fabulous' available in common usage, and he shows by implication how a fabulous event or person carries an inside story or a plot that is worthy of retelling. The phrase 'the fab four' is in that sense not only an expression of enthusiasm but also shorthand for a story that would include the 1960s, Liverpool, the Cavern Club, the relationship between Lennon and McCartney and so on. Fabulous, at once spectacular, there for all to see, and also made up, a fiction in the sense of a narrative, part of the culture. I warm to the uncertainty of not knowing what's to come with a group. After three months we might become bored with each other, but the first weeks? That's different. That's unknown territory.

As with travel, so with literature, it's impossible not to find oneself using a sexualised vocabulary, and at some stage I realise something else is stirring, especially among the female students in a group. Or perhaps, with my own repression and my feminine anxiety to absorb difference, it is just my own psyche that is on display here. An undiscovered country. Coming into the country again. For a male tutor conscious of an understandable reticence on the part of some female students in this area, the situation can be tricky. 'What does he know about our bodies, the way we really think, the unwritten codes and subterfuges we resort to? Or come to think of it, is he a pervert or what?' And then in mixed company – as Joyce himself, who was given to blushing according to Sylvia Beach, was the first to recognise – there are things that can and cannot be said. Not unaware of these tensions that undermine the authority of my position vis-à-vis the different authority of theirs, I proceed.

Always with my students I begin by attending to the words on the page, and what they tell us about how Molly perceives her body. We move on at some point to her past sexual encounters and then to more intriguing abstract questions, such as what it would be like to be a man (or a woman). I pursue a path that eventually leads into what I imagine will be a safe intellectual discussion about sexuality and textuality. The class allow me the space to talk about French feminist theory, Virginia Woolf and gender ambiguity in writing. I raise the issue of how 'Penelope' was written by a man about female experience, and whether that makes any difference to their reading. All the great modern novelists in this regard, whether we think of Flaubert or Thomas Hardy or D.H. Lawrence, repeatedly remind us that it

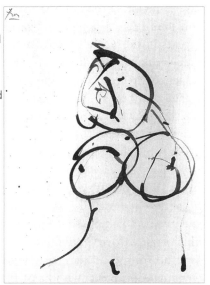

Robert Motherwell's sketch, 'Molly Bloom, 1982.' Here modern abstract expressionism meets the ancient art of portraiture. The head to one side has a calming effect, a reminder perhaps of an earlier generation of Modigliani, Picasso and Brancusi. The overlapping circles recall Euclid's geometry and Joyce's use of them in the Lessons chapter of *Finnegans Wake*. Circles in our culture, whether found in the art gallery or as graffiti on the wall or pavement, have a capacity to give us in a couple of strokes the female breast or bottom. But Motherwell does more. The unique individual in the universal, the universal in the unique individual. Molly as woman, Molly as a woman. In Motherwell's sketch, the circles are not so much suggestive as articulate, impossible to avoid, the nipples in their midst calling out to be noticed. No arms to get in the way or interfere, a body in the round, with an eight o'clock nose and eyes still closed. The body at rest. The eye of the viewer travels down the female body. Without the genitalia she would lack something, the breasts so lined, the genitalia so hidden, a large open staple. Join it all up – that's Molly. A still canvas of desire.

Source: Dedalus Foundation, INC/DACS, London/VAGA, NY 2007

is possible for a man to render female experience, but Joyce seems to want to delve further, and it is that delving that perhaps constitutes a worry. Each of these authors has a different investment in the female voice, but, arguably, what none of them invites is the suspicion that we are being presented with a peepshow or that intimacy is to do with revealing all. Delving and spanning. Adam and Eve.

I quote the class a passage from a student essay: 'Molly's gender is put into question with her need for sex and the explicit way she describes it. She almost becomes masculine, just as Stephen is feminine with his feminine way of thinking.' The crossover is suggestive. Is making explicit what men do and what women shy away from? Does Joyce succeed in his attempts to convey female experience? Or does his 'meandering male fist', as he describes it in *Finnegans Wake*, get in the way? The class decide to abandon for the time being such probing and come at the identity issue head-on, sensing that, like them, I'm looking for something that touches them.

Invariably, it's a moment of truth, a space for something to emerge, and eventually one of their number breaks rank. 'Was Molly a slapper? I mean, do you think she was a slag, a slut, a tart, a tramp, an easy lay? How can someone who thinks like that not be?' Gosh, I wasn't expecting that, and it catches me off-guard. Candid, frank, a slapper, not a word I use, and yet I have sometimes begun my class on *Ulysses* in York by playing 'My Girl's A Yorkshire Girl', a popular Edwardian song about female infidelity, which appears in the 'Circe' episode and which links dear dirty Dublin with the plain-speaking English county. 'Eh! by gum, she's a champion' as the song has it. My first teacherly response is to deflect the question. 'How do others in the group feel about this question?' But I realise even as I ask the question that they know this is but parrying and that what they're really after is their tutor's opinion.

I start by rehearsing in general terms the talk in our culture about affairs, how men converse about women, and how Molly considers her past lovers. 'Who doesn't consider their past lovers', I add, and I'm not expecting an answer. My first instinct, then, is to defend Molly. 'Man dear', I find myself recalling, 'did you ever hear of buxom Molly Bloom at all', which is how Joyce's tribute to her in his song 'Molly Brannigan' begins. And the song continues, seemingly with tutors like me in mind: 'Now every male she meets with has a finger in her pie'. As for her getting into bed that afternoon with Hugh 'Blazes' Boylan, I ask if that makes her a slapper. And if it is the onset of a relationship, what then? And if this is her first affair, how does that affect things? I retell the story of a leading Joyce critic Hugh Kenner, how in *Dublin's Joyce* (1955), he was persuaded

Chorus for 'My Girl's a Yorkshire Girl'.

by the following passage from 'Ithaca' to conclude that Molly was sexually promiscuous:

Assuming Mulvey to be the first term of his series, Penrose, Bartell d'Arcy, professor Goodwin, Julius Mastiansky, John Henry Menton, Father Bernard Corrigan, a farmer at the Royal Dublin Society's Horse Show, Maggot O'Reilly, Matthew Dillon, Valentine Blake Dillon (Lord Mayor of Dublin), Christopher Callinan, Lenehan, an Italian organgrinder, an unknown gentleman in the Gaiety Theatre, Benjamin Dollard, Simon Dedalus, Andrew (Pisser) Burke, Joseph Cuffe, Wisdom Hely, Alderman John Hooper, Dr Francis Brady, Father Sebastian of Mount Argus, a bootblack at the General Post Office, Hugh E. (Blazes) Boylan and so each and so on to no last term.

(*U* 17:2133–42)

For a while, Kenner's view sparked debate among Joyceans, but to my mind such a view was always wide of the mark. Mulvey at the head of the list has some credibility, especially when in her soliloquy Molly tells us that 'Mulveys was the first', where the possessive captures both the crude schoolboy at work as well as the uxorious Joyce in his late twenties anxious about Nora's former partners. Even though we don't catch him in action in the bedroom, Boylan, with his sky-blue socks and dandy tan shoes, cannot be denied, but with the possible exception of a liaison with a farmer at the Royal Dublin Society Horse Show (for which there is no actual evidence in the text), the other names between Mulvey and Boylan are so unlikely that the accuracy of the series as a whole should always have been doubted. Father Corrigan, her confessor, has spent too long in the confessional, asking ridiculous questions about where the man had touched her, to handle a woman like Molly. It's just a humorous list in a seriously funny episode positioned just before the ultra realism of 'Penelope'.

You can hear Joyce at some stage when he was at work on the novel saying to himself: 'Imagine all the partners Molly might have had. Let's put all those in somewhere. Ithaca is where Odysseus lands prior to his arrival home. Let's put it there and imagine it through Bloom's jealous eyes.' Ever the compulsive dabbler, Joyce also builds into this episode something else, supplementing the Greek theme with the Roman. In its question and answer format, 'Ithaca' reminds us of the Catechism. Who made you? Why did God make you? Years ago, every Roman Catholic child had to learn the Catechism by heart before receiving their First Holy Communion. Equally, as an Irishman, Joyce had been shaped by a puritanical form of Catholicism, but, as suggested in Chapter 8, his sojourn in Catholic Europe had opened his eyes to the scurrilous. No-one in Catholic Ireland or indeed Protestant Britain knows how to swear on the Host. Some words, such as 'bloody' (by Our Lady) or crikey or gorblimey carry within them a Catholic past, but only one or two select phrases such as 'hocus pocus' – 'hoc est enim corpus meum', the Latin words of the priest at Mass when the bread is changed into the body of Christ – continue to resonate from a former anti-Catholic period and ideology. Catholic Europe, on the other hand, doesn't know how to stop swearing on the host. '¡Hostia!' as Fernando Bauluz (1951–2004), a dear student from my year spent teaching English as a foreign language with the British Council in Madrid, would blurt out as he burnt his fingers stubbing out his *Celtas* cigarette in a container outside the classroom on Calle Almagro. 'Damn' meant nothing to the talented future film director as he flicked back his blond hair and cursed out loud the dirt-cheap cigarette which was double-wrapped and which had a tendency on reassembly to come apart in your hands. What could be more scurrilous in an episode which draws on the format of the religious Catechism than imagining all the lovers Molly might have had and then deliberately subjecting the list to exaggeration?

Kenner didn't ask what Molly would be doing with a bootblack from the General Post Office. Just exactly how would she have invited such a person back to her house? 'Would you care to come and have tea with me and do my other shoes?' Or to underline the ridiculous nature of the list, we can delay with some more such mockery. Imagine how things might have started with the figure who cannot hide his rather ridiculous sexual prowess, an Italian organgrinder. 'Would you care to do some grinding at my house on Eccles Street? Four would be an excellent time. I'll have my organ ready.' The exaggeration is Joycean, the extension isn't. It's too absurd and too crude. Any approach by Lenehan, who is rebuffed by the barmaid Miss Kennedy and who, as we have seen in his previous incarnation in 'Two Gallants', spends his evening walking listlessly round the streets of Dublin and eating a plate of peas by himself while his friend Corley gets the girl, would have been spurned. Lenehan is a leech but has his moments, and the novel would be poorer without him. In the Ormond Hotel in the afternoon, in the Music episode that is, Boylan is about to embark on his encounter with Molly, and it is Lenehan, in his familiar role as the sponge-like gallant, who asks in his crude but lively way, 'Got the horn or what?' Whatever we think about the 'brute' Boylan slapping her bottom in the bedroom, Molly has taste, horn or no horn.

The list in 'Ithaca' is a wink-wink, nudge-nudge, male fantasy, which perhaps rebounds on itself. It appears in the same episode where an absurd comparison is made between Bloom and Stephen, and between Bloom and the rest of his school, in the art of urinating:

> The trajectories of their, first sequent, then simultaneous, urinations were dissimilar: Bloom's longer, less irruent, in the incomplete form of the bifurcated penultimate alphabetical letter, who in his ultimate year at High School (1880) had been capable of attaining the point of greatest altitude against the whole concurrent strength of the institution, 210 scholars: Stephen's higher, more sibilant, who in the ultimate hours of the previous day had augmented by diuretic consumption an insistent vesical pressure.

(*U* 17:1192–8)

Joyce's eighteenth-century Irish predecessor, as we have seen, was also obsessed with the body's entrances and exits, and in *Gulliver's Travels* (1726) Swift famously imagines his protagonist in giant mode extinguishing a fire at the Emperor's palace on the island of Lilliput by urinating on it, the delicious wine called Glimigrim consumed the previous evening acting as a diuretic. The comparisons Joyce indicates in this passage are also graphic

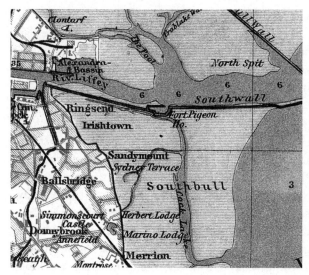

Map of Sandymount Strand and surrounding area. On this beautiful and informative German map, published in Leipzig in 1905, the numbers refer to the depth in metres of the water in Dublin Bay and the Liffey basin. The map highlights not only the actual existence of somewhere called Cock Lake – Dubliners like Joyce must have had great fun with such names as this and others, such as Ballsbridge, Stillorgan, Dollymount and Ringsend – but also how much water there is in this part of the coastline and how the tides therefore play havoc for those seeking clear definitions or distinctions between land and sea. 'Lagoons of sand', as Joyce puts it in a phrase that captures the action of the sea on the land. Yet another example of Proteus, the shape-changer, at work on the physical landscape and on the way language works through metaphors. In keeping with the fate of the poor Irish in their own country, Irishtown occupies, here as elsewhere in Irish towns, the low-lying part of the city, just below Ringsend and just above Sandymount.

My photograph of Sandymount Strand, the sibilant setting for the 'Proteus' episode of *Ulysses*, looking south towards Dun Laoghaire. This is where Stephen wanders by the shore in the company of his poetic narrator: 'In long lassoes from the Cock lake the water flowed full, covering greengoldenly lagoons of sand, rising, flowing' (*U* 3:453–4). Nothing defies Joyce's imagination.

but they require some extra thinking, and we realise just how absurd the world can become in fiction. Stephen wins out on sound, his urination being more 'sibilant' than Bloom's. As with fiction, so with explanation and association. Joyce takes care to explain the medical reasons for it being more sibilant – 'an insistent vesical pressure'. But for most readers the explanation will require yet another explanation and recourse to the *Oxford English Dictionary* to look up 'vesical'. The breaking wind at the end of 'Sirens', the so-called Music episode, reminds us that Bloom is associated with plosives. Stephen, on the other hand – as 'Proteus', the shape-changing episode, underlines throughout – belongs to the sea and the 'wavespeech' (*U* 3:457) made by his body's effluence.

Questions regarding Bloom's prowess remain, and perhaps they will be asked only by those given to asking such questions. How exactly did Bloom in 1880 achieve top marks against his contemporaries at school? And how would such a competition have been arranged? As an end-of-term event? On sports day? Or did the pupils throughout the term chalk up their 'highest altitude' against a designated outside wall? Or was it carried out inside after school assembly? And would their form masters have been there to verify that there had been no cheating? And how would they have encouraged the participants? 'Now, boys, no cheating and show what you can do.' And how would Bloom have been crowned? The highest pee-er in the whole school to shouts of 'No peer to match him!' His name would then be inscribed on a plaque in the entrance hall to dazzle parents with their children, visitors and future generations. The highest altitude. Wow.

This is schoolboy humour in the Joycean mould. My male students enjoy this kind of thing but, at least in mixed company, it appeals to few female readers. I reassure the class that the passage is absurd and so too, for different

Vote Bloom. Years ago somewhere in Yorkshire someone was standing for the British Labour Party and had the engaging name of Bloom. He would have got my vote.

reasons, is the proposed list of Molly's putative lovers. A comparison in the novel between prowess in urination among the males is in keeping with the characters involved, but this is not the case with Molly's list of lovers. The list suggests it has been drawn up by someone else, some male figure, imagining this for her. In her defence, we might agree that her sexual fantasies are too urgent and too divergent to be contained by a list. After all, she is a modern woman who is spectacularly promiscuous in her mind and who knows how to flirt and show off her body, but there are limits. Mrs Marion Tweedy is not a streetwalker or indeed a slapper. Molly entertains the thought of picking up 'a sailor off the sea thatd be hot on for it' (*U* 18:1412), but what woman in her right mind would entertain stepping out with someone called Andrew (Pisser) Burke, who comes complete with knowing brackets round his nickname? Maggot O'Reilly's first name doesn't even merit brackets or inverted commas. Pisser and Maggot are in their own way 'street names', serving at once to caution and define. In a small town like Dublin, once assigned, they carry such names to the grave. In the revised edition of *Dublin's Joyce* published in 1987, Kenner candidly admits his error. It's one of many cautionary tales in the history of Joyce criticism, and I remind my students not to ignore their instincts in reading, for Joyce makes us all, even so-called experts, equal before his daringly original and frequently crude imagination.

'It is a slim book,' Joyce declared of *Chamber Music* to his brother Stanislaus, 'and on the frontispiece is an open pianner!' (Gorman, 1948, 175). As a collection of verse, *Chamber Music* combines the delicacy of music with the seriousness of a young aspiring writer. It's the other side of Joyce, his head full of madigrals, intense moments, weary love, and the sound of an army charging across the land. Not his best writing. Too delicate and remote. Slim. Even before he met Nora, in a letter to Gogarty on 3 June 1904, Joyce tells us he had plans to sing in a concert with this title; all he needed from Gogarty was the loan of a suit or cricket shirt. It's this undercutting sentiment that perhaps most appeals about Joyce. The qualification of second-hand realism, when he drops a register. With Nora on the scene, the idea of chamber music took on a realistic twist, when the punster Joyce compared the noise Nora made when she peed into her chamber pot to chamber music. That wasn't the end of the matter, for Nora/Molly had their revenge when, by way of a properly earthy response to the boys' games with altitude in 'Ithaca', Molly opens the floodgates to allow through not only water from the bladder but also menstrual blood from the vagina. No bifurcated 'y' dribble here, and twice as much music going on. And no suggestion of 'Violence', the word used by Swift to describe the 'Torrent' issuing from the Man-Mountain Gulliver on the island of Lilliput.

You can almost overhear Nora exclaiming in the Barnacle/Joyce flat in Trieste: 'have we too much blood up in us or what O patience above its

Title page of Joyce's first book of poetry, published in 1907.

pouring out of me like the sea' (*U* 18:1122–3). 'Up in us' and 'out of me'. Up, out. Blood mysteries. If language has its origins in the body, it's certainly closer to the female body. As a Latin-American critic has recently suggested in a book with the engaging title *Mujeres de Babel* (Women of Babel): 'Bajo una recurrento invocación lunar, *Ulises* es un enorme tapiz habitado por motivos y surgerencias femininas' (Moreno-Durán, 2004, 89) (under a re-curring invocation to the moon, *Ulysses* is an enormous tapestry filled with swirling, feminine motifs). *Surgerencias*, surgings. You can feel the power of that word even before it gets translated into English. Bloom has altitude, Stephen sibilance, but Molly has *surgerencias*.

Only my students know if what I'm saying is relevant, convincing or passes muster for a professor of English. We've already strayed some way from a normal discussion in literature classes. This is what the defiant Joyce does to literature: he warps it, breaks taboos and in the process he stimu-lates animated discussion, not all of which can be defined as literary or especially high-flown. As Kain suggested 60 years ago, 'One must always

'The Young Joyce Inspecting the Future Hero', sketch by Guy Davenport. From Hugh Kenner, *The Stoic Comedians* (1964). Male voyeurism, full of shifty looks.

beware of taking *Ulysses* too seriously' (Kain, 1947, 136). Some years ago I was staying in a bed-and-breakfast guest house in an area just to the north of the North Circular Road in Dublin. It was a very small terraced house. In truth, it was really someone's house that had a guest room, a family house, and I was the intruder. In the morning when I came down to 'full Irish' breakfast I got chatting with the landlady, or rather she got chatting with me. She was in possession of a beautiful Galway accent, which I invariably fall for, and she reminded me that when in Dublin I always wish I was in the west, the roar of the Atlantic Ocean in my ears, the big skies overhead everchanging. Almost at once I could hear the accents of Molly and Nora. The country was going to pot. It must have been the 1980s. Young people, out late, not going to church, not doing their homework, not yet taking drugs. My landlady, who was in her forties, was, like Molly, also having problems with her teenage daughter. 'Was it the same over?' Oh yes, I said, and I could see in her hovering that she wanted frankness if not counselling from her cross-channel guest. Seamlessly we moved from one topic to another without interruption or pause for thought amid the toast and bacon.

I don't know how it happened but we arrived almost without prompting or embarrassment at unwanted pregnancies and abortion. Yes, I volunteered,

7,000 young women with Irish addresses sought clinics in Britain every year. 'Was it that many?' she wanted to know. And then the conversation took another turn. 'Joyce and Nora', the couple who emigrated without marrying. 'Nora Barnacle. A Galway girl. Wasn't that a nice name?' she mused, almost as if she knew what John Joyce had quipped about Nora's qualities of attachment. Then came what I can only describe as her pièce de résistance, the *copa de la casa* as the Spanish might say. 'Emigration. Yes.' At that point, there was then a slight pause, an interruption in the flow, followed by a slightly defensive sigh. 'Ah sure, don't we export all our problems?' I still don't know how I didn't choke on the jelly marmalade. My reply gave nothing away: 'Oh, I'd never thought about it like that.' I regret now I didn't ever return to tape her reading a selection from Molly's soliloquy, for she would have made an ideal reader of Joyce – even if Molly couldn't have spoken with a Galway accent.

Normally, I find myself rallying to Molly's defence as if she were a real person and someone I've got to know and like. She deserves our sympathy. The bloom of youth is over, her father is dead, her mother, 'Lunita Laredo', 'whoever she was' (*U* 18:846–7), is an absent figure in the novel. She lost a son, Rudy, in infancy, is sexually unfulfilled, the subject of innuendo and male gossip, and she gives the impression she has few friends in Dublin. Whatever my Galway-to-Dublin landlady thought about the couple who years ago emigrated to live in sin, it's rare to encounter that mixture of charm and prejudice among my students. But how do any of us read Molly? Never ever, I suspect, with identical eyes. I inject a contrary view, cautioning my students for example, that to my mind Angeline Ball, who plays Molly in Sean Walshe's film *Bloom* (2003) (which we watch together), is too knowing by far, that Joyce's Molly keeps her thoughts to herself, and that she would have been horrified to find herself the subject of classroom discussion round the world. To us as readers she breaks certain taboos by putting thoughts into words, but because they are her thoughts to herself, does she break any taboos, any confidences that is? When it's the self speaking to the self, is frankness ever on display? Honesty, yes, but frankness? Away from the classroom, when students have more time to reflect, they come to their own conclusions:

> At first sight the major theme of 'Penelope' is jealousy in Molly thinking Leopold Bloom is committing adultery. However, Joyce soon shows how although men can have fun and sexual encounters women can have double the amount of fun. Joyce reflects the exact way women feel when their husbands are ill: 'theyre so weak and puling when theyre sick they want a woman to get well if his nose bleeds youd think it was O tragic and that dying look'. This opinion made by Molly is true of men, and the fact that Joyce a male wrote this is significant. For a male writer to be able to write in such a feminine way shows the gender system to be arbitrary. Joyce himself could be labelled a feminist.

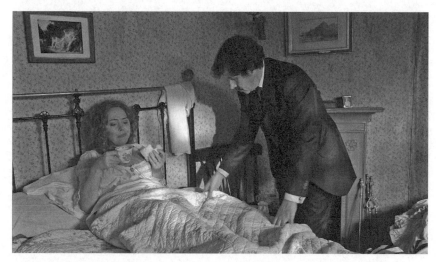

Angeline Ball in bed in a darkly-lit room, with the *Birth of the Nymph* above her.
Penelope as Calypso. Breakfast in bed. Stephen Rea as Bloom has his head down, hands
on the bedspread, thinking ahead. Crumbs. From Sean Walshe's film *Bloom* (2003).

The German Emperor

Some male students adopt a different viewpoint from the outset. Molly's
behaviour prompted one student to come to Bloom's aid:

> I feel that the reader cannot prevent feeling sympathy for the male character of
> Bloom, who is treated so badly by Molly. Her soliloquy at the end of *Ulysses* is
> filled with graphic sexual and bodily references such as 'make a whore of me'.
> The reader realises that Molly makes no secret of her sordid affairs and thus
> Leopold's suffering at the hands of his wife must be immense.

The particular passage the student has in mind is located near the beginning of the episode:

> a young boy would like me Id confuse him a little alone with him if we were Id let
> him see my garters the new ones and make him turn red looking at him seduce
> him I know what boys feel with that down on their cheek doing that frigging
> drawing out the thing by the hour question and answer would you do this that
> and the other with the coalman yes with a bishop yes I would because I told him
> about some dean or bishop was sitting beside me in the jews temples gardens
> when I was knitting that woollen thing a stranger to Dublin what place was it
> and so on about the monuments and he tired me out with statues encouraging
> him making him worse than he who is in your mind now tell me who are you
> thinking of who is it tell me his name who tell me who the german Emperor is it
> yes imagine Im him think of him can you feel him trying to make a whore of
> me what he never will he ought to give it up now at this age of his life simply
> ruination for any woman.
>
> (*U* 18:85–98)

It's one of several densely scrambled passages in 'Penelope' and not that easy to follow. Let me set it out in full sentences with punctuation and with what I assume is the identity of the speaker:

> Molly: A young boy would like me. I'd confuse him a little. Alone with him, if we were, I'd let him see my garters, the new ones, and make him turn red looking at him. Seduce him. I know what boys feel with that down on their cheek, doing that frigging, drawing out the thing by the hour. Question and answer. Would you do this, that, and the other with the coalman? Yes. With a bishop? Yes I would, because I told him about some dean or bishop was sitting beside me in the Jews' Temple's Gardens when I was knitting that woollen thing. A stranger to Dublin. What place was it? And so on about the monuments, and he tired me out with statues. Encouraging him, making him worse than he is.
>
> Bloom: Who is in your mind now? Tell me. Who are you thinking of? Who is it? Tell me his name.
>
> Molly: Who?
>
> Bloom: Tell me who!
>
> Molly: The German Emperor, is it?
>
> Bloom: Yes. Imagine I'm him. Think of him. Can you feel him?
>
> Molly: Trying to make a whore of me. What! He never will. He ought to give it up now at this age of his life. Simply ruination for any woman.

Molly sets the context for what is to come. She's imagining seducing a young boy, but then finds herself thinking of more mechanical, routine things such as question and answer and the forms of seduction Bloom employed with her. Yes, she would do such and such with a coalman, and indeed with a bishop. (This could be set out with separate entry for Bloom, but the phrase 'such and such' suggests it is Molly recalling or censoring what he originally said.) The use of 'because' at this point is interesting not least because what follows is not a reason but simply the mind working by association. We learn that the dean or bishop – presumably it is his words she hears – is a stranger to Dublin and he wants to know about places where they're sitting and the identity of the statues. The 'jews temples gardens' sounds confused on Molly's part, as if she had misheard something the dean or the bishop has said, possibly about trips to the Holy Land. It's the Alameda Gardens on Gibraltar where she is kissed by Mulvey. A Moorish not a Jewish garden. But it's surprising she can't recall the name of a Dublin garden with statues. Perhaps she was concentrating on knitting a woollen jacket for her son Rudy, who later died in infancy. As another of my students pointed out to me, the attitude of the bishop or dean towards statues stands in marked contrast with Bloom's more physical and sensual attitude as evidenced by his fixation on nude statues in the National Museum. Different views on fixation, one celebratory of human endeavour, the other an adjunct for the muse. The digression aside, Molly is bored with the good man's questions, and her mind switches again to a scene of seduction with Bloom.

She encourages him, 'making him worse than he is', a phrase that could refer to Bloom or possibly to the young boy (in which case there is another switch). We move on, back with Bloom in 1888. 'Who's in your mind', he asks? 'Who are you thinking of?' She becomes slightly irritated with his repeated questioning. 'Tell me his name', Bloom insists. 'Who?' she asks. 'Tell me who?' he demands. I've then assumed it is Molly asking if it's 'the German Emperor', to which he replies with a Molly word, 'Yes'. But it could be set out differently. It could be Bloom asking if it's the German Emperor and Molly replying 'Yes'. In which case, 'Yes' is her attempt to end his line of questioning. Or it could be Molly interjecting 'Yes' as she draws back a little in reminiscing about her past. Or, there's yet another possibility. It could be an exasperated Molly declaring 'Tell me who (for God's sake)'. And then continuing with 'The German Emperor is it? Yes.' At which point the dialogue reverts to Bloom: 'Imagine I'm him'.

Whatever the case, there is then another switch, for Bloom and Molly seem to be making love in this remembered scene. Imagine I'm the German Emperor, says Bloom. What's the name of the German Emperor? (1888 was the year when Wilhelm I was succeeded first by Frederick and then by Wilhelm II, so it was, quite legitimately, a confusing time.) Then Bloom tells her to imagine he is the German Emperor, adding 'can you feel him'. I assume 'him' is his penis inside her ('the thing' she has just mentioned in connection with the young boy). It is at this point that Molly's self-preserving, more proper thoughts seem to take over: 'trying to make a whore of me'. The insertion of 'what' then seems to be another expression of exasperation as Molly realises what Bloom is asking of her, and then comes her resolve: he never will make a whore of me. Her thoughts then return to the present with the conclusion that 'he ought to give it up now at this age of his life simply ruination for any woman', where 'it' could stand for seduction of servants (which Molly has just been thinking about), or for his dirty talk, or for other forms of sexual behaviour. The addition of 'simply ruination for any woman' is one of those delightful moments in Molly's soliloquy as Bloom's behaviour brings out the woman in her. Her husband is 'simply ruination for any woman', but in her almost affectionate use of 'simply ruination' she betrays he is not wholly to be condemned for that.

It's a complex passage and open to interpretation and misinterpretation. It helps to identify the trigger points in her mind. The reference to the bishop and the statues in the park seems to anticipate the reference to the German Emperor, public figures who do little for Molly. In contrast with her own personal life, the public world lacks something. Is that the trigger? The public world, for example, couldn't openly discuss 'frigging' by boys or the role of the German Emperor in the fantasy life of the bedroom. And yet such things have significance for the participants and also remind us of the power of Molly's thoughts when confronted with the official public world of men and boys. The historical context is also important. The mention of knitting a woollen is a late insertion, as if Joyce wanted to fill out and stress the historical moment, to help the reader in the movement back and forth between past and present. Molly returns in her mind to their early courting days in 1888, 16 years previously, when Bloom played games that seemed to involve role-play and sexuality. If I'm right, 'make a whore of me' is Molly resisting that particular line in dirty talk. What of course is striking is not only the candour but also the humour. Unless it was Bloom, how could any man think it was a turn-on for his female partner to imagine he was the German Emperor while they were making love? Unless, that is, there was popular gossip at the time about the prowess of the German Emperor in such matters.

During the 1880s, according to his modern biographer John C.G. Röhl (1982), Wilhelm led a very active sexual life, but, thereafter, he was praised as a paragon of marital virtue. There is something elusive about his character, however. He remained ambivalent in his attitude to women, and modern commentators have suggested he might have been a repressed homosexual. How much of this found its way into becoming general knowledge at the time is another matter. For our purposes, it fits, however, with the public – private theme in 'Penelope' With his own Hungarian, middle-European background, Bloom presumably also responded to Wilhelm's cult of personality, his colourful character, as well as to the handlebars of his fine moustache. Earlier in the day, when passing the optician Yeates and Son, Bloom thinks about getting his old glasses repaired: 'Germans making their way everywhere' (U 8:555). Germans everywhere. Moustaches and glasses. *Ulysses* marks the high point in the European novel of association with label attached 'Follow That'.

The student's response constitutes a general reminder that reading is a peculiar activity and that one's own interpretation contains at times unconscious and unwarranted assumptions. It's always worth remembering that some views will not be shared by others, and some, especially in the area of gender, will need arguing for. That Molly might want someone to make a

THE GERMAN EMPEROR

Stuart Richmond

Postcard of the grandson of Queen Victoria, the German Emperor, Kaiser Wilhelm II. In November 1902, when Wilhelm made a visit by yacht to see his 'kinsman' King Edward, the visit was recorded with some relish by the *Pall Mall Gazette* which included a sketch with moustache and fetching hat and feather: 'The morning was chilly and his Majesty wore a long military cloak with the hood thrown back. He was looking extremely well.' Although it's not specifically mentioned in *Ulysses*, my own view is that Bloom did sport a moustache in June 1904. At breakfast in 'Calypso' he takes down the moustache-cup his daughter Milly had given him for a birthday present. More convincingly, in the sketch Joyce drew of him, reproduced in my *James Joyce's Ireland* (1992), he takes care to show him thus attired, and look at all the moustaches in *The Freeman's Journal* composing room on page 255. In the passage we've been looking at, 'can you feel him' also suggests a close identity and show of force: the whole of Prussia, Germany and the Austro-Hungarian Empire driving forward to a man. Molly doesn't tell us if she enjoyed that part of it.

whore of her would be her way of saying 'I want some real physical experience that lies outside the marriage bed and in the arms of a stranger. Touch me in my soul.' If that's 'sordid' then I suspect so too is a large part of human sexual fantasy. A young male student, intent on keeping sexual encounters to himself, might be reluctant to recognise this or be genuinely innocent in such matters. But impersonality, playing roles or imagining being someone else or being watched or being entered by another man in your mind while your partner is in your arms – all this is but part of the psychology of lovemaking, one suspects.

Undaunted, the student decides it is Molly imagining she wants someone to make a whore of her, but, as I've just indicated, it's the reverse: it's Molly thinking Bloom is trying to make a whore of her. But in one respect, the student's reading does link with something threading its way through the passage as a whole, its general drift, that is. A few lines after 'make a whore of me', Molly has a wish: 'I wish some man or other would take me sometime when hes there and kiss me in his arms theres nothing like a kiss long and hot down to your soul almost paralyses you'. Why she would want Bloom to witness this moment is, again, part of this discourse on role-playing; it also reflects a desire to remind her husband how to make passionate love.

Such a move constitutes another marital game, this time more mean-spirited, which involves not giving him satisfaction and getting her own back on him. After years of marriage – the last time they enjoyed sexual intercourse together was in 1893 – and after years of pretending she enjoys lovemaking, we can feel her pain when she lets slip 'pretending to like it till he comes and then finish it off myself anyway'.

Another claim the student makes is that 'Molly makes no secret of her sordid affairs'. Actually, she does keep all this secret. Behind the student's assertion seems to be the fear that women can be indiscreet, and how indiscretion can exacerbate the plight of the cuckolded husband. An observation by a female student is worth quoting at this point for another perspective: 'The only audience she does offer her words to is God. She makes repeated reference to "O Lord" in her monologue. There is no other audience. The effect is one of voyeurism of the reader encroaching on Molly's private thoughts.' Again, this isn't quite right. Molly's repeated use of 'O Lord' is not really an invocation or a prayer but simply a mild form of exasperation or expletive. Synge's plays, which are full of references to God, Jesus, the Blessed Virgin and the saints, reflect the religious world of the Irish country people, but this isn't the case with Molly. However, this student is on the right lines and draws our attention at once to the peculiar form of voyeurism that inheres in 'Penelope' and to the peculiar position assigned the reader by Joyce/Molly. In Molly's soliloquy all we hear, therefore, is the communication she has with herself. Everything is filtered through her. Ironically, even the privacy of the confessional is revealed to us. Her soliloquy is not therefore a confession, for confessing one's sins to a priest is an act of deliberation and Molly is not telling someone else her sins. In the soliloquy she's not really telling herself, for that suggests she is weighing up things, consciously deliberating, passing judgement, when her monologue is a sequence of random, connected thoughts and associations, not all of which can be called conscious or self-conscious or indeed random.

As for the male student's choice of the word 'graphic' and the phrase 'at the hands of', this perhaps reminds us of something else. When writing about Molly and Bloom we frequently find ourselves unconsciously activating the literal. Bloom does suffer at the hands of his wife, and this in both a figurative and a literal sense, for it is the image of her hands holding Boylan in an embrace that Bloom has difficulty blocking out of his mind. The use of the word 'graphic' is also resonant here, for Molly's soliloquy is 'graphic' in the sense that the student intends, but it is also 'graphic' in that it is written down. In this way, a connection is unwittingly drawn between fear and taboo, between male fears about women and taboos in the culture about what can be written down and what should not.

A literary bombshell

Students new to Joyce are frequently able to get to the heart of the matter more quickly than established critics. Here is another student writing about Molly:

> In *Ulysses*, Joyce shows the perverse effect on the public's consciousness by literary repression of sexuality. *Ulysses* must have been a literary bombshell when published, as Molly's stream of consciousness expresses the liberation of a female. Her thoughts are explicit in their promiscuity and fantasy, liberal in their attitude to adultery. Again, this shows Joyce's integrity in his desire to render life truthfully, although some critics have of course interpreted Molly's desires as a male fantasy. One hopes that being privy to another individual's thoughts remains the preserve of literary fiction rather than scientific fact.

The movement of thought here is both forceful and intriguing. We are reminded of a camera taking a series of snapshots of a person, a first encounter. Each part of the body, the writer in this case, is recorded, summed up, and a judgement made about the whole. The particular effect this student homes in on – and I assume it is a female student – is 'perverse', and we realise this refers not to Joyce's writing, which is how that is sometimes seen, but to something in the culture. What she notices is the public's consciousness, not the consciousness of the individual. Again, this is right. *Ulysses* belongs to the public domain and it deliberately criss-crosses public and private spheres. In this sense, *Ulysses* is a very private book which is also very public, a book that has effects, therefore, in the public arena. The next phrase, 'literary repression of sexuality', is also arresting, for the student is seeking to distinguish the literary from some other form of repression of sexuality, a recognition that, whatever is attempted by way of censorship in the literary sphere, sexual practices among the general public have a life of their own. This is how I read that, and almost at once the student comes to Joyce's aid, noticing how the bombshell concerned 'the liberation of a female'. It is more, for 'Molly's stream of consciousness expresses the liberation of a female'. The use of 'expresses' is a suggestive word here, the two phrases on either side of the verb linked and at some level equivalent: Molly's thoughts and woman's liberation. But there's even more to it than this, for it is not Molly's 'stream of consciousness *is*' but Molly's 'stream of consciousness *expresses* the liberation of a female'. This is Joyce's bombshell, not Joyce the pervert (as he was seen by the courts) but Joyce the advocate of female experience. Needless to say, we are a world away from Mary Colum's view.

'Her thoughts are explicit in their promiscuity and fantasy, liberal in their attitude to adultery.' The word of interest here is 'explicit', carrying as it

Joyce, ashplant in hand, and the diminutive figure of Sylvia Beach, the daughter of a Presbyterian minister from Princeton, New Jersey, outside her bookshop on rue de l'Odéon in Paris. Sylvia Beach had launched her English-language bookshop and lending library in 1919, first on rue Dupuytren, then on rue de l'Odéon. Within a few days of arriving in Paris in 1920, Joyce had been introduced to her. 'We shook hands', Sylvia recalls, 'that is, he put his limp, boneless hand in my tough little paw' (Beach, 1987, 35). Joyce was despondent about ever getting *Ulysses* published after copies of *The Little Review* containing extracts from the novel had been seized in New York. In a youthful moment full of courage and opportunism, Sylvia stepped in with a now-famous invitation: 'Would you let Shakespeare and Company have the honour of bringing out your *Ulysses*?' Today, the plaque above her shop reads simply 'En 1922, dans cette maison, Mlle Sylvia Beach publia "Ulysses" de James Joyce'. Who would have guessed that one of the great encounters of European Modernism was to occur here in Paris between a tough American woman and a limp Irishman newly arrived from Trieste? Paris of the exiles, with Sylvia one of the midwives of Modernism and Joyce one of its chief exponents. Shakespeare and Company had secured its place in the history books.

does the sense of something forbidden being revealed, the ploy of the publicists to put on the cover of a risqué novel or autobiography. The use of the word 'explicit' is fairly widespread today among the young, but in its mixture of the precise and the forbidden it hasn't lost its force. The coupling of promiscuity and fantasy also invites comment, as does the liberality in her attitudes to adultery. This student knows a thing or two and doesn't need a professor to tell her how to read 'Penelope'. The next sentence is also revealing in the way it immediately returns us to the author and his 'integrity', a moral value here aligned with being faithful to reality, precisely what Joyce sought in his early career. The student delays momentarily on the thought that Molly's desires may belong to a male fantasy, and it is a thought which in fact, like Molly's flow, gets sidetracked with a closing comment surprisingly unlike the rest of her piece, beginning as it does with the impersonality of 'One': 'One hopes that being privy to another individual's thoughts remains the preserve of literary fiction rather than scientific fact.' It's as if the student enjoys reading about such intimacies in novels, but what she doesn't

George Whitman's Shakespeare and Company today on the banks of the Seine across the road from Notre Dame. Sylvia Beach's shop, which the Nazis effectively closed down in 1941, lives on in the name. The present shop began life in 1951 and it is still home to American visitors and to some of the 10 million people who visit Notre Dame each year. Under the patronage of Walt Whitman and City Lights Books in San Francisco (founded in 1953), the modern Shakespeare and Company has a down-to-earth quality reminiscent of a past era before the book chains took over. Photograph by David Pierce.

View of rue de l'Odéon today. Photograph by David Pierce. A one-way street, the writers, intellectuals and revolutionaries gone, history cleaned up or cleared out. Shakespeare and Company was half-way down on the right, next to the house where Tom Paine lived at the time of the French Revolution. Adrienne Monnier's bookshop, La Maison des Amis des Livres (the house of the friends of books), was on the left. Starboard and port, as Archibald MacLeish, looking up the short street in 1923, quipped. Further up the street, at number 18, Sylvia and Adrienne shared a fifth-floor apartment from 1921 until 1937. Adrienne, too, was a pivotal figure in the Joyce story, not least because of her involvement in translating *Ulysses* into French, a task that took a number of collaborators five years from 1924 until 1929. The Odéon Theatre at the top of the street, with seating for 1900 people, has been restored to its former glory. It was here in the Place de l'Odéon that the Café Voltaire played host to the preceding generation of artists and poets, including Gauguin and Mallarmé.

want is to encounter anyone in real life with the capacity to get inside her own head. A return in other words to the separate spheres that she had called into question in her opening remarks. Meanwhile, the insertion of the attitudinal adjunct 'of course' registers a familiarity and a certain impatience with critics who would limit the discussion unnecessarily to a first stage sort of criticism. I've read all about that but it doesn't really interest me. That's not where the real issue of 'Penelope' lies.

Breathless

Another student writes this about Molly:

Molly's monologue, her first and the last words of the book, is comprised of a breathless unpunctuated stream of consciousness. Her unchecked words are in contrast to the more careful musings of Stephen and Bloom. Rather than a tidy and considered conclusion, the reader is subjected to an exhausting journey through Molly's mind. Arguably, the most inconclusive feature of the Yes which ends Molly's monologue is the doubt over what precisely it is that she is affirming. The question for the reader to ponder is whether Molly is affirming her past life or whether she is reaffirming her choice to commit to Bloom. If the reader considers it is the latter, further questions arise over the extent of an affirmation based on the thought 'as well him as another'.

Molly's words. The phrase should be paused on and given the attention we devote to the words of great literature. Actually, Molly's words in 'Penelope' are not her first words. As early as the fourth episode 'Calypso' we hear Molly talking with Bloom, and, as with Bloom's carrying on with one the servants, she returns to such moments in 'Penelope'. It's true that she does speak the last words of the book, but it's not true to say, therefore, that her words don't appear in the other episodes. Sometimes her words are filtered through Bloom's consciousness but her presence, her words, can be felt throughout the novel. Her monologue, or to be more precise, her interior monologue is single-minded. It is not a voice that collects together all the other voices in the novel; if anything, it's a counter to all the other male voices such as Stephen and Bloom. Equally, it's not a monologue in the sense of a person going on at length. At least not for most readers. Moreover, her monologue is not a dramatic monologue which you might encounter on a stage or in a poem by, say, Robert Browning. And yet her monologue is in its own way a staging of female experience and it is personal or open to inspection – as if every part of her body is being attended to: sights, smells, feelings, and particularly internal openings and passages, the 'sweet unclose' as Joyce puts it in his continuing fascination with the female body that constitutes *Finnegans Wake*.

This is why I respond to the student's use of 'breathless', a word that captures the physical passage from the lungs to the mouth. The word in this

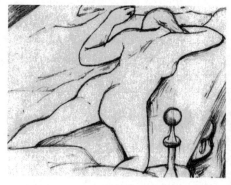

Richard Hamilton's 'Yes', 1988–91, a sketch of Molly in all her glory face down, the chamber-pot sticking out from under the bed, the bedknob impossible to ignore. Detail from *How A Great Daily Organ Is Turned Out*.

STUDENT RESPONSES TO MOLLY BLOOM   291

context means quick, without stopping, flowing ever onwards, perhaps in that sense 'exhausting', but it also invokes its opposite, namely full of breath, full of breathing. In and out. 'Quite breathless the way he swept me off my feet.' 'A sharp intake of breath.' Molly isn't short of breath. The day has been humid, sticky, something Bloom feels throughout the day. After all, as Bloom reminds us in 'Lotus-eaters', there is a heatwave in Dublin. At night, Molly sighs, draws breath, expresses air. In that sense her monologue is not 'breathless'. But it is 'breathless' in that she is full of desire and for that reason seems out of breath at times. 'Yes', as she repeats to herself on 89 occasions in her monologue, drawing back from one memory before launching into another. Words and breathlessness, the two go together in Molly. No breathing, no rhythm, no words. Words can only come with breathing in and exhaling. Interestingly, as I assume it would have been for Joyce's Galway partner Nora, the intake of breath on a word or phrase among my relatives from the west of Ireland is a constant accompaniment to their speech and utterly beguiling in its randomness. In her interior monologue Molly utters perhaps only a single word out loud, when she comes with a climax on the word 'Yes' at the end. 'Breathless' can then be seen as characterising the whole of her monologue as it moves towards its finale. In contrast with the image of the skull that punctuates Lucky's speech from Beckett's *Waiting for Godot*, hers is the one word 'Yes', an open-ended gesture rather than a poignant image, not death but life, not premonition but affirmation. Only a formalist could see this as marking the end of something.

The phrase 'unpunctuated stream of consciousness' reflects a conventional way of describing Molly's soliloquy. 'Penelope' contains but eight sentences, eight being the number of entry-points into the female body, eight being the mathematical sign with two holes that rounds endlessly on itself, eight, if laid on its side, having, on reflection, the look of a female bottom with joined lines. Another student is intrigued by the link between gender and writing and how bodies together resemble punctuation marks:

> Molly discusses her disappointment in the female form: 'whats the idea making us like that with a big hole in the middle of us'. The word 'hole' here puns on the word 'whole' suggesting the need for intimacy with another. Strange perhaps then that this is a marriage in which there is no longer a sexual relationship as they can be witnessed sleeping like a pair of question marks head to toe.

'Molly's narrative,' yet another student writes, 'defies the laws of punctuation as Molly herself defies the laws of conventional female thinking.' Frankness aside, the first impression that most readers experience on encountering 'Penelope' is one of racing, perhaps breathlessness as the eye races to discover some full-stop. As one of my students once suggested, 'It almost feels like we are trying to read at the same speed as Molly's thoughts'. Such an impression is followed by a certain reassurance when sentences can be punctuated by the mind, and meaning, or what amounts to the same thing, namely delay, thereby restored.

The irony is that consciousness itself has no punctuation. Rebecca West, in a famous 1928 essay designed to cut *Ulysses* down to size, maintained that sentences not words constituted 'the foundations of all language' (West, 1928, 32). According to West, Joyce composes 'strings of words as if they corresponded to the stream of one's consciousness; as if, should one resolve to describe one's impressions as they came, one would produce isolated words and phrases which would not cohere into sentences'. This is the least convincing part of her spirited attack. The mind works with all kinds of material – images, an overheard comment, a remembered phrase, a smell recalled from one's childhood, an advertising jingle, sounds out of the window, a clock striking, a bodily tic, a stored impression awaiting incorporation, the night sky, phth. Everyone must judge this for themselves. For myself, I rarely hear full sentences in consciousness, except when I become conscious of advertising jingles or snatches from songs or similar examples from a clingy consumer culture that won't let go. Molly's soliloquy in particular reminds us that perhaps language is only punctuated when written down. If a person speaks in slabs of grey prose, as one of my former college principals did, this is to do serious injustice to the way language works when spoken.

Let me insert at this point some remarks made in a letter sent in October 1975 to the German artist Jürgen Partenheimer by the art critic and historian Carola Giedion-Welcker (1893–1979). In the 1930s in Zurich Giedion-Welcker became a close friend of Joyce, and she was indeed the prime mover in persuading the authorities to allow him back into Switzerland in autumn 1940. Here she looks back on the course of modern literature from Dujardin to Beckett, and provides a telling insight into that development from the viewpoint of someone who had lived through it all:

> Just now I have received 'Les Lauriers sont coupés' by E. Dujardin from a local antiquarian. Quelle chance. These emotional outbreaks in their expression and formlessness were only able to flourish in this era of psychology. The nearness of Freud for Schnitzler's 'Lieutenant Gustl' (1901) and for Dujardin's work the libertinism in the more independent language of the music of the symbolists – le vers libre – Mallarmé etc. have initiated and encouraged the process in poetry. Also the 'automatisme' of the surrealists did swing along at the edge . . .
>
> And as a present topic take Samuel Beckett's anti-rational view of the world. A dark, contemplative clown of soul with steady 'kicks' against ratio-intellectuality

and the external world in order to be able to brood in the microcosm of the psyche!

How much more profound is all of that than the sociological over-interpretation and new-interpretation of art.

The emphasis on the subjective viewpoint has a warrior-like quality here, as if a new world was being fought for in all its various manifestations. You can see why Joyce would have fitted in with his perspective, the writer who was central in forwarding the idea of consciousness and the 'microcosm of the psyche'. The anti-rational element in Beckett is exaggerated by Giedion-Welcker, as is the opposition between sociology and psychology, but she does convey precisely what was at stake for the front-line of criticism during the heyday of the avant-garde.

As for stream – and it is a stream, never a lake of consciousness – such flowing we know is never punctuated in reality. That is a metaphorical usage. A stone, as Yeats reminds us in his poem 'Easter 1916', can interrupt the flow of a stream, but the stone he has in mind is revolutionary commitment and not the flow of consciousness. In consciousness, thoughts are punctuated, that is interrupted, and are themselves a form of punctuation, a stopping of an ongoing momentum or movement. Stream, however, conveys the idea of connectivity, and without such an image of fluidity we might not be able to make much of the unity of our sensations. Even when we speak of fragments, we invoke fluidity and unity, as when we encounter in a novel or autobiography a phrase such as 'Fragments float into consciousness'. Edmund Husserl, who together with Franz Brentano founded modern phenomenology, at one point resorts to the phrases 'stream of consciousness' and 'stream of experience' (Husserl, 1962, 161, 108). Philosophers,

Carola Giedion-Welcker. This photograph by Franco Cianetti appears on the back cover of *Carola Giedion-Welcker Schriften 1926–1971*, a collection of essays edited by Reinhold Hohl (1973). 'Little Gidi' is how Joyce called her. For a recent biography, see Iris Bruderer-Oswald, *Das Neue Sehen: Carola Giedion-Welcker und die Sprache der Moderne* (2007).

too, who spent years thinking conceptually about such matters, needed streams and metaphors to describe consciousness.

In defending his use of interior monologue in his novel *Les Lauriers Sont Coupés* (1887), a novel that Joyce took care to acknowledge in his own development as a novelist, Édouard Dujardin also invokes a similar metaphor of flow: 'la vie d'âme est un continu emmélement de lyrisme et de prose' (the life of the soul is a continuous entanglement of lyricism and prose) (Letter 21 April 1887, cited in McKilligan, 1977, 83). Dujardin's protagonist, Daniel Prince, *flows* through the streets of Paris. 'Now and Here', Daniel the flâneur thinks, for consciousness and the soul both need an idea of time as passage, of time as space. Interestingly, when Stéphane Mallarmé contemplated Dujardin's novel, he alighted on the metaphor of seizure: 'l'instant pris à la gorge' (the moment seized by the throat) (cited in Dujardin, 1990, xviii). I think this is right. The phrase 'stream of consciousness' raises problems to delay us. Or rather it should do, for when we reflect on the novel of consciousness and interior monologue, we realise that here and now, flow and seizure, belong together.

At some point, and Molly Bloom's soliloquy raises this in acute form, we arrive back at base and confront a more fundamental question. What is consciousness itself? What exactly is this? Most of the time we are conscious, we are not conscious that we are conscious. That is one of nature's delights, the alternation between movement and arrest, between the workings of consciousness – 'musings' as the student puts it – and being conscious. A pattern of thought – and speed is of the essence here – can continue for many seconds before being recalled, as it were, by the mind. Tracing the movement of a thought can prove difficult not only because of the speed but also because thoughts often don't have a natural departure

In June 1929 a lunch, organised by Adrienne Monnier, was held to celebrate the French translation of *Ulysses*. Dujardin is seated next to Nora, Paul Valéry next to Joyce. Joyce insisted there should be no speeches.

point and a natural destination point. They start, and before we know why or how, we arrive at a particular point. 'How did I end up thinking that?' – such is a frequent query for most people, I suspect. Lightning without thunder. Autochthonous, floating free, rather than tied to earth, Antaeus-like. Too swift to catch or determine. For the modern associationist Dujardin, the life of the soul is 'un continu emmêlement' (an unceasing entanglement). For Molly, her chat keeps going and going, entangling everything in the world around her. It's not so much exhausting to my mind as inexhaustible. She could go on for ever, and, presumably, her soliloquy was only brought to a full stop because Joyce wanted the novel published by his fortieth birthday in February 1922.

But the question remains and, as ever, I tend to get stuck on approach work. Whatever Marx claimed about social being determining consciousness, what exactly is consciousness? Interestingly, while it is possible, through an accident, sleep or drugs, to become unconscious, from birth to the grave it seems impossible, when awake or half-awake, for the flow of consciousness to be stopped. Isn't this one of the nicest ironies about 'Penelope', that it represents what happens to us all, and all the time, but it's written in a way that seems unique and never encountered before? A shock to the system. Brentano and Husserl insisted that consciousness is always consciousness of something. At the outset of his reflections on such matters, Husserl stressed the concept of intentionality, a word whose meaning here stems from the Latin word *intentio* or *intendere*, that is 'being directed towards some goal or thing'. Consciousness in other words is invariably *of* something. Molly's soliloquy never escapes from 'of'. That is one of the problems for the reader: there is too much intentionality in her consciousness, but we are not always sure what it is directed towards. The fragments come at us as fragments, but at the same time we know they belong to the stream, the drift, of her consciousness.

In a chapter on 'General structures of pure consciousness', first published in 1913, Husserl later suggested that the treatment of single experiences is 'governed by the "teleological" view of its function in making "synthetic unity" possible' (Husserl, 1962, 231). In 'Penelope', if there is a teleology at work, some higher goal towards which her thoughts are heading, this has the look not of 'synthetic unity' but of a half-way house where she gestures toward the future but where things remain largely unresolved or circumscribed by memory. As one student rightly argues: 'Arguably, the most inconclusive feature of the Yes which ends Molly's monologue is the doubt over what precisely it is that she is affirming'. There is truth in this observation, but Joyce takes care to ensure the word is capitalised, so that it carries a stronger affirmation than simply 'yes'. 'Yes', her orgasm come at last, Molly cries out. A release of tension. Urgent. Loud, reflecting some kind of commitment, and expressed through the interplay between the spoken and the written. 'Yes', a word written down but heard. Perhaps expressive of life as a whole, her wish for Boylan, whom she hopes to see again on Monday, her commitment to Bloom in spite of all his faults. It's true, there is a doubt about her commitment, especially as the student notices in the light of the phrase 'as well him as another'. But that is Molly, a woman who is, according to another student, 'slightly obsessed with the loss of her youth, and spends the day in bed reminiscing about past love affairs and anything else that enters her mind'. In spite of all her doubts, 'Yes'. It too is an 'unchecked' word (as indeed, for different reasons and with different effects, are Bloom's words). Right at the end also, Molly's word escapes the censor, the mind's quality control inspector, and it supplies an answer to life's reversals and frustrations, to what Virginia Woolf in elevated mode might call the inadequacy of human relationships. 'Yes' emboldens her, and it registers the honesty of a continuing response, a gesturing to the future as well as a judgement on, but not a line under, her past.

Other students have a different take on consciousness. One student is overwhelmed by the vertiginous headiness of it all: 'By overwhelming the human brain, Joyce effectively challenges the superiority of human intelligence and makes the reader question their consciousness'. Yes, unpacked, there's some truth behind this. But perhaps Joyce doesn't so much question a reader's consciousness as make him or her aware of the way the mind works. As for the issue of Joyce and human intelligence, if Joyce overwhelms the human brain that is only because the latter has the capacity to be overwhelmed. Marx, the heir to the Enlightenment, believed that humanity only creates problems it can solve. Something similar can be said about Joyce. Things at times got out of hand during the composition of *Ulysses* and *Finnegans Wake*, but this was to do with his own limitations, his need to triumph over adversity, and his characteristic inability to stop when the point is made. In the end he only created problems he could solve. As for human intelligence on display in Joyce's writings, this is always only human. It is not divine and, as with Molly and Bloom, it is full of human limits, which is another way of saying it's full of humanity. Stephen's most philosophical thought in 'Proteus' is when, on seeing a midwife with a bag, he imagines how the 'cords of all link back, strandentwining cable of all flesh' (*U* 3:37). A reference to 'mystic monks' follows, but it is the physical image that grabs us, the sheer humanity of consciousness and flesh combined that in turn binds us all together in an ever-changing, protean embrace.

Equally, Joyce is not Albert Einstein, and, while he enjoys playing with numbers and scientific ideas and theories, you will look in vain for a new

From its first mention in 'Calypso' when we learn Molly is to sing this at a concert arranged by Boylan to its closing moments, 'Love's Old Sweet Song' threads its way through the consciousness of *Ulysses*. It's a sentimental Edwardian song which yet manages to affect us. 'Though the heart be weary, sad the day and long / Still to us at twilight comes Love's old sweet song.' Not young love but old love. What's that like? At 22 you can only imagine. At the bottom of the front page of this music score, we read 'THE PUBLIC PERFORMANCE OF ANY PARODIED VERSION OF THIS COMPOSITION IS STRICTLY PROHIBITED'. It's as if Boosey & Co. also knew something from the outset, for the song in *Ulysses* can be viewed as what it is or as an insidious form of satire. Perhaps Molly sings it at the concert without any personal thoughts of Bloom or Boylan or Mulvey. After all, it's 'just a song at twilight'. In spite of everything, Molly and Bloom look as though they will stay together. They give us a snapshot of a modern marriage, sometimes sentimental no doubt, at other times they go their own way. They share enough, however, and enjoy shared memories. Bloom will continue to right her breakfast things, and she no doubt will continue to harbour thoughts of seeing Boylan again and of enjoying his arrangements. Who knows if they will make it to their golden wedding anniversary? Or, better, who knows but they might make it to their golden wedding anniversary.

theory about the nature of the universe. *Finnegans Wake*, the book that we are about to consider in the next chapter, is arguably the most difficult imaginative text to be found on the shelves of the British Library or the Library of Congress, but it's nothing by comparison with life itself or with scientific attempts to define life. Indeed it merely reflects something of life's complexity and texture. What Joyce, we might add, undermines is the patter that passes for most versions of the world.

The novel to end all novels

Let me end this chapter with two extracts from the work of Anthony Green, one of the brightest and most unassuming students I had the privilege to teach.

> The novel to end all novels is Joyce's *Ulysses*. This novel could be seen as the ultimate novel, the peak of novel writing and therefore part of a tradition, dating as far back as *Tristram Shandy*, which in itself was not a linear story. *Ulysses* can also be seen as the death of the novel, and of literature itself, as it seemingly

crams in all the traditional styles of English literature over the past two hundred years, and does them in such a way that cannot be outdone, while at the same time mocking them. Joyce creates his own new styles, such as his unique, then unique, take on interior monologue. This taking of something old and modifying it was part of Modernism (and part of any successful movement perhaps). *Ulysses*, written at the height of what we have come to call Modernism, is both a celebration and a rebirth, and at the same time a funeral or elegy . . .

Joyce has created a novel, which although it will keep his memory alive for the rest of time, is something independent of himself. It has taken on a life of its own. The novel has been said to have a self-rejuvenating quality, in which it can never be fully read: there is always something new to discover. The novel also spreads beyond its own boundaries, overflowing into the notes and into the many books written upon it. This is definitely not an incomprehensible novel of experimentation, but a complex, highly dense network, formalised in a way (as a look at Joyce's schema shows) but hugely innovative.

Text and context – the best students invariably have their own take on this relationship and are never content with stating the obvious or reducing one to the other. As far as the novel as a form is concerned, is *Ulysses* a rebirth or a funeral? This is what Anthony wants to know and you can see his mind working at it. He begins with the assertion that *Ulysses* is the novel to end all novels; it is the ultimate novel, where 'ultimate' carries a double meaning, the apex as well as the last. He then remembers Sterne's novel, but before he embarks on a comparison with *Ulysses*, he realises that *Tristram Shandy* is not a linear story. The history of the novel may itself not be a linear story either. Undermining is a more secure tack, and Anthony moves quickly on. Joyce's mocking of styles echoes Eliot's remark in conversation with Woolf in September 1922, how *Ulysses* 'destroyed the whole of the 19th century. . . . It showed up the futility of all the English styles' (Woolf, 1981, 56–7). Both a celebration and a rebirth. That is right, but then Anthony adds 'and at the same time a funeral or elegy'. His sets of discrimination don't stop there. Notice the repetition of 'unique, then unique'. This is clever. Joyce's use of interior monologue, though it was, as he took care to insist on, derived from Dujardin's 1887 novel, was in 1922 unique, and, by stressing this aspect, Anthony shows how *Ulysses* is also part of an ongoing tradition but how it also needs to be understood in the context of its time: 'unique, then unique'.

In the second extract from the same exam answer, Anthony makes something of the eternal aspect of Joyce's *Ulysses*, that it 'will keep his memory alive for the rest of time' and he then adds that 'It has taken on a life of its own'. There are writers one studies who elicit such a response. Shakespeare we recognise is for all time, but modern writers often await a canonisation by the reading public. Anthony feels Joyce is for all time; it's only a claim but one he is keen to assert, and it makes studying Joyce very special.

Through all the years to come, Joyce will be read by those generations who succeed us. You can feel Anthony touching the hem of the great writer's garment, but he's also detached enough to admit Joyce has a life of his own. And *Ulysses* does have the capacity to repeat its effects on different generations of readers. 'The novel also spreads beyond its own boundaries, overflowing into the notes and into the many books written upon it.' This, too, is intelligent, a reminder that the novel is not destroyed by notes and commentaries but spreads naturally 'beyond its own boundaries'. What I'd give to be able to write like that under pressure!

There is something special in the way *Ulysses* not only constitutes a journey in terms of a narrative but also embodies a journey for the reader. And, at one level, the same is true of *Finnegans Wake*, a text that invokes several journey narratives or crossings, including Tristan and Isolde and the Egyptian Book of the Dead. Most journeys have clearly discernible departure points and a clearly marked destination. It should be like catching a train from Dublin to Cork, as Joyce did as a boy with his father, or boarding a 21-knot steamer from Newhaven to Dieppe, as Joyce did with Nora, but one suspects for most people the Ulyssean journey is full of fits and starts where nothing is quite as gripping or as telling or as final as it perhaps should be.

At the first secondary school I attended in 1958–60 in Purley, Surrey, which was named after the sixteenth-century English martyr John Fisher, I remember vividly one of my teachers, Fr Fawcett, reading for us extracts from Homer's *Odyssey*, perhaps in the Butcher and Lang translation that Joyce used. Every week the lesson was given over to his reading out loud accounts of the various situations the protagonist had to confront. What I enjoyed about those classes, which I assume lay outside the normal timetable, was not only the idea of self-contained accounts but also the emphasis on other-worldly adventure read by a teacher who was kindness itself but who almost never smiled and whose severity was at times quite chilling. Years later in my late teens, when I met up with him again, I recall discussing the issue of married priests. The celibate wouldn't be drawn; all he would observe was 'there but for the grace of God go I'. There was no discussion in class after the reading, no writing up, no summarising or comprehension exercises. 'This is a text in the culture' was what I picked up from the tall, silent disciplinarian, 'and you should enjoy it for what it is, in its own right.' I was 12 at the time, still in short trousers, but never realised then that the boy's adventure story, which I perceived had no actual relevance to my life as a boy, though it was read to me as if it had, would accompany me for most of my adult life. I appreciate all that now, and indeed all my Catholic education, for where would I be without all those secular priests who, with all their cultivated obsessions and lonely careers, were the chief architects and models of my interior life – those uptight missionaries in black who laid the foundations for my own defiance and resistance to both secular and religious authority and who made it possible for me to appreciate the renegade who wrote in *Ulysses* 'the bluest book in baile's annals' (*FW* 13:21–2)?

Joyce's *Ulysses* is a different kind of experience to Homer's *Odyssey* and difficult to prepare for. Here in these chapters I've focused on aspects of the text that might prove of benefit to a wide range of readers. I've divided the material into three chapters and given space to three characters – Stephen, Bloom and Molly – and three places – Homer's Greece, Joyce's Paris and Joyce's Dublin. My concern has been to enable the reader to gain a purchase on the novel and at the same time to show some of its characteristic traits by working with particular passages or words. So pattern and theme are important, so is Homer, so is Paris, so is gender, so is the movement round the city of Dublin, so are time and place, so is work and so are situations. It must be obvious that I have only touched on a small amount of what's there, but, as I mentioned in Chapter 1, I hope I've done enough to encourage others to explore the novel for themselves. 'Keep putting it down and picking it up again' is good advice for reading this book and the one we are about to investigate.

The novel itself is in some respects unfinished. Joyce wanted it published by his fortieth birthday on 2 February 1922, and consequently, especially with all his corrections and additions to typescripts and placards, the pressure he put on Maurice Darantiere, his printer in Dijon who didn't speak English, was enormous. This in part explains the huge number of errors in the first edition – some 5,000, according to Hans Walter Gabler, the editor of the so-called Corrected Edition published in 1984. But I'm not really thinking of the errors and what we do with those, for we shouldn't forget that Joyce spent part of the following 12 months correcting many of them himself, and those which remained he saw in subsequent editions and perhaps chose to ignore. No, by unfinished I mean it was up to the reader to supplement, resolve, notice, adjudge, or just enjoy. It ends on 'y' not 'z'. By selecting to write about but one day in the life of a group of people or a city, almost of necessity implies that the reader will have a central role; you couldn't possibly have an ending that was conclusive in those circumstances. Beginnings are often made in the middle of things, but endings sometimes underline where things don't meet. Where Stephen goes after leaving Bloom's house in the early hours of 17 June is for the reader to decide. However, endings also underline where things do meet, and it is on this interrupted note I want to end these chapters on *Ulysses*. In one sense it is unfinished, and yet the more we think about the novel the more it reveals not only its rich sense of patterning but also its (un)believable harmony.

CHAPTER 11

Figuring out
Finnegans Wake

An unknown cargo

If we're honest, most of us would agree that, unlike his 'usylessly unreadable Blue Book of Eccles' (*FW* 179:26–7), *Finnegans Wake* is simply unreadable. The whole world says so, sometimes with a sigh, sometimes out of despair, and sometimes with relish. I once overheard a distinguished professor of English concede without a fight, 'That's one text I don't feel embarrassed about not having read'. 'Life's too short, anyway', she might have continued, 'and people say it's impossible, so why should I bother? After all, I've read his other books. Isn't that enough dedication to a single author?' Even the experts can't agree among themselves about its merit, and Joyce didn't exactly help his cause when he admitted that the ideal reader of *Finnegans Wake* was someone 'suffering from an ideal insomnia' (*FW* 120:13–14). The waking day is enough of a struggle, let alone having a book at bedtime that is also a struggle.

As with everything connected with Joyce, if you discover something you can appreciate, you read on. If you don't, the text will remain simply a curiosity, one of the great unreads to gather dust on the shelves in a library. Here in this chapter I offer some ways into reading *Finnegans Wake*, but perhaps I should stress at the outset the sound qualities of this book. It's a book given over to sounds and odd-looking words. Constantly throughout the book we hear a 'voise from afar' (*FW* 407:14) and find ourselves searching for the source or sources of meaning. It's linked to something else. How do you convey in writing the sounds of English and other European languages? And what happens when you try? Writing is silent, but supposing you believed the ear was as important as the eye. We can divide a language into four levels or components: grammar or syntax, phonology or the sound system, lexis or vocabulary, and semantics or meaning. If you teach English as a foreign language, as Joyce did all the way through his twenties and thirties, you know that each of these levels requires attention, but especially the sound system. You then repeatedly encounter something else, for the written system of English, its orthography, is often at variance with the sound system.

Finnegans Wake was produced by a teacher in a Berlitz school who spent hours in a classroom situation on substitution exercises and explaining the rules of English and why some words such as 'earth' and 'hearth' or 'count' and 'country' have similarly spelt syllables but different pronunciation, and why some words such as 'grieve' and 'leave', or some syllables such as the initial one in 'phoenix' and 'fiendish' are spelt differently but pronounced almost the same. Such activity must have made him realise a number of things: that meaning, for example, in terms of explanation, is in some respects a last resort, that the sound system obeys rules of its own, and that prescriptive grammarians such as Lindley Murray (1745–1826) often showed they couldn't handle a living language. But one thing above all others the near-sighted Joyce must have continually recognised was that language is composed of sounds, some of which come to us independent of meaning. Listen to the construction of sounds in *Finnegans Wake* and develop an appreciation for language simply on that one level. What can you hear? is good advice, then, to begin with. Not, what does this sentence mean? but simply, what am I hearing in this word or phrase or sentence? and use that as an anchor to something else. A language is more than sounds, we know, but this text is like an interactive machine which thrives on sounds being accessed in new ways.

There is of course a wider context for Joyce's experiment with sounds and with language as a whole. With the coming of mass society and mass culture, what the Modernists sought was not so much distance as resistance. There are many reasons for why and how this came to pass, but this isn't the place for such an inquiry, and neither can we afford to be delayed here by the gulf that opened up in the period of Modernism (say 1890–1940) between mass culture and the arts. From Picasso to Joyce the line that links them all was a conscious refusal to allow their work to be paraphrased. It wasn't so much to steal the language from humanity, which we might identify with Flaubert's project, but to resist or deny the possibility of paraphrase. As Beckett recognised from the start in a famous essay on the language of the new work in progress, it was 'not *about* something: *it is that something itself*' (Beckett, 1972, 14). Get little magazines like *The Little Review* (1914–29) and *transition* (1927–38) to advance your aesthetic, and let the world come back to you if it so wishes. With their feet still planted in the era of Modernism, two early commentators on the *Wake* declared: 'James Joyce did not subscribe to the journalistic fallacy that everything should be made easy to understand' (Campbell and Robinson, 362). To some extent they were right, though I wouldn't quite express it as they do. Ignorance after all can be dangerous and there's always a need for good journalism.

My own view is that whether we are students, tutors or general readers, we should avoid the word 'accessible' when writing or thinking about Modernism, for that tends to trigger a set of predictable responses designed to confirm prejudice and retard thinking. In an art gallery, you keep walking round a piece of sculpture noticing things. Do the same with a Modernist text. Be curious and don't retreat into a room marked 'accessible', that is to reading only those things that are deemed 'accessible'. Don't, in other words, shut down your options in the name of something which you think is for you simply because it appears 'accessible'. Be challenged, unsettled, and live with the sounds of the language around you. Spend your life enjoying them. Notice things and light up the world.

Pound and Yeats, Wyndham Lewis and others took their resistance into reactionary politics when they effectively declared UDI in their slogan 'no compromise with the public', or in Lewis's case in the one-word curse 'Blast', the loud title of his short-lived journal in 1914–15. But this was not the view of everyone in the avant-garde. Distinctions, therefore, have to be drawn, even as we seek to establish the common ground linking figures in this remarkable generation of writers and artists. *Finnegans Wake* carries forward the defiance on display in *Dubliners*, but it's combined with something else, namely difficulty and the whole expansion of what I have called elsewhere in connection with the 'Sirens' episode of *Ulysses* 'local disturbances' (Pierce, 2006, 117ff). No reassuring hand is offered to the reader, so that we are again positioned as observers who are there presumably to participate but given almost nothing by way of support to cling on to. In his Preface to *Tales Told of Shem and Shaun* (1929), C.K. Ogden, who was himself particularly interested in linguistic experimentation, as *Basic English* (1930) serves to remind us, speaks of Joyce inviting the reader to penetrate 'the night mind of man' (xii). But such an invitation can be simply lost amid the difficulty which appears insurmountable. In *Dubliners* the sentences look unfinished but we understand them or, rather, we understand them as gestures, perhaps part of the epiphany motif which Joyce writes well about. By contrast, in *Finnegans Wake* the sentences come fully formed, but they are like vessels freighted with unknown cargo.

There aren't too many photographs of Joyce where he is looking at the camera. Away is a characteristic pose that unites the man and the writer. Away from the camera, sideways, looking past the camera, to the side of the camera, with his back to the camera in the famous shot of him taken by

Carola Giedion-Welcker in Zurich. Substitute 'reader' for 'camera' and you get an idea of where the reader is variously positioned in *Finnegans Wake*. In the first chapter alone there are some 194 exclamation marks, 60 question marks and 54 brackets. As ever, Joyce takes things to extremes because even the possibility of an idiot's guide is removed from us. In some respects the best we can make do with is Roland McHugh's *Annotations to Finnegans Wake* (1991), a line-by-line compendium of the meaning of various words or phrases, and an extraordinary achievement in its own way. Unwrap the parcel but never get to see what's inside – that's what consulting annotations and some commentaries can resemble, however.

I recall the first conference on *Finnegans Wake* I attended at the University of Leeds in 1987, and listening to Bernard Benstock, fresh from his new base in Miami, on what we still don't know about Joyce's text. Well, quite a lot, was his answer. In its own way I found it encouraging. After all the groundwork conducted in the 1960s and 1970s by an earlier generation of *Wake* scholars in *A Wake Newslitter* (1962–80) – scholars who included Adaline Glasheen, James Atherton, Fritz Senn and Clive Hart – the large questions still remain. What does it all mean? Or, more basic, what constitutes the narrative of *Finnegans Wake*? And what about the issue that also relates to reading, but this time to strategies of reading? Working on particular passages can be fine, but how does one go from detailed commentary to an overall interpretation? – and by that I mean not simply how a passage ties in with a recurring theme. This is never an easy question in Joyce, as we have witnessed in relation to the idea of a series in *Dubliners*, or to consideration of the Cubist perspective in *A Portrait*, or to the use of Homeric themes in *Ulysses*. In some respects, we might agree, this was Joyce's persistent problem: how to structure things so that it all fell out and made sense.

Every guide, every commentary, every observation tramples on one of the author's original planks marked with the word 'paraphrase', and constitutes therefore a form of betrayal against the great era of Modernism. That's fine by me, for I have no wish to be a spokesperson for anyone, let alone for 'possibly the most arrogant writer that Ireland has produced' (Gorman, 1926, 6). And in case you thought this a rhetorical ploy, I've no intention of proceeding to outline what *Finnegans Wake* is about. What I can comment on, however, are the books on the *Wake* I have found helpful, and also the notes I made when I first began reading the book in earnest in the mid-1980s. Others will choose their own course, and that's as it should be, but how did I go about first reading this unreadable book? What was my critical journey in this respect?

The first thing I did was to make a card template of 36 lines and put it inside my copy of *Finnegans Wake*. Every edition of the text carries 36 lines per page and every edition has 628 pages. I thought: I may not be able to understand the book but at least I can accurately assign a reference! As I have been doing throughout this book, when critics refer to *Finnegans Wake* they cite the page number followed by the line number. I then began what I always do, which is to embark on reading without anything else beside me. No guides or commentaries, and see how far I could get. I would read as many pages as I could before I arrived at a point which I can only describe as a fog, an image I referred to earlier in this book in relation to the reading experience of *Finnegans Wake*. A blank, nothing coming back at me. I then returned to the beginning and started again, all the time hearing more of the rhythms and discerning more of the meaning of the book. In today's computer terms, I was in the process of downloading the book not in one go but over time, and on each occasion I accessed it the download cursor seemed to go further across the screen from left to right. I found this also encouraging, especially when the download wasn't aborted. This went on for weeks and weeks, but I didn't give in. 'Cry not yet!' (*FW* 20:19) at the start of a paragraph screamed at me early on, and I assumed I was being addressed directly by Joyce. As Jean-Michel Rabaté has rightly suggested in a related context, *Finnegans Wake* 'constantly creates the illusion of an illocutionary dramatization of its utterances' (Rabaté, 2002, 37). I drew breath. Keep putting the book down is good advice, and reflect: the text I was reading seemed to be about the act of reading itself.

I don't know why, but I then cheated and got myself a guide. I photocopied and stapled the ten-page working outline in Benstock's *Joyce-Again's Wake: An Analysis of Finnegans Wake* (1965), and ensured it was always in place when I came to read the book. I can't remember why I hit on Benstock's working outline. Perhaps it was because I had picked up a paperback version of the book (price $2.10 plus tax) in Logos Used Bookstore in Santa Cruz in 1982 before the earthquake that destroyed the store in 1989, and I returned to it again when I began reading the novel in earnest. We're never far from coincidence and what's to hand when *Finnegans Wake* is under discussion, and the text did seem to resemble an earthquake in the culture. Anyway, I found the outline useful and took to relying on it. It draws on Campbell and Robinson's *A Skeleton Key to Finnegans Wake* (1944), but it is more informative than their 'Synopsis', and I liked the way Benstock insisted that it's not a guide but a working outline.

Of course, in some respects the most appropriate introduction to *Finnegans Wake* is via the pages of *transition* (1927–38). This was the journal, edited by Eugene Jolas, that carried instalments of what was then known as 'Work in progress'. Each month in the first phase of the Paris-based

A *Working Outline* of Finnegans Wake

CHAPTER 1 (pp. 3-29)

3:	Statement of themes
4:	Battle in Heaven and introduction of Finnegan
5:	Finnegan's fall and promise of resurrection
5-6:	The City
6-7:	The Wake
7-8:	Landscape foreshadows H.C.E. and A.L.P.
8-10:	Visit to Willingdone Museyroom
10:	The Earwicker house
10-12:	Biddy the hen finds the letter in the midden heap
12-13:	Dublin landscape
13-15:	Pre-history of Ireland—the invaders (including the birth of Shem and Shaun, p. 14)
15-18:	Mutt and Jute recount the Battle of Clontarf
18-20:	The development of the Alphabet and Numbers
21-23:	The Tale of Jarl van Hoother and the Prankquean
23-24:	The Fall
25:	Finnegan's Wake revisited
25-29:	Restless Finnegan is told about the present age
29:	H.C.E. introduced

CHAPTER 2 (pp. 30-47)

30-32:	The genesis and naming of Humphrey Chimpden Earwicker
32-33:	Gaiety Theatre production of *A Royal Divorce*
33-35:	Rumors about H.C.E.'s indiscretion
35-36:	The Encounter with the Cad
36-38:	The Cad dines and drinks

Summary of Chapter 1 of *Finnegans Wake*, taken from Bernard Benstock, *Joyce-Again's Wake* (1965).

Source: University of Washington Press

magazine from 1927 until 1930, sections of the new work by 'the quintessential modern revolutionary artist' were broadcast as it were to the world (Fitch, 1990, 14). Equally, as has recently been suggested, *Finnegans Wake* was 'directly shaped by the tangled history of its serial publication' (Crispi and Slote, 2007, 17). In retrospect, what's surprising is how much of the original text was in place from the start; the positioning of the extracts was another matter, for the overall structure needed considerable adjustment by Joyce before its publication as a single work in 1939. The resistance Jolas clearly felt from his readers was what what most people today feel about the text: what was it all about? Give us some clues. Jolas's problem was more urgent, for he had a journal that was largely dependent on Joyce's strange language, and to support his project he needed to solicit help from critics almost from the outset.

Issue 8 in November 1927 carried William Carlos Williams's 'A note on the recent work of James Joyce', followed in the next issue by Elliot Paul's 'Mr Joyce's treatment of plot'. Frank Budgen's essay 'The work in progress of James Joyce and Old Norse poetry' appeared in issue 13 in Summer 1928, and then in the Spring/Summer double issue in June 1929 came the group of essays by Stuart Gilbert, Samuel Beckett and others, which were published separately by Shakespeare and Company under the heading *Our Exagmination Round His Factification for Incamination of Work in Progress*. This was followed in March 1932 by 'Homage to James Joyce', which included Cesar Abin's famous sketch of Joyce in the shape of a question mark. Seeing the new work unfold in this way, alongside art work by Picasso, Brancusi, Klee and Man Ray, in a journal with a title in lower case prominently displayed, helps to situate Joyce among the European avant-garde, marching under the banner that Jolas and others defined as 'the revolution of the word' (Jolas, 1949, 173–4). But the historical context also reminds us that the text needed a community of readers from the start to rally round and insist on its significance, a situation which in many respects is no different today.

Although the most appropriate introduction to *Finnegans Wake* may be through the pages of *transition*, many of us would prefer something less challenging at first. Books, then, with basic information that I have also

Cesar Abin's caricature of Joyce.

found helpful include John Gordon, *Finnegans Wake: A Plot Summary* (1986) and Danis Rose and John O'Hanlon, *Understanding Finnegans Wake: A Guide to the Narrative of James Joyce's Masterpiece* (1982). It's important at the start to be in possession of a wider framework of how to read this book, and the essays in *A Conceptual Guide to Finnegans Wake* (1974), edited by Michael Begnal and Fritz Senn, still retain something of their freshness. Information about how the book came to be written and what books Joyce drew on in its construction – this is also what one needs close to the start. James Atherton's *The Books at the Wake: A Study of Literary Allusions in James Joyce's 'Finnegans Wake'* (1959) is a labour of love and an extraordinary display of erudition both on Joyce's part and on the part of the Wigan schoolteacher. The recent interest in genetic criticism in Joyce studies has resulted in a set of informative and up-to-date essays edited by Luca Crispi and Sam Slote under the umbrella title *How Joyce Wrote 'Finnegans Wake': A Chapter-by-Chapter Genetic Guide* (2007). Armed with all this material, the reader new to *Finnegans Wake* can embark on a voyage of discovery, confident that the text will yield something more than its resistant quality.

Preliminary notes

As for my own notes, these are the record of one person's first tentative steps in understanding *Finnegans Wake*. What they represent are things that struck me going along, and, unlike my annotations to other books, they record incremental stages in my early reading. They are the work of an amateur reader of the *Wake* and perhaps for that reason valuable in the way that the native is to the anthropologist. I once caught sight of Charles Peake's copy of *Finnegans Wake*, one which dated back to the 1940s when he first began reading the text. There wasn't a centimetre of white space; every page had been mercilessly, and no doubt expertly, annotated. No, I said to myself, in the years to come, my copy will remain clean, the work of an enthusiastic amateur or wary neophyte. I'd never be able to match such knowledge and I'd no intention of trying. I'll just insert notes in the back for quick reference and as a record of what was in the text that appealed to me at the time and which phrases or words were of more than passing interest.

Every text reads us as much as we read it. I like the opening, the rhythms, the odd associations coming at you from all sides, but I made no notes on my first stab. 'Irenean' is the first word I jotted down, together with a reference to Joyce's *Selected Letters*. Often it's the case, as happens with 'gnomon' on first reading 'The Sisters' for example, that unusual words are

First page of notes from my copy of *Finnegans Wake*.

things that stand out. In the huge linguistic mound that is *Finnegans Wake*, I alighted on a word that now baffles me not so much in terms of its meaning but on account of why I chose to put it in my notes. 'Irenean' sounded like an unknown Middle Eastern sect or grouping, closer to Nazarene than modern Iranian. But then other, more relevant, meanings came to me. Ire, Irene, Ireland, eirenic, Eire. I didn't need Joyce's note to Harriet Shaw Weaver on 13 May 1927 to tell me as much, but it was nice to see the author's stamp of approval. There's a play on the name of Ireland and on how it carries two other meanings, one associated with anger, the other with peace. Not Irish but Irenean. A necessary defamiliarisation if identity is to be reassembled for more peaceful pursuits in the modern world. I must have been picking up on the constant use of reciprocity and doubling in the text, but I must also have been trying to read it politically. Reading passively and reading actively. There's plenty of ammunition in *Finnegans Wake* for whatever view you espouse.

'Here Comes Everybody' is a phrase that recurs in *Finnegans Wake* and I knew before ever opening the book that the initials HCE are scattered everywhere, and it's something I return to below. In trying to decipher the plot, I eventually encountered something definite: HCE is accused. At this point I see I have inserted no line numbers. Perhaps I was hedging my bets in this first run-through. The text seemed to be about a misdeed, followed by an accusation. A tormented text, full of guilt and shame, but such a view I was only glimpsing at this stage. The cad in the park was a continuation of this theme, but now this event is portrayed through the reassuring filter of a story. Next to 'They tell the story' I'm recalling the incident in 'Hades' when the caretaker at Glasnevin cemetery tells a joke about some drunks confusing one of the headstones of the Saviour with the man in the grave: '*Not a bloody bit like the man*, says he. *That's not Mulcahy*, says he, *whoever put it up*' (U 6:730–1).

So I was absorbing what I later observed was a common feature, how different events, different scenes, different characters, or perhaps, as in a dream, the same character under different guises, were being recycled. Not so much stories within stories but stories where material was being reconstituted. I don't know how to explain this adequately, but it is like a sequence of dreams where there is no original but only versions, and I understand why early commentators – such as Frank Budgen in his 1928 essay in *transition*, or Edmund Wilson in his essay 'The dream of H.C. Earwicker' (1941) – were attracted to this idea, for it does help to express something of the reading experience. In narrative terms it seemed to involve mining the same quarry, as we can see happening in *Ulysses* when an echo of a passage from an earlier episode is distantly evoked or recycled.

Page 35 must have got me excited because I also note the word 'Hesitency'; on a subsequent reading I see I added 'HeCitEncy'. I knew what Joyce was getting at here, or at least I knew enough of the historical record to sense that this is what he was drawing on. For what purpose? That was another question, and always worth asking when a source has been identified. In an attempt to discredit the leader of the Irish Parliamentary Party, the London *Times* ran a series of articles in 1887 under the heading 'Parnellism and crime'. Parnell was accused of supporting terrorism in Ireland. A letter purportedly written by him in 1883 expressed regret for the murder in the Phoenix Park of Lord Cavendish, the chief secretary for Ireland, but not for Mr Burke, the under-secretary. The letter was a forgery and it was exposed in court when the perpetrator Richard Piggott was asked under cross-examination to write one of the words used in the original letter. The word in question was 'hesitency', and Piggott, as he had done in the letter, spelt it wrong again. It's a nice story and vindication for Joyce's hero, the uncrowned king of Ireland. It was proof that, as we read elsewhere in *Finnegans Wake*, 'Every letter is a godsend' (*FW* 269:17).

Hesitancy, hesitant, hesitation. This motif also tells us something about what is happening in *Finnegans Wake*. We hesitate as we read. Indeed, we are forced to hesitate at each turn. Even as we get to the original story, as here with *The Times* controversy, there is a certain doubt as to how it is being used or how it functions in the text. HCE hesitates, he stutters, as if the accused is always guilty. HCE is the father-figure who is compromised, and he hesitates. Guilt. Perhaps, even as we hesitate, we too share something of humanity's doubt in the face of the world and in how we go about interpreting the world, and we also share or express something of its guilt. The cad in the park, the park where Cavendish was assassinated and where a murder might have been committed in Sheridan Le Fanu's novel *The House By The Church-yard* (1863) – Irish history, Irish fiction, the Irish imagination, and further back original sin. Language, history, psychology, religion – written into all of them, the Jesuit-educated Joyce discerned, was guilt and betrayal. Not for nothing do we encounter a reference to Adam and Eve on the first page of *Finnegans Wake*. 'Be sure your sins will find you out', parents caution their children. Eventually, the past will out. One letter, as happened to Piggott, is sometimes enough to betray you. But, equally, in a peculiar form of reciprocity, the victim sometimes shares the guilt of the perpetrator.

The guilt is there from the outset of *Finnegans Wake*. On the first page, the fate of the giant Finnegan, who is Irish or Erse through and through, is linked with the children's nursery rhyme. Finnegan, who was once a solid man, arse solid that is, has a heavy head after his fall, but he manages to enquire after his 'tumptytumtoes', which can be found in the Phoenix Park, where orange and green, unionist and nationalist, have been laid to rest since Dubliners first loved the River Liffey. 'The great fall of the offwall entailed at such short notice the pftjschute of Finnegan, erse solid man, that the humptyhillhead of humself promptly sends an unquiring one well to the west in quest of his tumptytumtoes: and their upturnpike-pointandplace is at the knock out in the park where oranges have been laid to rust upon the green since devlinsfirst loved livvy' (*FW* 3:18–24). Appropriately, Joyce's last work begins with a fall, an 'offwall' or awful fall or simply offal, with a knock out, with Humpty Dumpty, with a 'pftjschute', a chute, a parachute that didn't open, or the sound of quick-exiting waste matter shooting through the back passage. The word 'pftjschute' after all was a late insertion by Joyce. This is how human history perhaps began and how the head feels after it has imbibed too much. A once solid arse, 'entailed', is now liquid. Ah, where are my feet? I'll send a message down. Still in the same place. Thank God. Toes pointing up. Tight. HCE in his first guise. Prone.

When we return to the notes, it's clear my first run-through of *Finnegans Wake* was anything but systematic. That's as it should be. Wilde thought he could get the gist of a three-decker novel in 30 minutes (Ellmann, 1987, 21). It's impossible to do that with *Finnegans Wake*, but in general there's something to be said for just promenading at first, accumulating in carefree fashion knowledge and confidence. In a recent study entitled *James Joyce and the Act of Reception* (2006), John Nash, in a passage where he discusses Jacques Derrida's idea of the bad reader anxious to be 'determined', concludes that the *Wake* allows for the hurried reader and for a reception that is 'distracted' (120–1). This is especially true with the promenader, for the text keeps distracting us.

'I have met with you too late', a phrase mentioned in Chapter 2 of this book, is what Joyce is supposed to have said to Yeats in 1902. McHugh (1991) misses the Yeats connection but he does notice how the phrase echoes Wilde's sad confession to Bosie, Lord Alfred Douglas, in a letter full of recrimination sent from Reading Gaol and later incorporated into *De Profundis* (1905): 'I met you either too late or too soon' (Wilde, 1962, 487). In the actual text of *Finnegans Wake* at this point, it reads 'I have met with you, bird, too late, or, if not, too worm and early' (*FW* 37:13–4), and in the same sentence Joyce adds a reference to T.S. Eliot 'tag for ildiot'.

Joyce's image of Yeats as a bird is not without justification. Wearing the cape he was often seen in at the turn of the twentieth century, Yeats cut a dashing figure. His writings are full of birds, as can be seen in the titles to some of his books, such as *The Speckled Bird*, a semi-autobiographical novel finished in 1900 and unpublished in his lifetime, *At The Hawk's Well* (1916), a play with dancers in bird costumes, and *The Wild Swans at Coole* (1919), the volume that was to usher in the great verse of his middle and late period. Joyce himself, the 'hawklike man' (*U* 9:952), was no stranger to birds, as his early pseudonym Daedalus reminds us. As for Eliot, the note on page 62, with its play on *The Waste Land* (1922) and the emigrant's view of his or her native country, confirms that Joyce was always looking over his shoulder at his contemporaries or near-contemporaries. And from Paris in the 1920s and 1930s, Paris of the exiles, he had an extraordinary vantage-point. Too early or too late. It didn't make any difference in the end, for Joyce had established himself as the equal of anyone. The defiance at 22 had paid off. As for Wilde, the depths of his distraught state had been

The Polidor restaurant on rue Monsieur-le-Prince in Paris, a two-minute walk from rue de l'Odéon where *Ulysses* was published. Photograph by David Pierce. It was a favourite restaurant of Joyce, and his friends in Paris ensured its image featured in the 1949 exhibition catalogue at La Hune Gallery. I took this photograph in August 2006. The restaurant retains the look and character that Joyce would have been familiar with in the interwar years. The name 'Polidor' derives from two Greek words, namely *poly* and *or*, much gold, many riches. The Greeks brought him not only luck but, as we have seen in previous chapters, also chords. Odysseus is described by Homer as *polytropos*, many-sided, which is what Bloom is, someone with many sides to his personality. For me, and perhaps also for Joyce, 'Polidor' also echoes two Spanish words, *pollo*, with two 'l's, and *oro*: *pollo de oro*, a golden chicken. Birds again. The day I was there, a notice in the window carried a journalist's praise for one of their menu items 'Fricassée de poulet à la crème de morilles'.

forgotten but not the plucked phrase, which Joyce reuses again and again, perhaps most cruelly in 'We have meat too hourly' (*FW* 60:29–30).

The Earwickers of Sidlesham

The other notes I made on this first page can be left as they are. With its play on de Valera, the 'devil era' was a phrase that stood out for me and in time I began collecting all the references to the Irish leader whom Joyce in part blamed for the Irish Civil War in 1922–3. I write more about this in *James Joyce's Ireland* (1992). I must have noticed 'honeybeehivehut' because of the reference to 'hive for the honey bee' in Yeats's poem 'The Lake

Isle of Innisfree' and also what happens when you join three or four words into one – the power of association deriving from the power of combination. This is the place, however, to say something about the 'Glues etc' which appears on page 30. When Joyce began thinking in earnest about *Finnegans Wake* in the summer of 1923, he was on vacation in Bognor Regis, a coastal resort in West Sussex. He must have picked up the Ward Lock *Pictorial and Descriptive Guide to Bognor* and started perusing it. One of the villages nearby is Sidlesham, and the church there is described in the 1918 third edition.

Sidlesham lies between Chichester and Bognor. Just to the east of Bognor is the village of Felpham, famous for the cottage where William Blake stayed in 1800–3, but there is no record in Ellmann's biography of Joyce visiting it. Manhood End, another unusual name, lies to the north-west of Sidlesham. The Hundred of Manhood comprised, among others, the ancient parishes of Birdham, Earnley, West Itchenor, Selsey, Sidlesham and the Witterings. Surprisingly, 'Manhood' has nothing to do with manhood or virility but is a corruption of Manwode or common wood, a derivation Joyce, the diligent researcher, draws our attention to later in *Finnegans*

Sidlesham Church, a mile north of the old mill, is an Early English structure worthy of notice, and an examination of the surrounding tombstones should not be omitted if any interest is felt in deciphering curious names, striking examples being Earwicker, Glue, Gravy, Boniface, Anker, and Northeast.

Sidlesham, as it appears in the Ward Lock *Pictorial and Descriptive Guide to Bognor* (1918).

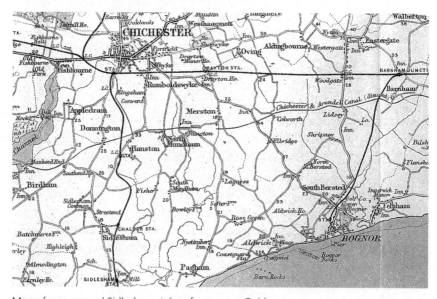

Map of area around Sidlesham, taken from same *Guide*.

An overdressed Joyce with
goatee beard and moustache,
looking directly into the camera,
Bognor, 1923.

Wake when we read 'manowhood' (*FW* 329:9). Wood to manhood via wode – when you go back in history and retreat to a time before surnames, you find a wholly unfamiliar world, but, equally, it is a world where the names, corrupt or otherwise, continue to taunt us. 'Make sense of that will you' is the injunction history bequeathes to us, especially evident when it comes to placenames and surnames. One corruption followed by another. And yet in spite of everything, as *Finnegans Wake* repeatedly demonstrates, we are all, as Stephen notices in 'Proteus', whether we like it or not, linked to the 'strandentwining cable of all flesh' (*U* 3:37).

What caught Joyce's eye in the guide book was not only the graveyard at Sidlesham but also the series of names. If I'm going to call it *Finnegans Wake*, what other names should I use for my male protagonist HCE? Sidlesham's fame, according to the guide book, rested not on its village or its church or some other monument but its cemetery. That must have tickled Joyce, but it was as nothing compared with the run of names to be found in the graveyard: 'Earwicker, Glue, Gravy, Boniface, Anker, and Northeast'. Now see how that series surfaces in *Finnegans Wake*: 'pivotal ancestors as the Glues, the Gravys, the Northeasts, the Ankers and the Earwickers of Sidlesham in the Hundred of Manhood' (*FW* 30:6–8). The names are made

High tide at Bognor in the 1920s, with ladies' bathing machines ensuring privacy.

plural, Boniface is cut (later, at 329:10, he's recalled as 'bonzeye') and the phrase 'in the Hundred of Manhood' is added, but we can't help being reminded of the run of names is as it appears in the guide book.

The names are certainly curious, even odd, but then any English telephone directory will yield more than its fair share of curious surnames. Glue is in fact from Old English *glēaw*, meaning wise or prudent (Reaney, 1967, 254). Gravy also stands out, but further research suggests the author of the guide book might have got it wrong. According to the Sussex Online Parish Clerks Burial Register Database – which covers the period 1793 to 1901 for Sidlesham – there's no Gravy in St Mary's graveyard at Sidlesham. Indeed, there are only three people with that name in the whole of the 1901 Census for England and Wales. On the other hand, there are several people named Grevett in Selsey and Littlehampton, areas adjacent to Bognor, but none as far as I can see buried in the graveyard at Sidlesham. In *The Surnames of Sussex* (1988), Richard McKinley claims that 'Gravely has survived as a Sussex surname' (128), but the 1901 Census shows only one Gravely in the vicinity of Sidlesham. Glues are plentiful. Boniface, however, is more common in East Sussex. There is one reference to Northeast being buried in the graveyard, and there are four Anchors but no Ankers as far as I'm aware. More securely, some 20 Earwickers are buried in the graveyard at Sidlesham.

The editors of *How Joyce Wrote 'Finnegans Wake'* (2007), in a book directly concerned with genetic criticism – that is with the printed material Joyce drew on in writing the *Wake* – claim: 'Earwicker (pronounced "Erricker") is the name of an old family in Sidlesham, Sussex, that Joyce might have heard of during his trip to nearby Bognor in the middle of 1923' (Crispi and Slote, 2007, 9). There is no 'might' about it, for the evidence is compelling, as compelling as Joyce's repeated raids on the eleventh edition of the *Encyclopaedia Britannica* for his description in the *Wake* of 40 or so cities from around the world. As he freely admitted, complete with exclamation mark, he was '[t]he last word in stolentelling!' (*FW* 424:35).

As for Earwicker being pronounced 'Erricker', again the editors are relying on an article by Clive Hart in *A Wake Digest* (1968), where the claim is made that 'The old, correct, pronunciation of the name is "Erricker" – hence Joyce's use of variant names like "Herrick or Eric"' (22). I assume this is based on P.H. Reaney's *A Dictionary of English Surnames* (2005) where a similar claim is made about how Earwicker is pronounced Erricker (148). For someone brought up in West Sussex, I must confess I didn't find this terribly convincing. I was also sceptical about what constituted the orginal name and what the variants. According to my source, Maureen Earwicker (née Luxton), who is an expert on the Earwicker genealogy, Earwaker is the most common form of the name, followed by Earwicker. When the name is first found in Sidlesham in the sixteenth century it was spelt in both forms, Earwaker and Earwicker, and even today there are families that use both spellings. The early spellings in Sussex included Earwicker, Earwaker, Erricker and Erwicker, but by the late seventeenth century it is rare to encounter any spelling other than Earwicker and Earwaker. Earwaker was a person ever watchful, a boat watchman, or watchful as a boat. In Old English the name appears as Eoforwacer, the name of a tribe of people living, according to my source, in what is now Weston-super-Mare in Somerset. Reaney suggests 'boar-man' as a translation of Eoforwacer, a view also shared by Patricia Hanks and Flavia Hodges in *A Dictionary of Surnames* (1988). Interestingly, if you change 'yor' to 'eofor', you have Earwicker's connection with my own city of York. This I suspect is not quite the intention behind 'York's Porker' (*FW* 71:12), one of the terms of abuse listed in Chapter 3 of Book 1 and connected with the emblem of Richard III, but it might have been if Joyce knew everything. Who first owned the name is uncertain; before the coming of the Danes, there were several tribes named Eoforwacer in the south and north of England. As for the Arwakers in Essex, they may be related to the Earwickers or Earwakers.

Until I got in touch with my source in April 2007, I assumed the name was Scandinavian and that wick was a dwelling, a parish or a village. Like most Joyce critics, I delighted in Earwicker, a Scandinavian name for a writer who came from a city founded by the Vikings in the tenth century, a city, as we have recently learnt, which contained in the area now occupied by the Royal Hospital at Kilmainham the largest Viking cemetery outside

Scandinavia. But the name I'm afraid is 'pure' English. Erriker is a variant, but rarer, and out of a total of 57 with this name in the 1901 Census, there are only five people with Sussex connections. As for the evidence adduced by 'Herrick or Eric', as Hart claims, that looks like an example of special pleading. Joyce could work with almost any sound, and if we wanted to list all the sounds that remind us of Earwicker in the *Wake* it would produce a whole battery of words awaiting incorporation or comment: Errievikkingr, Erriweddyng, earpicker, earwakers, earwanker, earwax, earwigger, earwuggers, earwugs, E'erawan, E'erawhere, eerie, eeriesh, eeriewhigg. In neighbouring Hampshire, the first syllable in Earwaker is closer to Erwaker when pronounced, but in Sidlesham in Sussex you can hear the ear in Earwicker.

I suspect Joyce felt he didn't need to visit the graveyard; he had what he needed from the book in front of him. And what he had was the 'pivotal' name he could hang a book on. With its impression of weighing a mass of evidence, 'pivotal' gives the game away, for Joyce was an expert at throwing false scents, or attempting to. Anyway, he had what he needed. Earwicker.

My photograph of the Earwicker family tombstones in Sidlesham Parish Church, taken some time after 1985. In spite of the flowers, the Earwicker family seem to have died out in Sidlesham, which is a shame given how important the name has become for *Wake* scholars. An extract from a letter about the family written by Gertrude Earwicker is reproduced in Clive Hart (1968). The tombstone of her brother Arthur, who died in 1979, is in the foreground of this photograph. Older tombstones are in a separate part of the graveyard and also inside the church by the altar. Photograph by David Pierce.

Eriwicker. Eire. Ireland. Humphrey Chimpden Earwicker. HCE. Here Comes Everybody. Like Finn, a sleeping giant and seemingly ubiquitous. As it was for me, the name was rich in association for Joyce. As an adjective, 'wicker' is something made of twigs, a wicker basket for example. But as a suffix, it might also refer to someone who lived in a 'wick', a *wîc* in Anglo-Saxon, or *vicus* in Latin, a town or village. My city: Eboracum, Yorvik, 'Yorick', York, the town of the wild boar, Sterne's city, modern York, once Roman, once Viking, once Norman. Waz iz. A 'wick' or 'wich', especially when located on the coast, can also be Norse for a bay or creek; in modern Norwegian the word is *vik*, and a Viking was someone from a *vik*. Closer to Joyce, Wicklow was a Viking meadow. Howth derives from *hovda* or head, and Leixlip is a salmon leap. Wood Quay on the banks of the Liffey was a Viking town, while Oxmanstown derived from the 'ostmen' or men from the east. The parallels are persuasive: underlying Dublin and underlying *Finnegans Wake* is a Scandinavian kingdom.

As *Finnegans Wake* never stops reminding us, 'waz iz', what was is. Everything from the past, including the corruption of surnames and place-names, comes along with us as we move through life, awaiting recognition or activation. A wick is also a candle-wick, something that lights up the dark. When it gutters, the light fades and dies, so again we have a scene of a wake. A wick is a wake or, alternatively, a wick – when lit, like a dick or a 'mickey' in Irish slang – is awake. Earwick is close to earwig and an earwig is close to sounds in the ear burying away. Earwicker, therefore, could become an earwigger, someone who's doing the earwigging or someone on the sharp end of being told off or losing an argument. By extension, an earwigger could also be something you put over your ears not to hear things, perhaps taunts by others.

As I say, technically, Joyce based all the Earwicker material on several layers of confusion. Earwicker is an English surname and related to Earwaker. Leaving aside 'wild boar', the first syllable, as we have seen, signifies ever or always; the second the person who is awake, on guard. If he had come across the idea of a watchful boatman, Joyce might well have developed it into a motif in the *Wake*. But his ear was seduced by hearing, so that when he mentions 'earwakers' at 351:25 he does so in a hearing context with 'eye-dulls or earwakers'. At 173:9–10, there is a reference to rooting with 'earwaker's pensile'. If he'd done some more rooting while staying in Bognor in 1923, he might have discovered he had in 'Earwaker' an even more appropriate name for his protagonist. Humphrey Chimpden Earwaker. He would have lost all the Scandinavian and Viking associations, all the earwig stuff, and much more of the comedy, but he would have gained something else. As noted earlier, Joyce believed the 'ideal reader' of his book was someone 'suffering from an ideal insomnia' (*FW* 120:13–14). Earwaker is precisely that person, always on guard, never asleep. On the other hand, the spelling was perhaps a little obvious, especially when placed alongside Earwicker, and it didn't appear in a guide book. So, we might well conclude that in hitting on Earwicker for the name of his protagonist, Joyce was hitting on a name with extraordinary resonance for him, a name that could run and run without ever being called to account.

Finnegans Wake, then, is a book of sounds rooted in spellings and printed material. The ear is what we use to hear, and inside the ear things are

This indenture (a legal document drawn up by a legal representative in which a pledge is made between two parties) shows John and Elizabeth Earwicker of the Parish of Sidlesham and Elizabeth's brother Henry Bolton, a blacksmith in the Parish of Compton, agreeing to sell a dwelling house and land adjacent to Merston Common to Joseph Straker of the Parish of Pagham and a Yeoman of the County for the sum of £ 630 of 'lawful money of Great Britain'. The document, which is dated 10 October 1769 and witnessed by William Foster, I came across some 20 years ago in an antiques shop in Chichester in Sussex. I think I paid about £15 for it. I thought it was worth it, if only to have in my possession something about Earwicker that Joyce knew nothing about. I also wanted a copy of Earwicker's signature for my records.

heard. Brancusi was right to settle on a spiral ear for his iconic image of Joyce. Eliot speaks of the auditory imagination, and if you want an example turn to any page of *Finnegans Wake*. Things get inside the head and stay there, sometimes for weeks and months before they are detonated or understood. With its elongated body and many-jointed antennae, the earwig works through concealment and persistence, and the words and phrases of the *Wake* do likewise. We pick up things as we read but some meanings or references come to us long afterwards. With Earwaker in mind, 'Wake up!' could serve as a motto for this book of words, a book where we might agree we constantly encounter a 'sound seemetery' (*FW* 17:35–6). Symmetry in a cemetery. Sidlesham (pronounced as if it were spelt Siddlesham) contains in its final syllable the name of Shem, one of HCE's two sons and often seen as the figure closest to Joyce himself. Jem, Shem. Shem, sham. The evidence is before our eyes and inside our ears: 'Shem was a sham' (*FW* 170:25).

The paradigmatic ear

As I look at the next two pages of my notes (read from right to left), I notice that my reading was Irish-inspired. I must have been thinking all the time of

Example 2 from my notes.

Irish history and politics. Page 28 sees 'angry scenes at Stormount'; people on high horses at the new Northern Ireland Parliament, which then links up with 'price partional' on page 264, the cost of partition. References to Sinn Féin can be heard on pages 36, 42, 58, 149 and 258. The Civil War context – another reminder of the origins of *Finnegans Wake* in the aftermath of war – is depicted on page 329 as a dispute between 'Freestouters and publicranks', between Free Staters, who accepted the Treaty partitioning Ireland, and Republicans under de Valera who didn't. Further attacks on violence come on page 338, when Erin Go Bragh, the rallying call of the Irish, is satirised as 'For Ehren, boys, gobrawl!', where *Ehren* is German for honours. If it weren't for the way the phrase is ridiculed in Martin McDonagh's play *The Lonesome West* (1997), 'Take a step back' might afford one of the little lessons to emerge from a reading of *Finnegans Wake*. More seriously, as soon as we open the book, we find ourselves in a war museum that Joyce, with the Duke of Wellington in mind, calls the 'Willingdone Museyroom' (*FW* 8:10). 'Willing, done', says the soldier. Watch your hats going in; you might not have one coming out.

I must also have been responding to Joyce's reflections on language and the practice of writing. *Finnegans Wake* is indeed 'nat language at any sinse of the world', where 'sinse' carries a demotic Irish accent and 'world' is substituted for 'word'. Nat. Equally, Joyce 'murdered all the English he knew', a surprisingly threatening remark coming from a man who abhorred violence. Word and world, language and people – *Finnegans Wake* constantly draws our attention to issues of identity in a way that is nothing if not dramatic and in our face. In the light of my comments on the Wild Geese in Chapter 8, the reference on page 71 to mourning 'the flight of his wild guineese', which is here joined to the black stuff, will have familiar echoes. References to Synge, Yeats and Le Fanu I also jotted down, and there are also mentions of Lewis Carroll, Michael Cusack, the model for the Citizen in *Ulysses*, and Freud's Oedipus complex.

Joyce lost precious little. From 1920 or so he was working full-time as a writer. Such concentration produces its own effects, and one of them in Joyce's case was to drive forward a tendency to which he was already prone, which was to recycle material. Hence the references here to the 'Penelope' episode on page 123 and her 'penelopean patience'. What he was actually doing in 'Penelope' as a male author writing about female experience is critiqued on page 123 in the reference to 'meandering male fist'. The run of words on page 278 reminds us of the sound of a leather ball on a cricket bat that Stephen hears in *A Portrait*, something I write about at some length in *Light, Freedom and Song* (2005), and the sequence can be heard again on page 358, this time in connection with Swift's *Tale of a Tub*.

The titles to the stories of *Dubliners* are also corralled for one last look by an author who can now mock his achievement with a certain detachment: 'Petty Constable Sistersen' ('The Sisters'), 'arrahbejibbers' ('Araby'), 'foul clay in little clots' ('Clay' and 'A Little Cloud'), 'boardelhouse' ('The Boarding House'), 'painful sake' ('A Painful Case'), 'countryports' ('Counterparts'), 'murder' ('A Mother') (*FW* 186:19–187:14).

Because of his compulsion to recycle material, we might be forgiven for seeing everything in *Finnegans Wake* as essentially nothing more than such material. Even the wake itself can then be seen as recalling the wake of Fr Flynn in 'The Sisters', only now it is more loquacious and given to argument. The father–daughter relationship between Bloom and Milly, which is full of hints and suggestion in *Ulysses*, resurfaces in *Finnegans Wake* in more troubled terms in connection with Izzy, the daughter in the family, and we can't help being reminded of Joyce's own daughter Lucia (who was to spend nearly half her life in a mental hospital in Northampton). Anna Livia Plurabelle is an older version of Molly, washing the sins of her husband into the river of life. And as with *Ulysses*, the bedroom is at once off-stage and centre stage, with the chimney acting as a noisy conduit between parents and children.

The geometry image, which appears in the 'Lessons' chapter on page 293, recalls the gnomon in 'The Sisters'. It also reminds us of Molly in her role as geomater, mother earth, geometry. Like the gnomon, overlapping circles also have a shaded area, filled now by a triangle, the female delta. ABC. Whether in his Jesuit single-sex schools or at home in a family of ten children crowded into small terraced houses, wherever he turned, the lesson Joyce imbibed during his boyhood and adolescence was inescapable. Women are the circles and triangles, while Shem 'still puerile in your tubsuit with buttonlegs, you got a hand-some present of a selfraising syringe and twin feeders' (*FW* 188:29–30). Puerile and yet constitutive of childhood,

Overlapping circles in Euclid's geometry, taken from *Euclid: Books I-IV*, a textbook edited by Rupert Deakin (1897). In *Finnegans Wake*, Joyce reproduces the same diagram, but he changes the lettering and adds a broken line to form another triangle below the one given. Instead of ABC he uses Greek π where A is positioned, Aα where B is, and λL where C is. At the lower intersection of the two circles he inserts a P. In this way, ALP, the initials for Anna Livia Plurabelle, dominates Joyce's diagram, transforming geometry into a female anatomy lesson.

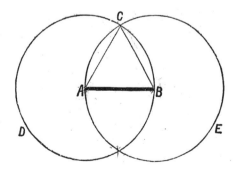

of being a *puer* (Latin for boy). We don't have any word in English with positive associations for the Latin word *puer*; puerile is invariably derogatory. *Puer* in Latin, though, is different. 'Puer natus est' (a boy is born) sings the Church at Christmas (and so did Joyce in a famous poem on the birth of his grandson in 1932). Reverse two letters and for *puer* you have pure. Add two and you have impure, something Joyce was told by his priests to avoid at all costs. But Joyce constantly reminds us of the impure *puer*. Like the boy he was, one part of him never grew up, and hence his fascination with things like smut, which belong to growing up. Where, however, would we be without Joyce? For a start, he imparts a wholly new dimension to what we imagined was going on in geometry lessons at school.

My third page can be quickly glossed. I see my attention on a subsequent reading was again drawn to things I'd already noted, as with 'hesitency', 'Stormount', 'ildiot'. But I was also gathering other sounds. The advertising jingle 'Guinness is good for you' is given an Indian inflection on page 16. Other jingles take the form of songs or rants, as with 'Follow Me Up To Carlow' on page 53 and 'The Wren, the Wren,' the Mummers' recitation on St Stephen's Day, and, as can be observed from my notes, they recur. 'They

Example 3 from my notes.

will be tuggling for ever' is an echo of what the Poor Old Woman says at the end of Yeats's play *Cathleen ni Houlihan* (1902), that those who fight in Ireland's cause will be 'remembered for ever'. 'Tuggling for ever' is how Joyce renders this, not quite an heroic struggle but more like tugging at something. In case we missed the patterns in history, Joyce tells us on pages 226 and 277: they keep recurring in the form of the 'same renew'. The Celtic Twilight is roundly abused as a concept on pages 344 and 492, and the sacrilegious Joyce has fun with the Hail Mary on page 502 and the Bells of Shandon on page 483. I don't know how I missed 'dumbestic husbandry' (see page 38) on my first reading, with its satire on domesticity and modern marriage. Dumb beast, husband dry. As you would expect from the semi-detached Joyce, Dublin's motto – 'obedentia civium urbis felicitas' (the obedience of the citizen, the happiness of the city) – is played with mercilessly throughout the text. One of my favourite *Finnegans Wake* 'sayings' I also collected from early readings: 'It was life but was it fair? It was free but was it art?' (94). The auction houses think they know, and people often think of value in monetary terms, so that if something is free it's often considered worthless, but isn't it quite absurd to put a commercial value on something like art? As for life, yes, it is unfair for most of us, but especially for the poor.

Finally, let me conclude this section by saying something about Joyce's reflections in the text on what he was doing in *Finnegans Wake*. The phrase 'paradigmatic ear' on page 70 is a fairly accurate description of the use of language in this text. We saw that in relation to Earwicker's name, but it's true of most of the portmanteau words as well. Try and hear the other words inside the word as written down. As I suggested in connection with the phrase 'foenix culprit' in Chapter 1, get to the chords that are playing

Wren boys, Athea, County Limerick, 1947; courtesy of the Department of Irish Folklore, University College Dublin. Wren boys dressed up on St Stephen's Day in disguise and went round the countryside performing tricks and singing songs in aid of charity or just for the crack.
Source: The Department of Irish Folklore, University College, Dublin

and never be afraid of guessing. Can you hear behind 'The latter! The latter!' on page 100 the phrase I drew attention to when discussing the Greek opening to *Ulysses*? What was that phrase that the Greek soldiers shouted on their return from the Persian wars? *Thalatta! thalatta!* the sea, the sea. Syntagmatic relations are horizontal relations, they travel across the page, as with subject – predicate relations or the order in a series of adjectives. If we just had the single phrase 'The latter!', we might have difficulty hearing *Thalatta!*. The repeated word guarantees the echo is heard as intended and it links immediately with 'letter', a word and concept that has particular significance in the *Wake*. Sometimes, therefore, a syntagmatic relationship helps to enforce a paradigmatic one, and it's for this reason that we need always to judge if such a relationship is relevant, even as we focus on the vertical relationship. Joyce constantly reminds us of the use of substitution exercises in foreign language teaching. Words in a sentence are in this sense in vertical relationship with other words that could potentially be positioned there. Joyce exploits the empty-slot idea and fills it with word association. To put it simply, there's merit in considering *Finnegans Wake* as a study in vertical relationships or, better, as a study in vertical and horizontal relationships.

To develop this point, consider the following sentence: '[He] believes in everyman his own goaldkeeper and in Africa for the fullblacks' (see page 129). The sentence structure is, as I said above, unexceptional, and presents no problems for us; it's the cargo, the content, that sometimes does that. Combined thus, not 'every man' but 'everyman', this might delay us, and we might be reminded of the HCE theme or the medieval morality play by that name, or the Everyman Theatre in Liverpool. Let's leave all that on one side and concentrate on 'goaldkeeper'. A goalkeeper keeps goal. Fine. Insert the letter 'd' and you have gold keeper. Goal, gold: what's the connection? We're held up by this example of something impinging on our 'paradigmatic ear' and want to delay more. A chord is being struck and we pause. Throughout this book from my remarks on the unfinished sentences of *Dubliners* onwards, I have been delayed by the concept of delay, and now in *Finnegans Wake* I'm allowed to delay as much as I like! It's a book that invites delay, especially in the way it exploits the concept of the paradigmatic ear.

It's good advice in life. Keep attacks out, stand proud in goal, and let nothing past you. The gold motif is more problematic because this could be the motto of a usurer, or in the Irish context a gombeenman, or someone like Silas Marner in George Eliot's novel who hoards his wealth and is consequently destroyed. 'Look after number one' was no doubt a motto Joyce would have sympathised with, but it raises issues for us. We read on, for he also believes in Africa for the fullblacks. The chord being struck here is governed less by sport and personal ethics and more by sport and politics. When New Zealand play rugby, they are known as the All Blacks on account of the black kit they wear on the pitch. Apart from the indigenous population of Maoris, New Zealanders tend to be in fact all white; the kit is in this respect a mask. The only 'All Blacks' on the planet come from Africa. And they are not all or half but full. Mr Browne in 'The Dead' is brown all over, but Africans are indeed black all over. Fullblacks. Not full back, the position in a game of rugby or football, and linked therefore with goalkeeper, but 'fullblack'.

In combining the two words into 'fullblacks', the focus, then, shifts immediately from New Zealand sport to African politics. Africa belongs to the native Black population and not to the White Europeans. Joyce didn't know when he wrote this sentence how intertwined sport and politics in South Africa would become in the era of apartheid from the 1940s to the 1990s, but, from his experience of being brought up in a colonial city, he knew enough about marginalisation to express sympathy with marginalised peoples outside Europe. Everyman, humanity, the individual, keeper, gold, goal, full, blacks, race – in this one sentence, delayed by the paradigmatic ear, we have a microcosm of what's going on in *Finnegans Wake*. An exploration of identity and difference, told through the changes rung on words in their paradigmatic and syntagmatic relations. One Joycean inference we might subsequently draw by way of a half-way resolution to the tension in the sentence between the individual and the collective is this: you're defined by your race but then you need to look after yourself.

Closing moments

Is it possible for any of us to know how much we know about *Finnegans Wake*? Or, alternatively, is it possible to know how much we don't know? The answer to both questions is probably no. If we can get to understanding say 95 per cent of *Ulysses*, perhaps more, then the figure must be below 50 per cent I suspect for *Finnegans Wake*. Perhaps less. Brecht rightly asserted that what you don't know yourself you don't know, but living with things you don't know, or accepting that you'll only ever get to somewhere below a half, this is quite reassuring in its own way. *Joyce's Book of the Dark* (1986) is the title of John Bishop's remarkable study of the *Wake*, where he dwells on the various stages in the text related to sleeping and dreaming and reads it accordingly. It is incredibly dark at times inside the *Wake* but, as my relation Tom Haugh might say about someone who gives up too soon, 'Well, s/he didn't put up much of a fight'.

What I like about *Finnegans Wake* is the way Joyce rearranges the known world and draws our attention to the artificial nature of the identity of word and world. It's true that things could be other than they are, but Joyce never stops stressing that the known world is itself constructed through language. Goal, gold – it's language that brings them into the same orbit, or, if you follow Nicholas of Cusa (1401–64), you might believe it's a 'coincidence of opposites' with philosophical or theological implications. I tend to be more sceptical than Joyce in this regard, whose influences in philosophy and the philosophy of history on display through-out the *Wake* include Nicholas of Cusa, Giordano Bruno (1548–1600) and Giambattista Vico (1668–1744). If one took to extremes the idea of a 'coin-cidence of opposites' or certain arguments about design, then the world is an egg. Only someone under the influence of something could believe that, in the ur-language created by God, 'goal' and gold' had some necessary connection. To most people, after the collapse of the Tower of Babel, the world was never the same again. The position assigned to us as readers of the *Wake* seems to me to be akin to the predicament of the boy in

Translation panel at the 2006 International James Joyce Symposium held in Budapest. From left to right: Rosa Maria Bollettieri Bosinnelli (University of Bologna, Italy), Jolanta Wawrzycka (Radford University, USA), Irena Grubica (University of Rijeka, Croatia), Radica Ieta (University of Western Ontario, Canada), Laurent Milesi (University of Cardiff, Wales), Teresa Caneda (University of Vigo, Spain), Barbara Laman (University of North Dakota, USA), and Patrick O'Neill (Queen's University, Canada). All the languages of Europe – and we would do well to remember non-European languages invoked by Joyce – have an interest in Joyce and especially in the feast of languages on display on every page of *Finnegans Wake*.

'The Sisters' and how he struggled to 'extract meaning' from Mr Cotter's unfinished sentences. Stick with language therefore, the sceptical goblin inside tells me, and leave cosmology to the age of the gods. Or alternatively, when thinking about myth and history, hold in play – and by that I mean tension – the relationship I discussed in Chapter 7 on *A Portrait* between 'once' and 'once upon a time'.

Why you would put your reader through such struggles is another matter. Couldn't you just say that you believe you should look after number one and that you also believe that Blacks should run Africa? Well, it's pretty obvious that the statement in the *Wake* has more power and resonance and that its political message rebounds or detonates long after the book has been put down. But, then, no-one goes to the *Wake* for a reading of African history. On the other hand, if globalisation has now problematised the whole issue of identity, then perhaps reading Joyce's last work can serve to remind us that interdependence has as long a history as hegemony and that nothing can be touched without invoking something else, perhaps its opposite, thus providing another example of Joyce's 'economic' way of being that I referred

Cover design for a collection of essays by Carola Giedion-Welcker edited by Reinhold Hohl and published in 1973. Joyce in good company, that is with the modern movement in the arts. The first section of essays is devoted to Joyce and Brancusi. The way Joyce bends words or warps his material reminds us all the time of Hans Arp. All these figures transformed our notion of representation, and if their work still speaks to us, it is because they remain our contemporaries.

Joyce during his Paris years, when his eyesight continued to deteriorate.
Source: James Joyce Collections at Morris Library/Southern Illinois University

to in Chapter 1. But awareness of interdependence should lead not to quietism in the face of injustice but to something else. Put simply, in its extraordinary attempt to include everything, the book should teach us fear and humility not in a handful of dust but in everything it touches.

A wake is a time for bidding farewell. Joyce began his writing career with a wake and he ends it with a wake. We have been attending the wake not of Fr Flynn but of Tim Finnegan, the hero of the Irish-American ballad, and of Finn MacCool, the ancient Irish mythological figure, who according to one legend lies buried under the city of Dublin, his head underneath the Hill of Howth, his toes out in the Phoenix Park. But in the *Wake*'s closing moments, Joyce's father, who died in 1931, comes once more into view. For the sake of neatness, Joyce returns to the father who peered at him in the opening moments of *A Portrait* and told him a story. Once upon a time a boy fell into history, and now at the end of that particular line of history the boy has his own story to tell about the father who once told him a story: 'And it's old and old it's sad and old it's sad and weary I go back to you, my cold father, my cold mad father, my cold mad feary father, till the near sight of the mere size of him, the moyles and moyles of it, moananoaning, makes me seasilt saltsick and I rush, my only, into your arms' (*FW* 627:26–628:4). In his searching for words and the right kind of rhythm, the sentimental Joyce reveals something of the depth of feeling for his sentimental father, whom he loved in spite of all his faults.

Joyce wraps his tenderness in feelings of fear for his father and how he was an inveterate moaner, but he also attends to his own feelings as an exile and the never-ending problems connected with his poor eyesight. In memory, some of our first impressions are of bulk, for it takes time to develop a sense of perspective. As an adult, with deteriorating eyesight, Joyce's 'near sight' is what remains. This is what I take from the phrase 'the near sight of the mere size of him'. Miles and miles the exile travels from home and miles and miles the waters flow from rivers out to sea. 'Silent, O Moyle, be the roar of thy water' is the first line of 'The Song of Fionnuala', a melody by one of Joyce's favourite composers, Tom Moore, and the one that is being played 'heedlessly' outside the Kildare Street Club when Corley and Lenehan in 'Two Gallants' pass. No one understands counterpoint better than Joyce, and in this closing moment he manages to invoke not only a song about exile and return but also the beginnings of his career as a writer. In Moore's note to the song we read that 'Fionnuala, the daughter of Lir, was, by some supernatural power, transformed into a swan and condemned to wander, for many hundred years, over certain lakes and rivers in Ireland, till the coming of Christianity, when the first sound of the mass-bell was to be the signal of her release'. Moyles and moyles of it. There is

Leaving again. The harbour at Howth and Ireland's Eye, seen from the port side of a Ryanair jet. Sea and sand. Silt and isthmus. Myth and history. Overlaid. Everything comes together in the end. Photograph by David Pierce.

no end to the sense of exile for the exile. Many hundred years in fact. But now the tide is rushing out and he finds himself beached in the silt formed by the retreating waters.

   Joyce is back where he started as a boy along the banks of the Liffey, the boy's adventure in 'An Encounter', walking by the strand in *A Portrait* seeing the wading bird-girl, and enjoying the lassoes from the Cock Lake and his own 'wavespeech' in 'Proteus'. 'Bussoftlhee, mememormee!' (*FW* 628:14). But softly, me, me more me, an echo in its own way of 'murmuring mournfully', a phrase from 'The Song of Fionnuala'. The memory is so powerful that he feels sick again, not so much seasick as 'seasilt and saltsick'. 'riverrun', the *Wake*'s opening word with its lower case like *transition* prominently displayed, begins a forward momentum, but the *Wake* ends in powerful memories which prevent the flow of a steady rhythm, and, impulsively, he rushes into his father's arms. His father is now quite simply 'my only'. Not 'my only father' or 'my only friend' or the only one who might have understood him, but simply 'my only', where the unfinished sentence reminds us both of a characteristic gesture on Joyce's part and of the suppressed lyricism that underlies his whole work. 'Yes. Carry me along, taddy, like you done through the toy fair!' (*FW* 628:8–9). After all the 'lashons of languages' (*FW* 28:32) on display throughout *Finnegans Wake*, and indeed Joyce's work as a whole, after all the time spent in this book attending to a phrase such as 'once upon a time' or 'illumined portholes', or to the sentence in 'The Sisters' about extracting meaning, or to a word such as 'palaver' or 'gesabo', we are back in the world of childhood and the time when Joyce was learning how to get into language. 'taddy', not yet 'daddy'.

Afterword

The last book Joyce was reading before he died in January 1941 was *I Follow Saint Patrick* (1938) by Oliver St John Gogarty. It's a book that traces the saint's travels through Ireland in the fifth century. Gogarty was Joyce's former sparring partner in the Martello Tower and the model in part for Buck Mulligan. Joyce, as we have seen, never cut the umbilical cord, and in reading about Gogarty's modern-day journey through Meath to Mayo, he was returning to beginnings again, to St Patrick and the coming of Christianity in Ireland, to St Patrick and his encounter with the ancient Irish mythological figure of Oisin, to Oisin and the Fenians, to the Land of Youth, to the Yeatsian territory where the Irish Literary Revival in part began in the 1880s with *The Wanderings of Oisin* (1889). Was he looking for a template for a new narrative? The Land of Youth which he in one sense never left? Who knows? Perhaps he had nothing more to give the world. But, as *Finnegans Wake* reminds us, St Patrick was never far from Joyce's thoughts.

Indeed, on the very first page we encounter 'thuartpeatrick' (*FW* 3:10). 'Thou art Peter,' Jesus told his leading apostle, 'and upon this rock I will build my Church.' As has often been noticed, the Church is built on a pun in that in Latin Peter is *Petrus* and stone or rock is *petra*. St Peter and St Patrick, however, are here joined by Joyce in an embrace most Irish Catholics will feel is appropriate. St Patrick brought Christianity to Ireland, drove out the snakes, and laid the foundations not only for the spread of the new religion but also for the special site of pilgrimage at Croagh Patrick in County Mayo. In his narrative poem Yeats tends to side with Oisin and ancient Ireland before the coming of Christianity, and one can understand this, for, with his crosier, talk of hell and quiet assurance, St Patrick must have resembled a figure ushering in a new era and consigning Oisin and the Fenians to history and myth. On the other hand, the boy who was captured as a 16-year-old by raiders from the sea and taken to Ireland went on to establish a remarkable rapport with his followers, not least because his Christianity allowed for continuity with their pagan past. Today, 17 March is celebrated throughout the world with the wearing of the green and with the display on the lapel of the three-leaved shamrock, which the saint had used to explain the theology of the Trinity.

When Joyce 'confronts' St Patrick, Oisin's father, the playful Finn, isn't far away: 'thuartpeatrick'. The happy coincidence of the first three letters 'thu' reminds us of the mid-point between Latin *tu* and English 'thou'. I also like the way this portmanteau word carries the material world that Joyce had left behind. A rick in rural Ireland is a stack of some kind, a rick of hay, for example, or a rick of turf beside the house. The humour is continued in a later reference to 'Puddyrick' (53:30). Peat, too, is a playful word, and sometimes can be encountered in an Irish bull, as in the question by a naïve foreign visitor looking at turf: 'Is that peat?' Answer: 'The very man'. Joyce, as we observed with the Cork/cork painting in his Paris flat, must have enjoyed this play on peat, which until recently was the staple fuel in a country without coal deposits, and Pete, the name of a person. 'Thou art peat, Patrick' is also an affectionate way of thinking about him, the ancient saint associated here with what is burnt in Ireland to keep people warm. Appropriately, at this point in the *Wake* there is a reference to Moses and the burning bush. Peat, Pete, burning bush, Moses, Patrick, all the patriarchs in place before the modern world begins.

The original pun in Aramaic by Jesus was in a sense a 'trick', a conceit, but one that Joyce is not out to expose but to celebrate. By contrast, the Irish Jesuit priest, George Tyrrell, who was excommunicated by the Papacy for his Modernist heresy, a heresy which he defined as an attempt to 'find a new theological synthesis consistent with the data of historico-critical research' (Petre II, 1912, 356), once facetiously suggested that 'Tu es Petrus' could be translated as 'You're a brick' (Petre, 1920, 298). What Tyrrell was seeking was a separation of religion and Catholicism, of 'food and form', as he put it in a letter to Monsignor J. Augustin Loger in November 1908 (ibid., 96). By the time he came to write *Finnegans Wake*, Joyce had developed a more relaxed attitude toward Catholicism and the contrast with Tyrrell serves to remind us of his essentially comic vision and his wish to reimagine the world in terms of identity rather than difference. If he needed support, Joyce had it to hand, because for many Irish speakers, those initial two letters 'th' might see it pronounced not 'thou art' but 'two art', which is another way of rendering Peter and Patrick. Two art. Too.

If the patriarchs, the peatricks, were ever to return to modern-day Dublin, what would they find? Joyce imagines it like this:

> Everything's going on the same or so it appeals to all of us, in the old holmsted here. Coughings all over the sanctuary . . . . The horn for breakfast, one o'gong for lunch and dinnerchime . . . . Coal's short but we've plenty of bog in the yard. And barley's up again, begrained to it. The lads is attending school nessans regular, sir, spelling beesknees with hathatansy and turning out tables by mudapplication.
> (*FW* 26:25–36)

Finnegan would be better off staying where he was, taking his leisure like a 'god on pension'. Nothing's changed. The regulated world is still in place. The same old music. Horns, gongs, chimes, bells pealing out across the city. The priests and altar boys are still coughing all over the sanctuary, food's short, as is coal, but they've plenty of 'bog in the yard', that is they've either plenty of peat from the turf-bogs of Ireland or they've plenty of boggy soil in the garden or, God forbid, they've plenty of toilet space in the garden. The children are still learning their tables at school, not so much by the art of multiplication but by the much cruder use of the soil with 'mudapplication'. Everything's going on the same, only now spelling bees and the beesknees have been hopelessly confused to produce 'spelling beesknees'. The adjective 'nessans' perhaps recalls 'nicens', the word Stephen's father uses at the beginning of *A Portrait*, while those with an acute eye for correspondences might hear in 'holmsted' *The Irish Homestead*, the weekly paper that published Joyce's earliest stories. As for 'hathatansy', we are back via a lisp to 'hesitancy' and the attack on Parnell by the London *Times*, explored in the last chapter. We might also detect a reference to T.S. Eliot, who elsewhere in the *Wake* is ribbed by Joyce in 'Tansy. Sauce. Enough' (164:22). Joyce also seems to be having fun with the mystical form of eastern therapy on offer at the end of *The Waste Land*: not the relaxing hatha yoga but the slightly bitter hathatansy. When you're dead it's better to stay dead and not go walking abroad and risking upset in 'Echoland' (13:5).

In 'Ephemera', an early poem by Yeats that reveals a great poet in the making, he puts these words into an autumn idyll about a love that is fading:

> Before us lies eternity; our souls
> Are love, and a continual farewell. (Yeats, 1889, 63)

Wherever he turned, whether in the field of religion or literature, Joyce had people reminding him that life belonged to someone else or something else. This is partly why I couple his stress on the quotidian and his attention to realistic treatment with the word 'fabulous', for, as Yeats also recognised from the outset, there's more to the world than ephemera. Whether you believe in the afterlife or not, it is the case that 'before us lies eternity'. Yeats steers us away from the *carpe diem* or seize-the-day idea towards something more profound. Our souls are themselves, not simply spiritual but, more importantly, they are or have the potential to love, and because they are involved in relationships they are also 'a continual farewell'. We are only 'ephemera', temporary, but the poet manages to dignify our temporariness also by the word 'continual'. With each encounter, with each departure, 'our souls/Are love, and a continual farewell'.

An afterword, too, is a farewell, and Joyce returns us as a matter of course to his Irish Catholic roots, and this includes not only St Patrick but also St Peter and the Gospel stories. As *Ulysses* confirms, Joyce is good at returning, and, as 'Eveline' and the end of *A Portrait* testify, he's equally good at saying goodbye. At the very end of *Finnegans Wake*, Joyce evokes the scene when Jesus entrusted the keys of the kingdom of heaven to St Peter: 'The keys to. Given!' (*FW* 628:15). This is a remarkable moment and we can perhaps sense its importance by the interrupted half-thought. The idea is lifted as we know from the Gospels by the writer who was both a heretic – a follower of Pelagius in this case – and a plagiarist. As he freely confesses in *Finnegans Wake*, Shem was a 'pelagiarist' (*FW* 182:3), but he was also an expert at knowing what to do with what he had stolen. Unlike the more vulnerable and other-worldly Yeats, Joyce bids farewell through the language and imagery of religion. In a curious way, however, the phrase carries more pathos than it does in the Gospels, for in its intensity we catch a glimpse of the suppressed lyricist behind all the defiance. A farewell, and then a memory, which reminds us of something we all say at times: what have I done with the keys? Ah, yes, Joyce says, I've given those – and he leaves it blank as to the recipient. In the beginning was the word, but at the end just an exclamation mark.

In 1965, the American artist Tony Smith (1912–80) completed a sculpture in steel painted black to illustrate this moment, and he called it simply

Tony Smith, *The Keys to. Given!* (1965). Steel, painted black, 96 × 96 × 96 inches / 8 × 8 × 8 feet / 244 × 244 × 244 cm, edition of 3.

Source: © ARS, NY and DACS, London/Tony Smith Estate, courtesy Matthew Marks Gallery, New York.

The Keys to. Given!. Its measurements are h: 96 × w: 96 × d: 96 in. (h: 243.8 × w: 243.8 × d: 243.8 cm). I spend a lot of time looking at an image of this 8-foot high sculpture. I find it enormously comforting. It's such a solid, uncompromising, interlocking object and at the same time it reaches out to fill the space of a large room. It reminds me of a huge key to a huge gnarled medieval door, but I spend no time on the door only on the key. For a text that is so resistant to meaning or one that invokes so many different meanings, suddenly, in this one stunning piece of sculpture with its sleek black lines, something that is full of pathos has the capacity to speak to me in an utterly straightforward way. Equally, Smith's work allows me an opportunity to connect what I've been saying so far with my final reflections on the covenant that Joyce has established with his readers today and the sense of posterity that inheres in his work.

The Old Testament Jews had a covenant with Yahweh. It protected them from His wrath and gave them protection on their journey through life to the Promised Land. When they had failed Him they could remind Him of the covenant He had made with them and stay His hand. If things failed completely they could establish a new covenant. Christians believe that with the coming of Jesus a new covenant, a new era, was initiated. A covenant, then, is a reminder of a particular history connected with Judaism and Christianity. A bargain is struck between one side and the other. If you keep to your side of the bargain, I will keep to mine. It's in that sense a contract, more powerful than a legal contract or a tax-saving arrangement because more is at stake. A whole people and their God. Humanity as a whole and the Divine.

As I mentioned in Chapter 1, I like to think of Joyce as offering a covenant with his reader. 'The keys to. Given!' To my mind what Joyce is saying here is: 'I've given the keys to what I have written to the reader. Eventually, after all the puzzles and enigmas which I've inserted into the books to keep the professors busy for centuries to come, after all my silence and refusal to say what I mean, after all the criticism that my work is difficult to understand, here at the end I've done the right thing and given the keys to my kingdom to those who want them. Whatever I've written can be understood.' We might detect a slight panic on Joyce's part, but there is an answer to his question 'Is there one who understands me?' and the 'one' has to be more than the author himself. 'Given!' But the covenant can only work if the reader is willing to participate; otherwise, there's no covenant and the keys will remain, like Fr Flynn's chalice in 'The Sisters', idle. Joyce, then, is a faithful writer. He never cut the umbilical cord with his country and religion. He returns, as I say, at the end of his life to St Patrick – or this is how I like to imagine his reading of *I Follow Saint Patrick* – and at the end of his last work he returns to St Peter. But, more importantly for my purposes here, he keeps faith with his reader.

However, when he speaks of the reader it is invariably an 'ideal' not an actual reader. As already noticed, in his famous remark about the reader of *Finnegans Wake*, he suggested that 'the ideal reader' was someone 'suffering from an ideal insomnia' (*FW* 120:13–14). In his correspondence with Grant Richards at the beginning of his career, when he was hoping to persuade him to publish *Dubliners*, again it is an ideal reader he is looking to or has in mind, a new kind of reader, that is, who sought something more mature in the depiction of the modern world. Similarly with his impatience with his aunt over *Ulysses*, for he believed that if his book wasn't fit to read, life wasn't fit to live. Life and literature. Literature and life. This is Joyce's covenant, a devotion to an ideal community of readers and a refusal to endorse the easy option. That's his commitment, and, once entered into in his late teens and early twenties, he never reneged on it.

To my mind, it is this covenant he wants to have with the reader which lies behind his defiance and it also helps explain why he remains an enigma. Equally, it was appropriate that in his last days on earth he should be reading about the saint who is synonymous with his country. For Joyce's covenant was not only with the modern community of readers but also with the past, which he filtered largely through the prism of his own country. What is perhaps surprising is that, given all the rivers and all the cities round the world and all the bridges over the Seine and all the songs of Tom Moore and all the other lists mentioned in the *Wake*, he didn't see fit to include all the placenames in Ireland associated with St Patrick.

Eugene Jolas (1949) believed that with the so-called 'revolution of the word' a new era had been ushered in, no doubt with Joyce as some kind of avatar or John the Baptist figure. This isn't my view. Joyce offers something new but it isn't a new dispensation and I don't believe he heralds some kind of paradigm shift. To those who would proclaim the unutterably new or, alternatively, to those tempted to adopt a condescending view towards history, he has the one fabulous, deflating, riposte: 'Everything's going on the same'. Still the same old business. Coughing all over the altar. Sin business. Failure. Sexual misdemeanours. Guilt. Rivers. The same renew. The same anew. As for the revolution of the word, turnips was a topic he would prefer to talk about rather than literature. Anything but literature, therefore. When he was feted in 1929 at the lunch marking the French translation of *Ulysses*, he refused to allow speeches.

Joyce creates many different kinds of readers, which is another way of saying that many different kinds of readers, both plain and specialist, can get something out of Joyce. Those who consider Joyce the 'bees-knees' are one kind of reader. In the words of my student Anthony Green, Joyce wrote in *Ulysses* 'the novel to end all novels'. That's fine by me, but I've never been sustained for long by the language of inflation when it comes to Joyce. What's any of that got to do with 'unfinished sentences', or with the image of the German Emperor, or with a phrase like 'foenix culprit', words and images I have been forced to delay on throughout this book? Joyce had in mind the ideal or potential reader, but I would come at this from a slightly different direction. Joyce is for all kinds of readers, and not all of them suffer from insomnia. Take up the challenge. Be curious. Come up with a question. Some enjoy him for his unknown or ambivalent status in the culture, the rebel with or without a cause, the renegade who showed the world how to survive four decades of writing without compromising his beliefs. I could go on with other kinds of fabulous readers, but let me conclude with the enigma himself: Joyce to my mind is worth the delay, and the history of his reception has still to be written.

It's a good, soft place to end on, the boy who learnt how to transform the world into language and himself, the me in 'mememormee', into memory. An enigma to the end. Let's start again. In the closing moments of his final almost impenetrable work, Joyce asks a question that many of his readers over the years must have thought about him, 'Is there one who understands me?' (*FW* 627:15)

Select bibliography

Joyce texts are listed first; secondary sources follow. The Joyce texts are given in order of their first publication, with the main text first, then other English editions and translations (in chronological order).

James Joyce texts

Chamber Music (London: Elkin Mathews, 1907).

Dubliners (London: Grant Richards, 1914).

'Dubliners': Text, Criticism, and Notes (eds Robert Scholes and A. Walton Litz) (New York: Viking, 1969).

Dubliners: An Annotated Edition (eds John Wyse Jackson and Bernard McGinley), (London: Sinclair-Stevenson, 1993).

Dubliners (ed. Jeri Johnson) (Oxford: Oxford University Press, 2000).

Dubliners: Viking Critical Edition (ed. Margot Norris) (New York: Viking, 2006).

Gens de Dublin (Lithographies Charles Bardet) (Lausanne: La Guilde de Livre, 1941).

Dublinois (trans. Jacques Aubert) (Paris: Gallimard, 1974).

Dubliners (trans. Rein Bloem) (Amsterdam: Van Gennep, 1987).

A Portrait of the Artist as a Young Man (New York: Huebsch, 1916).

A Portrait of the Artist as a Young Man (London: Egoist Press, 1917).

'A Portrait of the Artist as a Young Man': Text, Criticism, and Notes (ed. Chester Anderson) (New York: Viking, 1969).

Dedalus: Portrait de L'Artiste Jeune Par Lui-Même (trans. Ludmila Savitzky) (1924; Paris: Gallimard, 1943).

Retrato del Artista Adolescente (trans. Dámoso Alonso) (1978; Madrid: Alianza, 1993).

Exiles: A Play on Three Acts (London: Grant Richards, 1918).

Exiles (intro. Padraic Colum) (London: Granada, 1979).

Les Exilés (trans. J.S. Bradley) (Paris: Gallimard, 1950).

Ulysses (Paris: Shakespeare and Company, 1922).

Ulysses (London: Egoist Press, 1922).

Ulysses: A Critical and Synoptic Edition (ed. Hans Walter Gabler with Wolfhard Steppe and Claus Melchior) (New York and London: Garland, 1984).

Ulysses (ed. Jeri Johnson) (Oxford: Oxford University Press, 1993).

Ulysse (trans. Auguste Morel with Stuart Gilbert) (1929; Paris: Gallimard, 1957).

Ulysses (intro. Carola Giedion-Welcker) (Zurich: Rhein-Verlag, 1956).

Uliks (trans. Zlatko Gorjan) (1957; Zagreb: Zora, 1965).

Ulysses (trans. Hans Wollschläger) (1975; Frankfurt am Main: Suhrkamp, 1981).

Uliks (trans. Luko Paljetak) (Opatija: Otokar Keršovani, 1991).

Ulises (trans. Francisco García Tortosa) (revised edition) (Madrid: Cátedra, 2003).

Pomes Penyeach (Paris: Shakespeare and Company, 1927).

Pomes Penyeach (London: Faber & Faber, 1933).

Finnegans Wake (London: Faber & Faber, 1939).

Anna Livia Plurabelle (intro. Padraic Colum) (New York: Crosby Gaige, 1928).

Tales Told of Shem and Shaun: Three Fragments from Work in Progress (Paris: Black Sun Press, 1929).

Stephen Hero (ed. Theodore Spenser) (London: Cape, 1944).

Stephen Daedalus (trans. Georg Goyert) (1958; Frankfurt and Hamburg: Suhrkamp, 1965).

Giacomo Joyce (intro. Richard Ellmann) (London: Faber & Faber, 1968).

Letters of James Joyce (ed. Stuart Gilbert) (London: Faber & Faber, 1957).

Letters of James Joyce, vols II and III (ed. Richard Ellmann) (New York: Viking, 1966).

Selected Letters of James Joyce (ed. Richard Ellmann) (New York: Viking Press, 1975).

The Critical Writings of James Joyce (eds Ellsworth Mason and Richard Ellmann) (1959; New York: Viking, 1966).

Secondary texts

Arnold, Matthew, *Culture and Anarchy: An Essay in Political and Social Criticism* (London: John Murray, 1869).

Atherton, James S., *The Books at the Wake: A Study of Literary Allusions in James Joyce's 'Finnegans Wake'* (1959; Carbondale and Edwardsville: Southern Illinois University Press, 1974).

Aubert, Jacques and Maria Jolas, *Joyce and Paris 1902, 1920–40, 1975* (Paris: Éditions du CNRS, 1979).

Austen, Jane, *Sense and Sensibility* (ed. James Kinsley) (1811; Oxford University Press, 2004).

Ball, Robert, *Story of the Heavens* (London: Cassell, 1897).

Banville, John, 'Bloomsday, Bloody Bloomsday', *The New York Times*, 13 June 2004.

Barrington, Jonah, Sir, *Personal Sketches and Recollections of His Own Time* (1827; Dublin: Ashfield, 1997).

Bartholomew, J.G. (ed.), *The Survey Gazetteer of the British Isles* (London: George Newnes, 1904).

Beach, Sylvia, *Shakespeare and Company* (1956; London: Plantin, 1987).

Beckett, Samuel et al., *Our Exagmination Round His Factification for Incamination of Work in Progress* (1929; New York: New Directions, 1972).

—— *Krapp's Last Tape* and *Embers* (London: Faber & Faber, 1959).

Begnal, Michael and Fritz Senn (eds), *A Conceptual Guide to Finnegans Wake* (Pennsylvania and London: Pennsylvania State University Press, 1974).

Benstock, Bernard, *Joyce-Again's Wake: An Analysis of Finnegans Wake* (Seattle and London: University of Washington Press, 1965).

—— *James Joyce* (New York: F. Ungar, 1985).

Best-Maugard, Adolfo, *A Method for Creative Design* (New York and London: Alfred A. Knopf, 1929).

Bishop, John, *Joyce's Book of the Dark: Finnegans Wake* (Madison, Wisconsin: University of Wisconsin Press, 1986).

Blamires, Harry, *The New Bloomsday Book: Guide Through 'Ulysses'* (London: Routledge, 1996).

Borges, Jorge-Luis, *Inquisiciones* (Buenos Aires: Editoria Proa, 1925).

—— 'James Joyce', *El Hogar*, 5 February 1937. In *Textos Cautivos: Ensayos y Reseñas en 'El Hogar' (1936–1939)* (Barcelona: Tucquets Editores, 1986).

Bruderer-Oswald, Iris, *Das Neue Sehen: Carola Giedion-Welcker und die Sprache der Moderne* (Vorw. Gottfried Boehm; Beitr. Andres Giedion) (Bern: Benteli, 2007).

Budge, E.A.Wallis, *The Egyptian Book of the Dead* (New York: Dover, 1895).

Budgen, Frank, 'The work in progress of James Joyce and Old Norse poetry', *transition*, 13, Summer 1928.

—— *James Joyce and the Making of 'Ulysses'* (1934; Oxford and New York: Oxford University Press, 1972).

Bulson, Ed, *The Cambridge Introduction to James Joyce* (Cambridge: Cambridge University Press, 2006).

Butcher, S.H. and A. Lang, *The Odyssey of Homer: Done into English Prose* (London: Macmillan, 1897).

Byrne, John Francis, *Silent Years: An Autobiography with Memoirs of James Joyce and Our Ireland* (New York: Farrar, Straus & Young, 1953).

Campbell, Joseph and Henry Morton Robinson, *A Skeleton Key to Finnegans Wake* (1944; London: Faber & Faber, 1947).

Caprani, Vincent, 'James Joyce and the grandfather', *Ireland of the Welcomes*, Jan.–Feb. 1982.

Carleton, William, *Fardorougha the Miser* (London: W. Curry, 1837).

—— *The Black Prophet, a Tale of Famine* (London: Simms & M'Intyre, 1846).

Clarke, Austin, *Twice Round the Black Church* (London: Routledge & Kegan Paul, 1962).

Colum, Mary, 'The confessions of James Joyce', *The Freeman* (New York), 19 July 1922.

Costello, Peter, *James Joyce: The Years of Growth 1882–1915* (London: Kyle Cathie, 1992).

Crackanthorpe, Hubert, *Vignettes* (London: John Lane, 1896).

Craig, Maurice, *Dublin 1660–1860* (London: Cresset, 1952).

Crispi, Luca and Sam Slote (eds), *How Joyce Wrote 'Finnegans Wake': A Chapter-by-Chapter Genetic Guide* (Wisconsin: University of Wisconsin Press, 2007).

Cummins, Maria Susanna, *The Lamplighter* (London: G. Routledge, 1854).

Deakin, Rupert (ed.), *Euclid: Books I–IV* (London: University Tutorial Press, 1897).

Dettmar, Kevin J.H., *The Illicit Joyce of Postmodernism* (Madison: University of Wisconsin Press, 1996).

Downing, Gregory, 'Taking tips from Taxil: an edition with translation and commentary of chapters I through V of Léo Taxil's *La Vie De Jésus*, for use by students of Joyce's *Ulysses*', *Hypermedia Joyce Studies*, 3:2, 2003.

Duff, Charles, *James Joyce and the Plain Reader* (London: Desmond Harmsworth, 1932).

Dujardin, Édouard, *We'll No More to the Woods* (intro. Leon Edel; trans. Stuart Gilbert) (New York: New Directions, 1990).

Eglinton, John, 'The beginnings of Joyce', *Life and Letters*, 8:47, December 1932.

Eliade, Mircea, *Cosmos and History: The Myth of the Eternal Return* (1954; New York: Harper Torchbooks, 1959).

Eliot, T.S., *The Waste Land* (New York: Boni & Liveright, 1922).

Ellmann, Richard, *James Joyce*, revised edition (1959; Oxford and New York: Oxford University Press, 1982).

—— *Ulysses on the Liffey*, corrected edition (London: Faber & Faber, 1984).

—— *Oscar Wilde* (London: Hamish Hamilton, 1987).

Faerber, Thomas and Markus Luchsinger, *Joyce in Zürich* (Zurich: Unionsverlag, 1988).

Field, Saul and Morton P. Levitt, *Bloomsday* (London: The Bodley Head, 1972).

Fitch, Noel Riley, 'Introduction' in *Transition: A Paris Anthology* (London: Secker & Warburg, 1990).

Fitzpatrick, David (ed.), *Oceans of Consolation: Personal Accounts of Irish Migration to Australia* (Cork: Cork University Press, 1994).

Ford, Ford Madox, *The Good Soldier* (ed. Martin Stannard) (1915; New York: Norton Critical Edition, 1995).

Forster, E.M., *Howard's End* (1910; Harmondsworth: Penguin, 1968).

French, Marilyn, *The Book as World: James Joyce's Ulysses* (London: Abacus, 1982).

Freund, Gisèle and V.B. Carlton, *James Joyce in Paris: His Final Years* (preface Simone de Beauvoir) (London: Cassell, 1966).

Freyer, Grattan, 'Major Dermot Freyer's report on *Dubliners*', *James Joyce Quarterly*, Summer 1973.

Fritzsche, Peter, *Reading Berlin 1900* (Cambridge, Mass. and London: Harvard University Press, 1996).

Gheerbrant, Bernard, *James Joyce, Sa Vie, Son Oeuvre, Son Rayonnement* (Paris: La Hune, 1949).

Gifford, Don, with Robert J. Seidman, *Ulysses Annotated: Notes for James Joyce's Ulysses*, 2nd edition (Berkeley, Los Angeles and London: University of California Press, 1989).

Gilbert, Stuart, *James Joyce's Ulysses: A Study* (London: Faber & Faber, 1930).

Gissing, George, *New Grub Street* (London: Smith & Elder, 1891).

Gogarty, Oliver St John, *As I Was Going Down Sackville Street* (1937; Harmondsworth: Penguin, 1954).

—— *I Follow Saint Patrick* (London: Rich & Cowan, 1938).

Gordon, John, *Finnegans Wake: A Plot Summary* (Dublin: Gill & Macmillan, 1986).

Gordon, Mary, *The Other Side* (New York: Penguin, 1989).

Gorman, Herbert S., *James Joyce: His First Forty Years* (London: Geoffrey Bles, 1926).

—— *James Joyce: A Definitive Biography* (London: The Bodley Head, 1941).

—— *James Joyce* (London: Rinehart, 1948).

Green, Jonathon, *The Cassell Dictionary of Slang* (London: Cassell, 1998).

Griffith, Arthur, *The Resurrection of Hungary: A Parallel for Ireland* (Dublin: James Duffy, 1904).

Groden, Michael, *Ulysses in Progress* (New Jersey: Princeton, 1977).

Guggenheim, Peggy, *Out Of This Century: Confessions of an Art Addict* (London: André Deutsch, 1980).

Gunn, Ian and Clive Hart, *James Joyce's Dublin: A Topographical Guide to the Dublin of 'Ulysses'* (London: Thames & Hudson, 2004).

—— 'Rearranging the Furniture at 7 Eccles Street', James Joyce Quarterly, 44: 3, 2008.

Hall, H.S. and F.H. Stevens, *A Text-Book of Euclid's Elements For the Use of Schools* (London: Macmillan, 1898).

Hanks, Patricia and Flavia Hodges, *A Dictionary of Surnames* (Oxford and New York: Oxford University Press, 1988).

Hardy, Thomas, *Tess of the d'Urbervilles* (intro. P.N. Furbank) (1891; London: Macmillan, 1974).

Hart, Clive, 'The Earwickers of Sidlesham' in Clive Hart and Fritz Senn (eds), *A Wake Digest* (Sidney: Sidney University Press, 1968).

Hayman, David, *'Ulysses': The Mechanics of Meaning* (Engelwood Cliffs, NJ: Prentice-Hall, 1970).

Hill, Geoffrey, *Collected Poems* (Harmondsworth: Penguin, 1985).

Hohl, Reinhold (ed.), *Carola Giedion-Welcker Schriften 1926–1971* (Köln: Verlag M. DuMont Schauberg, 1973).

Homer, *The Odyssey* (trans. S.H. Butcher and A. Lang) (London: Macmillan, 1897).

Hoult, Norah, *Coming From The Fair* (London: William Heinemann, 1937).

Husserl, Edmund, *Ideas: General Introduction to Pure Phenomenology* (trans. W.R. Boyce Gibson) (New York: Collier, 1962).

Hutchins, Patricia, *James Joyce's World* (London: Methuen, 1957).

Ibsen, Henrik, *Prose Dramas*, vol. II: *Ghosts, An Enemy of the People, The Wild Duck* (ed. William Archer) (London: Walter Scott, 1890).

—— *When We Dead Awaken* (trans. William Archer) (London: Heinemann, 1900).

Jackson, John Wyse and Peter Costello, *John Stanislaus Joyce: The Voluminous Life and Genius of James Joyce's Father* (London: Fourth Estate, 1997).

James, Henry, *The Portrait of a Lady*, 3 vols (London: Macmillan, 1881).

Jameson, Fredric, 'Cognitive mapping' in Amitava Kumar (ed.), *Poetics/Politics: Radical Aesthetics for the Classroom* (New York: New York University Press, 1999).

Jesuits (Ireland), *A Page of History: Story of University College, Dublin 1883–1909. Compiled by Fathers of the Society of Jesus* (Dublin and Cork: Talbot Press, 1930).

Jolas, Eugene, 'My friend James Joyce' in Sean Givens (ed.), *James Joyce: Two Decades of Criticism* (New York: Vanguard Press, 1948).

—— (ed.), *Transition Workshop* (New York: Vanguard, 1949).

Jones, Peter (ed.), *Imagist Poetry* (Harmondsworth: Penguin, 1972).

Joyce, Stanislaus, 'Open letter to Dr Oliver Gogarty', *Interim* IV:1–2, 1954.

—— *My Brother's Keeper* (ed. Richard Ellmann) (London: Faber & Faber, 1958).

—— *The Dublin Diary of Stanislaus Joyce* (ed. George Harris Healy) (London: Faber & Faber, 1962).

Joyce, Weston St John, *The Neighbourhood of Dublin* (Dublin and Waterford: M.H. Gill, 1913).

Kain, Richard, *Fabulous Voyager: James Joyce's 'Ulysses'* (Chicago: University of Chicago Press, 1947).

Kenner, Hugh, *Dublin's Joyce* (1955; London: Chatto & Windus, 1956).

—— *The Stoic Comedians* (London: W.H. Allen, 1964).

—— 'The cubist portrait' in Thomas Staley and Bernard Benstock (eds) *Approaches to Joyce's 'Portrait': Ten Essays* (Pittsburg: University of Pittsburg, 1976).

—— *Dublin's Joyce* (New York: Columbia University Press, 1987).

—— *'Ulysses'* (1980; Baltimore and London: Johns Hopkins University Press, 1987).

Lawrence, D.H., *Women in Love* (1920; Harmondsworth: Penguin, 1982).

Le Fanu, Sheridan, *The House by the Church-yard* (1863; London: Anthony Blond, 1968).

MacCourt, Edward, *Home is the Stranger* (Toronto: Macmillan Company of Canada, 1950).

Malcolm, Janet, *Reading Chekhov: A Critical Journey* (New York: Random House, 2001).

Malton, James, *A Picturesque and Descriptive View of Dublin* (London: J. Malton, 1792–9).

Mamet, David, *Glengarry Glen Ross: A Play in Two Acts* (London: Methuen, 1984).

McAlmon, Robert, *Being Geniuses Together 1920–1930* (rev. Kay Boyle) (London: Michael Joseph, 1970).

McCabe, Colin, *James Joyce and the Revolution of the Word* (London: Macmillan, 1979).

McCarthy, Michael, *Priests and People in Ireland* (Dublin: Hodges & Figgis, 1902).

McCormick, Kathleen and Erwin R. Steinberg (eds), *Approaches to Teaching Joyce's Ulysses* (New York: Modern Language Association of America, 1993).

McCourt, John, *The Bloom Years: James Joyce in Trieste 1904–1920* (Dublin: Lilliput, 2000).

McDonagh, Martin, *The Lonesome West* (London: Methuen, 1997).

McHugh, Roland, *Annotations to Finnegans Wake*, revised edition (Baltimore and London: Johns Hopkins University Press, 1991).

McKilligan, Kathleen M., *Édouard Dujardin: 'Les Lauriers sont coupés' and the Interior Monologue* (Hull: University of Hull, 1977).

McKinley, Richard, *The Surnames of Sussex* (Oxford: Leopard's Head Press, 1988).

Mink, Louis O., *A Finnegans Wake Gazetteer* (Bloomington: Indiana University Press, 1978).

Mitchell, Flora H., *Vanishing Dublin* (Dublin: Allen Figgis, 1966).

Montague, John, *Selected Poems* (Oxford: Oxford University Press, 1982).

Moore, George, *Confessions of a Young Man* (London: Swan Sonnenschein, Lowrey, 1888).

——*The Untilled Field* (London: T. Fisher Unwin, 1903).

Moore, Thomas, *A Selection of Irish Melodies* (Dublin and London: 1808–34).

Moreno-Durán, R.H., *Mujeres de Babel: Voluptuosidad y Frenesí Verbal en James Joyce* (Bogotá, Colombia: Jaurus, 2004).

Muldoon, Paul, *Quoof* (London: Faber & Faber, 1983).

Murray, Lindley, *An English Grammar Comprehending the Principles and Rules of the Language*, 2 vols, 4th edition (York, 1819).

Nash, John, *James Joyce and the Act of Reception: Reading, Ireland, Modernism* (Cambridge: Cambridge University Press, 2006).

Nicholson, Robert, *The Ulysses Guide: Tours Through Joyce's Dublin* (Dublin: New Island Books, 2002).

Noonan, Robert, *The Ragged Trousered Philanthropists* (London: Grant Richards, 1914).

Norburn, Roger, *A James Joyce Chronology* (Basingstoke: Palgrave Macmillan, 2004).

O'Brien, Joseph V., *'Dear Dirty Dublin': A City in Distress, 1899–1916* (Berkeley and Los Angeles: University of California Press, 1982).

O'Casey, Sean, *Inishfallen Fare Thee Well* (London: Macmillan, 1949).

O'Faolain, Sean, review of Hugh Kenner, *Dublin's Joyce* in *The Listener*, 14 June 1956.

Ogden, C.K., *Basic English: A General Introduction with Rules and Grammar* (London: Kegan Paul, Trench, Trubner, 1930).

O'Neill, Jamie, *At Swim, Two Boys* (London: Scribner, 2001).

Ovidius Naso, Publius, *Ovid's Metamorphosis Englished* (trans. George Sandys) (Oxford: J. Lichfield, 1632).

Peake, Charles, *James Joyce: The Citizen and the Artist* (London: Edward Arnold, 1977).

Petre, M.D., *Autobiography and Life of George Tyrrell*, 2 vols (London: Edward Arnold, 1912).

—— (ed.), *George Tyrrell's Letters* (London: T. Fisher Unwin, 1920).

A Pictorial and Descriptive Guide to Bognor (London: Ward Lock, 1918).

A Pictorial and Descriptive Guide to Paris (London: Ward Lock, 1905).

Pierce, David, *James Joyce's Ireland* (London and New Haven: Yale University Press, 1992).

—— *Yeats's Worlds: Ireland, England and the Poetic Imagination* (London and New Haven: Yale University Press, 1995).

—— *W.B. Yeats: Critical Assessments*, 4 vols (Robertsbridge, Sussex: Helm Information, 2000).

—— *Irish Writing in the Twentieth Century: A Reader* (Cork: Cork University Press, 2001).

—— *Light, Freedom and Song: A Cultural History of Modern Irish Writing* (London and New Haven: Yale University Press, 2005).

—— *Joyce and Company* (London: Continuum, 2006).

Potts, Willard (ed.), *Portraits of the Artist in Exile: Recollections of James Joyce by Europeans* (Seattle and London: University of Washington Press, 1977).

Pound, Ezra, *Selected Letters 1907–1941* (ed. D.D. Paige) (New York: New Directions, 1971).

Pritchett, Victor S., review of Richard Ellmann's *James Joyce* in *Encounter*, 82, July 1960.

Rabaté, Jean-Michel, 'Modernism and "the plain reader's rights": Duff-Riding-Graves re-reading Joyce', in John Nash (ed.), *Joyce's Audiences* (New York and Amsterdam: Rodopi, 2002).

Reaney, P.H., *The Origin of English Surnames* (Routledge & Kegan Paul, 1967).

—— *A History of English Surnames*, 3rd edition with corrections by R.M. Wilson (Oxford: Oxford University Press, 2005).

Renan, Ernest, *La Vie de Jésus* (Paris: Michel Lévy, 1863).

Richards, Grant, *Author Hunting: By an Old Literary Sportsman* (London: Hamish Hamilton, 1934).

Röhl, John C.G., 'The emperor's new clothes' in John C.G. Röhl and Nicolaus Sombart (eds), *Kaiser Wilhelm II: New Interpretations* (Cambridge: Cambridge University Press, 1982).

Rose, Danis and John O'Hanlon, *Understanding Finnegans Wake: A Guide to the Narrative of James Joyce's Masterpiece* (New York and London: Garland, 1982).

Russell, George, *The Living Torch AE* (ed. Monk Gibbon) (New York: Macmillan, 1938).

Scott, Bonnie Kime, *Joyce and Feminism* (Bloomington: Indiana University Press; Brighton: Harvester, 1984).

Sebald, W.G., *The Rings of Saturn* (trans. Michael Hulse) (London: Harvill, 1998).

Senn, Fritz, 'Taxilonomy', *James Joyce Quarterly* 19:2 (Winter 1982).

Shelley, Percy Bysshe, *The Necessity of Atheism* (Worthing: C. and W. Phillips, 1811).

Somerville-Large, Peter, *Dublin* (London: Hamish Hamilton, 1979).

Sterne, Laurence, *The Life and Opinions of Tristram Shandy, Gentleman* (eds Melvyn New and Joan New) (1759–68; Florida: The University Presses of Florida, 1978).

—— *A Sentimental Journey Through France and Italy by Mr Yorick* with *The Journal to Eliza* and *A Political Romance* (ed. Ian Jack) (1768; Oxford: Oxford University Press, 1989).

Strauss, David Friedrich, *The Life of Jesus, Critically Examined*, 3 vols (trans. Marion Evans) (1835; London, 1846).

Strong, L.A.G., *The Garden* (1931; London: Methuen, 1945).

Swift, Jonathan, *Gulliver's Travels* (ed. Claude Rawson) (1726; Oxford: University Press, 2005).

Taxil, Léo, *La Vie de Jésus* (Paris: Librairie Anti-Clericale, 1882).

Tennyson, Alfred, *In Memoriam* (London: Edward Moxon, 1850).

Thiong'o, wa Ngũgĩ, *Decolonising the Mind: The Politics of Language in African Literature* (London: Currey, 1986).

Thom's Official Dublin Directory (Dublin: Thom's, 1904).

Thom's Business Directory of Dublin and Suburbs for the Year 1906 (Dublin: Thom's, 1906).

Thom's Commercial Directory 1979/80 (Dublin: Thom's, 1980).

Thom's Dublin and County Street Directory 1981/2 (Dublin: Thom's, 1982).

Tindall, William York, *The Joyce Country* (Pennsylvania: Pennsylvania State University Press, 1960).

Townsend, Horace, *The Mergenthaler Linotype Company: The Story of Printing Types* (New York, 1915).

Tysdahl, Bjørn, *Joyce and Ibsen* (Oslo: Norwegian Universities Press, 1968).

Urquhart, Jane, *Away* (Harmondsworth: Penguin, 1995).

Vegh, Beatriz, 'A meeting in the Western canon: Borges's conversation with Joyce' in John Nash (ed.), *Joyce's Audiences* (New York and Amsterdam: Rodopi, 2002).

Vidocq, Eugène Vincent, *Mémoires of Vidocq* (Bruxelles: Chez J-P. Jonker, 1829).

West, Rebecca, *The Strange Necessity: Essays and Reviews* (London: Jonathan Cape, 1928).

Wilde, Oscar, *Intentions* (Leipzig: Heinemann and Balestier, 1891).

—— *The Picture of Dorian Gray* (London: Ward, Lock, 1891).

—— *The Letters of Oscar Wilde* (ed. Rupert Hart-Davis) (London: Rupert Hart-Davis, 1962).

Wilson, Edmund, *Axel's Castle: A Study in the Imaginative Literature 1870–1930* (New York and London: C. Scribner's Sons, 1931).

—— 'The dream of H.C. Earwicker' in *The Wound and the Bow* (1941; London: Methuen, 1961).

Woolf, Virginia, *A Writer's Diary* (ed. Leonard Woolf) (1953; London: Triad/Granada, 1981).

Yeats, William Butler, *The Wanderings of Oisin* (London: Kegan, Paul, Trench, 1889).

—— *The Celtic Twilight: Men and Women, Dhouls and Faeries* (London: Lawrence & Bullen, 1893).

—— *Poems* (London: T. Fisher Unwin, 1895).

—— *Plays for an Irish Theatre: The Hour-Glass, Cathleen ni Houlihan, The Pot of Broth* (London: Bullen, 1904).

—— *Reveries Over Childhood and Youth* (London: Macmillan, 1916).

—— *The Tower* (London: Macmillan, 1928).

—— *The Winding Stair and Other Poems* (London: Macmillan, 1933).

—— *The Letters of W.B. Yeats* (ed. Allan Wade) (London: Rupert Hart-Davis, 1954).

Young, Filson, *Memory Harbour: Essays Chiefly in Description* (London: Grant Richards, 1909).

Index